good
wok Tweedie

WINNER'S
DINNERS

Michael Winner (signature)

WHERE'S MY MAIN COURSE!?

GIMME MORE.

WAITER!!

WINNIE
THE MULTI-HEADED-AND
-ARMED MONSTER SETS OOT

WINNER'S DINNERS

THE RESTAURANT AND HOTEL GUIDE

OVER 600 PLACES TO VISIT, NOT TO VISIT, TO LOVE, TO HATE!

MICHAEL WINNER

JR
BOOKS

First published in Great Britain in 2009 by
JR Books, 10 Greenland Street, London NW1 0ND
www.jrbooks.com

A catalogue record for this book is available from the British Library.

Photos © Michael Winner Ltd 2009. Front cover photo by Michael Winner and Geraldine Lynton-Edwards. Back cover photo by Geraldine Lynton-Edwards.

Cartoons © Michael Winner

Staff photographed on front cover are from the Belvedere restaurant, Holland Park, London W8 6LU

ISBN 978-1-906779-30-6

3 5 7 9 10 8 6 4 2

Printed by MPG Books, Bodmin, Cornwall

All entries are believed to be correct at time of print – please call before visiting a restaurant to ensure that details have not changed.

Contents

WINNIE
AWARDS
HIMSELF
FIRST PRIZE

WINNER'S AWARDS

BEST RESTAURANT IN THE WORLD: HARRY'S BAR VENICE
This is a much-criticised Award, but the critics are wrong. Every course, every meal I've had there is perfect. The service is beyond belief efficient and speedy. You have to sit in the downstairs bar to get the full atmosphere. Upstairs it's posher but somewhat dull.

BEST RESTAURANT IN LONDON: THE RIVER CAFÉ
A lovely room, food tastes of something, immaculate, not over-fussed cooking. A joy.

BEST RESTAURANT OUTSIDE LONDON: THE ROYAL OAK PALEY GREEN
Dominic Chapman is more than master cook, he's historic. Everything he does in this well decorated pub is superb. The scotch eggs are miraculous, the hand cut chips in a class of their own. The desserts spectacular. It's owned by Michael Parkinson and his son Nick.

…. AND THE FRENCH HORN, SONNING
Owned by Carole and Ronnie Emmanuel and brilliantly run by them and their children Michael and Elaine the food is old fashioned in the best sense. Top class fresh produce, roast duck beyond belief, scampi like nowhere else. Plus a beautiful River Thames setting.

BEST RESTAURATEUR: RICHARD CARING
Richard owns The Ivy, Le Caprice, Scott's, Annabel's, Harry's Bar in England, and some forty other places. His triumph was the creation and ongoing success of Scott's. They laughed when he went from the schmutta trade into restaurants. They ain't laughing now.

RESTAURANT I GO TO MOST: THE WOLSELEY
An iconic, bustling, celebrity hangout, beautiful large room, great service, food gets better all the time. It's the most fun dining in Britain.

BEST RESTAURANT MANAGERS: ROBERT HOLLAND AT THE WOLSELEY AND CHARLES PULLAN AT THE RIVER CAFÉ
It's important to have someone in charge you trust, to whom you can ask pertinent and irrelevant questions. Robert Holland is a nattily suited professional from the Jeremy King and Chris Corbin school of excellence. Charles Pullan is more preppy and has been known to screw up a food order big time. But they're both exceptional.

BEST WAITING STAFF: THE RIVER CAFÉ
They smile, they're friendly, they're efficient. And they all look good.

BEST HOTEL IN THE UK: THE RITZ PICCADILLY
Where other hotels have vandalised original excellence of design, the Ritz is grand and classic without being snooty. Chef John Williams is one of the best.

BEST UK HOTEL GROUP: VON ESSEN HOTELS
Some thirty hotels from Cliveden to Sharrow Bay, Amberley Castle, Ston Easton Park. Each one reflects the enthusiasm and control of owner Andrew Davis.

BEST HOTEL IN EUROPE: THE VILLA FELTRINELLI, LAKE GARDA
A villa on Lake Garda, once requisitioned and lived in by Mussolini. Stunning location. Great food. Lovely pool and lakeside gardens.

BEST HOTEL BOSS PERSONALITY: DANIELLE ROUX AT LA COLOMBE D'OR, ST PAUL DE VENCE.
In this marvellous hotel garlanded with artwork by Picasso, Braque and other biggies, Danielle can dismiss guests with a raised eyebrow. Picasso et al gave the paintings to the hotel when they couldn't afford to pay for the food.

WORST MEALS EVER: THE ATHENAUEM HOTEL PICCADILLY, THE MARRIOTT GROSVENOR SQUARE, THE DEVONSHIRE ARMS YORKSHIRE
Athenaeum and Marriott provided the dreariest, been in the deep freeze forever, inadequate food. The Devonshire Arms Michelin-starred restaurant does over-fussed, over-decorated, tired horror-story courses.

WORST FOOD, SERVICE, ATTITUDE, EVERYTHING: THE CLIFF, BARBADOS
Beyond belief snooty, arrogant waitresses and managers, ghastly food, very few tables worth sitting at, overall a horrible experience.

BEST VERY PERSONAL, WIFE COOKS, HUSBAND DOES FRONT OF HOUSE: FISHER POND GREAT HOUSE, BARBADOS
Set in an elegant mansion in the sugar cane fields, a touch of the very best of old Barbados. Tasty local food brilliantly prepared by Raine Chandler. Hubby John is host with the most. An example of everything a restaurant should be.

MOST AMUSING LETTER-WRITER: BARRY MCKAY
This reader started off insulting me non-stop. Now he is my greatest email pen-pal.

SEE MOROCCAN SECTION

INTRODUCTION

I became a food writer only to get revenge on Terence Conran. I'd been a guest at his Pont de la Tour restaurant by the Thames. Everything had been diabolical. We got the wrong orders, my fish tasted old and tired, the staff argued if you dare make a complaint. Finally, and there 12 of us, two waiters stood gazing at a tray of coffees, all getting cold. They had no idea who ordered what. The restaurant manager was arrogant. At this point I did raise my voice, something which rarely happens in spite of rumours to the contrary. I stood up, the restaurant manager was in the main room, and said loudly 'Excuse me!' He turned away. There was no escape. I followed him a few paces. 'I'm talking to you,' I said. He walked further away. Now I was shouting in a voice that, if the wind was in the right direction, would have been heard in Australia. 'I wish to talk to you!' I demanded. The manager then had to listen to my view of the proceedings. The next day I wrote a very polite letter to Terence Conran saying in general I always liked his restaurants, and told what had gone on the night before. Terence wrote back sarcastically, 'Thank you for your film script. I will investigate.' That was sixteen years ago. I assume the investigation is still ongoing. I never got a result.

When *The Sunday Times* asked me, 'Anything you can write for us?' I suggested a piece on catastrophes I'd had in restaurants including at La Pont de la Tour. This was printed and caused an enormous furore. Other writers took it up, the public wrote en masse to *The Sunday Times* detailing their restaurant problems. That led me to a regular column which, I'm happy to say, still produces great angst among the readers and some of the funniest letters ever, many of them directed against me. The phone rang one evening a couple of years after I'd been blessing the world with my views on eating out. It was Gordon Ramsay. 'Whatever you read in the *Daily Telegraph* tomorrow, I didn't say it,' he explained. I knew Gordon had shot his mouth off (a habit he retains) and regretted it. The *Telegraph* published his comment: 'Michael Winner knows nothing about food.' They rang me to ask for a response. 'God, the truth hurts,' I said. I know something about food. I know what I like. So do you. You have as much right to your opinion as any so-called professional critic and you're probably more right than they are. Sure, I don't know the constituent ingredients of the sauce. I can't give you a chemical analysis of what's in every dish. I give a playlet on what happens and my opinion. I pay for all my meals and hotels as a normal punter –

no freebies. I am not reimbursed. Readers go where I recommend but sadly don't stay away enough from places I condemn. For many years Terence Conran wrote very rude letters about me to the press, including ones to go with my *Sunday Times* column. I slagged him off, too. Then about five years ago, I was by the pool of the Cipriani hotel in Venice. It was rather quiet, but there, sitting not far away was Terence Conran and his wife Vicki with another couple. Having done Question Time and Any Questions I knew that feuding politicians behaved very cordially outside of the battlefield. So I wandered over to say 'hello' to Terence. His face was awash with dread. 'Was that terrible Michael Winner going to make a scene? What a thing to happen on holiday!' In seconds Terry was my new best friend. So much so that in the evening his wife rang my suite and said, 'We're going to Harry's Bar tonight. Terence can't get a seat downstairs. Can you help?' Harry's Bar in Venice is terrific at the bar level, that's where all the stars and Italians go. The upper rooms are posher but lack the bustle and sparkle. The owner, Arrigo Cipriani is a great friend. It took seconds to secure Terence his downstairs table. We've been pals ever since.

As we sail into another Winner-Guide, this time with the world in financial meltdown and restaurants declining to pay their suppliers, going bust, struggling, moaning, pretending all is well when they know it isn't, I am still bemused by the number of letters I receive and tales I hear told of how utterly arrogant, rude and uncaring restaurant staff and often owners are of their customers' interests. To complain invariably produces threats that you'll never be allowed back or that wonderful phrase, 'No one's ever complained about the food before.' The implication being, 'There must be something wrong with you.' The so-called hospitality industry is peopled by the most inhospitable examples of humanity on the planet. From receptionists who look at you as if you're rubbish and say 'Have you got a reservation?' to waiters who bring the wrong food after an endless wait. You know what happens, you've had a dreadful meal. Some of your group got the wrong food, you've been saying how awful it is. Then over comes the maitre d'. 'Is everything alright?' he asks. 'Oh yes, lovely thank you,' everyone says. Well, come out with guff like that and you deserve what you get. It took me at least 50 years to pluck up courage to give my true views. So I guess I can't blame you. Now if I'm asked if it was OK and it wasn't I just say 'Read about it.'

Your views are just as good as anyone else's. Don't be afraid to let them be known. Anyone who eats is entitled to an opinion. I really don't think there's any such thing as a food expert. There are people who analyse what's in the sauce, give you details of what makes what. The only thing that matters is: does it taste good? Are you enjoying it? If the answer to that is Yes, you've won for the evening or lunch. If not you're in the poo. This book will guide you, not to every restaurant on the planet, but to a vast selection of places in the UK and abroad. What I say to you is what I say to my friends. I hope this leads you to some good places – and helps you avoid others.

HOME

WINNIE GOES TO THE
IVY RESTAURANT

LONDON

A lain Ducasse is a famous three-Michelin-starred chef with his main restaurant at the hotel Plaza Athénée in Paris. Like many acclaimed chefs, running one kitchen is not enough. They feel the need to increase income by spreading their name to the winds. So it settles on establishments all over the place, run by their pupils, acolytes, disciples or passing garbage collectors who feel like having a go with a mixing bowl.

Thus **Alain Ducasse at the Dorchester,** its full name as printed on my bill, charged £252 for a three-course lunch for two, the only alcoholic drink being a buck's fizz. I don't normally care about bills, even though I pay them myself without reimbursement. But this one had me reeling, and writhing.

I went with my delightful friend Adam Kenwright who owns London's second largest theatre advertising agency. The Ducasse room has been widely criticised, as has its food. I found the premises very pleasant. But not much else.

We got a freebie of tiny choux pastry with Swiss and parmesan cheese. Not interesting. Then came pumpkin ravioli. That was terrific. The bread was boring. We were served, in a crockery egg, 'royal of broccoli, crunchy raw vegetables and a black olive condiment.' A waste of time. For our real starter we both had 'steamed langoustines, artichokes, truffled parmentier jus'. Adam said, 'Wonderful, very good.' He left most of his sauce. The langoustines were fine. The sauces throughout were utterly tasteless.

My main course was 'Dover sole fillets florentine-style, shrimps with Paris mushrooms, Château Chalon sauce.' It was five little pieces of fish, shrimps and bits of veg. What looked like curly cheese straws appeared, but they were potatoes. The whole lot tasted of total zero. Adam had 'fillet of beef with seared foie gras, rossini, sacristain potatoes, périgeux sauce'. He asked for green vegetables. As he was finishing, a tiny bowl of overcooked vegetables arrived for an extra charge of £10. Adam liked the foie gras, said the beef was 'nothing special. And the potatoes have no taste at all.'

There were many empty tables. At the prices they charge for tasteless twaddle, the word is obviously out. I was advised to try the 'rum baba like in Monte Carlo.' I've never had it in Monte Carlo, but their London version was very good indeed.

Adam had 'apple composition' – a slow-baked apple, green apple sorbet with meringue and a soft almond cake filled with green apple jelly. He liked his dessert. The after dessert was 'Devon cream sorbet on top of fresh and dried grapefruit with a fresh orange infused in Grenadine.' Awful. Some petits fours arrived but I was too exhausted to dictate more into my tape.

When I went to see a production of *The Lady from the Sea* at the splendid Almeida theatre in Islington I had a first course before the show at Conran's **Almeida** restaurant opposite. It was a mixture of salamis, other sausages, pâté and ham, all very good indeed, with exemplary service in a well-designed room.

For my next visit I suggested Terence and Lady Conran might like to join us. I was switching to a larger table when they came in. May I make one thing clear: the food at the Almeida is absolutely sensational. I say this not so Terence and I can remain blood brothers, but because it's true. It's a great credit to Terence and to Ian Wood, then the chef. Everything I ate was stupendous. Simple, no plate decoration, close to divine.

'This is what Elizabeth David taught me,' explained Terence, 'to love French bourgeois food.' That was too classy a statement for a poor boy from Willesden. I don't know what he was talking about. The restaurant, like the food, is uncluttered and very pleasant to look at. If you live near Islington, make a detour.

I had the marinated herring from the set menu. I also had ris de veau, which is the glands of something or other. I had the salami selection again, a frog's leg from Terence's plate and a snail from Geraldine's. I only complained about the mushrooms. By the time they came I'd almost finished my main course. 'Bringing them late was a nice additional surprise,' said Terence. 'Surprise! They'd forgotten them!' I responded.

I finished with a historic chocolate tart. 'I think you should have a thin sliver of prune tart too,' said Terence, 'just to keep you regular.' You see, once we were enemies. Now he cares about me.

As in so many parts of London we have our Arab restaurant. This one's called **Al-Dar III**. Apparently two other Al-Dars are on the Edgware Road. One featuring music and a belly dancer. I can manage lunch without that.

We sat near the door facing the bustle and buses of the high street. An extremely professional, cheerful and welcoming Palestinian waiter, Mohammed Ali, brought some Evian water and ice.

There's a long counter full of delicious-looking stuff from pizzas to hummus. Behind it beef and lamb roast on separate spits. There's also an enormous menu. I started with the little pizza from the counter (pretty good). Geraldine had the vegetarian hummus, moutabal, tabbouleh, falafel and fatayah spinach. I nicked a bit of each item. Excellent.

As her main course Geraldine chose chargrilled boneless baby chicken with garlic sauce. I had a kind of in-between moment, with thin slices of beef from the spit. These were almost historic. My main course was chicken cooked with vegetables and served with rice. A sort of stew. Perhaps I was in a particularly good mood (rare, I assure you) but I found it extremely tasty.

They've only got paper napkins, which I hate, but they intelligently change them after the first course.

My dessert was baklava, cheesecake and other delights where nuts and honey featured heavily. Geraldine said they did milkshakes so I ordered a banana one. I think it had real banana in it. Tasted too much like a health drink for me.

In restaurants, on average, a bottle of wine costs four times the purchase price plus VAT. This has become a problem for me, because if I am to drink out what I enjoy at home, the price is ludicrous. So I seldom order wine in restaurants. However, I found the answer to my prayers: a Persian restaurant that serves no wine but invites you to bring your own. It is called **Alounak**, in Russell Gardens, near Olympia, and is run by the brothers Janzamini. I left it to them to decide what we ate, and a series of totally fresh, highly likable dishes appeared as well as newly baked naan bread. It was all pretty good. They also had the extreme good sense to give me, for two of us, a table for six. The napkins are blue paper. This is bad.

Why do I bother to go to new restaurants? I hardly ever like them. So what on earth was I doing visiting **Amaya** in the Halkin Arcade, Belgravia? Either someone recommended it, invariably a disaster, or it was the idea of my friend, theatrical agent Michael Linnit. Geraldine and I attended with Michael and his wife, the excellent singer Jenny Wren.

I don't know why anyone who's not an expert bothers to read Indian restaurant menus. They mean very little to me. 'Cod and chips' I understand. 'Sausages and baked beans' – that's clear as a bell. A lot of fancy Indian stuff, described in terms that are utterly incomprehensible, goes right over my head.

Michael Linnit said he'd had the introductory tasting menu before. 'You can't beat that,' he assured us. I'm easily led. 'Okay,' I said. Saved a lot of trouble asking, 'What's this?' and 'What's that?'

We got some poppadoms, which were fine. When are they not? Then minced chicken wrapped in lettuce leaves with sweet chilli and coconut sauce, chicken tikka and three different naan breads. 'Sweet potato something with yoghurt and tamarind sauce,' I dictated. Grouper came in a pandan leaf, whatever a pandan leaf is. Then the pandan leaf appeared again with an osso bucco. 'They've obviously got a lot of pandan leaves,' I observed, 'perhaps they fell off the back of a lorry.' Linnit said: 'There's a tree in Belgrave Square.'

Somewhere in the middle of this plethora of courses Michael Linnit said: 'Now can we have some clean plates?' Jenny chipped in: 'I asked him to say that. By now we should have clean knives and forks too.' She was absolutely right. It's horrid that these places keep bunging food in front of you, lots of different courses, and you're supposed to eat off congealed plates and congealed cutlery.

The restaurant was getting grossly noisy. It's at best a room that isn't nasty. To my surprise the desserts were very good. First time I've ever encountered that in an Indian restaurant. I had lime and mint tart and a coconut crème brûlée. Linnit had the French pomegranate granita. They were all fantastic.

I was glad to see the chef, Karunesh Khanna, was fat. I always assume a fat chef likes his own food so much he eats a lot of it.

'Gets very noisy, doesn't it?' said Preman, the restaurant manager, as we left. 'Certainly does,' I agreed. Far too noisy for me to return, that's for sure.

Best China plates

Andrew Lloyd Webber looked at me with a mixture of regret and disdain. 'I'm not sure you're a real foodie, Michael,' he opined. His Lordship was absolutely right. Compared with Andrew, I'm nowhere. He has an incredible interest in food, he understands its component parts, he's an avid collector of new places to eat. I care nothing about the make-up of what I consume, only that the overall result be pleasing. I'm not greatly interested in new restaurants, having been let down so often by recommendations from professional critics and ordinary people. But I do value Andrew's opinion.

He said he liked **Aroma II** in Shaftesbury Avenue, because they served offal and funny bits of animals. So I rang them up. We drove up Shaftesbury Avenue, past trinket shops blasted with rock music, to a garish site named Aroma II. It was large and bustling. They'd reserved a good table for me by the window. I sat facing the room, my friend opposite, with a view of the street. She liked that. If I'd faced the street, people would have been waving and smiling all night as they recognised me. That's nice, but ultimately tiring.

I was glad to see a lot of Chinese people eating there. That's comforting. Particularly if it's a Chinese restaurant. Ken Lee and his wife, Kitty, the owners, were working the room like crazy. She offered me duck tongue, deep-fried pork intestine, chicken feet, pork knuckle, jellyfish, smoked fish and marinated beef. 'Have a bit of each,' advised Kitty. I'm easily led, so I said, 'Fine'.

My friend ordered jumbo prawns, sweet-and-sour chicken, duck with pancake (which we never got) and other ordinary stuff. 'I don't eat chicken feet, thank you,' she announced.

My exotic first course arrived. Five neat little ducks' tongues were laid out. I took one and bit it. Kitty said 'Be careful of the bones', by which time I was traumatised. This tongue is all bone. The rest of the display was rather jolly. I liked the deep-fried pork intestine, though it won't go on my regular diet.

Thereafter, more good food arrived in waves. Scrambled egg with seafood, braised grouper mandarin-style, baked quail, Singapore noodles, veal chop with honey and pepper sauce. It really was very tasty. You finished and then kept going back to take a bit more – before they came to clear the table.

We finished with toffee apples, ice cream and a fruit bowl with coconut mousse. As I left, saying goodbye to Kitty and Ken, a large group of men at a table started saying goodbye as well. 'Goodbye Michael, goodbye,' they chanted. An unusual sort of evening.

Essex appeal

Asia de Cuba, the restaurant at the St Martins Lane hotel, is a well-designed room. Circular bookcases, ceiling high, are littered here and there, other round pillars have photos of Cubans on them, or are covered with potted plants or pleated silk. Dim, bare light bulbs hang low over the diners. It looks like a 1950s canteen, with wooden chairs to match. Also extremely noisy, with throbbing music and a lot of Essex-type people. I like them, they've got energy.

The restaurant manager recommended the calamari salad and a rock shrimp salad to start. The portions are enormous; quite enough for four people. They're put in the middle of the table, so if there were a lot of us we could have shared. The food was very tasty, even the salad was made interesting. And the fresh orange juice – aficionados please note – was first-rate. To follow, I had a thin piece of meat described as palomillo of lamb brushed with mojito – the verbiage went on forever. It was excellent. My friend had Latino spiced chicken with coconut rice, banana leaf, tamarind sauce, egg noodles, old Uncle Tom Cobleigh and all. Salads were again plonked on top of everything.

The Cuban coffee brownie was almost historic, the banana and chocolate mousse poor. The Mexican doughnuts I ordered didn't turn up. But overall, it was an interesting and worthwhile meal. If they served it in Kensington High Street without my having to put up with 150 people and the row, I'd be there a lot.

Booking good

It is rare that I am pleasantly surprised. Upset, yes. Disappointed often. Appalled, not infrequently. To find a restaurant almost beyond criticism, practically unique. I was recommended an Italian restaurant above a pub in Notting Hill Gate by someone whose views of culinary matters I suspect. Why I even went I cannot imagine.

Assaggi is in a street of pleasant Victorian houses with a pub, nicely lit, suddenly appearing on the left. That's if you're going south; if you're going north, it's on the right! There's no sign, so I entered the pub, wooden-modern but pleasant, quickly realising this was not it. Round the side there's a door under an arch. You go up stairs covered in rough matting, bright red walls, squares screwed onto them that could be decoration or could be modern art. This leads to a large room with a wooden floor, wooden tables, no cloths, wooden chairs, no padding, three high windows looking onto the street, tables well spaced, similar squares of 'art' on the walls. Rather nice.

I was greeted most warmly by the owner, Pietro Fraccari, who had served me at Cecconi's. His partner Nino Sassu, the chef, also used to be at Cecconi's.

Assaggi provides quite the most marvellous food. I have recommended it effusively to many of my famous friends (yes, I do have famous friends!), but none of them has eaten there. This is because when they phone up, Pietro tells them he's full! When I go back I say: 'Pietro, how can you turn away so-and-so?' He just shrugs and says : 'There was no room.'

This is largely because there are only 10 tables and 35 seats. Pietro only takes bookings for that number. He doesn't try to fill any table twice. If someone finishes early, or someone doesn't turn up, and you phone or drop by, then you might get in at the last minute. Otherwise it is not easy.

On a recent visit I started with pane carasau, which is crisp, almost poppadom-like bread, Parma ham, grilled vegetables in olive oil, then tortelloni with buffalo ricotta and a little tagliolini with sea urchins. Vanessa had brill with spinach, capers and lemon peel. My main course was prawns wrapped in pancetta. Pud for madam was figs in red wine with cinnamon and lemon peel, for me chocolate truffle cake with white chocolate ice cream. It was all historic, the cake being as good as I've ever eaten, even in Harry's Bar in Venice, which is my all-time favourite for everything.

P.S. Table numbers and diners seem to have increased. I hardly go now as it's so noisy.

Star turns

People I know are divided on **Aubergine** in Park Walk, Chelsea. Eighty per cent say 'wonderful', the rest 'dreary food, awful service'. My friend Michael Caine wanted to go there, so I phoned. 'This is Michael Winner speaking. I'd like to book a table next Wednesday for myself and Michael Caine and his wife.'

'It will be a great honour to have Michael Caine here,' said a man with a strong French accent. 'What about me?' I replied. 'Won't it be an honour to have me?' There was a pause. 'It will be nice to have you as well,' said the Frenchman dismissively. 'What time would you like to come?' 'Eight o'clock,' I said. Another pause. 'Could you make it 7.45?' said the Frenchman. 'Look,' I said, 'if it's a great honour to have Michael Caine, do you think we should really ask him to come at a time he doesn't want?' 'It will be all right at eight o'clock,' said the Frenchman, 'but 7.45 is better.'

I put the phone down in stupefaction. 'This is what eating out in London has come to,' I said to myself. The customer is a pawn for the convenience of the restaurant.

For a starter I had langoustine soup, which was exceptional. Sarah had a tian of leeks and scallops, sauce champagne (that's how the menu put it!). She pronounced it good. My main course was pigeon pôché, purée of swede and wild mushroom ravioli, jus Madeira. As pigeon goes it was impeccable. Sarah had fillet of sea bass roasted with braised salsify, jus vanille. I didn't understand the menu at all, but she liked it greatly. We had a bit of free chicken soup to start with, and all of us voted the food thus far tiptop. I found the desserts a considerable let-down. The orange tart was heavy, the crème brûlée jus Granny Smith marginal, the millefeuille of vanilla with red fruit okay at best.

We adjourned to the front bar area for a gossip and coffee. An enormous, tough-looking man in white, wearing a chef's hat, appeared. He turned out to be the owner, Gordon Ramsay. I was glad I could say I genuinely liked his cooking. He kindly offered us the meal free. I should obviously go out with Michael Caine more often. But it was my turn to pay, so I said, 'Thank you, no,' much encouraged by Michael Caine, who said: 'Let him pay, he's a millionaire, he won't notice it.' Overall I found the atmosphere in Aubergine rather tepid. No buzz, although our group was a delight.

P.S. Gordon Ramsay is gone. But it's still good. Has one Michelin star.

It's the real thing

Without Robert Summer and his wife, Susan Kasen Summer, I would never have become a food-life writer. Bob and Sue are marvellously eager-beaver New Yorkers who know far more about London restaurants than I do.

Bob and Sue take me to many London restaurants I would never have gone to, thinking they were largely for tourists. They took me to **The Avenue** in St James's, a place I would normally have stayed away from. Not because it's touristy, quite the contrary – it was full to overflowing with young semi-trendies, all enjoying themselves greatly and making a lot of noise in the process. It's a typical mid-1990s, cavernous, sheer-surfaced, minimalist room with hard chairs and a white tiled floor. Lights of various colours play on the walls. Bob had booked, so The Avenue didn't know it was getting me. When I saw the table offered for five people, they did. I pointed to something much larger. After a hurried whisper, we were allowed to sit there.

My first course eventually arrived: bruschetta of sardines with wilted dandelion leaves and pancetta. This was good, old-fashioned sardines on toast (which

I always liked), with some horrid stringy things that I took to be the dandelion leaves. Bob observed he was eating 'a real risotto'.

My next course was vegetarian spring roll with chilli plum sauce. I decided not to eat it. I tried a couple of fried veggies and some champ potatoes, which were fine. My mascarpone ice cream, rhubarb compote, ginger syrup was adequate. People gave me bits of theirs, which I thought were much better.

There's a large space to the left of the entrance to Chelsea Cloisters, a block of flats on Sloane Avenue. It used to house a Chinese restaurant owned by a nice man called Laurence Leung. Many years passed, and now it's called **Awana**, which is Malay for 'in the clouds'. Considering it's on the ground floor I couldn't quite figure that out. But tiring of bland English food I decided to give it a try.

You go up a few steps to enter and are faced by what looks like a cinema kiosk selling movie magazines. You continue through a bar with red leather chairs, then into a canteen-like room with shiny tables, no cloths, and with a kitchen just visible at the end.

'Your starter will come first and then your main course,' our waiter Jeff Oh explained. He obviously realised, quite correctly, I had no idea of restaurant procedures at all.

From an enormous menu Jeff recommended for Geraldine prawn satay with a spicy peanut sauce and for me corn-fed chicken satay. Jeff assured me they used the chicken thigh instead of the chicken breast, which is apparently better. He also brought some little squares of garlic bread with dahl sauce. It was an absolutely wonderful first course. Tasty, different, delicious. I was pleasantly surprised.

Our main-course plates were hot, which is more than they are in many posher places. What went on them was sensational. I had slow-cooked tender beef rendang, meltingly tender slow-cooked rib in coconut milk curry, accompanied by a bowl of coconut yoghurt, Awana blended herbs and some coconut rice. A total delight. Geraldine had asam kari lautan seafood curry simmered with tomato, okra and Asian herbs. I tasted that. Sensational.

There was a large dessert menu including gin and tonic sorbet. Jeff, who was now my new best friend, suggested the roti tisu – thin, sweetened crispy bread served with cinnamon ice cream and chocolate sauce. So along came this enormous cone-shaped pancake, totally crisp, supported on a metal frame. The chocolate sauce was poured over it and you broke bits off. Geraldine, who never eats desserts, other than crème brûlée, was breaking off bits of this crisp whatever covered with chocolate sauce as if her life depended on it. 'It's disgustingly delicious,' she rightly observed.

Even our starter prawn crackers were wonderfully spicy. Without being pretentious, Awana is simply terrific. With service far more efficient and charming than at most grander places.

Balans, in High Street Kensington, is part of a chain scattered around posh areas of London. It's bright, with an art-deco feel to it, a very lively place. There are lots of specials on a blackboard. The service was quick. I received, fairly smartly, robust eggs benedict with bacon, two large servings. Miss Lid had blueberry pancakes with fruit salad. The difference between this and New York snack places, which I greatly like, is that there they offer so much more space. You get large booths for four or six people, often inhabited by only two. In Balans, I'd chosen the poshest section, central and opposite the bar, which was just acceptable spacewise. The rest of the place was crammed. This is fine for the owner, but indelicate for me. Balans is not the Ken High Street of old. It's the sort of place I'll go to about three times a year.

P.S. I didn't, but my staff like it.

Bellamy's in Mayfair received quite a few rave reviews. Friends of mine said: 'So what? It's no good.' The score: critics nil, friends 1,964.

I entered Bellamy's with the ever-sensational Joan Collins and her extremely nice nusband Percy. Gavin Rankin, the owner, led us to a table with banquettes on one side. It was ridiculously small and absurdly close to the adjacent tables. The water was poured. A great deal of it went on the table. The whole area around Joan Collins was deluged. The head waiter put a wet cloth over the mess and in doing so knocked over the lamp on the table. The lampshade went on the floor. That shows how cluttered the space was.

Things got worse. Joan took a sip of her onion soup and gasped. It was boiling hot. 'They should warn you if the soup is that hot,' said Joan most reasonably.

My whitebait was all right. Joan said: 'Whitebait is dull.' I think that's a peg down from 'all right'. Things improved somewhat with the main course. But not for me. My fish was horrid. I expected to get a nice juicy sole. Instead it was in little, rubbery fillets curling up at the edges. Overcooked and unlikely to have been a first-class fish originally.

Gavin's mother, Lady Bayliss, makes fantastic chocolate cake. I used to order it from her house. So my dessert, made by mum, was terrific. We were given some little chocolate things at the end of dinner. Paola said: 'They're Galaxy Minstrels from a packet.' The head waiter confirmed that. Why not chocolate mints or something else classier?' I wondered.

Just face it, Simon, I'm the one they idolise

Unless you've just arrived from Mars you'll know Simon Cowell is very famous on television and has, deservedly, made millions. We met recently for lunch at the **Belvedere** restaurant in Holland Park. I've known this place since 1946 when I moved into a house (mansion really, but I'm feeling modest) a few yards away.

At first Holland Park was closed and its slightly bombed Jacobean mansion left to rot. Eventually it opened as a public park where the Belvedere, for decades, served some of the worst food ever put before an unsuspecting public.

It has recently improved beyond belief, having been bought by Jimmy Lahoud, whose name sounds like a Damon Runyon character, but is a very pleasant and extremely professional restaurateur.

He has a first-rate chef. He even took my advice and got in a pianist. Things are looking up. It's still a bit gloomy in winter, the more so because Jimmy refuses to floodlight the area.

As we sat in the elegant main room Simon said to me, 'You look very good, have you had botox?' He then asked Geraldine if I'd had botox, adding to me, 'You look like you had a face-lift or something. Are you sure they didn't sneak up and do it?'

Then Simon turned to more serious matters, recommending and ordering the kipper pâté. Geraldine had foie gras. I'd asked for chilli con carne, which wasn't really on the menu that day. We all had that as a main course. It was superb but could have done with some grated cheese and onions. It's a very big menu (unwieldy in my view) so the chef was obviously too busy for these extra bits and pieces.

The set weekend lunch, including roast beef, is £28.06 for three courses, including the 'optional' gratuity. There are 24 items on the set menu and an enormous à la carte.

Then a woman came over to me and said, 'I've always respected you and it's an honour to meet you today.' As she went Simon said, 'You paid her to do that.' 'She obviously had no idea who you were, Simon,' I said smugly. Simon thought for a mini-second before adding, 'She's also drunk.' She wasn't really, I hasten to add. Just a lady with exquisite taste.

We all enjoyed our lunch. I finished with a warm chocolate muffin with vanilla ice cream and double cream. Not only can you eat well at the Belvedere, it has a car park, which is a great help.

I hate not paying for lunches and dinners. Simon put down one of those unbelievably special credit cards glistening with diamonds and gold. 'Don't take it, ' I ordered the waiter. 'Put this lunch on my account.' Simon told him not to. The waiter obeyed Simon. This is clear and depressing evidence that he is more highly regarded than me. In limited circles only, of course.

Leslie Linder was a successful film producer – *10 Rillington Place* and others – in the 1960s. He was also a restaurateur. His White Elephant, in Curzon Street, was the great show-business hang-out of the 1960s and 70s. He owns **The Berkeley Square Café** in Mayfair. A 'gang' based in the late Doug Hayward's nearby tailoring establishment often lunches there. Other masticating members are Johnny Gold of Tramp, Terry O'Neill, photographer, and Philip Kingsley, hair expert. So there I was with the Doug gang, in the light and airy Café, eating a cobb salad, which is a pleasing replica of one they served at the famous Brown Derby in Hollywood. The ingredients include chopped chicken breast, crispy bacon, lettuce, Stilton cheese, tomato, avocado and Brown Derby dressing, whatever that is. 'You won't eat anything else, it's huge,' said Leslie. He was right. I left half and all I could manage to follow was a fruit salad. This was big enough for four and one of the freshest and best fruit salads ever. The Berkeley Square Café will soon sport a sushi bar in the basement. It's a good place.

Charm counts for a lot. You couldn't call the food at **Biagio** in Charing Cross seriously excellent. But Bekim, from Yugoslavia, was such a jolly waiter it made up for the bland spaghetti (we couldn't decide if it was vongole or bolognese), the tired salami and mortadella, and the After Eight mints that were so frozen you could double them over and they still didn't snap. The strip lighting was particularly odd. It was heavily smeared in what looked like blood. Didn't really go with the endless hanging Chianti bottles. Nor did it complement the album of greatest hits signed by Diana Ross: 'Biagio restaurant lovely, thanks for staying open.'

Restaurants often open in a blaze of glory and maximum volume from the chattering classes. Then, even though they keep going, depart totally from chatter radar. Thus it is with **Bibendum**.

Over 20 years ago my friend Paul Hamlyn, Terence Conran and Simon Hopkinson opened Bibendum in an old tyre salesroom on Brompton Road. When I eventually went I found it remarkably good. It was much talked about. For years it hasn't been.

When I visited recently memories flooded back. Marlon Brando declining to sit facing the room because he didn't want to be recognised. Another friend, Burt Lancaster, being followed to our table by some nutty fan. Burt gave him short shrift.

But the greatest star-moment for me came when I was asked to dinner by top Hollywood director Oliver Stone. I took the ever-lovely, ever-cool Joanna Lumley. There we were with Oliver, his Hollywood agent and assorted biggies from across the pond.

Oliver is a bit of a male chauvinist. That's putting it mildly. He was spouting off about this and that. Joanna sat being gracious as ever. I can't remember exactly what Oliver said, or even if it was directed at Joanna. Either way, with great dignity, and far greater fury, she let Oliver Stone have it. Everyone was stunned. She reduced him to an oil slick.

Bravo, I thought, nobody would dare do that to him in Los Angeles where success breeds mute acolytes.

On my current trip to Bibendum, David Mellor was at the next table. I greatly like his classical music programme on Classic FM. After we'd greeted each other I turned my attention to the menu.

I was pleased to learn Matthew Harris, the chef, was actually in the kitchen. His predecessor, Simon Hopkinson, had cooked with splendid simplicity that was memorable. After seven years, Simon had a kind of mental collapse in Bibendum's kitchen and walked out, never to return. He wrote an immensely successful cookbook. He's quite unlike most chefs in that he's both sane and pleasant.

Matthew Harris was Simon's sous chef before taking over. Matthew's brother Henry is chef at nearby Racine. Their food is not pretentiously described on the menu. There's nothing overegged on the plate when it's delivered. It's just marvellously full of taste.

Geraldine ordered endive salad with Roquefort dressing and toasted walnuts, then she chose confit of duck with puy lentils and fried artichokes. Mine was chilled cucumber and yoghurt soup and then deep-fried haddock and chips with tartare sauce. My dessert was gooseberry fool with warm butter cake. I ordered a lime sorbet for Geraldine so I could eat it (she didn't want a dessert).

Everything, and I mean everything, was beyond belief excellent. My soup was utterly delicious. The fried fish was juicy and full of taste with a perfect batter. The chips were probably bought in, but very good anyway. Geraldine thought her duck confit superb.

We had a stunningly good meal. A great credit to my departed friend Lord Hamlyn.

One of the worst dinners I ever had in my life was in a basement called Downstairs at 190 in Queen's Gate, SW7. The chef was Antony Worrall Thompson, and my host was a well-known movie star. Everything went wrong, from very slow food delivery to courses that were so heavy that if Worrall Thompson had been chef on the *Titanic* it would have sunk long before hitting the iceberg. I am prepared to accept that was an off-night, which we can all have, because Mr Worrall Thompson has flourished. He rarely cooks now, but is the 'creative director' of his six restaurants, one of which is **Bistrot 190**. This is a jolly spot with a lively atmosphere, located just above my earlier disaster. When I went there, the first table I was offered was too small, and the second, ostensibly for four people, was so squashed that even with only two of us my head kept hitting some dried-flower arrangement hanging from the wall.

P.S. Worrall Thompson is not associated with these places now.

Table manna

It didn't go down too well when my location manager, Michael Harvey, asked for ice cream at **Bloom's** kosher restaurant at Golders Green Road. 'In this place, not allowed anything with dairy,' explained Leon, the waiter. 'Don't mix ice cream with meat.'

Leon's a Greek Cypriot who looks Jewish. 'You even sound Jewish,' I observed. 'You've got to with the people here,' said Leon. 'After 32 years, I think I'm one of them.'

The restaurant itself is a marvellous time warp, reminiscent of New York delis and every bit as good. Over there, you have The Stage, the Little Carnegie (Woody Allen's favourite), the 2nd Avenue deli, Barnie Greengrass and Sammy's Rumanian, to name a few. In London, since the original Bloom's in Whitechapel closed following a furore because they were found serving non-kosher meat, not much is left of the deli world. 'It was all a mistake,' said Leon. 'The man accidentally delivered meat he had for himself. It closed when business fell off as the Jewish community diminished.'

At Bloom's, and their rival Harry Morgan's in St John's Wood High Street, business always seems pretty good. Not that I'm a regular. I hadn't been to Bloom's for about 10 years; then, I'd found the latkes rather greasy and the mixed chicken soup with lokshen, kneidlach and kreplach poor. This time they were outstanding and the salt beef superb. If they did a Jewish Michelin Guide this would get three stars.

Shortly after we sat down on the chrome and brown-leather chairs, Leon said: 'Three mixed soups and then we'll discuss business.' Off he went and returned to put some amazingly good, large pickled cucumbers on the table. 'They do them here: cucumber, nutmeg, whole pepper, plenty garlic, kosher salt, concentrated vinegar, leave them in cold water for 24 hours. The best.'

Mr Harvey ordered a Bloomburger and onions. Crispian and I opted for salt beef, latkes and tzimmes – a particularly wonderful way of doing carrots with little dough balls thrown in. 'It's sort of melting,' said Crispian of the salt beef, probably the best I've ever eaten. Leon gave Mr Harvey some salt beef with his Bloomburger. 'I can't get through all this,' said Crispian, looking at me. 'I'm glad to see you can't, either.'

We didn't actually want desserts, but Leon came with two enormous slices of lokshen pudding and two vast apple strudels. 'Oh my God!' said Crispian, as Leon cut a third of both and gave them to Mr Harvey. It was all terrific.

'This bit, I can wrap it up for you, take it home,' said Leon of the leftover salt beef for three and much of Mr Harvey's Bloomburger. 'Why should we waste this beautiful beef?' he added, as he returned with a blue plastic bag. 'I give you half a loaf of bread, I put the cucumbers in there and everything.' 'I shall enjoy this tonight with my friends,' said Mr Harvey.

'Now I give you, compliments of the house, three black coffees to wash this down,' said Leon, expansively. I'm so glad he did. At last I had something to complain about. I know you shouldn't look a gift horse in the mouth, but the coffee was awful.

Hot stuff – but I've got cold feet about the kulfi

It's sad hotels and restaurants feel obliged to tart up, make over, redesign. For decades I've gone to the **Bombay Brasserie** in South Kensington. That's now had a redo. The bar area is better. What was a dowdy but respectable dining room now resembles a flash hotel lobby. Enormous, bowl-like chandeliers. Undistinguished smart furniture. Absurdly, it's dumped the pianist. Worst is the conservatory. This was exceptionally pleasant. A lot of plants, some in hanging baskets, a real delight. Now the plants have diminished. There's an open show kitchen in the middle, with chefs cooking. I don't want to observe staff working while I eat. I can see that at home.

It's lost one of my favourite restaurant managers, Adi Modi. His number two, Arun Harnal, has taken over. 'Knifed out Mr Modi, did you?' I asked cheerfully. Arun assured me Adi had retired.

On Saturday and Sunday the Bombay Brasserie always had sensational buffets. Now it doesn't have it on Saturday, thus the place was more or less empty.

I've never had a bad meal at the BB. Lunch started with superb poppadoms made with lentils and some other bits and pieces, all excellent. Arun offered me a drink, but I have to cut down. My liver is one of many organs packing up. So I got fantastic fresh sugar-cane juice with a minty taste. Then a freebie of spiced water with tamarind poured onto a small wheat puff pastry filled with chopped potatoes. Marvellous. The delightful fried spinach had creamy sauce. Geraldine said it contained tomato and onion. Also chicken tikka, tandoori prawn, scallop and salad. Food was batting 100%. Then it dived with a horrific 'palate cleanser' of tamarind sorbet. Dry-ice 'smoke' spurted from the bowl like at a rock concert or pantomime. Smoke effect was good. Sorbet beyond belief awful.

My main course chicken pilau wasn't bad, but I should have ordered my favourite, chicken biryani. The pilau chicken was too mushy. The chef, Prahlad Hegde, has been there 18 years. I've been going much longer.

Then catastrophe – Indian ice cream called kulfi. It tasted like terminally ill cold cornflakes. If you see 'kulfi' on a menu, run screaming for the exit. For a while, on my advice, BB took Marine Ices. They're the best. Go back to them, fellas.

We finished with ginger and lime: 'Our own blend of tea,' explained Arun. 'It's good for the digestion.'

'Are you suggesting your food gives people indigestion?' I asked.

'It makes you feel lighter,' said Arun. He's certainly got the dialogue.

Good news: the Bombay Brasserie still lives. Bad news for it: I shall return.

I both like and admire Gordon Ramsay. But from time to time we have our little tiffettes, like a couple of old queens. We ruffle our feathers, strut about, smooth them down, and are friends again.

I was particularly looking forward to Gordon's latest excursion, into what was Vong on the north side of the Berkeley hotel, Belgravia. There he's opened the **Boxwood Cafe.** In interviews Gordon spoke of doing hamburgers and other cafe-like food. The food resembles cafe fodder as much as I resemble Elizabeth Hurley. As Gord and Winnie are going through one of their love-ins, I won't report him to the Trading Standards Office for misrepresentation under the Trade Descriptions Act. Instead I'll say that the highly posh restaurant named the Boxwood Cafe is very good indeed. That's if you want another highly posh restaurant with staff creeping about with peak discretion in an elegant room where you can hear yourself talk.

The night I went, Gordon came to the table and showed us some River Wye elvers in a shallow bowl of water. They looked like hair-cuttings. When Gordon prodded them, they wriggled. He served them on thyme toast. One of the great tastes.

We got a freebie of some parmesan-fried courgette flowers with San Daniele ham and sweet onion. This was delicious and totally un-cafe-like. You won't get a cuppa tea and a bun from our Gord at the Berkeley.

Geraldine got a freebie smoked salmon and sevruga caviar croque monsieur with cream cheese. Another regular cafe dish, I don't think. But it was marvellous. For my main course I had the grilled rib-eye chop with marrowbone and braised shallots. Absolutely superb. Then, when everything was going so well, the meal took a plunge over the precipice.

For dessert I ordered warm sugared doughnuts with blood orange yoghurt sorbet. The sorbet was fine. The doughnuts were among the most revolting things I've ever forced myself to eat. The outside was both hard and chewy. They were clingy and revolting. Any discernable taste was horrid. I was given three. I left two and a half.

It was my neighbour, the lyricist Don Black (*Diamonds Are Forever* and *Born Free* among his many hits), who, some years ago, offered me serious advice. 'The best salt beef in London is at Selfridges,' he said. The menu at **The Brass Rail Salt Beef Bar** in Selfridges announces: 'All the cattle used to make our salt beef are hand- and grass-reared in southern Ireland and supplied from a sustainable source.' Unlike at Harry Morgan's the salt beef was served hot. Don Black was absolutely right. It was superb. A generous portion, it came with some marvellous pickled cucumbers, which were bought separately. Actually, the best salt beef in London is at Rueben's in Baker Street.

La Brasserie in the Brompton Road is a very bustling, atmospheric place genuinely in the style of a real French brasserie. There are globe lights, fans twirling from the ceiling, French posters on the wall, waiters that look like they've served in Montmartre for 40 years. Written in chalk on a wall mirror was 'Speciality today is terrine de foie gras with onion marmalade and brioche'. Geraldine ordered the foie gras, then smoked chicken salad. I chose French onion soup followed by scampi provençal with rice. The baguette was fine. The French onion soup superb. Full of clingy bits of cheese that stretched forever. Geraldine said of her foie gras, 'Mmm, that is perfection.' My scampi were a tiny bit soft, the sauce and rice were lovely. A perfectly pleasant dish. Our desserts were crème brûlée (hers) and lemon sorbet (mine). Both were extremely good.

The Brasserie St Quentin (now **Brompton Bar and Grill**) is in premises I used to visit a lot in the 50s when it was the Brompton Grill. Did incredible lamb chops, was all red plush and owned by a very nice Polish man.

This time a very smart hospitable lady, Elena Tramonti, greeted me. It's a nice room. Wooden floor, tables well spaced apart, red leather studded banquettes, very simple. Quite posh. Various old photos on the wall, some of Paris, some of London.

The set menu is £18 for three courses plus the dreaded 'discretionary' service charge of 12.5%. I noticed they sneaked in 'sides' costing extra. These seemed to be all vegetables. There's à la carte stuff printed on the same card. Geraldine ordered a salad of spinach, green beans, poached egg and pancetta. Then Shetland organic salmon, fennel salad and tomato dressing. I chose tomato tart with rocket, followed by steak, frites and 'salade'. The baguette was so good I ate two slices. My tart was superb, very flaky pastry, delicious interior. Geraldine greatly liked her salad.

Elena explained the place is owned by Lord somebody and Anthony somebody. Elena said: 'I'm sure you know him.' She thinks I know people. I don't. It's named after Quentin Crewe, who was the original owner. He was a wheelchair-bound food critic who knew what he was talking about. Unlike me, who assuredly doesn't.

Now, would you believe it? They put a baby in a high chair, right opposite me. After a short time the baby slumped to its right. 'Do you think it's dead?' I asked Geraldine. 'If so, we'll all be held as suspects. Hercule Poirot will turn up and quiz us endlessly.' 'It's asleep,' explained Geraldine. Thus it stayed throughout the meal. I think all children under nine should be put to sleep the minute they enter restaurants, thus saving sound-sensitive diners, such as myself, the wailing and other strange noises they emit.

Our main courses were close to perfect. Even though the chips were bought in. For dessert I had hot chocolate fondant, burnt orange ice cream. Geraldine chose raspberry brûlée. They were both above excellent. There's no doubt St Quentin is first-rate. It's changed ownership and its name but is still good.

'We must go to Southall,' said gourmet and television writer Laurence Marks. 'It's like little India, and there's the best Indian restaurant in England, **The Brilliant**.' 'Oh,' I said, less than enthusiastically. But somehow or other on a Friday night there we were in the Ferrari on our way to Western Road, Southall. Not a place I plan to spend my holiday in. The Brilliant is a large, highly unattractive room with tables laid out in rows as if waiting for a major function. It is run by Kewal Anand and his younger brother Gulu, who is also the chef. We sat on nasty red chairs, eating very good rice, terrific jeera chicken with cumin seeds, pickled carrot and mango, prawns masala, karahi gosht lamb, mushrooms, peppers and kulcha bread, which nobody else makes! All excellent, but worth travelling to Hounslow for? Definitely not.

I'm weak-willed and easily led. When I read Prince William took his girlfriend Kate to **Brinkley's** on Hollywood Road, Chelsea, I decided to give it a bash. The thought of lunching next to the future King of England and his debbie-type date sent me all a-quiver.

My heart was racing as I looked at a more or less empty dining room one recent Saturday. The two other people in the room were pleasant-looking but unlikely to have royal blood. So I settled for a corner table facing the door and the bar. Behind me was a canvas-covered yard with tables. It's a very nice place, simple, friendly.

Geraldine started with pâté de foie gras with red onions, marmalade, toast and rocket. She thought it superb. I tried some and agreed. I had 'hot smoked salmon with home-pickled cucumber, dill and sour cream'. A good starter.

To follow, Geraldine had Caesar salad with corn-fed chicken, anchovies and croutons. I had the hamburger. A considerable disappointment. It was far too compacted. They put melted blue cheese on top of fried onions, thus moisturising the onions.

To finish Geraldine had white and dark chocolate mousse. I tried the dark chocolate mousse. It was historic. I also had hot coffeecake with ice cream. It was pleasant school-food stuff. Not fine dining, but none the worse for it.

Hey, big spender

When my friend Sir Philip Green, one of the great retailers of all time, asked me to have fish and chips with him in **British Home Stores**, which he owns, I was confused. Georgina had told me Bhs served very good food in Kensington High Street. That branch closed down.

I ordered fish and chips, baked beans and a Yum-Yum Donut. 'Afterwards?' asked Philip. 'I'll have the doughnut now,' I replied. 'I'll have a few peas as well.' It all arrived. The batter was fresh and crisp. The beans were HP, not Heinz, but they were good. My cod was excellent.

I was offered strawberry tart, chocolate gateau, mixed fruit tart and lemon meringue pie. I chose apple tart. It was fine. Not Gordon Ramsay, but extremely pleasant nonetheless.

A lady customer came over and said to me: 'I want to tell you how good the lamb is. It's the third time I've come here. Lamb on the bone with peas, carrots and roast potatoes.' Then off she went.

As we left, I gave our waitress, Nola, £50. 'That's not necessary,' said Philip. 'It's for me,' I replied. 'I won't take a free meal.'

Rocco Forte bought **Brown's** hotel in Mayfair, spent millions on 'improvements' over two years and then reopened it. I went for Sunday lunch with Anna who shortly thereafter suffered a setback. She became my PA.

At Brown's the restaurant is a nice old-fashioned dining room. It's not trying to be clever. It isn't up its own rear. Panelling, wooden pillars, decorated plaster ceiling. There's a historic restaurant manager, Angelo Maresca, who was at the Savoy Grill. He'd kept two places for me, one by the window and a banquette opposite. I chose the window table. Very comfortable green padded chairs. White roses on the table.

They offered Evian and Malvern mineral water, both excellent – and the dreaded Hildon. A feeble selection of bread. I took a roll. At least it was warm.

The Sunday three-course lunch is £35, 'service charge not added'. Anna ordered fennel with baby spinach, mozzarella and rocket salad with balsamic vinegar from the à la carte. She's very posh. She described it as 'lovely, a very interesting mixture.' I had smoked salmon and gravadlax. The smoked salmon is sliced in front of you. It came from Forman in the East End. They're the best. The gravadlax was very good too. Some rather white melba toast arrived.

We both had roast beef from the trolley. The beef and red cabbage were just about quite good. The Yorkshire pudding was fine. Anna said: 'My mother makes it better,' adding 'the gravy is a little tasteless.' It was awful.

For dessert Anna had Agen prune and matured armagnac crème brûlée. Me – baked orange and lime tart with confit kumquats and coconut sorbet. The tart was about passable. I left a lot of it.

In summation (I've never done a summation before) I'd say the food is not awful but it isn't good enough.

I offer Rocco Forte some advice. Change your meat supplier to H.G. Walter of Baron's Court. Get the chef who was at the Dorchester Grill and is now doing general catering there – Henry Brosi. He's exceptional. Or the previous Dorchester chef, Willi Elsener. He was marvellous too. Then take restaurant manager Michael DiFiore. He had a great following at the Dorchester Grill. Angelo Maresca is fantastic, but he won't stay for ever.

*

The **Brunello** restaurant in the Baglioni hotel is the worst. The most miserable example of mismanagement, decor and dreary food I've ever encountered. The hotel faces Hyde Park near the corner of Palace Gate. It's one of those pretentious places that thinks it's very chi-chi but is, in fact, beyond belief abysmal.

The room itself was like some backward child had been given free rein to commit design hara-kiri. There was a variety of chandeliers, most of which seem to be metal sprayed with glossy black Dulux paint. There were black curtains, yellow curtains, rough-hewn grey pillars in what looked like cement. It was a nightmare. I've never seen an uglier room.

My first course was an utterly dreary version of spaghetti al pomodoro. Geraldine was silent about her ham and buffalo mozzarella but liked the olive oil. My main course of grilled chicken paillard was lifeless and bland. The vegetables were ludicrous. Geraldine quite liked her red onion tart with slow-roasted tomatoes, goat's cheese and rocket.

Their brochure says, 'Our menu offers an original and inventive interpretation of authentic Italian dishes, utilising only the freshest and most interesting ingredients to ensure that the memory lingers with you long after you have left the restaurant.' The memory indeed lingers with me. Like a bad dream.

Bumpkin is a restaurant in Notting Hill owned by the people who have Boujis, a nightclub that is either frequented by royalty or page three girls, or both. Bumpkin serves good old-fashioned English food. On the Saturday lunch we went it was full although its three upper floors were closed. The ground floor is very pleasant. A bar, a view of the kitchen, exaggerated Victorian-type wallpaper, wooden tables and floor.

Geraldine chose the Bumpkin breakfast of bacon, sausage, black pudding, tomatoes, mushrooms, beans, eggs any style (she chose fried) and toast. We both started with an excellent rocket and parmesan salad. The waitresses all had T-shirts with 'Country girl' on the back. Bit twee but pleasant. At the next table people were eating enormous cow pies. They looked fantastic. The cow pies, not the diners.

The service was not speedy, to put it mildly. After 40 minutes I didn't have my main course. To pass the time I ordered a chocolate swirl cocktail consisting of chocolate and espresso shaken with rum, cream and sugar. I could become an alcoholic if all drinks were like that.

Geraldine said, 'This makes me think of a New York restaurant.' I agreed. 'It would improve if we could only get some food,' I added. The minute I come in my food should be put ahead of everybody else's. So we're not served in rotation. I get mine first.

Eventually my fish and chips arrived. They were totally marvellous. The chips utterly memorable. 'This is comfort food at its best,' said Geraldine tucking into her Bumpkin breakfast.

The General Manager of the whole premises, which I strongly advise you to visit, is Dariush Nejad. Both he and Louise Lovell, the charming restaurant manager, were working like mad serving customers, which was just as well as a mass of waiting people collected at the bar.

For dessert I ordered treacle tart. A big letdown. 'There's hardly any taste of treacle in it at all,' I moaned to Geraldine. 'If I was given this on a blind tasting I'd be hard-pressed to say what it was.' Seeing this Louise told me later, 'I've taken it off the bill.' 'Which you didn't have to do, but it's very sweet of you,' I replied.

I'm apoplectic because two food critics, writing for 'respectable' publications, said the hamburgers at my local dump, **Byron**, were the best in London. They're the worst ever.

Byron is beyond belief terrible. Which is a pity as the premises, overlooking Holland Park, were previously inhabited by Ask, which was rather good. (Byron is owned by the same group that has Pizza Express and Ask.)

Like the canaries sent down the mines to test the air, my lovely PA Ruby checked out Byron. She came back smelling of cooking fat. She went back (forced under threat of dismissal) with me, my assistant Dinah May and my adorable fiancée Geraldine. She said, 'I hope the smell doesn't attach itself to my jumper.'

We got them to open a window, but the people at the next table objected. Some fried courgettes arrived. A clumsy and heavy batter. Very poor. The menu declares, 'Our buns are baked by a fourth-generation family baker in the East End. They are just the right size and taste great, the perfect partner for your hamburger.' Both bun and hamburger were awful. The meat was dreary, tasteless, heavy. Everyone's bun was cold. 'All that nonsense about them being made in the East End,' I said. 'They taste like they were made in the fridge.' To add insult to insult we ordered at 1.10pm and it took 40 minutes, in a restaurant far from full, for our burgers to be served.

The 'home-made cheesecake' was sickly and clammy. 'It really is appalling, this place, absolutely appalling,' I dictated onto my tape. Yet two food critics said it was the best. They're bonkers.

Rowley Leigh worked for years at Kensington Place, a noisy moderate restaurant. But very successful. Then he was head chef at West Street, a disastrous dump a few doors from the Ivy. Rowley ventured solo with **Le Cafe Anglais**. Unfortunately he took premises in Whiteleys shopping mall in Queensway.

At the restaurant reception I said my friend Matthew Norman, food critic of the *Guardian*, who'd raved about Le Cafe Anglais, had booked. Surly girl studied the computer as if I'd asked for Einstein's theory of relativity in ancient Greek. The computer wasn't telling her anything. Why don't they have a reservations book? A man joined her in staring, helpless, at the screen. I walked into the restaurant. If I don't I'll be late for dinner, never mind lunch, I thought. I was eventually shown a nice booth.

Matthew arrived. We ordered kipper pâté, parmesan custard with anchovy toast ('outstanding,' said the waiter), pimientos de padron, salsify fritters (which turned out to be off because the fryer had collapsed) and rabbit rillettes with pickled endive. The parmesan custard was brilliant. The rest, okay.

'There's something very dangerous in this rabbit,' Matthew reported. 'It's as though there's shot in it or someone's lost a tooth.' My friend Jeremy Irons met me at the Queen's dentist, whom I also frequent, and said, 'You're too old to have teeth, Michael.' If I had eaten this rabbit I might not have had any. Or choked. So I stopped.

My beef hash with poached egg was cloying, stuck together far more than it should be. Matthew ate most of mine. The main course was a disaster. Grilled sardines tasted of cotton wool. The red cabbage was beyond belief ghastly. 'It is poor,' admitted Matthew.

The dessert chocolate soufflé was stupendous; the pistachio ice cream the best ever. Matthew raved about his mango and rhubarb sorbets. There were many empty tables. Surprising, as I keep reading it's always packed. I don't like it.

To be fair, **Cafe Pasta** in Kensington High Street is not run for the likes of me. It was full of energised shoppers and secretaries, who probably thought the tagliatelle with fresh asparagus and cream was fine. I found it totally resistible. No taste, no texture, asparagus could have been anything, cream bland to the point of extinction. Rum and raisin ice cream was uninteresting, and I finished with a rather insipid cappuccino.

Cafe Tarte on Kensington High Street is one of those places that multiply all over. I bet there's at least one of them near you. It's the sort of place that defies conventional wisdom that everything must be salt-free, preservatives-free, fat-free and taste-free. The window is awash with cakes as if they were entrants in a Woman's Institute baking competition. On the top shelf are little models of bride and groom to go on wedding cakes. That made me nervous.

The menu is enormous; their microwave must be on overdrive. I ordered the jacket potato with baked beans, cheddar cheese and scrambled eggs. Even I couldn't eat the vast serving that came to me. I had to ask for another plate to put half of it on. The jacket potato was all right, skin not really crisp, the cheese and baked beans were adequate. The microwaved scrambled eggs were lumpy, overcooked and inedible. I finished with a white-iced doughnut. Not that good and enormous. But I still ate half of it.

The cakes were described as 'home-made'. Although Cafe Tarte is a one-off I find it hard to believe the owner's wife is busy baking at home.

In my search for a decent Sunday lunch I thought I'd try the **Capital Hotel and Restaurant** in Knightsbridge. It has two Michelin stars. I arrived at the Capital with the Princess, aka Paola Lombard. Miss Lombard is no longer a girlfriend. She's a friend. I remain on very good terms with all my ex-girlfriends. This is because I'm such a wonderful person.

The dining room is plain, small and L-shaped. They offered a table in an area resembling a corridor. So I moved to where I could see through into the lobby and the lounge beyond to give a bit of perspective. Outside the window I had a clear view of my doctor's surgery.

Miss Lombard and I ordered salmon marinated in treacle with spices and coriander and deep-fried soft crab. Our starter had six tiny rolls of treacle-marinated salmon standing up like midget soldiers with a sprig of greenery planted at the top. Then the crab, a spring roll and a lot of plate decoration. It tasted fine. Except the salmon was in such miniscule bits it didn't add up to much. The crab was delicious.

My main course was a daube of beef with garniture grand-mère. I thought that meant boiled grand-mother. Paola had grilled fillet of red mullet with aioli and crushed potatoes. She rightly stated: 'The food is lovely but you can only have it every so often.'

I finished with blood orange jelly with chestnut chantilly and Jivara ice cream. I observed: 'It's a good meal but very prissy-dissy. I'm happy to come here once, but I won't be back.'

You should try it. There's no dress code. I was about the only man wearing a jacket. It's rare when I'm the best-dressed kid on the block.

At his Caprice

Le **Caprice** has figured heavily in my life. When I came on to the 'upper' end of the London scene in the mid-1950s, it was done out in red plush sofa-seating. A bobbing, smiling, small man named Mario Gallati (who had named it after his wife's bra) would greet evening-dressed celebrities after theatre and film first nights. Look to the left and you'd see Noël Coward, to the right Larry and Viv (Olivier and Leigh) and over there Rex Harrison and David Niven. It was all terribly 'dahling' and posh.

The room was bigger than it is now, a large part of what was a seating area being the kitchens. The fashionable bit was on to Arlington Street, where the entrance door is today. A large alcove opposite was the place for racial minorities and nobodies. I qualified for both, but got seated in the best part because I was for a few weeks a theatrical agent, and an important, ageing, blonde lady in the same office took a shine to me and had me with her. I was an embryonic toy-boy, although nothing naughty ever took place, even if 40 years on is a bit late for a denial.

Later Le Caprice floundered, as the era when you wore evening dress for almost every night out vanished. In 1975 it became a tea shop! The next owner changed the red plush to brown and in 1981 it was taken over by Christopher Corbin and Jeremy King, who respectively managed Langan's and Joe Allen's. A lot of black leather and chrome entered, a sparse, minimalist chic, and the showbiz group began to return.

It's now a noisy (unpleasantly so in the evenings), jolly and extremely well-run place. The food is cheap and cheerful, a description the owners would probably object to, but it's very good. The black wood chairs are rather chipped if you look closely, but other than that it retains a fresh appearance. The service is usually fine, although an occasional reminder that I'm an eccentric diner does no harm.

Regular diners wondered whether Le Caprice, the Ivy and J Sheekey would collapse with the departure of Chris and Jeremy. It's now owned by the oh-so-nice Richard Caring, ex-rag trader and general superguy. Le Caprice remains an absolutely marvellous place. The David Bailey portraits, the simple decor, the superb staff and comforting food are an immense credit to all concerned.

I lunched there recently with my guest Henry Wyndham, the chairman of Sotheby's. I had crispy duck and watercress salad (always great), braised ox cheek with beef steak, mushroom and celeriac mash, and muscat jelly with cream. I love jelly. A thoroughly pleasing meal!

Henry enjoyed eggs benedict followed by the restaurant's most popular item, salmon fishcakes. Other Caprice favourites of mine are sautéed foie gras with caramelised apples; deep-fried haddock with minted pea purée, chips and tartare sauce; and chopped steak Americaine – a hamburger minus the bun.

I greatly like their restaurant manager, Nick Roderick. In over 60 years I've never had a bad meal at Le Caprice.

My friend Peter Wood, boss of esure ('Calm down dear, it's only an insurance company') is difficult. Correction: he's not difficult, he's very difficult. Second correction: he's not very difficult he's stratospherically difficult. I approve of that totally. In my Who's Who entry under 'hobbies' I list making tablemats, washing silk shirts, eating and being difficult. Peter writes many robust letters of complaint. Good luck to him. I wish I'd kept the acidly biting letters of complaint I've written for over 60 years. They'd make an instant bestseller. Peter is also the best employer ever. All our deals for commercials – often for millions of pounds – have been consummated in a two-paragraph letter. He's the only person I know who pays faster than I do. Never mind that Peter's fired me six times. Once to bring in a horrific computerised mouse, which spoke with a strange American accent at a speed that made anything he said incomprehensible. As we sat in **Caraffini**, a pleasant blast from the past place in Chelsea, rather naughtily, I mentioned the mouse. Peter laid his hand on my arm and said, 'You were right.'

The restaurant manager there is Francisco Pedre. He remembered me from Al Gallo d'Oro, an Italian restaurant near my house, once owned by a man called Renato. I went there a lot. Often saw George Michael, before he came out, sitting with a boyfriend. The place slid from worse to terrible. Renato asked me to do a private report on it for him. I did. It was damning. I recommended he sell. He said 'Do you know anybody who might buy?' I recommended it to my friend Claudio Pulze, owner of many restaurants. He tried to buy it, but Renato insisted on staying in charge. So the deal fell through. A few months later I saw Gallo d'Oro had closed. Claudio had bought it and later turned it into Memories of China Kensington, which is absolutely terrible. Renato went off with the money from the sale. Claudio acquired a new restaurant. Did either of them send me a thank you note? No. Did they send a bottle of wine to the unpaid agent? No. The other day Claudio rang, after years of silence. He asked me to go to one of his restaurants, wanted a good review. I made my excuses and stayed at home.

'Er, aren't you dining with Peter Wood in Caraffini?' I hear you ask, 'Do you intend to tell us about it?' Okay. It's a pleasant, rather old-fashioned place. It's off the radar. No-one I know goes there or talks about it. Except for Peter. The food is early 1970s which is about the time it opened. This is not meant to be uncomplimentary. I had a faultless gazpacho, an enormous portion of cold poached salmon with potato salad, very good but far too much for me to finish. Dessert was cassata alla Sicilliana. You don't see those much today. They do a marvellous one at La Colombe d'Or in St Paul de Vence. The Caraffini version was fine, but lacked a band of pink ice cream. I like pink. All in all a charming meal, very well served by cheerful and professional staff. We ended on a sad note. Peter told me he wasn't doing any esure commercials in 2010. He is issuing thousands of rubber figures of me which, when pressed, say 'Calm down dear.' And there's talk of my doing some website ads for him. Do hope so. I'm still £6 million in debt. Every little bit helps.

At Heathrow, most of terminal 5's restaurants are 'airside'. That's after you've passed passport and security checks. In the public area I tried **Carluccio's**. I wanted to murder it. Carluccio spoke very rudely about me (who hasn't?) and many readers wrote in saying how awful his restaurants were.

Charming staff led me to a nice table. The place is cheerful with piped Italian music, which I found okay. They had highly respectable Panna and San Pellegrino water. The bread was tired and clammy except for the focaccia. That was excellent. I kept dunking it in the olive oil and eating away.

My only course was tortelloni di cervo, handmade pasta filled with wine-braised venison. It was very good indeed. Geraldine had a large 'antipasto di verdure' and declared it terrific. So I can't blast Carluccio's.

The superb, feared writer Lynn Barber asked if I'd have lunch with her and Tom Parker Bowles, son of you-know-who. Tom, who writes about food, apparently wanted to meet me.

Tom had chosen **Carpaccio** in Chelsea for our date. It was his neighbourhood restaurant. He liked it. I arrived first, Tom a few seconds later. Then Lynn arrived. 'We should all have something different,' said auntie Lynn, now running the show.

I started with maize and pulses soup with mushrooms. It was fine. I followed with spaghetti with tomato and basil. Also very pleasant. We also had fried zucchini on the table. That was good. I enjoyed the wine I ordered, Tignanello 1999 – whatever that is.

Lynn said, 'My 24-year-old daughter works at News International on the management side.' Before ordering a lemon sorbet I asked: 'Could she get me a raise?' [Ed: No] The sorbet was really very superior.

Who says pigs can't fly?

The true test of any restaurant is: having been once, do you go back? Often I quite like places, report them to you favourably, but never return. So it's considerable recommendation that within two weeks of visiting **Cecconi's** in Mayfair, I was there for a second dinner.

Cecconi's was very popular in the 1960s and 1970s. I took glitterati there ranging from Sean Connery to Dennis Hopper. Then, when it started packing in extra dining tables and adding them to the bar, it slipped into restaurant oblivion. For years it was, in my view, mediocre.

At the beginning of 2005 it was bought and redesigned by Nick Jones. Nick is a man of considerable taste. He has the amazing Electric cinema in Portobello Road and the Electric Brasserie and club attached thereto, as well as a posh country hotel, Babington House in Somerset, and Soho House clubs in London and New York.

As with many of today's super-rich, he dresses, as I do, like a load of old baggage. When I was young a millionaire looked like a millionaire. Now most of them look like hippies gone wrong or aged twits clinging to their youth. I put myself firmly in the latter category.

My first visit to Nick's Cecconi's was with Joan Collins and her exceptionally charming husband, Percy. Joan looked spectacularly good, even for her. We sat at a corner table on dark green, velvet-covered banquettes. The tables are well spaced apart. There's a bar in the middle and a nice buzz. It was unbelievably dark, like a night club. Then the lights rose a bit. They'd obviously heard me complaining.

They gave us an excellent freebie starter of shrimps, quail's eggs, oysters, langoustine plus this and that. I ordered tagliatelle with tomato and basil with some roast suckling pig on a side plate. The pasta was good, not historic but acceptable. Joan greatly liked her chicken with truffles and fried zucchini.

There was an amusing cabaret with the suckling pig. Giacomo Maccioni, the restaurant manager, brought the trolley over. Just as it reached our table, the front wheels came off. All the pig shot from the trolley onto the floor!

The pig itself was tip-top but the skin not crisp enough. 'Did they serve it from the floor?' I hear you ask. No. It wasn't a whole suckling pig. It was large bits, some of which had obviously been held back because Giacomo produced more on a silver tray.

On my second visit the skin was much crisper. Good, but not perfect as the suckling pig is at Sandy Lane. There it's historic beyond belief.

Desserts tried out included tiramisu (superb), a lemon sorbet (marvellous), a vanilla pannacotta (good), a fig tart (okay).

Nick advised: 'Nothing's ever gone wrong with the trolley until you came in. Then it has to collapse in front of you!'

I said: 'Put it in the garage now.' On my second visit it was fixed. That's called progress.

When David Tang, the Chinese entrepreneur supreme and general nice person asked me to a party at **China Tang**, his new restaurant in the Dorchester hotel, a series of e-mails flowed. I checked if I was to be seated willy-nilly, or at David's table. David assured me I'd be at his table, no more than two places from him.

Thus my ex-girlfriend Paola and I arrived in the basement bar of China Tang at 8.30pm. David showed me the private rooms and the elegant dining room. Then I returned to the bar. As I saw no sign of people going in to eat I said to Paola: 'This'll take for ever. Let's go in now.'

Paola and I ate a superb Chinese dinner. Other than getting Hildon water (ghastly) and no prawn crackers (one of my favourites) it was a historic meal. There were very light spring rolls, some excellent and fresh sweet and sour pork, which was the best I've ever had, fantastic crisp-skin chicken, stir-fried chicken with spices, pak choi (a Chinese vegetable), Cantonese fried rice, vegetarian fried rice and E-fu noodles, which are some sort of dumpling. I finished with peach sorbet.

Towards the end of the meal David Tang's party entered the room and various illustrious guests stopped for a brief chat, including but not limited to, Barry Humphries, Nick Mason, drummer with Pink Floyd, Lord Lichfield, and other glitterati.

I am always wary of going to places that are supposed to be chic. When people told me **Christopher's** in Covent Garden was 'in', I stayed out. I did eventually go, however, with Miss Seagrove and the TV sex therapist, Dr Ruth Westheimer. Make what you will of that! The parsley soup was thick, my hamburger and bun extremely good, and the lime pie more like cheesecake, but edible nonetheless. Miss Seagrove and Dr Ruth enjoyed their grilled sole. The owner, called, unsurprisingly, Christopher, is the son of Lord Gilmour, a former cabinet minister. It is always nice to see the upper classes forced to labour.

A TV programme I always enjoy is *Trouble at the Top*. It shows the progression of some business enterprise as it starts up. This frequently involves the finances running low, builders being late, everything going wrong and then an opening that is a fiasco.

The Cinnamon Club in the old Westminster library was a chosen subject. It looked a disaster. Some chefs were brought from India or Pakistan to a tiny flat in the East End and promptly fell on their prayer mats. A position they adopted before the opening night in March 2001 when the most important ovens conked out and the ragbag guests who turned up failed to impress the worried owner, Iqbal Wahhab, or anyone else. But almost two years later the Cinnamon Club is still there.

It was chosen by the famed former *Sunday Times* editor Andrew Neil for our lunch date. We were given a freebie starter, a mini rice pancake with sesame chutney. It didn't taste of much. I'd forgotten my glasses but using Andrew's, I was able to order smoked lamb kebabs followed by Gressingham duck with sesame tamarind sauce. To get in the mood I added stir-fried okra with dried mango and also a portion of cumin-flavoured yoghurt with cucumber. I was appalled to hear they had no poppadoms. How on earth can an Indian restaurant not have poppadoms?

I'm sorry to say, everything I ate tasted of nothing. This was definitely, and by a long way, the worst Indian meal I've ever had. Usually even a not-great Indian meal is tasty. You get some sauce or preparation with Indian food that gives it oomph. This had none. It was all totally sanitised.

I chose a dessert of mango brûlée with spiced nougat. It was, at best, mass catering standard. Very poor.

The room was largely occupied by men in suits. 'Why do they come here?' I mused. It was a pity. I saw Mr Wahhab go through so much angst on his way to opening this restaurant. All that, I thought, to produce the most bland food I've ever eaten.

My good friend Arrigo Cipriani, the Harry of Harry's Bar in Venice, told me he was opening a restaurant in London called **Cipriani.** I consider Harry's Bar in Venice the best restaurant in the world. Some of you greatly like it: some do not. Either way, the coming of Arrigo to London is a major event.

Cipriani is beautifully designed by David Tang, Arrigo's partner in Hong Kong. I had one minor objection regarding ambience: the wall candelabra were too bright. They gave the off-white room a clinical appearance. The dimmers could have been turned down 15%.

We all had Arrigo's famous Bellinis made with prosecco and white peach juice. Then over came Claudio Ponzio, a smiling, welcoming Italian recently relocated from Venice where he's been with Arrigo for 35 years. Arrigo himself, well in his seventies, walked the room meeting and greeting. He is unparalleled as a restaurateur. Six of his Venetian chefs are in the kitchen at Cipriani. Upstairs are some of his Italian front of house people.

The ethos of Harry's Bar and Cipriani food is its simplicity. The menu is not like reading an overblown recipe book describing a 'jus' of this and garnish of that. Arrigo relies on top ingredients, beautifully prepared. The plate looks like a food offering not an oil painting gone wrong.

We started with tuna tartar. I'm not usually mad about that. But this was delicate, and I loved it. Geraldine adored her grilled salmon main course. Dinah and I had meat ravioli with a light gravy and parmesan. A total delight.

Harry's Bar desserts are super-historic beyond belief. I was concerned whether they could match them in London. The renowned chocolate cake was superlative. It may or may not have been 1% less than in Venice. I could only tell that by having two slices side by side and gobbling them alternately. Suffice it to say, it was an addition to the London scene that I massively welcome.

We finished with some excellently prepared fresh mint and hot water. Not mint tea in bags, which is ridiculous. Real mint tea. Cipriani is a gargantuan triumph. Go there.

There is one important ingredient for an enjoyable meal that I never see in any write-up: the customers. I used to enjoy **Clarke's**, a Kensington establishment where Sally knocks out impeccable food in her see-through kitchen. When her set meals achieved media recognition, the jovial clientele changed to impeccably suited businessmen, mixed with over-expectant 'special occasion' groups. It scared me away.

The **Club at the Ivy** had a shaky start. Members complained to me endlessly. That was then. Now it's superb. I last visited the Ivy club with Peter Wood of esure. I had a fantastic chicken pie, marvellous white asparagus with poached duck egg and minted hollandaise, and a lovely rhubarb pie. Service is good, the menu mercifully simple. The first-floor bar also offers food; the second floor has the Library restaurant, above it a sushi bar. I'm not going there. Raw fish can be dangerous.

Only one problem with the Library: the three best tables have huge, soft leather chairs. You sink into them. You're out of touch with the table. As that's my only complaint, the place has to be pretty darned good. Ignore all critics, gossips and halfwits. Especially me.

P.S. There's a very glamorous glass lift. No buttons. It goes automatically to the first floor. The single door swings outwards electronically. There's an accident waiting to happen.

Near Smithfield meat market in the City is **Club Gascon.** It's not a club. It's a small restaurant with a lot of marble and mirrors so it looks like a toilet. It's quite famous and has a Michelin star. I went with Geraldine and Dinah May, our receptionist. It was full of men in suits. Not a buzzy crowd.

The menu offered eight types of foie gras, six soups and much more. It's £38 without wine, gratuity or coffee for five courses. Nobody rushed to take our order. Eventually I requested 'melting lamb delicacies, brain and tongue, creamy morels' and then 'hot and tasty pork bites.' We got a starter of sausage, sliced duck and some shellfish. It was delicious, but there wasn't much of it.

I asked the lady sitting behind, 'How did you get your bread?' She said, 'They offered it to us.' No one offered me any. So I asked for it. When it came it was unexceptional. We got another miniscule offering of jelly and tomato sorbet. Excellent.

No one seemed to be in charge of the room. It was appallingly run. After 45 minutes we didn't even have our first course. Geraldine said, 'I'm starving.' My lamb dish was tiny but exceptionally good. The ladies liked what they were eating. 'Just as well,' I said, 'You may never see food again.' Trays of food came from the downstairs kitchen. I looked, hoping they'd be for us. They weren't.

I was given a dessert menu. The ladies ordered cheese. I requested 'velvety chocolate and violets, crunchy praline, coffee sauce.' Geraldine said, 'I think it's lovely here. I haven't got enough to eat, that's all.' 'Well dear, it is a restaurant,' I murmured. I decided to ask for the bill the minute we got the cheese. Otherwise it could take an hour.

My dessert was another pleasant mini-item. I said to the waitress, 'Could I have the bill please.' She said, 'Do you want any coffee?' I replied, 'No, just the bill. I won't live long enough to get coffee.' Amazingly the bill came quickly.

Coast in Albemarle Street, W1, is indescribably noisy, decorated in a nihilistic style of non-decor. The food was fine. Except for the dessert, which was a number of rock-hard chocolate balls. 'Be careful,' the waiter said, 'they may shoot off the plate.' They did. So why serve them?

At **Coco Momo** in Marylebone High Street we sat at a large table, big windows, views of the high street. Seth Berry, an American waiter, came over. He was studying finance at Pennsylvania State University.

Seth recommended the cheeseburger with chips, and assured me they cut up the potatoes on the premises every morning and fried them just before serving. That's more than they do even at very posh restaurants. He also said, 'The freshly squeezed orange juice is squeezed downstairs. They put it in a container and bring it up.' 'So it was squeezed early this morning?' I enquired. 'No, sir, it was squeezed half an hour ago,' replied Seth. Tasted like it. Remarkable.

The burger was superb. The chips were real. Geraldine had toasted Mediterranean vegetables, baby leaf salad, feta cheese with croutons. She was pleased with everything.

Cont'd

My dessert was sticky toffee pudding. Remarkably light, excellent texture, a lot of toffee with it. The ice cream was Jude's from Winchester. Not as good as Marine Ices in Chalk Farm, but good.

Seth walked the room with purpose and speed. 'I don't know how you are at finance, but you can always be a waiter if things go wrong,' I told him. 'Duly noted, sir,' replied Seth.

My friend David, he who won't have his surname revealed, selected **Cocoon**. He explained a well-known multi-millionaire had recommended it. Proof that money can't buy taste. One word sums up Cocoon: ghastly beyond belief. All right, that's three words. Arithmetic was never my strong point.

It's on a first floor above Regent Street. It was quite jolly. Full of secretaries, shop assistants and very minor yuppies. Nothing wrong there. David said: 'You and I are the oldest by far.' We sat with an uninterrupted view of McDonald's. Wendy, David's wife, announced: 'I chose this table.' That was not a major achievement.

We got soft-shell crab with garlic and chilli. I thought it was okay. Then we received a horribly crude, lumpy duck roll with minced duck. It didn't even taste of duck. Our meat dim sum contained the same ghastly duck mince we'd had earlier. There then arrived wasabi prawns, jasmine rice, and a load of other mediocre twaddle. After one tiny bite of the atrocious Mongolian lamb main course, I couldn't eat any more.

I said: 'I don't think this food has been good.' Wendy said: 'It's like a British Airways version of trying to be Asian.' The negative vote was unanimous.

There are places wild horses could not drag me back to. High on the list is **The Collection**, the fashionable restaurant in Brompton Road. Within seconds I knew why I'd never return. It is terribly noisy. You have great difficulty in talking even to someone close to you. I understand that's what it's all about today: big noisy restaurants where you are swept away (or in my case swept aside) by the cacophony and spirit of others enjoying themselves. But not for me. And the food was no good.

P.S. Mogens Tholstrup is no longer associated with The Collection.

Hospital case

What I only go through. How I suffer. Unbelievable really. I'm referring to the food at the multi-million-pound refitted Lanesborough Hotel. It is grotesque, so awful as to be almost indescribable (though I shall try) and an absolute disgrace.

It all started when Mrs Hylda Gilbert, a close friend and wife of the film director Lewis Gilbert, rang me. 'Take me to lunch at The Lanesborough,' she suggested. 'It's the most beautiful room.' 'How's the food?' I asked. There was a pause. 'Average,' she replied. Now, I don't totally trust Hylda on rooms. She once told me the lobby of the Carlton Tower was the most beautiful room in the world. But when she said 'average', I knew the food would be dodgy.

Nothing ventured, nothing gained. So Vanessa and I picked up Mrs G and set off for Sunday lunch at The Lanesborough. The building, on the site of the old St George's Hospital at Hyde Park Corner, is severe Georgian. It looks from the outside like a home for the mentally unstable. Once you get in things perk up a bit. The Georgian lobby/corridor is classy, although I don't know why they've got one of those awful gas imitation coal fires. If Claridge's can have a real fire, why can't they?

The Conservatory is the name of the only restaurant in The Lanesborough. It is indeed a nice room. Rather camp, done out in Georgian chinoiserie with a lot of pink, models of mandarins, various Chinese lanterns and two enormous urns with palm trees and assorted plants in them. The ceiling is glass and high, the tables are well apart, the chairs are comfortable, the crockery is good with blackberry decoration. There is pleasant music from a real-live pianist and double-bass player on a little platform. If only they served food as well.

Guessing things would be in need of help I went totally mad and ordered a bottle of Château Lafite-Rothschild 1961 for £499. Before you think how utterly decadent, I drink very little but tend to spend a lot when I do.

I ordered Chinese duck cakes with oriental aioli to start. It might match the decor, I thought. This turned out to be no more than duck hamburger, with no sauce to help it. It was bland and dreary. Vanessa had asparagus soup. I tasted it, or rather non-tasted it. The flavour was nil, and it wasn't very hot either. Mrs G had smoked salmon. The service was fine – the room is run by John Davey, a great pro whom I knew at Bibendum and The Belfry.

For a main course I ordered a kedgeree of salmon and haddock with curry butter. It came with rice and, for some odd reason, boiled egg slices! It was totally uneatable. It is very rare I leave a main course. I pig out and then complain. This was so drab and tasteless I just nibbled a bit and gave up. Vanessa's chicken was dry and horrid, but the corn fritters with it were good. Mrs G had roast beef and Yorkshire pudding. She picked at a nasty-looking piece of overdone beef and from time to time pulled a face and looked round at the decor. At the end she left half of it; Vanessa left most of her chicken.

Dessert was cappuccino brûlée for me and Mrs G; thick and horrible is the best I could say. Vanessa had apple pudding and honey ice cream. I tasted it. Rather like it came from a packet, I thought.

They deducted everything except two set lunches at £23 each and the expensive wine from my bill as a gesture of regret. The next weekend a friend of mine went and his meal was so terrible they gave him two meals free. This, however, is not the point of a restaurant. After all, this is on one of the most expensive sites in London. If other London hotels can get in excellent chefs, why can't The Lanesborough? 'When they shut the hospital they should've kept the chef,' I said to myself as I left.

Clarendon Cross is a daft name, dreamt up by an estate agent to add glamour to an area at the junction of Portland Road and Penzance Place, Notting Hill. The centrepiece of Clarendon Cross was a restaurant called Orsino. It was beautifully and simply decorated, very light and airy, serving highly indifferent food. I wasn't surprised it closed down. The premises have now been taken over by adventurous entrepreneur Nick Jones.

Cowshed is more spa than restaurant. As you enter there's a counter with food on it, a tiny kitchen area behind and a lime green table with white wooden chairs for 10 diners. On your right is the cash desk with lots of potions on display. The ground floor is completed by three large chairs where people sit having their feet massaged. Downstairs are full-bodied massage rooms.

It's all far too elegant for a poor boy from Willesden. But ever wishing to invade a social class that is well above me, I dropped in for lunch accompanied by Dinah May and a recent addition to our ranks of office assistants, Jane Horn. She answered our ad in *The Stage* newspaper for new recruits.

There's a fairly small breakfast, lunch and tea menu. We all had leek and potato soup. Rather bland. 'Maybe because it's so healthy they don't put salt in,' observed Dinah. Salt and pepper were produced in attractive white shakers. That jazzed it up a bit.

Katherine Connolly, the manager, directed me toward the facial stuff. I bought 'Cheeky Cow rejuvenating facial moisturiser' and 'Cowshed Bullocks soothing moisturiser made by Babington House with grapefruit and palmarosa essential oils.' Apparently the cowshed was the only building left at Babington House hotel in which to place the spa. Thus the name. If I look more beautiful than ever in future photos, these products could be the reason.

Back at the lime green table I had roast butternut, feta, pecan and french bean salad. 'What's this I'm eating?' I asked Dinah. 'Rocket,' she said. It's nice to have an expert on call. As salads go it was pleasant.

The blueberry muffin, which I was told had been baked that day, tasted cloying and clammy. 'Not as good as Starbucks,' said Jane. The other muffin was coconut and something. That was absolutely superb. Close to historic. The chocolate brownie, definitely made the day before, was pretty good.

As we exited an assistant rushed out after me. I'd forgotten my moisturising creams. I wonder if I should have a face-lift or Restylane injections? These are problems I really shouldn't trouble you with. But if I do take the plunge, I promise to reveal all.

There was a great hoo-ha when Joel Robuchon came to London. As if it was important. It wasn't. The downstairs restaurant, called L'Atelier de Joel Robuchon, is highly unattractive. There's a counter facing the kitchen. The tables are in pokey alcoves, or are just pokey. The basic colour is bright red.

They'd reserved me two seats at the bar in the upstairs restaurant, **La Cuisine**, because, apparently, that's the fashionable place to be. Watching the chefs in the kitchen. I can see staff working at home. I don't need to go out for it. So I asked the very charming general manager (as opposed to the two lady receptionists who were the opposite of charm) what there was above.

Laurent Chaniac led me upstairs to the grander area. One of the most appallingly designed rooms I've ever seen. Here the colour is black and white. A narrow room has been divided by a useless counter, not for people to sit at, just laden with pots and green stuff. Thus punters have two narrow areas either side of this divide.

I was shown a banquette with a view of the kitchen. The heat from the wood-fired oven was blasting across me. 'I'll be medium rare before dessert,' I said to Laurent. I moved opposite.

Luckily when my guest, Laurel Powers-Freeling, UK boss of American Express, arrived she didn't seem to mind the heat. Perhaps she was used to it, working for Amex.

First food to appear was carta di musica, crisp Italian bread. I've never had better. The baguette that followed was miserable. Surprising for a French restaurant. It was also offered to me before Laurel. Don't they know the lady should be served first?

The rest of the food was incredibly good, but the place was far from full. I'd read you had to book months ahead. The premises, in West Street, adjacent to the Ivy, have been a graveyard for many restaurants. Monsieur Robuchon should worry.

I chose, from the à la carte menu, langoustine fritters with basil pistou and then roasted young duck, orange jus and endives. Laurel ordered crabmeat followed by young veal rib (they seem very keen on description 'young' here!), in wood oven, olives and purple artichoke.

We got a freebie mousse of foie gras topped with a reduction of port served with a froth of Parmesan. And some ham. They were both superb. Then I got something else I didn't order – two scallops baked in the oven and served with a citrus and seaweed butter. My duck was historic, tender, nice crispy caramel surface. Laurel said her veal was perfect.

We both chose meringue for dessert. Laurel the chocolate one called le black. I had white – crispy meringue, lemon and lime sorbet, avocado banana. It was perfection.

The chef here certainly knows what he's doing. I just wish he was doing it somewhere else with a better room design and more atmosphere.

I drew a total dud at the Athenaeum hotel in Piccadilly recently. Lunch. The worst ever. It was a Sunday. An extremely courteous doorman opened the door and an extremely courteous lady greeted me inside to lead me to the hotel's restaurant, named **Damask**.

The lobby is airy. The restaurant was a cacophony of colours and irrelevancies. Like a kitsch airport lounge gone wrong. The menu offered three courses for £20, including coffee and bitter chocolate truffles. There was no 'discretionary' service charge added. That appeared to be a good deal. After I'd eaten bits of the most awful meal ever presented to me, it seemed vastly overpriced.

My starter was pan-fried fishcake with caper butter and seasonal leaves. If this mound of pathetic, tired mashed potato had been within six million miles of a fish, I'd be surprised. It was tasteless muck.

It was 1.30pm and we were now the only people there. Damask is an absolute non-atmospheric restaurant. If you tried really hard for a hundred years you couldn't have a restaurant designed to give less sense of atmosphere.

Geraldine had peppered seared tuna steak with baby squash ratatouille and anchovies. The chef, and that's vastly stretching the use of the word, didn't know what seared meant. Her tuna was overdone, grey and ghastly. She described the so-called ratatouille as one green vegetable with some sort of tomato paste. She left nearly everything.

Mine was McDuff rib of beef with Yorkshire pudding and horseradish sauce, roast potatoes and summer vegetables. The beef was extremely stringy. The summer vegetables were cold and utterly tasteless. The roast potatoes were British Rail circa 1950. The Yorkshire pudding was adequate. I left nearly all of everything.

The final insult came with my so-called chocolate and orange pudding with vanilla ice cream. I took one tiny taste and reeled in horror. How can anyone serve stuff like this?

Thus ended the most disastrous meal in the history of my life. The owners of the Athenaeum should be thoroughly ashamed. Who says British food is getting better? It certainly isn't at the Athenaeum.

I knew **Daphne's** in the 1960s when it was opened by a theatrical agent and specialised in chocolate soufflé. The last time I went was after OJ Simpson's first trial when I took OJ himself. The *Daily Mirror* photographed me and OJ in my Rolls. Piers Morgan, the editor, captioned it, 'Britain's most reviled man . . . with his friend OJ Simpson.' I thought that was very funny!

Recently I was taken to Daphne's for lunch by Roderick Gilchrist, deputy editor of *The Mail on Sunday*, who I've known since the mid-1970s when he was a showbiz writer and did some exceptionally good profiles of me.

Rod sent a chauffeur car for me. A modest Mercedes was outside my house.

The sort given to junior executives with no hope of promotion. I thanked the driver and walked past to my Rolls Phantom V with my chauffeur, Jim, holding the door.

At Daphne's we were joined by Jesus Adorno, who's in charge of Le Caprice and Daphne's. He's a good restaurant manager. Jesus sat down at our table. I've heard of democracy, but it's a bit much when restaurant staff plonk themselves with the customers.

Jesus ordered fried zucchini. That was a great success. They were a tiny bit salty, but I loved them. My hands darted to the plate, grabbing them like crazy.

I started with commendable spaghetti as recommended by Jesus. Then on to meatballs. 'They're the fishcakes of Daphne's,' explained Jesus, referring to the most popular items at the Ivy and Le Caprice. They were excellent.

Jesus recommended the chocolate and pumpkin tart, which I'd rejected when reading the menu as it sounded a ridiculous combination. 'I'll have it, Jesus,' I said. 'Because you've done well on the food so far.' The tart was pleasant but unexceptional. It was a reasonable meal, nothing more.

As we left Rod indicated his own company Mercedes. It was like the one he'd sent for me. 'What's wrong with that car?' he asked defiantly. 'It's pathetic,' I replied, and wandered off to a quality vehicle.

Delfina is a charitable institution founded by Delfina and her ex-husband Digby. It's for subsidised artists in the studios above to have a cheap meal. They pay £1 for lunch. Normal punters pay full price. The restaurant also does catering.

The food was extremely good. If Delfina were in Holland Park I'd go regularly. Although, at Kensington rents, the tables would probably be an inch apart, instead of nicely spaced in Bermondsey. When the restaurant manager, Sadie-Jane Berinson, eventually appeared, she was charming. I chose 'pickled herrings, beetroot pancakes, crème fraîche, savage beets' as a starter. My guest, the beautiful actress Cherie Lunghi, had carrot and ginger soup and carrot-date wonton.' Both were splendid. My main course was chargrilled marinated kangaroo with aubergine, tomato, parsley salad and tahini yoghurt dressing. I asked for some mashed potatoes. 'Are these real potatoes?' I queried. 'Of course,' said Sadie. They were absolutely wonderful, some of the best I've ever had, with just a bit of butter hanging around. The chargrilled marinated kangaroo was cold. 'Rather like a duck salad,' observed Cherie. It was tender and tasty. I'd definitely have it again. Although I'm unlikely to return to Bermondsey. Nothing wrong with it, but I can eat perfectly well without a huge trek.

I become attached to restaurants. Some are old friends. The atmosphere, the food, the staff – all become a pleasing part of existence. Thus the Grill Room in Mayfair's Dorchester hotel enhanced my life for over 60 years. Now it's destroyed. Ruined. Violated. Savaged. Vandalised.

The new decor can generously be described as hideous beyond belief. The historic English menu has been transformed into ghastly, over-decorated rubbish. To ensure a triple whammy they've replaced many of the marvellous restaurant staff with gross incompetents.

The old **Dorchester Grill** was a marvellously kitsch re-creation of an 18th-century Spanish palace. The ceiling was ornately gilded and decorated. You expected to see Errol Flynn sword-fighting on the tables. The room was as one. It had character and style.

This has been replaced with beige walls featuring murals of enormous Scotsmen swirling whatever it is Scotsmen swirl. Tartan is predominant. There are red lamps on the tables.

A peer of the realm told me the place now resembled a bordello. I can't match the aristocracy on brothel expertise, but the red lamps look cheap. They remind me of a 1950s clip joint.

Amazingly, the old ceiling, with no style connection whatsoever to anything else, has been retained. It's as if the hotel's owner, the Sultan of Brunei, didn't have enough money to finish the job.

Worst of all are the bright luminous red banquettes with tall studded head-boards, and the shocking red curtains. This shrieking red is at odds with all the other colours.

Mercifully they haven't added extra tables so the acoustics are superb. You can talk about how awful the room is, how pathetic the service, how dreadful the food – and be clearly heard.

I took a highly intellectual young lady, Julia Stephenson, who was my constituency's Green candidate at the last general election.

A lot of new young men clomped about. One dropped a dirty knife and then a dirty fork onto the floor as he cleared our first course. Another plonked the wrong desserts in front of me and Julia.

The new chef is Ollie Couillaud from La Trompette. He's a total disaster.

The Dorchester used to have a fantastic bread trolley with at least 14 loaves. Now there's just a modest basket with a diminished selection of sliced bread.

The menu is also smaller than it used to be. Julia ordered 'smoked eel with egg yolk, raviolo, spinach and grain mustard hollandaise'. I had crisp pig's ears and sweetbreads. The ears were sickly, the sweetbreads second best. I left most of it.

My grilled Dover sole was the worst food item ever presented to me. It was small, dry, overcooked and tough. There was béarnaise sauce with it. The sole was too awful to eat. One small taste and I gave up.

The Grill Room used to have a staggering dessert trolley. Lots of scrumptious desserts, all tasting as good as they looked. That's rare with desserts. The trolley's gone, replaced by a limited menu selection. My sticky toffee pudding was clammy. I left nearly all of it. British Rail would have done it better.

I asked for fresh mint tea. 'Is the new chef saving on mint leaves?' I asked as the teapot went back for more. I've never dined at a disaster level like this. Never. There's a new chef. So what? The room is so hideous I'll never go anyway.

It's funny how even I, the ultra-sophisticate, am influenced by what I read. I saw a review of **Durbar**, an Indian restaurant, written by someone for whom I have no regard. This informed me that the chef, Shamim Syed, had won the International Indian Chef of the Year award. As Durbar is near Notting Hill, quite convenient for me, I decided to give it a try one Saturday lunchtime.

The restaurant was empty. Jaked Syed, the younger brother of Shamim, greeted us very pleasantly. We were served, on Shamim's recommendation, a starter of kachori, made from lentils and pastry, and vegetable samosas. The samosas tasted old and reheated. The Lorient special chicken and the lime chicken with coconut milk, lime juice, lemon grass and chilli tasted of very little. The rice was absolutely appalling, like hard pellets.

I began to wonder how the International Indian Chef of the Year award came about. I learnt it was created by Tommy Miah, an Indian restaurateur in Edinburgh. A long list of judges included Lisa Aziz and Michael Cole. Shamim read about the award and sent in a recipe. Five chefs were chosen to go to Edinburgh. By no means were all of the judges present on the day. The award, upon examination, meant very little.

Although I was disappointed with my Durbar meal, some of it was memorably good. The naan bread was as excellent as any I've ever eaten. The dessert, gulab jumun, served with syrup and ice cream, was splendid. The ice cream was Wall's; not classy, but I like it.

They gave me the guest book. This is tricky if you haven't enjoyed the food much. I wrote: 'I had a very nice time. Thank you. Good luck. Michael Winner.' That was true, because Shamim and Jaked were very personable and the chairs were comfortable.

For years, driving through George Street, Marylebone, I have admired the clean, white façade and the myriad hanging baskets of geraniums that make the exterior of **Durrants Hotel** so attractive. As we were filming at the Wallace Collection, Durrants was the nearest place for lunch. Sadly, it illustrated the old saying: 'You can't judge a book by its cover.' The dining room was pseudo, and the food of a type that I thought had disappeared from London decades ago. I started with mozzarella and tomato, difficult to mess up, but Durrants succeeded. It was soggy and of no known taste. I turned to the trolley: slices were cut from a little piece of pork that were tasteless and spoke of the deep freeze. A couple of bits of crackling were given separately; they lacked oomph. The vegetables were overcooked and boring. For dessert I chose some sort of pastry with cream and strawberries. I have pigged my way through many of the worst puddings ever. I left most of this. At least the service was excellent.

Asian gracefully

Charles Saatchi, a man of impeccable taste and grace, told me **e&o** in Blenheim Crescent is the new 'in' restaurant. I thought no more of it. I've been recommended more bad restaurants than I care to remember. A bit later, Georgina said: 'Why don't we try that restaurant Charles Saatchi told us about?' 'Why?' I asked incredulously. 'Because we always go to the same places,' replied Georgina. There's no answer to that: it's true. So I phoned and reserved for Saturday lunch.

e&o is just the latest fly-by-night trendy dump, I thought, ungraciously, as I directed the chaffeur to it. The place looked rather good. As with all new restaurants, it seemed they'd saved on decor by not having any. There was a large room separated from a drinking area by a sizeable bar. This gave a nice sense of perspective. The rest of it was plain, with windows down one side and mirrors down another. There's a row of booths for larger parties. We humble two sat at a table. Knives, forks, spoons and chopsticks were clumped together in a bowl in front of us. A good idea: it saves trying to find someone to bring them to you.

I was in the hands of the general manager, Alex Winchester, a good leader, not afraid to muck in and clear the tables. The place is part of a trilogy, the other two being Great Eastern Dining Room in Shoreditch and Cicada in Clerkenwell. e&o stands for Eastern & Oriental.

Alex described the food as 'Pan-Asian-Japanese-Chinese'. It's prepared by a charming and skilful man from Scotland, Ian Pengelley. We ordered crispy-skin chicken, crispy fried fish, prawn and chive dumplings, baby pork spare ribs, prawn phad Thai, tempura of avocado and sweet potato, tuna sashimi, chilli salt squid, stir-fried vegetables and sweet ginger noodles. (Actually, that was over two visits; it was so good we went back.) Everything ranged from excellent to fantastically tasty and delightful. The service was speedy and very friendly.

The only complaint is that I wanted the warm tamarillo crumble with white chocolate anglaise, but the waitress said it took 20 minutes. They should print that on the menu. Give us a chance to order early. Instead, I had lemon grass and vanilla brûlée, which was fine.

e&o is a really good place. Cheap and cheerful in the very best sense of the words.

Will Ricker, the delightful owner of e&o, asked me to try their sister restaurant **Eight Over Eight** in Chelsea. What a disaster! We ordered, and waited forever for two simple starters. Finally I said to the waiter, 'Please send a search party to the kitchen to find my food.'

At 9.15pm, over an hour after we'd ordered, crab soup and some walnut and date gyozas arrived. The gyozas looked a bit burnt, but the food was okay. The main course arrived at 9.40pm. Black cod. Which was good.

The place has low light and a rather dreary atmosphere. As we'd been put next to the bar there was endless plate clattering plus the noise of the electric mixer going. Not a nice spot to be.

The Electric is a cinema even better than mine at home. It has enormous leather seats with padded footstools. Between the seats are little tables and at the back double-bed sofas, so if the film's no good you can either sleep or snog.

Next door to the cinema is the **Electric Brasserie**, owned by Nick Jones and Richard Caring, who have many much-talked-about places, including Soho House and Babington House hotel near Frome in Somerset. The Brasserie is a big place with a glass front looking onto Portobello Road. It's open from 8am to 11pm. 'On Saturday we do a thousand covers,' Shelley Kleyn, the restaurant manager, explained proudly. Translated into civilian speak, that means they make a fortune.

I lunched there with my ex-girlfriend, the delightful Vanessa Perry. There's a very big menu, everything from steak sandwiches up, down and sideways. Our first course was 'small plates' consisting of duck rillettes, crispy squid, sautéed chorizo, chipolatas with mustard mayonnaise, Ortiz anchovies and shallots, aubergine bialdi, humus and flat breads, and snails in garlic. After that I needed a snooze in the cinema, but being a pig I carried on with grilled lamb chops, peas, bacon salad and butered Jersey royals. All my stuff was extremely pleasant.

In my Electric Brasserie notes, transcribed from carefully made contemporaneous tape recordings, I say: 'I'm going to have an apple crumble.' A few lines later it becomes: 'I liked my apple strudel.' Pathetic, isn't it? I must be demented.

I don't read restaurant guides much. I'm the only true prophet. But I was thumbing through the Zagat guide's good and bad comments from readers. Both the Zagat and Harden's guide offer nothing but praise for **Enoteca Turi** on Putney High Street. Zagat refers to it as 'a little gem'. Harden's: 'a memorable destination. The food bursting with flavour'.

I didn't read every word of both guides, that bored with life I'm not, but I found nowhere else receiving only praise. I went because it was reasonably close to Waterstone's in Putney where people had the unbelievable pleasure of seeing me sign *Michael Winner's Fat Pig Diet* book.

It's a pleasant room, wooden floor, wooden chairs, dreary piped music. Giuseppe Turi, the owner, was present and smiling. We were the only customers.

Our order was placed at 12.40pm. It came at 1.15pm. That's 35 minutes to get a starter. Not service that 'really goes the extra mile' as Harden's says. But we both thought the starters were very good.

At 1.20pm the number of customers doubled. Two more people came in. We waited endlessly for our main courses. Food finally came 55 minutes after we'd ordered. My pan-fried hake with fregola and seafood guazzetto was fish in a soup with beans, clams and tomatoes. Okay. Not 'bursting with flavour'.

Another delay. I threw a minor tantrum. 'We're only waiting for cold desserts, for heaven's sake!'

The food was generally good. But take your own coffin. You may die waiting for it.

Fait Maison, a restaurant on Stratford Road off Kensington High Street, is a small place with an impressive display of croissants, pain au chocolate, almond meringues and other stuff in the window. The manager said it was all home-made. It should be. 'Fait Maison' means made at home.

There's a counter with cold meats and salads. Also cakes: Belgian chocolate, carrot, cheese and pecan tart, fruit tart, fig tart, chocolate brownies and chocolate chip cookies. I took a chocolate chip cookie. It was a total delight.

In the back room there are nine tables. One has newspapers for customers to read. A smiley, welcoming waitress explained we should order at the bar. I had some freshly squeezed apple juice and a Spanish lamb stew with rice.

Mohammed Elbanna entered. He owns this place and a butcher's shop opposite called Miller of Kensington. He told me his croissants were awarded best in London three years running by a leading catering magazine.

'The man who makes our croissants brought the croissant to London 28 years ago,' added Mohammed. I don't know why, but I viewed that information with a degree of scepticism.

La Famiglia is owned and run by one of the greatest old-timers of the London restaurant scene. An admirable professional from Florence, Alvaro Maccioni. He opened his first restaurant, Alvaro, on the King's Road in Chelsea in 1966. Then he had the great 'in' place of the late 60s and early 70s, the Aretusa, also on the King's Road. All the stars went there. It was incredibly atmospheric and lively.

Alvaro opened La Famiglia, just off the King's Road, in 1975. It was always very popular. But not with me. I favoured San Lorenzo. I hadn't been to La Famiglia for decades. It's a pleasant place composed of a number of rooms with a garden at the back, which is covered over in the winter.

Tiled floor, tiles up the wall to dado rail height, real family photos on the walls. Alvaro recommended the 'zucchini flowers deep-fried.' I was hypnotised by the 'chopped chicken livers, capers, garlic on toast'. Rather than spend time on decisions it's easier to order everything and sort it out when the food arrives. So I said: 'I'll have them both.' For my main course I opted for 'roast organic rabbit with rosemary, garlic and a wine sauce'.

The starters were sensationally good. Then on came this bionic rabbit. It was so big! It didn't even taste like rabbit, more like veal. If that's 'organic' I'll have factory-farmed bunny any day.

Sweet trolleys are invariably deceptive. Everything looks good, but usually isn't. At La Famiglia there was wild strawberry cheesecake, which I chose without expecting much. Restaurant cheesecakes are usually dire. This was light and amazingly good.

I made a reservation some time ago at **The Fifth Floor Restaurant** at Harvey Nichols, went up there and was so appalled by the snotty, aren't-we-wonderful approach of the two girls on the desk that I fled without eating. Bravely, I returned with an American couple, he being terribly important at Sony Music. A tall, dark girl at the desk gave us a look as if a smile to her was like sunlight to a vampire, but another lady rushed us to the table before I could run for the lift. The room, which was crowded, is grey and looks like a canteen, but the chairs are extraordinarily comfortable. The menu is large and can't make up its mind whether it's in English or French. Words of both languages mix uneasily. I chose for my first course Henry's black bean soup – called that, I was told, after the chef's first name. Since it's the only dish he put his name to I had some hopes, but it was dark brown and desperately uninteresting. My American lady companion had grilled clams in garlic butter; I ate one, bland and of dreary texture. She agreed. My main course, described as 'Bury black pudding, potato, apple and bacon galette, mustard sauce and onion rings', was horrific. The black pudding was tasteless, difficult to get out of a tough sausage skin and oddly textured. The potato etc galette was soggy and tasted rather nasty. The onion rings were limp. In fact, the whole course was limp. Personally, I don't see any point in eating in a clothes shop. I mean, you wouldn't buy suits at Le Caprice, would you? I'm sorry to say my first impressions were right. The Fifth Floor may be fashionable, but it's absolutely awful.

Someone I must have thought highly of, or I wouldn't have gone, recommended **Floriana** in Beauchamp Place, Knightsbridge. So slave-like and easily led, off I went for Saturday lunch.

The general manager, Vincenzo Mortillaro, is extremely pleasant, but not a patch in the meeting and greeting league compared to Mara and Lorenzo Berni a few doors down at San Lorenzo, or Valerio Calzolari and Michel Lengui round the corner at Scalini.

It was 11 minutes past one and only two other diners were present. Possibly the excellence of the food had not hit the marketplace. 'Normally, Saturday they come in late,' said Vincenzo.

I was not over-impressed with the food. It all looked very nouvelle cuisine. They spent a lot of time organising the squiggles.

Floriana's front room seats 36 people. By the time we left around 2.30 it was pretty full. By comparison, San Lorenzo, which seats around 170, is always packed to capacity for Saturday lunch, with people standing shoulder to shoulder in the bar waiting for seats. The food is infinitely better and it's much better at Scalini, too. So there's no real reason for Floriana.

I've just had a really terrible, terrible meal. Ugh, ugh, ugh. I mean beyond awful. Where was this catastrophic waste of my lunchtime? At a posh place called **Foliage** in the Mandarin Oriental hotel, Knightsbridge. What's so amazing is that it's rated in the AA Restaurant Guide with five rosettes, the top rating. Only two other places in London get that, Gordon Ramsay in Chelsea and Pétrus in the Berkeley hotel.

According to the AA (who may be good at car breakdowns but are useless at restaurants) the chef, Chris Staines, ranks equal with Gordon Ramsay, Heston Blumenthal and Raymond Blanc. Not on what I ate, he doesn't. It's a pity because Chris is a delightful person and I'm sure, led in the right direction, could cook a meal worth eating.

The Mandarin Oriental is a grand hotel with marble halls and modern bits they've done up somewhat oddly. The staff were exemplary. We were shown a nice table overlooking Hyde Park. Just to prove it's 'foliage' there's a leaf under your see-through plate. The room is standard hotel nonentity, with a carpet that could have come from a pub in Bradford.

My first course was foie gras. Reasonable, but nowhere near top of the range. Followed by four tired scallops, which, in my view, had been far too long in the deep freeze. There was a bit of cauliflower purée with them. Who cares?

Then I'd chosen beef, Thai shallots and watercress. It just wasn't very good beef. Chewy, poor flavour. I left half of it and there wasn't much of it to start with.

I sat on my leather yellow chair, which looked like it came from a sale at House of Leather, and wondered what happened to real food. When was it that these mini portions of tarted-up plate decoration came to be taken seriously?

The place was far from full. Why should anyone in their right mind set out to a strange place like Foliage to eat enlarged canapés? There was no atmosphere at all. Geraldine said, 'You feel like you're alone, just the two of us in the middle of nowhere.' I've never been to nowhere, but it couldn't be worse than this.

Fortnum & Mason is a very good place.

Prince Charles, Geraldine and I recently went to the opening of the remodelled Fortnum & Mason. I was expecting total disaster as the designer, David Collins, is responsible for a mass of appallingly designed restaurants all over London. Most of them featuring a variety of dreary brown paint.

The Fountain restaurant has been re-done with shelves of crockery, clocks and a large bar. The menu is much as it was, including welsh rarebit, which they always did so well. The new Fortnum's is a delight.

I have always considered afternoon tea one of the great achievements of British culture. At **Fortnum & Mason's St James's Restaurant** they do it brilliantly. They have Gentleman's Relish, lovely scones and, a sight not often seen these days, the English toasted teacake. Crumpets, too. The pastries are not as good as they were in the old days, but what is?

On another day, I arrived with Vanessa at 1pm for lunch. We were dealt with, and I mean that in the best possible way, by a wonderful old (sorry, ma'am) Irish waitress, Frances McNamara, whom I've known for a long time – she's been there for 17 ½ years. She is exemplary. What a mover! We both had cold cucumber and mint soup. It was good. I then had Lady MacLean's beef stroganoff. I've no idea who Lady MacLean is, but she knows absolutely nothing about beef stroganoff. It was revolting. Tough, tasteless beef, a horrid sharp sauce. I won't go on or I'll get upset. I went on to bread-and-butter pudding. It wasn't awful, but it was well on the way. The event was not saved by some excellent choccy mints in silver paper.

Olympian appetite

My dad's office was a period house in Addison Bridge Place, a small cul-de-sac south of the railway bridge that leads you to Olympia. On the corner was **Frank's Sandwich Bar**, run, not unsurprisingly, by Frank, second name Cura, together with his son Frank Jr and a thin man with brilliantined black, sleek hair, Ronnie Oddi. Opposite was a small garage where dad bought my first car, a black Austin A35 with bright red seats. I have not been back to that spot since – oh, probably 1960. It's quite near my house, so I recently walked there for lunch to see if Frank's was still very good.

It used to be the original ticket entrance to Olympia station. It's still very 1950s. A few cracks have appeared in the large painted sign outside. They've added a couple of white plastic tables with matching chairs; otherwise it remains a time warp. I ordered a bacon, egg and sausage toasted sandwich from a young man who turned out to be Frank Jr's son Paul. Frank Sr has passed away, so Frank Jr is now called Frank and he's still there. The thin, sleek black-haired chap, Ronnie Oddi, is still there, too, only he's put on a bit of weight, lost most of his hair and what remains isn't black.

But the sandwich was terrific. So were the accompanying cups of tea, served in nice china cups with saucers and proper spoons. The place was packed with regulars who obviously know a good thing when they eat it, many of them taxi drivers, which I always take as a good sign. Frank's Sandwich Bar is the sort of place most people pass by. But if you're at Olympia, or just feel like dropping in, I think you'll find it excellent of its kind.

People often say, 'You must get special attention when you turn up.' To which I reply, 'I certainly hope so.' My reception at **Frederick's** in Islington proved that not always is any particular effort made. 'Do you have a reservation?' said a surly girl at the door. I stayed silent. 'What's your name?' she persisted. I told her. 'Table 52,' she called out, as if a train was to be shunted into a loading bay. We were shown through into a gloomy room with glass walls and ceiling. Once settled, after a long delay, our drinks order was taken.

And then came the food. There is a wonderful line in the play *Kean* when Edmund Kean has to see an audition by an aspiring actress. 'Was I awful?' she asks. 'My dear, you were worse than awful, you were quite good.' Thus was the food at Frederick's. The crudités were tired. My soup was bland but not nasty; Vanessa's hot asparagus wasn't hot. My liver and onions were okay but fairly tasteless; Vanessa's dover sole was a bit rubbery. I ordered an apple tart and if I'd been blindfolded I'd have had difficulty saying what it was. The service was slow to awful, and the restaurant manager crept about looking as if a smile to him would be like a silver cross to a vampire.

La Gaffe in Hampstead is a bit of a find. It has great individuality and atmosphere. The owner, Bernardo Stella, looks like what you imagine old Hampstead was: artists and writers, somewhat bohemian.

Upper Street, Islington, home to the King's Head Theatre, has more restaurants than I've ever seen in one area. 'There's nowhere any good to eat up here,' a lady said, coming over to me, as people tend to, with gems of information. She's right. Frederick's and Granita are supposedly okay. I found them pretentiously awful. The indefatigable Lionel Blair recommended **Gallipoli Again**. It's next to the King's Head.

I entered Gallipoli Again at 7pm and had to be out at 7.50pm for the theatre. I chose a table in the pleasantly muddled front room, which has a long bar, a lot of hanging lanterns, Turkish pots, chains running from the ceiling with candles in them, an old radio and masses of other strange stuff. I was led to a strange tent covering the back yard.

They produced a large menu. I ordered hellim, which is Cypriot grilled cheese. 'Then I'll have sucuk izgara [spicy Turkish garlic sausage, grilled], then mitite köfte [char-grilled minced lamb prepared with chopped onion and fresh herbs], tavuk kanat [charcoal-grilled marinated chicken wings], falafel [a mixture of ground chickpeas and broad beans toasted in spices], ispanak yumarta [boiled spinach with fried eggs] and Gallipoli special kebab.' I had enough for about 10 people.

For dessert I had a dry baklava without the usual gooey honey – I prefer the gooey honey – a milk pudding and an apricot filled with almonds and cream. With three Coca-Colas, the bill was £33.45, ex tip. Very cheap – and tasty.

On our next visit we were allowed to sit in the proper dining area upfront. They gave us even more dishes, including Albanian liver. We entered at 7.10pm and by 7.40pm we'd been served and finished an enormous multi-course meal. That's what I call zipping along. I can think of many grander restaurants that should learn about speedy service from Enver Uçar and his merry Turks.

When I arrived at the Hilton hotel, Park Lane, a cheerful doorman opened the car door. 'Hello Mr Winner,' he said. 'Welcome to the Hilton.' I was on my way to **Galvin at Windows** on the 28th floor.

I'd expected a dreary hotel-type dining room, but it was pleasant and elegant. We were led to the best table. Below was a large swathe of London, including Buckingham Palace and all its gardens.

Chris Galvin took over the restaurant in May 2006. He was the original chef at the Wolseley, then opened Galvin on Baker Street with his brother Jeff.

Unfortunately the first course, a 'ballotine of foie gras', was a disaster. There were blobs of this and that decorating the plate. It was all too clever by half.

I ordered Anjou pigeon for my main course. I consider myself an expert in only three food items: chocolate cake, ice cream and pigeon. I'm very fond of pigeon. Sometimes I stand in the garden with my mouth open, in flies a pigeon, chomp, chomp, and that's the end of it. Why restaurant pigeons always seem to come from Anjou I do not understand.

There was a very long wait for the main course. I noticed the flag was flying over Buckingham Palace, but I didn't see the Queen in her bikini cavorting among sun loungers on the lawn. When the pigeon arrived there was a nice sauce with it. It was good but not the best I've had.

Geraldine took some cheese so I joined in. There was white fig chutney and some others I can't recall. The biscuits were good. This was a nice course. Except I ate so much. I finished with an excellent sorbet.

It's a special event place, really. But not at all bad. If you could persuade Her Maj to put on a show in the garden, the superb view would be even better.

My friend, the theatre impresario Michael 'Chalky' White, suggested we should lunch at the **Gay Hussar** in Soho. Liked the thought of that. Any place that keeps the word 'gay', as meaning cheerful, jolly, carefree and not the other version is okay with me.

On its internet site, the Gay Hussar tells punters it has served national specialities and the finest Hungarian wines for more than 50 years and it's used by 'the UK's leading political figures, journalists and artists alike.'

When I entered the Gay Hussar there were very few people in the restaurant, all men. The water was Kingsdown. I looked at it suspiciously. 'It's not poisonous,' John Wrobel, the restaurant manager, assured me as he poured. 'I'll be the judge of that,' I responded.

As I was in a Hungarian restaurant, I started with smoked Hungarian sausage, followed by the goulash stew, which John assured me was very Hungarian.

> **Cont'd**
>
> I drank a good buck's fizz and my sausage was superb. My goulash was a bit too spicy; not good, not horrible. I wouldn't rush back.
>
> Chalky said: 'Michael Foot eats here. This hasn't changed in 50 years.' I agreed that was a plus. So was my sweet cheese pancakes, which was exceptionally good.
>
> The walls are covered with cartoon sketches of Gay Hussar customers. Ken Livingstone was one. I'm glad I didn't see that earlier. It would have put me off my food.

Lunch with Mo

It was so embarrassing. After 50 years Harrods cancelled my account. I only found out because my assistant, Dinah, was going to get me some sheets and pillowcases. Wanting to check everything was hunky-dory, I phoned Mohamed al-Fayed's super-efficient PA, Wendy Allen.

'I suppose Mohamed's abroad,' I started. 'He's here,' she said. 'I'm sure he'd love to talk to you.' Thus I was put through to his Pharaoship.

'I'm only phoning to check my account's okay,' I stuttered. 'Come to lunch,' said Mohamed.

Shortly thereafter I found myself sitting in his **Georgian restaurant** eating stag's testicles from his estate in the Highlands. The taste, shall we say, was unusual. Mohamed assured me they had great powers of libido revival.

The Georgian restaurant is a marvellous room. A large, elegant space, big tables set well apart, a pianist tinkling away. There's an excellent buffet, although our meal largely came from some of the 30 restaurants spread all over Harrods.

The meal continued with Mohamed's own recipe of lobster in a shell, a sauce with oysters, tomato relish, mozzarella, breadcrumbs, garlic and caviar. Fantastic. It came from Harrods oyster bar.

Then we had bouillabaisse fish soup from the Sea Grill bar downstairs. This too was outstanding. The main course was beyond belief. Really simple. Roast duck, saddle of lamb from the rotisserie and roast beef from the Georgian restaurant. All three were absolutely exceptional. They were organic and from Mohamed's Highland farm.

For dessert I was given bread and butter pudding. It was light, very tasty. I ate everything, sultanas and all. This was one of the best meals I've ever eaten. I'm not sure I'd ask for stag's testicles again, but the rest – beyond belief.

'I must pay,' I said. Mohamed waved his arm dismissively as we started our trip round the store. 'All right,' I said. 'What charity do you favour?'

'I do a lot for the Great Ormond Street children's hospital,' replied Mohamed. I sent him a £500 cheque for them. No freebies for me, thank you.

Waiting to greet us at **Getti**, on Marylebone High Street, was the manager, Simone Conti. He led us to a large round table by picture windows overlooking the high street.

The room is light and airy, white walls. There are more tables upstairs and downstairs and 18 tables outside, which, by the time we left, were nearly all occupied.

Getti is owned by a man who also has Zia Teresa opposite Harrods. This used to be very good indeed. When I last went it was beyond belief appalling. But this may have been before the Getti fellow took over.

My fish soup was not as tasty as some I've had in the south of France, but it was acceptable. My grilled sole with the inevitable horrid spinach was okay. Dessert was a triumph. Berries with a mixed berry jelly around. It had some fancy Italian name, but a berry is a berry and a jelly is a jelly.

The customers all looked like they came from a bus stop in Herefordshire. How the poor dears ended up in Marylebone I can't imagine. Perhaps they wanted to live closer to their medical specialists. Simone Conti has left and was replaced with a miserable woman.

'If you review this place, make sure you mention the pancakes were a bit tricky,' advised playwright Sir David Hare. We were in the **Golden Dragon**, a Chinese restaurant in Soho. David was trying to separate pancakes so he could take one for his duck. They were sticking together and tearing.

It was my pal John Cleese's lunch party. Another member of our group was John Myatt, the man responsible for 'the biggest art fraud of the 20th century', according to Scotland Yard. He got a year in prison for successfully forging famous artists. Now John sells his work as 'genuine' fakes for around £10,000 a canvas.

Our marvellous food was served on one of those swivel things. You helped yourself as it went round. I ate multiple dumplings, spring rolls, noodles with beef, duck in pancakes which, when released from each other, were fine, and cups of tea. I also had two Coca-Colas. All the other tables were full of Chinese people.

I've decided, after deep consideration, that Britain's greatest contribution to the world of food is fish 'n' chips. I've had second-rate fried fish and chips in posh restaurants, but never from local places with gleaming vats of oil. They often have glamorous names associated with old sailing ships. You fear that, when you return for seconds, the whole thing may be out at sea tossing in the waves.

Luckily the **Golden Hind** stayed anchored in Marylebone Lane. Its fried plaice with chips and mushy peas are a delight. The fish is succulent and fresh, the batter light and crispy. Mushy peas and chips are tip-top. I ate this accompanied by its excellent tomato salad with raw onions. A first-class meal.

The Golden Hind is extremely popular. It's a very old-fashioned set-up: a black and white tiled floor, wooden tables, a wooden coat and umbrella stand. You can eat on the premises or avail yourself of its takeaway menu. A wooden board lists the owners' names, starting with '1914–1947 Mr Esposito Italian' up to the current owner '2002 Mr Christou Greek'.

There used to be a newspaper ad with the slogan, 'They laughed when I sat down to play.' It showed a man on a piano stool who'd just taken a crash course in piano-playing. Everyone thought he'd be useless. Then he launched into a perfect rendition of Beethoven's 'Appassionata'. Jaws dropped. I always think of Richard Caring when I recall this ad.

Four years ago, Richard, whose previous experience was to pioneer the manufacture of clothes in China, bought some of London's most famous restaurants, including the Ivy, Le Caprice, and J Sheekey. The sneers, putdowns and insults from the so-called 'expert' restaurateurs flowed fast and furious. The fact that most of these twits couldn't run a whelk stall was neither here nor there. Venom, motivated by jealousy, poured forth and still continues. Now, as restaurants collapse all around as famous chefs liquidate companies, buy them back cheap from the liquidator and re-open, leaving their suppliers owed vast amounts, Richard sails on, acquiring restaurants and hotels all over the place. He currently has 39 with 10 more soon to open. His suppliers aren't out of pocket. There's no chance they will be. The more Richards, and the fewer arrogant dullards whose only skill is shooting their mouths off as their companies either collapse or dwindle, the better.

Richard suggested we lunch at **Goodman** in Mayfair. It's a steak house. Our date was for 1pm. I'm never late. When I turned up at 12.56pm Richard was already there. 'Have you bought the place yet?' I asked. 'No, but I'm going to open a steak restaurant in Mayfair. I wanted to check out the opposition,' explained Richard. Tell you something else I like about him, you always get a straight answer. No ducking and diving, no 'I can't tell you at the moment,' just open and real. Plus, he's got a great sense of humour. As for Goodman, it's okay. If Richard sets up offering similar fare, he'll win hands down.

The décor is dark wood booths with photos on the wall. Not offensive. The bread was warm and pretty good. They offered tap water, or in-house filtered. Could do better. The waiter brought an enormous tray of steaks. 'It's a US strip steak, a US rib eye, a British bone-in sirloin, an Irish T-boner and an Australian organic fillet,' he informed us, adding 'the difference is that the US meat is corn fed and wet aged. It's very mild, it's very sweet, it's very juicy.' 'He's getting swept away, this fellow,' I dictated into my tape. The waiter continued, 'The quality meat is grass fed, the Irish meat is grass fed, grain finished. You can mix and match, you can share steaks.' 'But Mr Caring wants medium well done and I want medium rare,' I observed. The waiter said, 'It'll be difficult to share, then.' 'The word I would use is impossible,' I volunteered. 'What if the chef does medium?' suggested the waiter. 'Then neither of us would get what we wanted,' I responded. This was getting into fantasy land.

I chose a bone-in sirloin, British, medium rare. Richard chose Goodman rib-eye 400 gram, medium well done. We both had béarnaise sauce. I ordered creamed spinach and hand cut chips. Service was speedy. We got a hefty steak knife. My steak didn't taste of much. Had it been in the deep freeze too long? The spinach was superb. The hand cut chips were not as crisp as they should have been. No oomph at all. I don't know why restaurants offer hand cut chips when they can't do them. Richard told me he was opening a chain of French brasseries called Cote. 'Really fantastic,' he said. Well, he would, wouldn't he? But I do hear well of them. There are five already and two more due before the end of the year. No crisis in Caring land. My dessert was 'Goodman best ice cream chocolate sundae'. It was utterly meaningless. A lot of dush and slush. No good taste. Little bits of dreary chocolate cake buried in it. Not great ice cream. I left 95%.

Richard found it highly amusing that I looked at the menu through one lens from a broken pair of glasses. 'Can't you afford a full pair?' he asked. 'As they're only £6 each wholesale, I can, Richard,' I informed him, 'but glasses in your top pocket make a funny shape in your clothing and I'm a funny enough shape already.' When we went for our photo I patted Richard's front. 'Your suit is so close it's practically painted on,' I said, 'Why bulge it out with glasses in your top pocket?' 'I think you're right,' said Richard. 'Marvellous,' I said, 'You've learnt something.'

Recently a stupid journalist came up with the nonsense that I shout at waiters. I don't. I'm the only food writer in history that mentions waiters by name, praising them for their contribution to the meal. Very occasionally I complain vociferously to inept restaurant managers. Normally I go in quietly, eat quietly, thank everyone and go. This disappoints some people sitting nearby who hoped for a tantrum display they could relate to their friends. You can't please everyone, can you?

When I entered the world of top-class restaurants, around 1940, cooks worked in the kitchen. I don't remember them as chefs. I'm certain they never spoke. If they did nobody took a blind bit of notice. As for them being so-called celebrities, this was inconceivable.

Since then we've tumbled downhill. We are now deluged with photographic images in the press and on television of these ridiculous people wearing white aprons. And they are giving opinions. It's beyond belief.

When I was young the word 'celebrity' meant something. You were a celebrity if your considerable achievements were known throughout the world. Now every nonentity on the planet is a celebrity. We'll soon have celebrity plumbers and celebrity traffic wardens. In order to sort out this plethora of grotesques, they are compartmentalised into degrees of celebrity. A-list, B-list, down, presumably to Z-list and beyond. The word celebrity no longer has any meaning.

I'm drawn to these thoughts while ruminating about my friend the admirable Gordon Ramsay. An extremely nice person with a beautiful and charming wife.

Gordon has wandered, I think unwisely, from his real métier as a chef par excellence to become a television buffoon.

There are thousands of professional smilers, inane autocue-reading insignificants and other motley morons filling hour upon hour of television time. Their pathetic mini-activities are recorded with reverence. Details, which should be of no interest whatsoever to sane people, fill pages of newsprint.

Is Gordon now so infatuated with being a celebrity that he's forgetting the talent which rightly gained him respect? That he could knock up a dinner that was stupendously memorable.

When I first met Gordon at Aubergine, he cooked. Regularly. I've been to his personal Chelsea restaurant, **Gordon Ramsay**, a couple of times. Other than nasty bread and the worst cup of mint tea ever produced, it was prodigiously wonderful. But when I went Gordon was in the kitchen. I wonder how often that happens now?

Gordon runs restaurants all over. Too many. It could all end in tears.. If I go to a three-Michelin-starred restaurant called Gordon Ramsay, I like to think the boss himself is slaving away over a hot stove. If he's somewhere else – and of course this applies to any major chef – should we have to pay the same for our meal?

I equate this to the art world. If I buy a Canaletto actually painted by the master I can pay millions. If it's a Canaletto school painting, executed by his highly trained workers, it looks good but the price is a fraction of the real thing.

How often do people have a meal at a famous chef's restaurant where the chef has made any direct contribution? Are we now in the extraordinary position where Michelin stars are handed out not to an individual chef, for his meticulous and brilliant work, but to an organisation where nameless minions are trying to remember what they were told to do?

Who ate all the pies?

I'm a fan of Gordon Ramsay. He's one of the great chefs in the world. By comparison, our other three-Michelin-star-cook, The Waterside Inn's Michel Roux, is fit only for motorway cafés. Gordon also possesses, in abundance, something M Roux does not: charm. He's enormously likeable, direct and warm.

I've been a fan of Claridge's for 60 years. But the marriage of Ramsay and the hotel worried me. I liked Claridge's restaurant as it was under John Williams. It was simple. The staff were delightful and straight-forward. I had some superlative meals there. However, life progresses.

As the Claridge's doorman opened the Bentley door, he said: 'Look, Mr Winner, it's buzzing.' Through the entrance doors, I saw a new Claridge's. They'd previously redecorated the lobby and the downstairs lounges; now they'd changed the restaurant and, above all, brought in Gordon Ramsay. The American owners should give him a major bonus. It's become a crowded, invigorated, exciting place. Little bars here, groups sitting at tables on the way to the restaurant. It's no longer a delightfully eccentric, cavernous club for elderly Establishment personae.

After inspecting the chef's table in the kitchen – which is not for me – I settled into the restaurant alcove where I'd sat so many times. The **Gordon Ramsay at Claridge's** room is glamorous, although I greatly missed the windows, now obscured by a wall. Low-hanging lantern chandeliers provide pleasant perspective. The colouring, carpets and ambience are fine. The immaculately dressed mingle with the tieless. One man wore a black jumper and no jacket. My guests were David and Wendy, who decline to exhibit their surnames. They're married. He's in business, she's in television.

We got many superb freebies. 'A sort of aubergine mush,' I dictated. Also cream cheese with white truffle. The menu offered 'Roast canon of lamb served with shoulder of lamb (cooked for eight hours), white bean purée, baby leeks, rosemary jus'. Georgina asked to have the eight-hour lamb, not the other. The restaurant director, Dominic Corolleur, froze. 'But canon of lamb is delicious,' he said. He tried again and again to persuade Georgina (and he called her 'Georgina', which was overfamiliar) to have both. 'She's told him what she wants,' I thought. 'Why not give it to her?'

Dominic became offensively snooty. 'I'll have to discuss it with the chef,' he said, as if dealing with a total moron. I remembered the critic for the *Independent* writing of this restaurant: 'My waiter was typical of French waiters, who know the customer is never right. His smile evaporated quicker than chloroform once he had taken my order. He then used the same script on the next table, like some double-glazing salesman working from a call centre in Cardiff.'

After the debate with the chef, Georgina was graciously permitted to have only the eight-hour lamb. She liked it. So did Wendy, who had the full monty. My first course was superb – haddock and quails' eggs with a vichyssoise of leek and potato soup. But I became saturated with the profusion of freebie mini courses. They fill you up and make you less ready for the main events. Nothing, however, could have made me ready for my main course.

I used to love the chicken pie at Claridge's. Either Gordon or his chef, Mark Sargeant, had made some. It was the worst chicken pie I've ever eaten. I left most of it. The chicken was in cloying cubes. There was no gravy or succulent taste, as with the old Claridge's pie. The pastry was white and abysmal.

After that, the dessert freebies were exceptional, but the bread-and-butter pudding, made with brioche, was too sweet even for me.

There's a saying: 'No good turn goes unpunished.' Gordon had kindly made both the chicken pie and some pommes soufflés for me. Pommes soufflés are blown-up fried potatoes. They were not as good as under the previous chef. Gordon should stick to what he knows.

Most of the food is good but it's 'event eating', served with great pomposity and utterly lacking the old restaurant's understated charm. Gordon should be knighted for services to the nation. But for a treat, I'll keep going to his place in Chelsea.

Airside at Heathrow's terminal 5 is **Gordon Ramsay Plane Food**. It's a beautifully simple restaurant with a great view of BA planes one side, a bar and see-through to the kitchen on the other. I started with a salad of watermelon and feta with toasted pumpkin seeds and lime vinaigrette. Very tasty. I loved it. Then braised lamb with honey and cloves, grain mustard mash. Tip-top. With some rather lukewarm and dreary buttered spinach. The handmade chips were excellent. Dessert was horrible. Valrhona chocolate fondue (which was superb, runny chocolate sauce) to be poured over miserable, tough, textureless waffles and heavy, cloying marshmallows. Gordon should visit Heathrow's Virgin lounge, where I had fantastically good waffles, free.

In *Travel and Leisure* magazine they recently listed the 10 best hotels in Europe. Number one was Inverlochy Castle, near Fort William. Been there, got the T-shirt. It's good but I wouldn't rate it best in Europe. Then it goes through various foreign hotels until, at number six, we have the only London hotel – the **Goring** near Victoria station. What happened to the Connaught, the Berkeley, Claridge's, I wondered? Obviously the list was rubbish. I'll go to the Goring and murder it, I thought. You might call that unfair – so what? Fair is boring.

I had a slight tremor of doubt as we arrived. It's in a lovely backwater street and looked immaculately preserved. It's an Edwardian place with the inevitable flags flying and window boxes of flowers. The restaurant manager Stuart Geddes, came out to greet me and led me through a marble tiled hall, turning left to the restaurant. An extremely elegant Georgian-style room, very discreet, very old-money, lots of windows.

Only one thing seriously tarnished the ambiance. There were four modern, cheap-looking, horrific chandeliers that looked like they were leftover Christmas decorations from a bad day at B&Q. They were totally out of keeping with the lovely plasterwork, the subtle furnishings and the overall excellence of what would have been, minus these electric, spindly lights, one of the best dining rooms in London. I was told the room had been redecorated by Lord Linley a couple of years ago and these atrocities were his doing. The hotel owner, Jeremy Goring, should get a stepladder and pull them down immediately. Be brave, Jeremy. Admit an error of judgement and put it right.

Enough of moaning, let's deal with the positives. That great musician Jools Holland was at the next table with his lovely daughter Daisy. 'I come here regularly because the food is like my gran used to make,' observed Jools. I know what he meant. This is English food at its best. Served in an atmosphere that Claridge's used to have in the days before it became Gordon Ramsified.

You could tell all the staff were, in the very best sense of the word, of the old school. As indeed were the clientele. Stuart Geddes had worked under Simon Girling at the Ritz. The chef, Derek Quelch, whom I cannot praise highly enough, had been number two to John Williams who moved from Claridge's to the Ritz. Both Girling and Williams are great role models.

Among the many foods I'm not an expert on, which in fact is every food on the planet, the one I know least about is jellied eels. But they were my starter, with a lovely sauce. I thought they tasted very good. Geraldine had smoked salmon followed by gâteau of spinach and wild mushrooms with roast garlic and baby vegetables. Both courses were exemplary.

My superb Castle of Mey roast beef was served from an old, slightly chipped trolley. It was as good as I've ever eaten. The gravy was delicious. The Yorkshire pudding a tiny bit tough, but still in the 'good' category, the roast potatoes excellent. I had a little copper pot of mangetout and another of peas and onions. Both perfection.

The pudding menu looked beyond belief tempting. I tried knickerbocker glory, a baked custard tart and a lavender pannacotta. They all looked like a coffee table cookery book illustration. They tasted just as they should.

There must be something more wrong with this place, it's just so great. Ah yes, Jools said, when Lord Linley re-did it they got rid of the pianist. That disappointed him. Didn't bother me.

I was absolutely wrong in my original bias. The Goring is very special indeed. Never mind being number six on the European hotel list, I'd put it number one.

Great Queen Street in Covent Garden is awful, ghastly, ill-run, absurd. For a start this dump is so pretentious it doesn't put its name or street number anywhere. Not on the window, not on the awning.

The room is okay. Wooden floors, wooden tables, long bar. We were seated in the window overlooking the United Grand Lodge of England. Whether you like freemasons or not at least they have the sense to label their building.

I ordered potted shrimps followed by hare ragù and noodles. My potted shrimps came in a tiny glass. I've heard of small portions but this was ridiculous. Then I got some very underwhelming pasta. Bunged into this was a meat, which was, of course, the advertised hare. Not only was it tasteless it was dangerous. It contained many very small tough bits of bone. Bite heavily on them and you'd crack a tooth. Swallow them and they could be fatal. What an appalling place this is, I thought. I left most of my hare and pasta.

Then, not unnaturally, we wanted to order dessert. It was impossible to catch the manager's eye. She was the sort of person who walked through the room, not looking around to see how the customers were faring or if they wanted anything. So she didn't notice me beckoning.

No one took any interest in giving us the bill, so I went up to the till. I'd forgotten the pin number of my Mastercard. Luckily Geraldine knew it. So we were able to flee.

'Go to **The Greenhouse** in Mayfair,' people said to me. I went. I wish I hadn't. At the end of their Sunday lunch I reckoned I hadn't eaten food like that since I was last on British Rail. It's a very posh place with far too much glossy cream paint inside. The poached egg salad with sauté potatoes and black pudding I shall spend a long time trying to forget. The deep-fried plaice was bland to the point of non-existence, and only became interesting when my guest, Dorrit Moussaieff, the international jeweller, tried to dab it with a tissue to take the excess grease off. Her roast beef looked good, but lacked any known taste, and the so-called chocolate steamed pudding was grossly inferior chocolate gateau with a watery sauce. The regular chef, Gary Rhodes, was off. I think the dish-washer stood in.

Twenty years ago, Simon Parker Bowles, brother of the famous one who married that woman, opened **Green's** in St James's. It's much favoured by picture dealers and others who visit Christie's. I'd never been there, so I went for lunch one Saturday. Green's is a sparse, clumsy, substandard Wilton's, but not unpleasant. There are booths with a studded, rust-red hessian-type covering, framed prints and a male-club atmosphere circa 1980. Not one of the great years for interior decoration. The food is comfort food – sausages and mash, fishcakes and, when in season, oysters, crab and sea stuff in general.

I started with a salmon fishcake, which was perfectly all right. Georgina greatly liked her goat's cheese and leek tart with salad. My main course was pan-fried fillet of sea bass with grilled spring onions and brandade. Mr Vickerstaff explained it was a cod brandade and 'rather salty'. That's the understatement of the decade, if not of the past 500 years.

I got extremely excited about dessert when I noticed one of my all-time favourites – Bakewell tart. I asked Mr Vickerstaff when it was baked. 'I'd guess yesterday afternoon,' he said. 'Why not go to the kitchen and check?' I suggested. He returned, saying it had been baked that morning. Unfortunately it was not made with the usual raspberry or strawberry jam but with large, chewy slices of apricot. It also lacked the icing and cherry that sometimes tops the almond sponge. The pastry and sponge, though, were superb. If they'd stuck to the classic recipe this could have been historic.

Green's is unexciting, certainly not terrible, but offering no major accomplishment in food or décor.

I said to Martin Magee: 'Let's have lunch in a London taxi shelter.' Martin drives me sometimes when my chauffeur's off. He works for an Arab prince (doesn't everyone?), but occasionally drives his modern black cab.

We set off for the **Grosvenor Gardens taxi shelter**, near Buckingham Palace. There's a 'rest rank' outside, where drivers can park without having to feed meters. The

Cont'd

shelters provide cheap food for London cabbies. They can take 12 people on bench seats facing a narrow shelf from which they eat. The dining area's on the left as you enter, the kitchen on the right. Martin and I squeezed onto one of the benches. A blackboard menu showed pork chop, £4.50, and sausage and mash with onion gravy and beans, £4. I had a mug of tea (good) and ordered the sausage and mash.

My sausages arrived. They were enormously long. I'd like to say it was a wonderful dish, but it wasn't. The sausages were soft. Not a good taste and no crispness on the skin. Wall's pork sausages, Heinz baked beans, a fried egg on toast – that's a great meal. These beans were weak in colour and taste, not Heinz. The potato was Smash or something like it.

Tina Jenner, the formidable chef-landlady, was a legal secretary before taking on the shelter two years ago. 'She's also our mum,' a cabbie explained. 'She sorts out all the arguments.'

I ordered Tina's home-made festive pie with ice cream. 'Where's the ice cream from?' I asked. 'Asda,' replied Tina. It was terrible. But the festive pie was sensational. Superb. At last, a triumph. It was a marvellous home-made pie with apple and raisins. I should have had an enormous portion of that and nothing else.

The company was great, and I had a very nice time.

When **Hakkasan** opened, some people described it as very chic. It's near the junction of Oxford Street and Charing Cross Road, in a gloomy alley named Hanway Place, where I once directed a movie with Billy Fury. The entrance looks like the back way into a carpet factory.

A Frenchman in a green suit stood behind a long desk. He didn't smile or say 'Good morning', just, 'Is there anything I can do for you?' 'I've come for lunch,' I said. This seemed fairly obvious as it was lunchtime, but perhaps he thought I was there to read the gas meter.

Things were saved by France Gendron, a charming and efficient waiter from Australia. We gave a complex order, including Chinese dumplings with chicken, Chinese chive, peanut and dried shrimp, which I think was called a chui chow dumpling, but don't rely on me. Then stir-fried roast udon with pickled vegetables in a xo sauce, poached Peking dumpling with chicken, prawn and dried shi'itake, scallop shumai with tobiko caviar, red rice organic pork with ginger and Shao Hsing wine, and so on. France came back saying: 'We've got some good food here, I guarantee you'll enjoy it.' The dumplings were good but a bit rubbery. The duck and noodles main course was pleasant, as was the pork. There's nothing precise about Hakkasan's food. It's jolly, canteen-like and very edible.

A few days later, I saw Hugh Grant eating at Hakkasan in the movie *About a Boy*. This has nothing to do with anything. I just thought you might like to know.

Lionel Blair, starring with style at the King's Head Theatre (a cause I donate to), said the Turkish restaurant next door was excellent. He'd even seen Ralph Fiennes there. I tried a Turkish place across the road, the **Harbour Restaurant**. They produced some rather good lamb and a salad with roast potatoes and a mezze for Miss Lid plus soft drinks and water – all within six minutes of our entering. The owner, Volkan Altinok, said he and his brother had been there three years. Their father had opened Britain's first kebab restaurant in the Holloway Road. 'It was very popular with Irish people,' he explained.

I find Mohamed al-Fayed a delightful eccentric who cheers up our national psyche no end. So let's progress to his Jewish-type delicatessen, the **Harrods Salt Beef Bar**. I've always wanted to try that. Particularly as, at the peak of his battle with Tiny Rowland, Tiny issued immaculate books to selected people detailing supposedly taped conversations in which Mohamed spoke as a dire anti-semite. I rather like the idea of an anti-semite running a salt beef bar. Even though I don't believe Mr al-F is anti-Jewish at all.

But I did find his salt beef odd. It's not bad. It tastes perfectly pleasant. But it in no way resembles the salt beef I have lived with. Offer this up at great New York delis, such as The Stage or the Little Carnegie, and they'd fall about with derision. It's sort of pressed salt beef. It has none of the succulence and texture of the salt beef I adore. The deli pastrami, on the other hand, is excellent, and the frankfurters superb, even though they weren't in the usual buns but in crusty French bread. The pickled cucumber and sauerkraut were tiptop. The only available dessert was described as 'wonderful New York cheesecake'. It was.

The posh people of London, the truly stylish, the highly elegant, the seriously rich, should erect a statue to the amazingly nice Mr Mark Birley. He's done more to satisfy their extravagances than any other person in catering, although to describe Mark as 'in catering', which he is, diminishes his true worth. Mark's three famous establishments are clubs. That stops the rubbish getting in.

Probably the most attended and talked-about venue in Mark's collection is **Harry's Bar**, in South Audley Street. As with all Mark's establishments, there's no sign outside indicating what's inside. Just the number 26 on a canopy. It is a very, very good Italian restaurant, although not a patch on the real Harry's Bar in Venice. (There's no connection between the two.) There's one serious problem with London's Harry's Bar. It's furnished for small children. This is odd, as most of the guests, being rich, are quite large and fat. The chairs are tiny, the space between tables is minimal, it's vastly overcrowded and noisy.

The restaurant is always packed with glitterati. At the next table were the Duchess of York, my old school friend Prince Rupert von Lowenstein and the TV writer Jeremy Lloyd, who played upper-class twits in my early movies.

The slices of salami and ham, and the cheese straws, which started our meal, were of exceptional quality. Georgina had asparagus with shrimps and peas, which she described as 'delicious'. I had asparagus with a fried egg, parmesan and truffles. It was fine. The bellinis were good, but nowhere near the quality of the Venice Harry's Bar, where they were invented.

My main course was tagliatelle verde with cheese. Waiters kept bumping into me as they walked by. The adjacent table, laid for four people, was suddenly relaid for six. A very plastic-surgeried group sat there. My dessert was a deeply memorable apple strudel. I eventually prised myself away and onto the pavement.

P.S. Mark Birley sold to Richard Caring, then died. I've visited under the new owner. Much the same!

Hot tip for fish lovers

Personally I find everything and everybody north of Hyde Park highly suspect. Until you get to St Albans that is, and I'm not sure about them either. But I do like **Harry Morgan's** Jewish restaurant in St John's Wood High Street. I hadn't visited for quite a while. But I was seduced back by my friends John Gold and Terry O'Neill. Johnny and Terry are an unlikely couple to lunch regularly on Saturday at Harry Morgan's – or Herschel's as they call it in honour of the owner, Herschel Havakuk, an Israeli. Terry is a nice Roman Catholic from somewhere in Ireland and Johnny is Jewish.

One recent Saturday lunch we assembled at one o'clock on the red imitation-leather banquettes, in front of the shiny tables, and ordered variously salt beef, gefilta fish, chopped herring, mixed chicken noodle, kneidlach and kreplach soup, some latkes, and a display of pickled cucumbers. All of this is totally delicious. In fact I have never had anything at Herschel's that was not delicious except for one Saturday when I asked for hot fried fish and he obviously didn't have any, and warmed up some cold fried fish and it tasted ghastly.

This particular morning we were surrounded by the usual Damon Runyonesque characters. As Johnny studied the racing form, one of them, called Monty Marks, offered up a tip. Johnny phoned his bookmaker and asked me what I wanted. I don't remember the name of the horse, but I do know it was Monty's tip. Having placed our bets, Johnny then listened to the race on the phone from the bookie's. When it was over, amazing and miraculous, I had won! My, or rather Monty's horse had come home for a change without a clear view of the rear of eight other horses and jockeys. I was so excited I ordered an apple strudel. Then I left Herschel's £300 richer!

The next time I was in, Monty was nowhere to be seen. As I knocked back some chopped liver, Johnny looked up from the paper. 'Carranita for the 2.10 at Doncaster,' he said. I pretended not to hear. It's the best thing, I assure you.

P.S. The food's still good, but they've rearranged it so it all seems to be communal tables, like a synagogue social club. Too much for me. I order takeaways.

My friend Adam Kenwright, whose ad agency expertly services theatre productions, went to **Hélène Darroze at the Connaught**. He grabbed my tape recorder and described it as thus: 'We've decided to have the tasting menu. The waiter said that would be the way to experience Hélène's special style of cooking. Hélène would recommend it personally. She was cooking that day.

'The first course was seafood something. The waiter stood by after lifting the domes off the plates. I asked, "Is there a problem?" He said, "I like to wait because Hélène is very proud of this dish. Hélène feels this is a special dish from Hélène and Hélène would like me to see how you react to her dish."

'I laughed and said, "You're not serious are you?"

'He said, "Oh yes, this is very special and Hélène is very special and this is her special dish, and captures Hélène's very special talent. She wants us to report to her how much pleasure you get from it'."

Adam said the waiter stood there through other courses, talking a load of twaddle, until he was asked to leave. Adam found the food very disappointing. There were four empty tables when they'd said no table was available at 7.30pm.

I read and heard of similar nightmares from other people who'd been there. So my visit to Hélène Darroze started in a very biased mood, made unhappier by the appalling redecoration of the Connaught, particularly the restaurant. This has various clashing shades of patterned yellow, tacky wall lights, horrific Seventies-type carpet and enormous central, high-backed banquette divisions, which obscure much of the room from my favourite corner table. It's all a total, ghastly, unrelieved, hideous mess.

Before what the general manager, Anthony Lee, described to me as 'a £70m upgrade' it was understated, distinguished and lovely. If that's an upgrade I'm an astronaut. But – and this is important – I suffered no verbose diarrhoea from the waiters and Hélène's food was all good to historic.

I had the three-course set lunch, which with freebies came to around 127 courses. There was cauliflower velouté, tuna with truffle, foie gras, the best pigeon I've ever eaten and chocolate carupas de Venezuela, which I was told was pure chocolate with 'crispy and creamy salted caramel ice cream, fresh candied kumquats'. I've only described a fraction of what passed from plate to tum. I'd need three pages to list it all. Boy, can this gal cook.

The maestra herself appeared. A blonde, tiny woman, charming and self-effacing. On her website it says: 'Children over 10 years of age are welcome.' That should be followed throughout the land. Or, 'Children under 10 visiting restaurants should be drugged and put to sleep.'

Occasionally Matthew Norman and I meet for lunch. His career has gone downhill since his diary days. He now writes the *Guardian*'s food reviews. Everyone knows food critics are at the absolute bottom of a deep pit. Thus two ocean-floor monsters went to lunch at **Hereford Road**, Notting Hill's newish, supposedly 'in' restaurant.

Cont'd

I started with potted shrimps, which were fine. Matthew had braised cuttlefish and fennel, which he was most enthusiastic about. For my main course I ordered braised beef cheek and pickled walnut. It was fine but not earth-shattering. Matthew had wood pigeon, sprout tops and lentils. I've got wood pigeons galore in my extensive garden. Maybe I should shoot them and flog 'em to Hereford Road's chef-patron Tom Pemberton.

Matthew then had rhubarb sorbet, which he liked. I had so-called treacle tart, which I definitely didn't. As we left I noticed Tom had great burns and slashes all over his arms. 'He's a self-mutilator,' explained Matthew. Tom assured us it was quite normal when you work in a kitchen. Never happens to me when I scramble eggs.

The **Hilton National London Olympia** is the sort of hotel for people I never meet. I walked there for lunch the other day. I was seeking adventure. You go up gold escalators past a bizarre chandelier of chrome and strip lights to the first-floor dining room. Strangely, I thought it all worked rather well. The dining room is large, bright, big windows, very comfortably furnished and with good-sized tables not set too close. We decided to go for the buffet, £11.95 inc coffee and mints! It looked all right. A cold table and hot tureens of lamb, turkey, chicken and what have you. I took a bit of this and that. The lamb was surprisingly good. I grabbed a lot of apple sauce and mint. The roast potatoes were noticeably better than The Ritz or the Four Seasons. My guest, Michael Guest, a film producer, had the scampi, which were okay plus. The veg were particularly fresh, tasty and crisp. Unbelievably, I found myself viewing things as almost excellent. We then had ice cream, a mousse (both good), an excellent red jelly with fruit and cream (I like jelly), plus fairly feeble meringue cake and weak apple and berry tart. Still, for the money, it was good value.

For the esure insurance commercials I travelled through parts of London I had no idea existed, to the Centrale Shopping Mall in Croydon. Peter Wood CBE, distinguished chairman of esure, was present to see I behaved.

'Let's go to my new restaurant, Post, in Banstead, for lunch,' he suggested. 'I've only got an hour,' I said, 'better we eat here.' 'I'm the chairman, you can have longer,' said Peter. 'No, no, I'm just a humble employee,' I retorted with proper modesty. Thus Peter, my assistant Dinah May and I ended up in the restaurant at the **House of Fraser** on tables 19, 20 and 21.

'This is what I'd call a respectable crowd,' I observed looking at my fellow diners. I wandered round the counters. There were olives, cheeses, meats of all kind, lots of bread and Danish with various fillings. 'Never knew Croydon was so sophisticated,' I thought.

Then I returned to my soup, which was dreadful. 'Like dishwater,' came to mind. My main course came, which was much like the soup but without liquid. A perfectly respectable dish if you're out shopping. Which I wasn't. We finished with hot apple pie and fresh cream. It came rather tepid. But wasn't bad at all.

I rarely read restaurant reviews, but I saw some for **Hush**, the Mayfair place opened by Roger Moore's son, Geoffrey, and one of my former lawyers, Jamie Barber. Even critics who are normally bland or relentlessly kind went bananas with their invective. A lot of it seemed to be, rather unreasonably, because the two young men who own it had never been in the restaurant business before. So what? Everyone has to start somewhere.

I had my moan before I got there. I found it impossible to locate. It's in an alley leading to a mews off Bond Street. I've heard of exclusive, but hidden is ridiculous. I found it, eventually, and thought it exceptionally pleasant. Downstairs, it's lively, canteen-like, with no tablecloths. Upstairs, it's grey, elegant and with a long bar.

Unlike some serious food critics, I liked what I ate. Hush is definitely good, but I think the menu could be more inventive. More different. I'm getting bored with British nouvelle cuisine. If I see another piece of grilled fish on a bed of spinach I shall vomit.

PS Geoffrey Moore is no longer with Hush.

Although he occasionally threw people out, Nico Ladenis is the sanest and nicest chef I have ever met. He and Marco Pierre White achieved their three Michelin stars on the same day and, by coincidence, handed them back the same week, Marco because he no longer wished to slave in the kitchen, Nico because he was retiring.

Nico was mentor to **Incognico**. He's now parted company with them. I'd been there a few times for a pre-theatre snack. It was always first-rate. The delicious warm apple pie is as good as you'll find anywhere, and the service exemplary. The room is a dreary brown, the favourite colour of the overused restaurant designer David Collins. Brown probably featured traumatically somewhere in his youth, and he's been taking it out on the rest of us ever since. On a return for dinner I was glad to see they had bought elegant, panelled glass mirrors and oil paintings to cheer the place up.

All the food was memorably good. I ate rather simply: gravadlax, an entrecôte steak with béarnaise and flat mushrooms with garlic and breadcrumbs, followed by champagne jelly with citrus fruits and ice cream. Georgina was more adventurous, with ravioli of goat's cheese followed by breast of guinea fowl with lentils. 'Extremely balanced taste,' she opined. Then, seeing the inevitable stains on my shirt, added: 'We should have taken the photograph before you ate.'

Prior to a theatre visit to *Fosse* (very good) one Saturday night, I decided to grace the **Intercontinental Hotel Coffee House Restaurant**. I arrived at 5.43pm. Kim, from South Korea, in a green blazer, greeted me most charmingly and said the buffet would be up until 6pm, but we could order from the à la carte. She said it would take 10 minutes to squeeze two fresh orange juices. I checked what was on display: a very fresh-looking fruit salad, desserts and some light and dark fudge in a bowl. I like fudge; it was good. Biljana from Macedonia, in a striped waistcoat, took our order. After that, food appeared all over the place. Miss Lid tried sushi from the buffet and said it was marvellous. I grabbed everything as the waitresses carried it in. 'What's that?' I'd call out and it would be brought over for me to taste. Cubes of sauté potatoes, stir-fried lamb and prawns in Thai curry sauce (got a bit of that on the tablecloth), carrots, clear chicken soup, egg and dumpling soup, confit of duck legs and then the ordered course of roast maize-fed chicken with bubble and squeak and shallot and white wine chicken jus. I finished with some very nice chocolate-chip cookies.

The food ranged from good to acceptable. The main problem is the room itself, which is stuck in an ugly part of the 1970s: sort of fake Georgian with prints of jockeys. I think a coffee shop should have more snacky things, be open all day, which this isn't, and not worry about tablecloths and flowers in little pots. The hotel PR is obviously aware of this, because she wrote to me: 'The current décor is rather old-fashioned and we hope to completely update it.'

P.S. They have. It is still good.

It's hard for anyone to join the Ivy league

I don't understand where all these extra diners come from to fill the seemingly endless new restaurants. Are they bused down from the Outer Hebrides, cleaned up, de-Scotchified and sent forth to multiply?

It made me wonder about the earlier 'in' favourites, such as the **Ivy**, which after eight years of bidding, Jeremy King and Christopher Corbin got from the freeholder, guitarist Mark Knopfler, in 1990. Corbin and King instantly got the Ivy back to its glory days.

The Ivy was recently acquired by Richard Caring, who swapped selling clothes for flogging fishcakes. I thought I'd see how this old lady was faring against the new competition. So I went on Sunday for lunch.

It was packed. No 'faces' (as my friend Terry O'Neill calls celebrities of all shapes and sizes), just perfectly pleasant-looking people who probably came from Essex.

As I settled into my usual table I noticed the wooden chairs were chipped. Like me, they'd seen better days. Perhaps they came from a builder's yard. I consider that an immense plus. Like the Ivy, they were ageing, comfortable and still performing a useful purpose.

I'm fed up with glitz and more glitz. The Ivy could not be called glitzy. The panelling looked relaxed and tired, the windows, largely plate glass, could have come from a sale of unwanted items in a minor Victorian church. I don't know when they last renewed the upholstery. I'd guess 1810.

That's what's so alluring about the Ivy. The easy-going atmosphere provided by staff and decor is near-perfect. Please Richard, don't buy new chairs. Don't give the Ivy a make-over.

The food hasn't changed since the early days of Jeremy and Chris. It's pleasing in a totally unostentatious way. It's diverse, yet never goes over the edge. It's also amazingly cheap. For Sunday lunch you get a three-course meal from the nine dishes on offer, which include rib of Hereford beef with Yorkshire pudding and roast potatoes.

The beef was cut thick, tender and of great taste. The Yorkshire pud was unbeatable and they even managed the roast potatoes to perfection. Carrots and cabbage came too. To start I had artichoke minestrone, delicious. And for pud a mint chocolate chip ice cream.

The Ivy remains a serious gem in the West End firmament. Frayed at the edges but with a heart of gold. Last time I went service was far too slow. Buck up, please.

I was expecting very little of **Izgara**, a Turkish restaurant in Hendon Lane. Miraculously, I enjoyed one of the best meals I've ever had, accompanied by exemplary service. At Izgara the high-back chairs look like modern versions of those designed by Rennie Mackintosh. Unframed paintings of sunsets and skies. Jolly Turkish music came unobtrusively from loudspeakers.

I ordered hummus, tarama, cacik, Patlican tava – fried aubergine and green peppers with yoghurt and tomato – falafel, Turkish feta cheese, ispanak tarator – fresh spinach with creamy yoghurt – and Atlana kofte – a spicy minced kebab grilled on skewers, served with salad. It was all beyond belief tasty. It came in a very few minutes without fuss. Everything was beautifully presented. Fresh is the key word.

My dessert baklava was far and away the best ever. It can be chewy. This was flaky with a fantastic flavour. A fresh pear cooked in syrup with nuts and blobs of cream was perfect.

The waiter even brought the bill in seconds. For three people it came to £39. I added a tip of £15. The waiter took a few steps, turned and said in quiet amazement: 'Fifteen pounds?' I waved my arms in a 'yes'. He was worth it. I've never had better service anywhere in my life. As we left Dinah said: 'I don't mind paying if it's like that.' 'Since you're not paying I don't know what you're talking about,' I responded.

A look west,
and a flight out

In 1969 Julie Hodgess, famous for designing Biba's, the 1960s rocket-up-and-down clothes superstore, went into the restaurant business. She opened **Julie's** in Holland Park, or rather what estate agents have now named Clarendon Cross. After a couple of years she threw in the towel, and the place has since been owned by the property people who had the head lease, Timothy and Cathy Herring.

I used to go to Julie's a lot in the early days. In their large back room with a table not unlike that used by King Arthur I would entertain the likes of Burt Lancaster, Marlon Brando, Robert Ryan, Ryan O'Neal and other luminaries of the cinema. Although the food was a bit ropey, they all liked it because of its atmosphere. It had a 1960s charm, inventive but safe, twee but delightfully odd. I went back recently and it had changed hardly at all. While the area had poshed up no end, Julie's remained a time-warp of dark cellar-rooms, tunnels, a sort of greenhouse white place and, of course, the old back room.

Even the food had moved up a notch. It is pleasant without reaching any serious culinary standards. My wild mushrooms in a pastry basket had very good pastry, my companion (there's a word I hate!) had aubergine and sour cream mousse with toasted pumpkin seeds. And liked it. My beef stroganoff was pretty revolting, old and tired beef strips in indifferent wild rice; the lady chose better with salmon baked in puff pastry with fennel and dill. The butterscotch crêpes with cream cheese and ginger could generously be described as adequate. But the overall feel of the evening was rather endearing. No-one wants major meals every time they go out, it would be too exhausting. Ambience and charm make up for a lot. I do wonder, though, about all those diners sitting in a corridor leading from the bar to the back room and the greenhouse area. I've decided that any restaurant that can sell seats in a passageway must have some secret of success.

I stopped going to **Kai**, a Chinese restaurant just off Park Lane, years ago because in a makeover my usual table vanished. There was no other acceptable spot to replace it. As I visit tables, not restaurants, I struck Mr Kai (as it was then called) off my list.

When I revisited, the meal was a disaster from start to finish. The table itself (they'd re-done the layout and decor yet again) was fine, the service charming and prompt. The food 100% disaster.

That's a tiny exaggeration. The first thing we got, fried seaweed, was fine. We then had spare ribs and spring rolls. Both horrid. I don't believe for a second they were cooked that day. The spare ribs were dried out and tough. The spring rolls tasted stale.

Our main course, crispy duck in a pancake, was beyond belief. The duck was totally dry and turgid. The pancake was like rubber. You couldn't cut it with a knife.

Further disaster was to come. The menu offered 'pumpkin cream with purple rice and coconut ice cream. A not to be missed speciality of Kai'. That was £10 plus service for a plate of white smoke hiding a smallish scoop of ice cream. Pumpkin cream was then poured over it. The only special thing about this dessert was its exorbitant price.

Pity the white smoke didn't set off the fire alarm. That would have put us on the street before we had time to suffer what was underneath.

The fantastic chef at **Ken Lo's Memories of China** in Pimlico, Kam Po But, is very low key and immensely pleasant. I left him to choose for me. We started with prawn crackers, one of my favourites. They were as fresh as anything. Then I had a prawn roll, also very good. Then deliciously light prawn and chicken dumplings.

Paola said: 'Let's try and eat slowly otherwise we get full so quickly.' I'm a gobbler. I gobble. Paola said: 'You make me eat fast in order to catch up.' She was using chopsticks. That's well beyond me.

We followed with roast duck cut up and in pancakes. It really is, when well done like this, exceptionally pleasing. I also had sweet and sour fish with vegetarian rice. Dessert was toffee apple and toffee banana.

Kam told me he opened the restaurant 20 years ago with Ken Lo and his wife. Twenty years of producing great food is quite a record. Kam should be proud.

At **Kensington Place**, on a day things had come to a halt, I ended up serving the entire restaurant with bread. I was so keen to get some for myself, I got up, took the basket from the serving area and then helped Alan Yentob, who was sitting some distance away. At that everyone called out for 'service', so I did the whole room.

P.S. I think Kensington Place became careless and dreary. I stopped going after I ordered the mixed grill three times in a row because I couldn't find anything more interesting. It's changed owners and I hear it's even worse.

Everyone should have a local Indian. Not a red one with feathered head-dress and a bow and arrow. Although that would be nice, too. I mean a restaurant. Mine is called 'The famous Kensington Tandoori, Indian Cuisine, air-conditioned'. It's just off High Street Kensington. I wandered round there with Miss Lynton-Edwards, ex-dancer supreme.

Time has stood still at the **Kensington Tandoori.** They have a lowered ceiling over padded side banquettes with chairs facing inwards on the other side of the tables.

Cont'd
There are green and yellow lights illuminating fake plastic leaves and lemons. Leaves are also on the wallpaper. Between the tables are glass divisions etched with Indians on horseback, playing sitar and dancing.

I've delayed telling you about the food because, sadly, I was unimpressed. The poppadoms were good. The naan bread adequate. But the rest had no oomph at all.

The dessert menu had colour photographs of what was available, which made it apparent they were all bought in. The four on the left-hand side came from Spain. Why Indian desserts should be shipped in from Spain I can't imagine.

Now I've seen everything. Never mind appalling food. Never mind bad service. Both of which I got at **L Restaurant and Bar** in Kensington. What about either an attempt to swindle me, or negligence so bizarre that I was overcharged anyway!

My guest and I both had the three-course set lunch at £16.50 plus 12.5% service charge. So the food bill should have been £37.12 for two. When I got home I noticed I'd paid £43.87! You're saying: 'Calm down, dear, it's only a difference of £6.75.' So you don't mind paying 18% more than the menu price each time you go out. Is that it?

Instead of being charged for the three-course meal, we were charged £14 plus service each for the two-course lunch, and the goat's cheese ice creams – clearly on the three-course lunch anyway – were charged as separate items at £5.50 each plus service.

I rang the owner, Eddie Lim, and made my feelings known. Later I received his cheque for the whole meal. That didn't help. I wasn't looking for a freebie. I simply wanted to pay the price announced on his menu. You'll be relieved to hear that, eventually, I got my £6.75 back! I bought a new Rolls-Royce Phantom with it.

L Restaurant and Bar, a silly name if ever there wasn't one, is off Kensington High Street in premises once occupied by a place called Trattoo, which was quite good. The place fell into disaster and many owners. Recently it has been redesigned (badly) and Mr Lim is offering a load of old rubbish.

In case you're saying, 'Just because he was inadvertently overcharged Winner's giving 'em hell!' may I point out that the brilliant and serious food writer Fay Maschler, who may or may not have been overcharged, said the only likable item she ate there was wok-fried spinach. She did better than me. I didn't like anything.

The last time I ate lunch at the Four Seasons hotel in Mayfair was on 5 November, 1995. I went some years later for tea, to be haughtily informed by the duty manager, Rachel Begbie, when I said, 'Why are you serving teabags?' that they only served loose tea, never teabags.

As she said this a second pot of tea arrived with teabag tags hanging out of it. She never apologised, just walked off in a huff as she'd been made to look ridiculous. That remains one of the most inept examples of hotel management ever. So I never went back. Until recently, when the adorable Geraldine, Ruby, my lovely PA, and I visited its **Lanes** restaurant for Sunday lunch.

In 1995 their chef was the dreaded Jean-Christophe Novelli. He later opened five restaurants in London, which were so awful they went broke. The bailiffs were called in. I hate to think of how many staff and suppliers were left unpaid.

Mr Novelli continued his downward fall by going to Auberge du Lac in Hertfordshire, where he got a miserable two stars from the AA Guide and was fired, according to the management. Mr Novelli, not unnaturally, claims he left of his own accord. He now has his name on a tacky pub in Harpenden where the sign outside says, 'A touch of Novelli'. 'A kiss of death' would be more appropriate. That's closed too! 'What a bitchy old queen you are,' I hear you say. Bitchy, yes. A queen, no. But who knows what the future has in store?

Back to the current Four Seasons restaurant. It looks terrific. There's an outer restaurant with bird prints. The main one has large windows overlooking Park Lane, very attractively rimmed in modern stained glass. There's a stained glass buffet lit from underneath, topped in marble.

The hotel manager, Annabel Shaw, greeted me, the restaurant manager, Gregory Viaud, took over and the executive sous-chef, Damien Chorley, added to the superb warmth of welcome and service.

I had smoked salmon and gravadlax from the buffet. Geraldine had an assortment, including marvellous smoked halibut pâté.

For real starters Ruby loved her scallops, Geraldine had nothing but praise for her whipped potatoes with globe artichoke crisps, Alba truffle and rocket leaves. My fried egg on a bed of creamed spinach topped with white truffles was unbeatable.

The atmosphere was buzzy and busy. Then we were all given an utterly marvellous Alba truffle and cep risotto. It was all going splendidly and continued so for Geraldine and Ruby with their main course: Ruby had lamb, Geraldine had black cod. Their praise was unbounded.

I, a true traditionalist, had roast beef from the trolley. I asked them to make me fresh Yorkshire pudding instead of stuff that was hanging about on the trolley. This could have been a mistake. It was the worst Yorkshire pudding I've ever eaten. Soggy, no crispness, no soft interior, just totally revolting. Whoever made it should be sent to Yorkshire for pudding lessons or demoted to wash plates. The beef wasn't much good either. No real taste. There's great roast beef at the Goring hotel, Simpson's-in-the-Strand – and it used to be fantastic at the now ruined Dorchester Grill.

Desserts weren't up to much either. My chocolate brownie with macadamia nuts and chocolate truffle was heavy and cloying. Geraldine, a world expert on crème brûlée, gave hers a weak mark. Ruby had cheesecake, which was okay but not splendid.

In spite of a few faults, Lanes is a very jolly place to go. I definitely recommend it.

What I like about **Langan's Bistro** on Devonshire Street is the food is plain and simple. I recently had a chicken and liver salad with crispy bacon. The liver was round and tender, without a streak in sight. The bacon and salad were exemplary.

This was followed by Langan's mixed vegetable pie, which looked like a vegetable pie should. Two pieces of crust on top of a tasty choice of vegetables, all of which had individual flavours.

I finished with bread and butter pudding with custard. It was not in slices but was extremely pleasant nevertheless.

On another occasion I had red onion and stilton tart, which was so good I left not a crumb, followed by smoked haddock with poached egg and hollandaise sauce, which was moist and near perfection. I finished with Mr Langan's chocolate pudding. Dark chocolate on the outside, white chocolate on the inside and a chocolate sauce. I've had massively less good desserts served at twice the price in famous restaurants.

I think Langan's Bistro clever to restrict the size of the menu. Therefore what they offer, they can actually do. At the top of the menu is a watercolour by Patrick Proctor of Peter Langan, looking out in a kind of glazed way. It is massively to Michael Caine's credit that he nurtured Peter and brought him to the West End and ran the show for so many years.

Opened by Peter Langan and Michael Caine in 1976, **Langan's Brasserie** in Mayfair remains one of London's most famous names. Though strangely, perhaps, it is one to which I never rushed. I've no objection to it. I've eaten perfectly good food there. I've also had quite adventurous times. I took my friend O J Simpson and his wife Nicole there after we'd been to see *Cats*. You may have heard they since parted in somewhat unusual circumstances.

Peter Langan was normally in the restaurant, performing his usual function, which was to wobble drunk down the aisle, fall on the floor and go to sleep. It was a colourful feature of Langan's that you had to step over this recumbent man in a white suit.

Peter was a great eccentric but, above all, he was a superb restaurateur. He opened Langan's Bistro in Devonshire Street and, adjacent to it, Odin's. Peter himself always told me with pride that Odin's served far and away the best food in the group.

P.S. Michael Caine has sold out his interest in Langan's. He's seldom, if ever, there.

All right Coq?

I have always been an admirer, though not a fan, of Langan's in Mayfair. I appreciate its professionalism, its continued popularity. I like the room, the staff, the party catering upstairs, but I've never been crazy about the food.

So when my friend Bill Tennant, the highly superior movie executive, suggested we go to **Langan's Coq d'Or** in Brompton Road for lunch, I was not enthusiastic. The room itself is extremely attractive. Sort of fake 1900 with nice brass hanging lights from the George V in Paris, pleasing oil paintings, photos of regulars to the 'old' Langan's, which of course don't include me, pink and yellow flowers and one odd thing – layers of paper cloths on top of a real tablecloth on the tables.

The room was pretty empty. Tara Palmer-Tomkinson appeared at another with the UK boss of TAG Heuer watches, Neil Duckworth. Apparently that nice-looking brunette lady ahead on my right, lunching with a gossip columnist, was Tara's sister, Santa. A table away sat a baroness from Brussels whom I like, but whose name I forget. A pleasing group.

I noted they had Langan's bangers and mash with white onion sauce on the menu. They're always very good. Bill ordered crab and ginger dumplings to start. I nicked some when they arrived; they were most pleasing. I asked for gravadlax with mustard sauce.

'That's adventurous,' said Bill, meaning it wasn't. Safe it may have been, but it was first-rate.

The bread was all right, not over-exciting. Bill declared his main course, grilled tuna, to be superb. I rated it good. I'd decided to forego the sausages for beef bourguignonne: it lacked that extra something.

By now the paper tablecloths were becoming a real bore. They kept rising every time I brought my arms up with my cutlery. I ended up eating my apple strudel dessert with one hand, while holding the paper cloth down with the other. This is something new in my vast experience, and not necessarily a plus.

I'd rate this a pleasant meal in very nice surroundings. I even made a note of the table number of my corner setting, which means I'd be happy to go back. Peter pointed to the other corner. 'That's Lord Archer's table,' he said, as if his restaurant had thus achieved the apex of distinction. I found that totally bizarre.

Laxeiro, a Spanish restaurant in Columbia Road, is owned by jolly Isabel Rios. She's had it for eight years and for 18 years before that ran it as a delicatessen. She lives above.

It was full and very lively. Isabel promised me a selection. Albondigas sounded odd, but apparently it's meatballs. I like meatballs. We had them, plus calamari, a sausage called chorizo alvino and a lot of other stuff that I enjoyed but failed to note properly.

The crema Catalana dessert was delicious. The Spanish do those creamy things wonderfully. 'Just the right texture,' I dictated, 'just the right crispiness of the thing on top.' They also had banana crêpes. They were pretty good, too. I can totally recommend a Sunday trip to the Columbia Road market.

Occasionally a restaurant is so awful I'm almost lost for words. But not quite. Thus it was with the **Ledbury**, a newish venue in Notting Hill. Local residents would be better served if the premises were razed to the ground and turned into a car park. That's useful. The Ledbury isn't.

I may have been more unimpressed with a meal. I can't remember when. Strange, because the Ledbury is part-owned by a marvellous chef, the two-Michelin-starred Philip Howard of the Square in Mayfair.

The Ledbury's chef, Brett Graham, worked with Philip. Either he wasn't attending or he decided when, mistakenly, given his own restaurant, to go to it alone. That's where he should be. And when I visited one Saturday for lunch that's how I was. More or less alone.

Buzz and atmosphere: nil. Not helped by pretentious décor with black pillars and mirrors, which at night would reflect black from outside.

Service throughout was superb. They just didn't bring anything worth having. Actually, I did like their first offering: the bread. After that it was downhill.

My first course was 'sardine beignets with wild rocket and aubergine caviar'. A pompous, overelaborate description of a ghastly concoction. The so-called sardines were mushed-up and covered in what looked and tasted like shredded wheat.

The next disaster was 'breast of duck with celeriac, beetroot and tart fine of peach'. What a load of old cobblers! Silly little slices of duck that could have been anything.

The house speciality was chocolate soufflé. I don't know much about food but I prize myself on being a world expert on desserts, particularly chocolate soufflé. This one was, by a long way, the worst I've ever eaten.

'The food is all too played about with,' I dictated. 'It isn't relying on the real flavour. It's hiding it.' We left before coffee. I was just so fed up with the place.

Chefs are stupid, egomaniac, vacuous morons. That's when they're not going broke thus defrauding their suppliers and staff of millions of pounds. I don't know why they're even called chefs. They cook. Why can't they be called cooks, restrained in the kitchen and just get on with providing food? My only interest in chefs is what they serve for me to eat.

There are a few exceptions. Giorgio Locatelli, for example. Giorgio (bet you guessed) is Italian. He has a superb Michelin-starred restaurant, **Locanda Locatelli** in Marylebone. He's charming, pleasant, intelligent, handsome, cheerful – and he can cook. When he opened in 2002 his wife Plaxy, a lovely dark-haired lady, was the brilliant restaurant manager.

We started with freebie fried artichokes, beans, olives and cured beef with lemon and as touch of olive oil. Marvellous. Then spaghetti alla chitarra, made with balls of tuna. Prior to the meal I'd watched Giorgio preparing these in the kitchen. He then ate them himself. Didn't fall down foaming at the mouth. So they were obviously safe. Also very good. I followed with marvellously moist cod, lentils and parsley sauce. My guest, a Welsh lady, had fillet of wild sea bass in salt and herb crust, green salad.

I can't mention why I was with this person. I have a contract that warns that if I say anything I'll be dismembered and my body parts will be delivered to various kitchens around London, where they'll be cooked and served as pork. A friend of mine who ate people in the jungles of Borneo, before the area became infested with McDonalds and Starbucks, assured me human flesh tasted just like pork. Valuable information if the credit crunch bites and you have to eat your neighbour.

I finished with Amalfi cream Eton mess. 'What's the difference between Amalfi cream and ordinary cream?' I asked. 'Amalfi cream is made with limoncello,' was the reply. The dessert had crispy meringue inside. Historic. Only downer: the restaurant décor lacks the warmth of he whom it is named after. Go anyway.

Lucio is extremely charming. He was the restaurant manager, or maybe something just under restaurant manager, at San Lorenzo in Beauchamp Place for 30 years. In 2003 he left. Mara Berni, the co-owner of San Lorenzo, one of the greatest restaurateurs and hosts ever, and by far the hardest working, was (Gordon Ramsay swear word) furious. Being a devoted admirer of Mara I did not join the fashionable set – I never have – and trot along to **Lucio**, the place he opened in Fulham Road. I stayed loyal to Mara, declining invitations galore, including one from the delectable Joan Collins, to eat at Lucio.

I succumbed recently when my friends, photographer Terry O'Neill and his lovely wife Laraine, suggested we go there for Sunday lunch.

The main room is thin and ill-proportioned and leads to an equally dreary second room, which in turn leads to the entrance. Lucio has wisely kept it simple – white walls and outstanding celebrity photos by Terry.

We started very well. I took a mini roll in the shape of a croissant, there was tomato-something bread and the focaccia was also terrific. Then we got some fried zucchini, which was all right at best. But I give Lucio brownie points for bunging stuff onto the table quickly. My orange juice also arrived speedily and was definitely fresh. By that I mean squeezed then and there.

I had risotto with aparagus and taleggio cheese. This was far too salty. The main course – chargrilled salmon fillet with new potatoes and asparagus – pulled them up a bit. It had some juiciness and a reasonable taste for salmon, which is not the most piquant of fishes.

Our dessert of warm chocolate fondant with vanilla ice cream was absolutely superb. Even tasted of chocolate, which a lot of them don't.

The greatest growth industry over the last few years is 'health' food. Everything has to be organic or at least labelled organic. Do we trust the labels?

Ever wishing to go with the flow I lunched a few days ago at **Luscious Organic** on Kensington High Street. This was acquired by a Yugoslavian lady, Dragana, who I understand will be appearing as the wicked witch in Humpty Dumpty on ice at some bizarre theatre in the north. She took over Luscious Organic in 2003 when the previous company went bankrupt. Among her partners are Boy George and a man called Simon Brown, whose book *Feng Shui for Wimps* was on display above my table.

Dragana certainly made a go of it. The premises used to be empty. Now they're buzzing. Elle Macpherson shops there. I know that because I was sent Elle's bill in error. It dwarfed my humble purchases.

Luscious Organic has five tables inside and another six outside (weather permitting). The shelves are full of packets of stuff so healthy I didn't dare read the labels. They even have organic wine.

Greg, the manager, produced the menu. I chose Caribbean vegetable soup followed by Moroccan chickpea and spinach stew, rice and salad. My soup and main course arrived at the same time.

The soup was absolutely superb. Very tasty. It said, 'I'm not only healthy but nice as well.' The Moroccan chickpea and spinach stew surprised me by also being excellent.

I went to Luscious Organic shortly after eating roast beef and Yorkshire pudding at home expecting just to taste everything for you. But it was so good, I stuffed myself.

For dessert Greg plied me with cakes. Orange and almond cake, moist and excellent; then carrot cake with lots of nuts, and an orange and banana cake with icing. That last one was a bit heavy. They have organic coffee and espresso.

Downstairs there's a clinic open seven days a week offering services that include face reading. As a finale Geraldine took a bottle of pinot grigio 'made with organically grown grapes from the living soil'. It was all so healthy I began to feel a bit queasy.

I hate going to new restaurants. They invariably disappoint. So when Geraldine recommended **Maggie Jones's**, situated just off Kensington Church Street, to say I was unimpressed is putting it mildly.

I decided to reconnoitre it on one of my nightly hour-long walks Geraldine forces me to take. These, plus the 30 minutes of Geraldine's Pilates class for one, imposed upon me every morning, have uplifted my health enormously.

I entered Maggie Jones's and sailed past two surly young men on the door who treated me as if I was just the sort of customer they didn't want. A charming and welcoming assistant manager, Christine Watts, then appeared and showed me round.

It looks very good in a fussy, over-decorated way. It's rustic. There are sideboards hung with chipped mugs and kettles. Hops, wheels and rakes dangle from the ceiling. The tables are all different. The cutlery is solid and disparate.

The crockery is old. When I ate there my plate, which didn't match anyone else's, was inscribed 'Johnson Brothers, England 1883'.

On my evening visit it was busy. I chose a first floor table for Saturday lunchtime. On the way out I spotted a much larger table on the ground floor, made up of strips of bleached wood.

'How many does that seat?' I asked Christine. 'Usually eight people,' she said, 'but we can easily get 10 there.' 'You're not busy on Saturday lunch are you?' I suggested with, as usual, no knowledge of what I was talking about. 'I'll have it for four people.' 'You'll be quite far apart from them,' said Christine nervously. 'Don't worry, I'll make myself heard,' I said.

Thus it was, promptly at 1pm – I'm never late – on the following Saturday I turned up at Maggie Jones's with Geraldine, her sister Wendy and Wendy's husband Ben.

Although it was a bright sunny day all the tables had lit candles in bottles. The wax dripped into a nice sculpture as it melted. The 'specials' board was on the floor. 'Odd that,' I thought, 'people have to go on all fours to see it.' When I spotted it and asked, they raised it up for me.

I ordered lamb pie preceded by stilton mousse. The stilton thing was excellent. The lamb pie was pretty good. It's all basic stuff. Ben had steak and kidney pie. We examined it closely, finally tipping its contents onto a plate, searching for the rather miniscule number of kidneys. Geraldine and Wendy had grilled salmon, which is the house speciality. They greatly liked it. We also got peas with bacon, potatoes, beans and cauliflower cheese.

Geraldine said, 'Did you see the shrimp cocktail? It looked fantastic.' I asked Christine, 'Have you got one you're handing out to anyone else?' She said, 'I'll go and pinch one back.' She showed it to me. It looked superbly 1950s.

My treacle tart was a major disaster. The pastry was thick and clumsy. There was mush on top that tasted like foam. If treacle had ever been anywhere near, it left no mark. The apple crumble was cloying but not terrible.

Maggie Jones's is so called because it is said Princess Margaret, who lived nearby, went there during her courtship with Anthony Armstrong-Jones. Apparently, when they married she'd phone and say, 'Maggie Jones here, table for two please!' Or something like that.

Because the Michelin Guide gave the **Malabar** in Notting Hill Gate a red M, which means it merits your attention, I attended. Very ordinary. Heavy naan bread, cloying sticky samosas, and only fair murg makhni and accompanying fried pumpkin, and sliced banana cooked with ginger and spices. It read better than it tasted. Not awful, but I wonder if the Michelin-Guide man had had a drink too many or was just feeling generous.

Mark's Club, in Mayfair, is as masterful an English restaurant as you'll find. It's in a building where Ziggy Sessler once ran a club. He was a fat, beaming host who attracted the likes of Frank Sinatra, Dean Martin and other luminaries in the 1950s. Mark Birley bought the place from Ziggy's widow. For the past decade he's employed Bruno Rotti, the greatest restaurant manager in the world. Near Mark's Club, in a Berkeley Square basement, is the discotheque Annabel's, which Mark opened in 1963. It offers the same gentleman's club atmosphere as Mark's Club, with excellent food and dancing for elderly toffs and, on occasion, younger ones as well.

PS This is now owned by Richard Caring. It's still good.

My first visit to **Marcus Wareing** was in September 2000 when he had Pétrus in naff premises in St James's. I thought the food excellent. I next encountered Marcus at the Savoy Grill. The meal had pluses and minuses. After court battles between Marcus and his old mentor Gordon Ramsey, what was Pétrus at the Berkeley Hotel is now called Marcus Wareing at the Berkeley.

It's in a room decorated by David Collins. Need one say more? Except that it's in full Collins style of totally horrible. Like a gloomy purple box relieved only by one wall of wine racks fronted by coloured balls on wires. The chairs are purple leather.

The canapés were fantastic. We decided on the £55 menu. Geraldine chose the omelette Arnold Bennett, one of Marcus's signature dishes. I've had that, it was brilliant. I chose Ardennes frog's legs with cumin and lemon confit served with white onion and garlic soup, grilled focaccia. It didn't taste of much. Before it arrived we got more freebies – a tiny gazpacho with a touch of vanilla and a mini brioche with foie gras. Both historic.

I'd expected a full grouse, little legs and all that. But I got just breasts. Nice, but I'd have preferred the lot.

We got a small portion of tarte tatin with clotted cream. As good as you could wish for. Freebie desserts were flowing. My main dessert was a peanut parfait with rice crisp crunch, Valrhona chocolate mousse, candied peanuts and chocolate sauce. It was memorable. There's no question, overall, this was a very good meal indeed.

In the kitchen I asked Marcus, 'Do you do chips?' He said, 'No. And we don't do pommes soufflées either.' People usually do them for me specially. Gordon did great pommes soufflées in the Boxwood Café. But Marcus was clearly raising his flag of independence. Good for him. Now he's left Gordon forever.

Let's start with a quiz. I recently had dinner at Gordon Ramsay's **Maze Grill** in Grosvenor Square. I was billed for a wagyu sirloin steak, medium size. I later spoke to Jeremy King, restaurateur supreme, who co-founded the Ivy, Le Caprice and J Sheekey in their present incarnation and now runs the massively successful Wolseley in Piccadilly.

'How much was my wagyu/kobe steak at the Maze Grill?' I asked. Jeremy thought about it, 'Sixty pounds,' he suggested. 'You're not a restaurateur,' I responded.

You guess now. How much was it? If you said £20, you're wrong. Fifty pounds, you're wrong. A hundred pounds, you're wrong. I'll put you out of your agony. This steak, alone, not including veggies or plate decoration, was – wait for it - £123.75, including the 12.5% service charge. On the menu it said 'market price'. So £123.75 was market price that day. 'It's a good job we weren't here yesterday,' observed my guest, Sir Michael Caine.

Did I like it? Yes. Rather gristly. I got this horrendous bit of gristle and thought, 'Shall I spit it out?' But I hate bits of removed food on the edge of the plate so I chewed relentlessly and swallowed.

The steak, when I avoided the gristle, was superb. But – and this is a big 'but' – a few days later I received a letter from John Cowan, general manager of W G White, which normally supplies me with caviar. He offered American wagyu/kobe beef, the same as I'd had at Maze. A sirloin steak, identical size, cost me £20. I usually get 10% off so it could have been £18.

Restaurateurs reckoned Gordon buys his wagyu/kobe steaks for £14. I grilled mine at home. So I missed the splendid company of Gordon and his excellent chef Jason Atherton.

Our Gord has said vociferously and at length that restaurants should serve locally produced food. I didn't see any Japanese cows (I'm told wagyu/kobe steak comes from them) chomping the grass in Grosvenor Square. Nor did his New York strip steak from Creekstone in Kansas emanate from near the Maze. I was told Gordon's wagyu/kobe came from Australia. That's local to Grosvenor square, innit?

As for the Maze, I thought it was marvellous. No table clothes ('Saves a fortune on laundry,' observed Michael Caine), wooden floor, bustling, full to overflowing. Who said there was a cash crisis?

Michael chose Gordon's 'local' New York steak and declared it the best steak he'd ever had in England. His cost a mere £39.37. I like a cheap guest. Lady Shakira was presented with a whole sea bass, including the head and tail.

I had two starters. The menu informed me they were tapas-size. I took that as meaning small. They were both enormous and absolutely terrific. One was pigs on toast, parmesan and rocket. That turned out to be chopped up pig's trotter. The other was confit tomatoes, chorizo, potatoes, bitter shallots.

I also tasted Geraldine's fried calamari – sensational. The french fries on the menu are bought in but the lobster chips served with the lobster are made on the premises. They're fried in duck fat. I had them with my £123.75 steak and some onion rings. All good. So was my dessert of red fruit Eton mess with mascarpone ice cream.

I have a somewhat limited association with **McDonald's.** My first of two visits was to the New Rochelle outlet in New York state on July 25, 1983. We were on a location reconnaissance for *Scream for Help*, a movie featuring a 17-year-old girl in trouble. I knocked on doors asking, 'Do you have a teenage daughter? If so, could I see her bedroom?' Many residents called the local police chief, whom I knew well, saying, 'There's a pervert on the loose.' 'I do wish you'd tell me when you're going out,' the police chief said pleasantly.

It was the first day of work and we lunched at McDonald's. I was massively disappointed by its Big Mac. It seemed all soggy. I phoned Lee Rich, boss of Lorimar, a massive TV and movie company in Hollywood making *Dallas* and other famous TV shows. 'How did it go?' he asked. 'Lunch at McDonald's was awful,' I replied. 'I never go there,' said Lee. Later his wife told me, 'He goes to the Beverly Hills branch every Saturday with the kids.'

A year ago I considered visiting McDonald's for this column. After lunch at the excellent chic Scalini in Belgravia I went round seven tables of elegant *Sunday Times* readers. 'Excuse me, do you go to McDonald's?' I asked. All of them said, 'Yes.' One man beckoned me back, adding, 'My children make me go there.'

Recently the TV producer for Sir Trevor McDonald (I'm told he's no relation to the hamburger bars) rang to ask if I'd give my opinion of McDonald's for his news programme. I turn down about 50 offers a year to speak about food on TV. Writing for you is totally fulfilling.

Strangely, I accepted this, insisting it be the Kensington High Street branch, which is closest to my house. So I ended up with a TV crew in the Kensington High Street McDonald's, which I'd passed endlessly in one Rolls-Royce or another for years.

The room was pleasant, fresh, with clean, wood-top tables. It's the chain's Forever Young brand, introduced two years ago. The staff looked nicely presented. They're soon to have outfits designed by my friend Bruce Oldfield.

I had a hamburger with M on the box. 'What exactly is it?' I asked. It was a Quarter Pounder with Cheese. The bun was squashy, the meat average. Not a patch on the Ivy hamburger.

I ordered two milkshakes, strawberry and vanilla. They were oversweet and sickly. Those at the Wolseley are far better. A McD rep told me all their food was organic and they'd cut down on salt and fat. 'You didn't cut down on sugar, did you?' I said, referring to the milkshakes.

Then I tried a chicken legend with a spicy salsa sauce, which was fine. The bun was different and of excellent texture, the lettuce was crisp. Top marks for that. The salad was also very good. Fresh-tasting. I'd have accepted it in any upper-class restaurant.

The chips, which I'd been told were terrible, were very acceptable. The Filet-o-Fish was encased in a horrid bun, the fish pretty good. They said it was sustainable hoki fish from New Zealand. Frankly, my dears, I don't give a damn. If it tastes good why should I care whether it's sustainable? I'm not in control of sustainable.

My final order was a Bacon de Luxe with tomato relish, batavia lettuce, a slice of tomato, garlic mayonnaise and three slices of bacon. On a scale of 1 to 10 it was a strong 5.

McDonald's earns a big plus for serving Vittel, a first-rate French mineral water. Yet diners at Scott's have to suffer the inferior Tufa.

If you had a milkshake (£1.29), a Chicken Legend (£2.89) and salad (99p) it would be a reasonable and filling meal for £5.17. No wonder McDonald's serves 54m customers a day in 120 countries. They won't see me again, so it'll be 53,999,999. They're unlikely to hold a prayer meeting about that.

I realised how lucky I was in the lifestyle I lead and the food I usually eat when I went for lunch at **Med Kitchen** in Kensington. It was beyond belief awful. Another world which, thankfully, I seldom enter. It was my cook's day off. Geraldine wanted to go to Edera which is north of my house. She said, 'It's owned by an Italian family who do the cooking.' 'I'll believe that when I see it,' I responded. Geraldine was in full flood. 'Med Kitchen is a chain and the food all comes in a bag,' she said. 'I'll look out for the bag,' I promised. 'You won't see it. It's in the kitchen,' Geraldine continued, adding, 'Microwave, have you heard of microwaving?' She moved her left arm in a gesture. 'All these chain places are the same,' announced Geraldine, 'they have an enormous kitchen in the cellar somewhere.' I couldn't work out how she knew it was in the cellar. 'And they send it out somewhere,' she said with finality.

At this point the Rolls arrived at Med Kitchen. Geraldine, my assistant Dinah and I alighted. It's a nice looking room. Very simple, large tin piping going everywhere. 'Excuse me, Geraldine,' I said, 'it's printed here on the menu "all of our dishes are freshly prepared on the premises with produce personally sourced by our chef including our fresh fish, corn fed chicken from normandy (sic) and our award winning beef which is selected first by Donald Russell from cattle that are reared on traditional farms then aged for 31 days to ensure maximum tenderness and flavour."' That failed to impress Geraldine. Nor did it mean anything to me.

I started with 'today's homemade soup, lentil and cumin'. Tasted of nothing at all. Or worse. They'd have been much better off buying it from Wholefoods up the road. I followed it with homemade salmon fishcake with tzatziki rocket and fresh cut fries. I was assured potatoes were cut up in the kitchen and fried. The fishcake was vile. Heavy, clammy, ghastly. Not on the same planet as those at Le Caprice and the Ivy. The chips would have been better bought in. They were white and underdone. Totally anaemic. I left nearly everything.

The menu announced 'homemade desserts freshly made by us'. 'When was this Banoffee pie made?' I asked restaurant manager Moustapha Khazari. He replied, 'I don't know, I'll have to ask the chef.' He did. Then informed me it was made on Wednesday. As it was Friday it was now two days old and had sat in the deep freeze.

I don't call that fresh. So I chose, from the blackboard, 'summer berries with ice cream'. Squashed looking mini-berries appeared in a small cocktail glass topped with a splat of revolting catering cream that squirts from a plastic container. 'Why is there no ice cream?' I asked Moustapha. 'Genuine mistake,' he said. Unbelievable. There was hardly anyone in the place. They could see me dictating my notes. They knew I was reviewing it. Yet they produce a dessert not as described. I ate one berry. It was revolting. So was the cold, textureless bread that had started the meal. Dinah said, 'I'm not too sure,' when asked about her sea bass. Geraldine described her poached salmon as 'over-cooked'.

Moustapha said there would be no bill. 'Yes there will,' I responded, 'I always pay.' It came to £75.54. I placed the ladies for our photo. They saluted to indicate they were ready for me to join them. I did. My chauffeur, Jim, took the picture. I thought they looked much better without me. Wouldn't anyone?

Chinese whispers

Memories of China in Kensington High Street was never as good as its sister restaurant in Pimlico, where the totally superb Kam Po But is the chef, but it's an okay neighbourhood Chinese.

Thus I went one day with Mrs Edge. Mrs Edge is a legend in her own lunch time, having been married to a musician in the Moody Blues. She went out for many years with Terence Stamp, and was even closely associated with a national newspaper editor of great renown. She's now a bachelor grandmother and truly glamorous. The day we went to Memories of China, the restaurant was involved in one of those newspaper offers where you get lunch for £10. It wasn't doing them much good, because, other than Mrs Edge and me, the only other customers were a party of four by the window and a single gentleman over the aisle from us.

The manager is a hospitable Italian named Giuliano Movio. On this occasion we had some prawn crackers and then a few starter orders, followed by the inevitable roast duck in pancakes. You know the sort of thing: a duck is cut up into little bits, you get these thin round pancakes, smear a bit of brown sauce on them, add the duck, strips of cucumber and spring onion, then roll it up. I've had it there, and at other places, many times. Now, as I dutifully served the duck onto Mrs Edge's pancake, I thought: 'This looks a bit tired.' But I didn't say anything. Then I took the first bite. It was dreadful. Old, hard, chewy. I called Giuliano over. 'This duck is a disgrace,' I said quietly. 'It's tired and old. Take it away.' He did so. Then Mrs Edge said, in her rather posh voice: 'And the pancakes were dreadful, too. Didn't you see, Winnie, they were all curling up at the edges?'

This was humiliating. I'd been shown up in my own neighbourhood in front of my guest. And at a restaurant that I regularly visit.

I've not been back. But I do go to Memories in Pimlico. That's terrific.

Show trials

I'm well known as an angel. Both in the sense of being personally angelic and as an investor in – and occasional presenter of – theatrical productions. The chance of getting any money back after investing in West End plays is minimal, unless Maggie Smith is starring. This does not deter me. Those of you with long memories will treasure my presentation of Paul Scofield in *The Tempest* at the Wyndham's Theatre, which miraculously made a profit. Other shows I produced were less fortunate.

I spend quite a lot of time at the National Theatre. Their **Mezzanine Restaurant** looks like a school canteen, with illustrated figure on a band around the walls. I once ate some awful sausages there with the impresarios Michael Codron and Sir Cameron Mackintosh. Later Michael Codron said they'd improved. So I gave it a try. The restaurant manager, Giuseppe Fortis, is exceptionally pleasant. He has been there 21 years. You feel no dramatic change has taken place during that period.

On a recent visit I had roasted peppers with goat's cheese (adequate) and steak baguettes for both of us. Nobody asked how we wanted them cooked, but we got one medium rare and one medium, which was okay.

I'm a great admirer of the National Theatre. The restaurant isn't appalling or anything, but it would be nice if the catering was upped to near the level of their productions. I'm sure Trevor Nunn will want to spend personal time achieving this.

I'd seen a chef called Brian Turner on television making a lot of sense in lauding fresh English produce. So I phoned the **Millennium** hotel in Grosvenor Square where he has his restaurant to book Sunday lunch.

A manager, Andre, said they were going to serve in the lounge because the restaurant was closed but it was Brian Turner's fare. I turned up with Geraldine, her actor son Fabrice and Geraldine's grandchildren, Benjamin 9, and Jesse, 6. I've failed totally in my pleading with Geraldine to give out only the age she looks – 42 – rather than the age she is – 104.

The menu was Mr Turner's but considerably downsized. We were the only diners until later a party of four came in. There was terrible piped music. I asked the restaurant manager, 'As we're the only people here can you turn the music off?' Mercifully he did.

I ordered 'pizza pollo ad astra' to start and then chopped steak burger, medium rare, with home-made fat chips and tomato and red onion salad. Fabrice wanted fusilli pasta chicken and mushroom.

We got there at 1pm and ordered at 7 minutes past. It was now 1.45pm and no pizza. I said to the waiter, 'Is there a problem in the kitchen?' He said, 'No.'

I said, 'There's a problem here. I'm going to walk out in a minute and go to the Wolseley where they're serving food.' After 40 minutes my pizza arrived. It was very good. We shared it.

Geraldine got a charcoal grilled chicken salad which she described as 'pretty tasteless'. My chips were excellent. The hamburger, okay.

It took forever for the plates to be cleared. Then the waiter cleared one plate, leaving four dirty ones behind. In clearing the main course plates he left a plate of chips, a plate of bread, a tomato and onion salad, mayonnaise and tomato ketchup. Then he gave us one dessert menu for five people. This was the worst service ever.

We ordered a chocolate 'negus' terrine, one coconut tart, nutmeg ice cream with raspberry sauce and one warm apple tart with clotted cream for me. The desserts arrived at 25 minutes to 3. Over an hour and a half after we entered. The apple tart was horrendous.

Jesse, understandably, became extremely bored. She used her napkin as an aeroplane, then she rolled up her menu and looked through it like a telescope, then she tried first to grab my tape recorder and then the camera.

Benjamin said the ice cream was horrible. Jesse reached out for my credit cards. The bill was headed, the Millennium hotel Mayfair Brian Turner bar. It totalled £155.70, including an optional service charge (for pathetic service) of £17.30. It was one of the most ghastly eating experiences of my life.

Mr Turner should spend less time spouting on television and get his act in order.

Michael Chow's sister Tsai Chin was in the oddest film I ever made, *The Cool Mikado* in 1962. She went on to greater things. Her brother Michael was a major Sixties figure, famous for **Mr Chow**, a restaurant in Knightsbridge much inhabited by the glitterati of the day, from Princess Margaret to Peter Sellers. Michael moved to Los Angeles and opened a successful Mr Chow restaurant there. The London one sank deeper and deeper into ghastly.

When I went in September 2002 the headline to this column was 'Ciao, Mr Chow – you won't be seeing me again'. I wrote of that visit, 'This is the worst Chinese food I've eaten in 100 years.' Readers with an IQ over 10 will realise I hadn't been eating Chinese food for 100 years in 2002. So what?

I heard recently that Mr Chow had considerably improved. Well, it could only go up. When Sir Michael Caine asked Geraldine and me to his wedding anniversary dinner there not long ago, his wife Shakira assured me it was now very good. I believed them. They know more about food than me. Mind you, so does a passing tourist from Mesopotamia. Does Mesopotamia still exist?

I duly turned up, the first of 10 guests, to be met with cold looks from all the staff who obviously had long memories and recalled my previous visit. The restaurant manager asked, 'Are you with Mr Michael Caine?' What's the point of being knighted if restaurant managers don't even know it happened? 'It's not

Mr Caine, it's Sir Michael,' I responded somewhat icily.

To reveal other bad points: they served Hildon water and had European piped music. I hate them both. After that though, a miracle. Everything was fantastically good. They must have fired everyone in the kitchen since my earlier visit. The service was fast beyond belief, just as I like it.

I never saw him order, but Michael said he'd ordered for the whole group. 'I didn't hear that,' I observed. 'I'm very quick and crafty,' responded Michael. 'You've ordered very well,' Shakira said to Michael. She was right. I should take him wherever I go. Save me reading the menu. Mr Chow is rumbling on. It's rather inconsistent.

I don't consider myself a world expert on food. ('You know [expletive] nothing!' I hear my dear friend Gordon Ramsay say.) But I do consider myself of unparalleled skill when it comes to judging ice cream, milkshakes, cakes in general and most sweet things.

For a long time my ex-girlfriend the Princess (aka Paola Lombard) sung the praises of **Morelli's Gelato**, which sells ice cream, sundaes and all things nice on the ground floor at Harrods. So we decided to visit. Bibi Morelli flew in from Monte Carlo to greet me. This is a minimum distance owners should travel to make me happy.

Bibi's dad started the business in 1907 selling ice cream from the back of a bicycle in Broadstairs, Kent. Bibi, now aged 32, joined the family firm three years ago.

I declined malt in my vanilla milkshake. It was very creamy, very rich. Delicious. We ordered two hot fudge sundaes and for my assistant Dinah, a berry pavlova sundae.

I kept dropping blobs of everything everywhere. 'I need more napkins!' I wailed. I can't remember how many things I tasted at Morelli's. I even tried an iced cake.

It took me back to 1953 when I first went to America and found heaven at a Howard Johnson ice cream parlour. From war-torn England to 55 varieties of ice cream – what a trip!

Give me a plonk of ice cream, a nice frothy milkshake, dessert biscuits from the Wolseley – and I'm happy. Then I get on the scales and I'm suicidal. There's no such thing as free ice cream, is there?

Eating out is quite a hazard, really. I was served with what looked like a nut and bolt in my pasta at **Mosimann's** in Belgravia. When I complained, the head waiter said: 'It came from the kitchen – we're doing some building.' 'I didn't think it came from Harrods,' I replied. We got four free champagne cocktails for that, but since we'd finished our main course, they seemed a bit inappropriate.

Cont'd

I've always liked tea places. London used to be full of them. Gunter's in Curzon Street was particularly posh. Prior to a theatrical outing, I visited **The Muffin Man**, in Wright's Lane, close to Barkers department store in Kensington High Street. Nowadays, I prefer to eat before the play and then go home to enjoy hot chocolate and Marmite on buttered toast. Does this imply senility? The Muffin Man sported a large display of cakes. The waitress assured me they were all home-made. I said: 'Bring over the cakes. I'm an official taster.'

Later the waitress asked, 'Don't you like the cakes?' because I'd left most of them. 'I'm only tasting a little bit of each,' I explained. 'That's my job. I never finish anything. I just taste.' This seemed to satisfy her. The cakes were very good.

I'm delighted to heap praise on Angela Hartnett, one of my all-time favourite chefs. She used to be at the Connaught but quit when they asked her to provide room service. Quite right. What would a nice girl like Angela be doing frying eggs at 6am for some visiting idiot?

Her newish restaurant is **Murano** in Mayfair. It's part of the empire (thriving or failing according to who you believe) of Gordon Ramsay. The Murano decor is exceptionally pleasant. Tables are spaced well apart so you can hear yourself talk. Rare these days. But it's nothing to do with Murano. No Murano glass that I could see. Just some demented 1950s-type metal chandeliers with strange bulb holders on the end.

Murano's wine waiter, Marc Andrew, cleverly wrote on the still water bottle of Panna the letter G. That means the gentleman is having the still water. He called me a gentleman. This is quite rare. I'm not often called that. Unfortunately another staff member came along during the meal, didn't read this carefully prepared warning, and sloshed Geraldine's fizzy water into my glass. This is not uncommon. It drives me totally bananas.

The staff were incredible – restaurant manager Jose Garcia, his assistant Paulina Trocha and the reception manager Maddalena Ciocca, to name a few. Charming, on the ball, nicely dressed.

I had a carnaroli risotto with two-year-old parmesan. I'm not normally told the age of the parmesan. This is not information I need to know. Then I note I had a truffle risotto. I don't think I could have had both, but who knows?

I did have truffles because the waiter said, 'The best truffles are the small red ones because they grow quite close to the tree.' They were incredible. The second time I went I also had truffles and the price had nearly doubled. None of this matters because they're not serving truffles again until October. So you've got time to save up.

I ordered roasted Anjou pigeon with pickled beetroot, lyonnais onions and semolina gnocchi. 'I'd like a pigeon that's been eating well prior to coming to me,' I said to Paulina, who's Polish. 'A well-feed one?' she asked. 'Exactly,' I replied.

I finished with apricot soufflé, amaretto di saronno ice cream. Geraldine had warm zabaglione with figs infused in red wine.

Take my word for it, Murano is utterly superb. They also give you lots of bibs and bobs, before, after and between. Never mind the credit crunch. Any money spent that gives you pleasure is worth it. That even applies to the parking tickets I got on both occasions, which cost me 60 quid times two. Who cares?

It's very big these days, isn't it? Save the planet, eat organic food, drive electric cars, use energy-saving lightbulbs that don't give out any light. If there's a hole in the ozone layer, why not just send someone up in a rocket with a bit of plaster and patch it up?

In Marylebone High Street (trendy area) there's the **Natural Kitchen** followed by the words 'artisan, organic and wild cafe'. It didn't look very wild to me. Downstairs a butcher's shop, lots of cheeses and, at the back, some tables. Surrounded by shelves of produce that was far too healthy for its own good, Geraldine and I sat at a table for four. There was music screeching, discordant, monstrous music.

'I can't believe it,' I observed. 'A place meant to be representing the country-side, with murals of cows and buttercups, and they've got this rubbish music.' The waitress, Orama, a lovely girl from New Zealand, said, 'The music drives me nuts.'

I had the smoothie of the day, a mixture of berries with fresh apple and orange juice. Reasonable. Then I asked for 'traditional homemade lemonade'. That was very good. My main course beef stir-fry was revolting. Tough, stringy beef. It may have been natural and organic. It tasted like nothing. Geraldine had chilli con carne. I thought it moderate. She finished the lot.

For dessert I ordered a chocolate cake and a flapjack. The flapjack was too healthy for me. The chocolate cake was ghastly beyond belief – dry, no taste of chocolate. Even the icing was bland. I left most of it.

As for Natural Kitchen, natural it may or may not have been. I'm certainly not going back to investigate.

I've had a somewhat mercurial relationship with **Nobu**, the oh-so-posh restaurant in Old Park Lane, Mayfair. I went there in 1997 and hated, hated, hated it. The service was amateur and diabolical, the food varied from too spicy to eat to just plain lousy. The waitress dropped things all over the table.

After that, chefs being petulant idiots, they didn't want me back, and I didn't want to go back. People I respected assured me I'd hit a bad night and an unusually dreadful waitress. I accepted that might be so, as Nobu remained the 'in' place, which it still is.

A few years ago, Michael Caine (not then 'Sir') asked me to his birthday dinner in Nobu's private room. That meal was superb in food quality and service. Still, I never went back to Nobu only because I find the low-ceilinged room and the noise rather oppressive.

Cont'd

I was looking forward to **Nobu Berkeley Street** because I read my least favourite restaurant designer, David Collins, had turned it into a forest. I expected a marvellously camp pantomime set. Instead there were a few streaks on one wall. They didn't look much like a forest to me.

Our waiter, Yoram Perez, was brilliant. He brought things speedily and was helpful without being intrusive.

First I asked for a knife and fork instead of chopsticks. 'Because I'm common,' I explained to Yoram.

I had rock shrimp tempura as a starter, then crispy pork belly with spicy miso and a bowl of rice. Vanessa chose black cod den miso followed by a tuna cut roll. Then 'faultless' mango. I also had a lemon, carrot and orange smoothie 'A juice for chronic fatigue synbdrome that helps boost the immune system,' intoned the menu. Tasted great.

The pork belly was better than perfect. Absolutely fantastic. Soft, succulent, crisp on top. Historic. All the food was good. My only criticism that the Mont Blanc Berkeley dessert had rather chewy meringue. I like it crisper.

I always book. I never drop into restaurants unannounced. Unless I'm on a movie location reconnaissance, then you don't know where you'll be at lunchtime.

Geraldine's plane from Milan was delayed because of 'rain at Heathrow'. That's a new one! So I waited for her and then we set out for Notting Hill. Lots of jolly places there. We'd just driven past what used to be Leith's, but is now the **Notting Hill Brasserie**, when Geraldine spotted a parking space in a pay and display area. She went to check the restaurant had room.

We entered the large Victorian house where a rude and dismissive restaurant manager, John Lacombe, passed us to a waiter who indicated a very small table. 'That's better,' whispered Geraldine, pointing to a table laid for four in a corner. 'I'd like to sit there,' I announced. The room was almost empty. It was after 2pm. 'You can't sit there,' said the waiter, 'there's a big group coming.'

No big group came in. The tables for four remained empty except for the one we occupied. Why, I wonder, are so many restaurant staff trained to be liars?

I checked the menu, three-course lunch £19.50 plus 12.5% service. An older waiter, Miguel Vazquez, came over. He proceeded to look after us very efficiently. I liked him.

We'd been sitting there quite a while. I was hungry. So I ate a bit of their superb olive bread. Eventually, and I do mean eventually, a freebie starter I hadn't ordered arrived. Sea bream with a creamy sauce. Excellent. A long delay. Still no sign of my Jerusalem artichoke soup. I asked Miguel, 'Where's the food?' 'Would you like some more bread?' he asked. 'No,' I said, 'I'd like the food.' Miguel went to check. Eventually the soup arrived. It was extremely tasty, delicate, a credit to soup-makers the world over.

Another delay. Then I got a double eggs Benedict. Absolutely marvellous. I finished with vanilla yoghurt with berry compote. This was the best yoghurt I've ever tasted.

'Good place,' I dictated into my tape, 'food service ridiculously slow, everything else fine.'

Jay Maggistro was a hairdresser who opened a restaurant called **No 5**. This occupies a large house in Cavendish Square. At amazingly, number 5. Vanessa suggested we have lunch there.

It's a pillared, 19th-century building, overdecorated far too brightly. But still quite nice. The dining room, on the first floor, is red with impressionistic pictures of people and horses.

Jay, the owner, appeared. He's very charming. 'To open this place, he must have done very well on tips,' I thought. I expressed it somewhat differently. 'I see you've found a backer,' I said. 'Big backer. Bloody right,' said Jay. I was told who the backer was, not by Jay, but I won't reveal his name. I doubt he'll make a fortune.

My veal chop arrived. It was very good. Just as I dictated, 'There's no sign of vegetables,' a man appeared carrying them. I took a bit of spinach. I don't know why. I detest spinach. Everything's on a bed of spinach today. When I was young we all hated spinach. The only way parents could get us to eat it was to refer to Popeye, the cartoon hero, who poured spinach down him from a can and then beat up all the baddies with spinach-induced vigour.

I don't know what they put into my lunchtime spinach, but it tasted better than any I'd ever had. It was a commendable main course. The beans and potatoes were good, too. The fig and marzipan tart was a letdown. The figs were sticky, the pastry horrid.

Vanessa rang me at 6.30pm and said, 'You didn't pay the bill.' This was true. I'm so used to having restaurant accounts, I'd just walked out. Nobody said anything. I phoned and had them fax it at once. I paid, as always, very promptly.

When I go somewhere new it's invariably a disaster. I don't know what madness overtook me one recent Saturday when I read in a newspaper about a hotel called **Number Sixteen**. The writer was wittering on about a lovely garden, design of great taste, load of twaddle, but I fell for it. So I drove a mile to 16 Sumner Place, South Kensington. There four white-painted, pillared Victorian houses have been made into what's known as a 'boutique' hotel. We walked through to a cramped conservatory leading to a small garden. Roses blooming. Little pond, goldfish, very tatty, cheap modern repro fountain of cherubs doing whatever cherubs do. Actually all they do is hold up fountains. Dull life, really.

Geraldine chose hummus and guacamole, followed by a chicken Caesar salad. I ordered hoy sin duck spring rolls to start. I asked the waiter, 'Do you think the beefburgers are good or am I going to be upset?' 'They're good, we get the best quality of beefburgers,' he replied. 'We'll see,' I thought, adding a fried egg.

The duck rolls were excellent. Probably bought in, but had a crisp, fresh taste. Geraldine liked her hummus. And later her Caesar salad. For me things collapsed totally after the first course. The hamburger, which I'd ordered medium, was far beyond well done. It was pulverised by over-cooking into a useless, inedible mass of stone. Why have a cook in the kitchen who can't even grill a hamburger? I'm pretty useless (correction, totally useless) but I can grill meat, chopped up or not, to perfection.

Bravely soldiering on in adversity I ordered carrot cake from the tea menu. It was terrible. Clammy, no taste of carrot or anything else and with a strange and highly unwelcome icing.

The review I read of Sixteen referred to it as like 'the private residence of a friend with great taste'. Nonsense. It's like a mish-mash of no taste backed up by a kitchen with no cook.

Mumsy came from Poland in 1932. This doesn't make me an expert on Polish food. Or indeed any other type of food. But I remember eating some of the best meals ever in the mid-Fifties in a marvellous little Polish restaurant on Thurloe Place, South Kensington called the Silver Spur. The owner looked like an ageing colonel in the Polish army. He wore a monocle and had a plump, beautifully spoken, English lady friend.

I hadn't eaten Polish for years until a friend recommended **Ognisko**, housed in a large mansion on Exhibition Road given to the Poles by the Duke of Kent after World War II. The restaurant is on the raised ground floor in a grand, if slightly distressed, room, looking onto a garden square and with an outside dining area attached.

Although our window table wasn't near the kitchen it was near to a loud-speaker where the waitress Ania Bouzid spoke to the kitchen and they replied. It was like hearing Polish resistance messages during the war.

For a starter I ordered borscht, which is beetroot soup, with dumplings. Geraldine had blinis with smoked salmon, sevruga caviar and cream. The borscht was the worst ever. Watery would be a complimentary way of describing it. Pathetic compared to the Silver Spur. If they can't deliver good borscht in a Polish restaurant, what hope is there for the world? The soup was accompanied by heavy bread and ghastly piped music.

I reckon the house is worth at least £35m, so no wonder they have exceedingly dull pictures of the Duke of Kent and family all round the dining room. For £35m I'd have the donor's family tattooed on my posterior and beyond.

My main course was knuckle of pork Bavarian-style, with rösti potatoes and red cabbage. The rösti potatoes were the worst ever, soggy, tasteless rubbish. The red cabbage also had no taste. It was weak and wobbly. Things were saved by the pork. It was historic. Soft, tender, absolutely delicious.

Ania suggested the dessert pancake filled with sweet cheese. It was fantastic. I dictated, 'It's sort of like a slice of meringue pie or pancake with sweet cheese and orange sauce.' This was as great a dessert as I've ever eaten.

You couldn't say I was a regular at the restaurant **One-O-One** in the Sheraton Park Tower hotel. I last visited in 1994. I returned last year because John Cleese was having his teeth fixed nearby and I foolishly suggested it.

One-O-One was ghastly in 1994. Fourteen years later I found it totally changed in every way except one. It was still ghastly.

The restaurant manager, Darren Neilan, asked if he could explain the menu to me. 'I can read, Darren, I think I'll probably manage,' I replied. 'But if I want to know anything I'll ask.'

The wine waiter offered to tell us about the restaurant. It was sitting there, plain, bland, hotel-like. What else did I need to know?

John received a massively decorated portion of steak tartare. My grilled line-caught mackerel goujons were less decorated. They were okay. We both had a main course of 'rabbit saddle with black pudding and pan-fried scallop, carrot purée, vanilla emulsion and jus gras'. John's dessert was goat's cheese. I had 'raspberry and pink champagne consommé jelly, white chocolate sorbet, pink foam'.

John summed up the meal: 'It's clever food. The shame is we have to eat it.'

I went to Terence Conran's **Orrery** restaurant in Marylebone and the manager, Greg Sapin, stared at me and said, 'Who are you with?' That's really welcoming attention! About as bad as you can get on entering a restaurant. Then Greg showed me to a table laid for three when I'd personally booked for four.

My guest, Roderick Mann, arrived with his 'last living relative', Antoinette. Roddy was a fantastic showbusiness writer from the 1950s to the 1980s, when he moved to California and wrote for the *Los Angeles Times*. His articles were witty. Not as witty as mine, of course. Roddy was the first person to write about me as a food critic. In the mid-1970s I graded private meals. At my agent's house in Beverly Hills his wife cooked one of the worst dinners ever. To be polite I gave it seven out of ten. The wife never spoke to me again and the agent dropped me!

At Orrery service was nil. No bread, no butter. I said, 'Who takes the order?' A waiter came without a pad. I asked him to get one. After 25 minutes the butter arrived. Still no bread. I asked the waiter, 'Do we get bread to put it on, or do we just look at the butter?' The bread was unspectacular to say the most. I'd guess it wasn't even good when it was baked yesterday.

The freebie starter was smoked salmon jelly with cauliflower foam. That was marvellous, delicate, great taste.

There were very few other diners. Geraldine had really excellent duck, crisp skin, I took a bit. Top marks. My saffron risotto had a lot of squiggle decoration but it was superb. Asparagus had something to do with it. Roddy said his pan-fried halibut was wonderful. I dictated, 'No question, it's very good food here.'

One thing let the food down with a heavy crash. That was my dessert, peanut butter parfait, bitter chocolate ganache. I specifically asked if it was made that morning. I was told, 'Yes.' Pull the other one! It had all the taste and texture of having been in the deepfreeze overnight. It was dried out, heavy and cloying. Absolutely dreadful. Other than that, and the bread, it was a very good meal indeed.

If you go to Orrery and the dumb restaurant manager asks, 'Who are you with?' answer, 'Michael Winner, I'm expecting him any minute.' That'll put a rocket up their you know what.

Orso's is a subterranean place in Covent Garden with adequate, quasi-Italian food and excellent service. On one visit I had a bit of a drama trying to persuade them to serve me an egg to go on the establishment's rather dry pizza. And this despite them serving eggs on my pizza for 10 years. I only succeeded by entering the kitchen and smiling at the chef. When I phoned Orso's boss, Richard Polo, the next day to ask why there was a problem, he said he didn't want to discuss it. This man was obviously frightened by a chicken at an early age. I suppose that's as good a reason as any to go into catering.

The people's Court

I don't like St John's Wood. But from time to time, people have strongly recommended to me a 'hidden' gem restaurant – **Oslo Court**. So I phoned them. A man said: 'Yeah.' 'Are you a restaurant?' I asked. He said: 'We are at the moment.' 'You mean you may not be next week?' I said. 'Who knows?' he replied.

'My name's Michael Winner,' I volunteered, determined to progress the conversation. There was a pause. 'I hear you have a very poisoned pen,' he said. 'Not on Tuesdays,' I responded. 'Everyone says I should visit you.' 'When do you want to come?' he asked. 'Tonight,' I stated. 'You're not serious?' he said. 'We've got nothing until 9pm.' 'I'm very old, I have to go to bed early,' I explained. 'Can you do 7.30pm?' 'We'll fix it,' he agreed. He turned out to be Tony Sanchez, father of the Spanish family who owns the place.

An hour later, I parked the Bentley between dull blocks of flats, entered the lobby of one of them, and was directed to the restaurant. Tony's daughter, Maria, an extremely charming girl, showed me to a small corner table. 'Can I go there?' I asked, pointing to a larger table in another corner. 'This is the best corner, trust me,' said Maria. I went to sit down, but Maria beckoned to another chair. 'I'd like you to sit there,' she said. I was so gobsmacked that I sat meekly facing the ladies' toilet while Mrs Lagoudakos, my long-suffering receptionist, got the best view.

The food started well. The bread with garlic butter inside was warm. Excellent melba toast was on the table. It went with the upright fanned-out pink napkins. The low ceiling made it claustrophobic; the tables were all set for six or eight people. When the diners arrived, it was very overcrowded.

There's an enormous menu, and they announce many extras. The service is superb and the staff are very nice. Mrs L had lobster cocktail, which she thought was chewy. I had whitebait, which were all right, and asparagus, which was a bit undercooked. My main course was half a crispy roast duck. It was a bit tough.

All the food was plonky. No finesse. Not refined cooking, but enormous portions. In fairness, I must state the place was packed with St John's Wood families. They clearly all loved it. Oslo Court is a wow in north London. Who am I to argue?

Miss Caroline Langrishe, actress of beauty and taste, told me she went to all the 'in' places, such as Bluebird and the Oxo Tower. 'If you phone, they say you can't have a table for six weeks,' she said. 'But if you turn up and say have you got a table, they'll look and say, you can have that one over there.' 'That may only work if you're blonde and beautiful,' I suggested. I have telephoned the **Oxo Tower** twice to make a reservation. All I got was classical music. It went on for ever. No human voice did I hear. This is ridiculous – if I want a concert, I'll visit the Albert Hall. I may only be a poor boy from Willesden, but why should I put up with that? I'd rather go somewhere less chic where they answer the phone. Thank goodness I no longer aspire to be trendy. It makes life so much easier.

Putting on the Ritz
for the world's best cuppa

They serve 420 teas a day in the **Palm Court of the Ritz** hotel in Piccadilly. People book months ahead for the five sittings. The Ritz is one of the last bastions of major dress code. No denim. No trainers. Jacket and tie essential.

I must be the only non-tie wearer in the world with a museum-worthy collection of 630 ties. They go back to the Forties, through the Fifties, where I sported bow ties with straggly bits hanging down, as in the Wild West, to thin, back barmitzvah ties, which Brian Epstein had the Beatles wear in the early Sixties, and wide actor-laddie ties of the Seventies. I've got ties in all shapes, colours and sizes.

The room is staggering. Gilded statues, decorated ceiling, grand chandeliers. It's exquisite. I know of no better room, except the Ritz dining room, or my bedroom, which was a famous artist's studio. Edward VII had his portrait painted there. He called it 'one of the most beautiful rooms in London'. Don't rush to book. Winner ain't serving tea.

The Ritz grub was impeccable. Marvellous Earl Grey tea; perfect fresh sandwiches; scones with jam and cream; chocolate cake; raspberry rounds; shortbread; fruit in a pastry bowl; gingerbread base with apple jelly on top; mousse; a chocolate macaroon. All stunning. A quality English tea is one of the great meals of all time.

A harpist was plucking away very gracefully. Note to all those dumps with piped music: a real harpist or pianist is better, even if more expensive.

Serving 420 teas at £37 is £15,540 a day. That's £5,672,100 a year. With that much coming in, the Ritz could go mad and hire a five-piece string orchestra.

I have around 400 oil and watercolour paintings on the walls of my house. One of my favourites cost £5 in an Ealing junk shop. I recognised it as a fine example of 19th century Austrian kitsch. It's a small oil-painted board in a gilded original frame. The subject is Leda (whoever she was) having intercourse with a swan. Both bird and Leda seem to be having a good time. This has been a popular subject for artists over the centuries.

Now Ms or Mrs Leda features in wood illustrations on the walls of the Ritz hotel's fairly new **Rivoli** bar. This art deco creation occupies a space vacated by shops facing Piccadilly. I'm not a great frequenter of bars, but a glossy magazine wanted to interview me in one. As the Ritz is my favourite hotel I thought, 'Why not there?' I'm pictured beautifully dressed (you can't see my pyjama bottoms) with a banana daiquiri and barman Alan Cook. This was a cocktail version, sharper and tangier than the smooth, superb BDs at Sandy Lane. At least the dreaded chef, Grant McPherson, who desecrated the food, didn't ruin their exotic drinks.

The Barclay brothers, Sir Frederick and Sir David, spent over £50 million restoring the Ritz to its Edwardian grandeur. They resisted the temptation to which other great hotels (Dorchester, Claridge's, Connaught et al) have succumbed, namely to replace what was elegant and historic with varying degrees of tat. The Rivoli bar is a delight. My Leda is better than theirs. But they display two versions. Numerically I'm inferior.

Compared to the new bars at the Dorchester (brown mush with red spears), Claridge's (awful) and the Connaught (the worst) the Ritz bar has class and style. I understand hoteliers need to maximise cash intake per square foot of space. Thus the Dorchester turned their lovely Italian restaurant into a bar; ditto Claridge's, their fantastic smorgasbord eatery. There's more money in drink than food. Another thing many hotels have done is change the lobby or lounge area, where guests could sit, meet friends and generally relax, into all day dining. More profitable than keeping a freebie space for room-renters. Claridge's has a chandelier which looks like Medusa on acid, the Dorchester has various heights of chairs and tables, none of which match.

In fairness (why should I suddenly be fair?) the Dorchester lobby, called the **Promenade**, has a bar at the end which seems to be a favourite for ladies who could be there for professional reasons. I hope so. Those girls always cheer the place up. I recently sampled the Dorchester 'afternoon tea tradition'. This is not cheap. The champagne afternoon tea costs £49 including service; without the glass of champagne, £38.50. I'd made a speech in the Dorchester Ballroom celebrating Lionel Blair's 106th year in show business. I didn't want to eat or sit through the lunch. Instead we listened to the pianist (very good) in the Promenade. I ate a hamburger, which was okay. Geraldine had a fried fish platter with lobster which she greatly liked. Then, as taster for you lot, I tried some sandwiches, scones and cakes. All excellent. The menu listed 24 different teas. By the time you finished reading about them, you'd be late for dinner.

Jimmy Page, leader of Led Zeppelin, the heavy rock band, came out of his astounding William Burges 'castle' next to my house with his handsome son, turned left and headed towards Kensington High Street. 'Where are you going, Jimmy?' I asked, coming out of my front gate. 'We're going to **Papaya Tree** Thai restaurant,' he said.

Jimmy is a good neighbour. He makes no noise. He keeps his house immaculate. He's a great expert on Victoriana. He has a second legendary Victorian house in the country.

We exchanged a few more words and Jimmy padded off towards Papaya Tree, which is between some rather uninteresting shops on Kensington High Street. I decided that, if it was good enough for Jimmy, I'd try it too.

The Papaya Tree is not imposing. A white basement, pleasant, flowers on the tables. But you have a feeling they know a thing or two about food. The waiter who looked after us was Songpol Chongsuwan. Unfortunately, I had left my glasses at home and so had Joanna Kanska, one of my lovely receptionists. It was the blind leading the blind.

I said to Songpol, 'We can't read because we didn't bring our glasses. Bring us quite a lot. We'll have at least four dishes. One chicken, one pork and then three other things that you choose. Actually, we'll have five dishes.' 'Five dishes will be too much for you,' said Songpol. 'It doesn't matter,' I said. It's a simple place but the taste of the food is excellent.

The **Mandarin Oriental** hotel is very grand. Marble pillars, lovely wrought iron, grand steps leading up from Knightsbridge. I once sat down in a chair there and placed my ex-employee OJ Simpson behind me. When we developed the photo, he was pretending to strangle me. For a double killer, OJ is a very nice man. When he came to my house I said to Geraldine, 'If he's got a knife, throw yourself in front of me.'

The entrance lobby and stairs are the only good things about the Mandarin Oriental. Except for the staff – they're pleasant. More than you can say of the restaurants.

Cont'd

Chris Rea, brilliant musician and lovely person (so's his wife but she can't play a note on anything), wanted Thai food. So I decided to try the **Park**. Worst decision of 2008.

The Park room is hotel-boring. All the food was horrendous. The spring roll was old and tired, tasted as if it had been deep frozen for ever. The dim sum were hard, rubbery and horrible. My main-course chicken and noodles were also hard and dried out. A total disgrace for a supposedly first-class hotel.

In the background, pleasing live saxophone music came from the bar. Later Chris Rea rang Geraldine and said, 'The saxophonist was better than the spring rolls.' A rotting horse would have been better than the spring rolls.

The Directors' Guild of Great Britain, a trade union of which I am the longest-serving founder-council member, was to honour Stanley Kubrick with its Lifetime Achievements Award. It was my idea. For the function I chose the **Park Lane Hotel** – their art deco ballroom and balconied cocktail area are particularly attractive.

After worrying about the menu and the seating, I worried about whether guests would turn up. My table was as nice a group as you could muster. I took the delightful Miss Cherie Lunghi, recently returned from foreign parts. On my right was Miss Joanna Lumley with her husband Stephen, very smart in a red jacket and looking like a musician, which is just as well as he is one. A conductor, anyway. Then there was the red-haired and very lovely Patsy Palmer, Sir Peter Ustinov and his daughter and, on the other side, Maureen Lipman and her husband, the writer Jack Rosenthal.

Dinner menus are always a bit of a joke, especially as, at any function for more than 300 people, you know it isn't going to be great. But I thought the Park Lane Hotel did well. Their Italian antipasto of roast artichokes, grilled vegetables, mozzarella, olive bread and rocket salad might not have won first prize in Siena, but for a catered event it was excellent. The inevitable chicken, in this case supreme of chicken (is any menu chick not supreme?), with a tarragon mousse and a wild mushroom cake, was rather good. The dessert was memorable, chocolate millefeuille with orange sorbet. Coffee or tea was accompanied by dark, white and milk chocolate truffles.

Sir Peter Ustinov made the best speech I've ever heard. His impersonation of everyone from Charles Laughton to Laurence Olivier to John Gavin at the script read-through of *Spartacus* was historically hilarious. He presented our trophy to Christiane Kubrick after her daughter Anya had spoken most movingly. *The Evening Standard* described my compering as 'brilliant' – so I should have been happy. But it is exhausting organising dinners for any size of group. I shall now retire to be, as before, the host with the least. It's a role I delight in.

The Royal Garden hotel in Kensington is functional rather than special and is most certainly not known for its great food. It is doggedly second rate in design and decor. But practical and quite buzzy.

The **Park Terrace** is the sort of meaningless room that should have a buffet. Furnished like a school, with wooden chairs and tables, but a nice view over the park. There's a large menu, including English specialities such as slow-roasted pork belly with a sweet glaze and apple mash. Then a lot of eastern stuff – sweet and sour prawns, et cetera.

The menu reads well. That means nothing until you eat the food. Then it all collapses. Nothing we ate was any good at all. I just don't know how a hotel with pretensions of grandeur can dish up stuff like this.

Vanessa had the best of the day with her starter of roasted beetroot salad with parmesan shavings. It wasn't good but it wasn't ghastly. My marinated salmon was tasteless. It had probably been in the deep freeze too long. My lamb stew was totally tasteless. Could have been cardboard.

There followed a lull with nobody offering to take our dessert order. I considered waving my napkin but I couldn't see any staff who'd even notice. So I rose to go into the kitchen and find someone.

I eventually got a spiced pear crumble, which was railway buffet standard. Vanessa ordered apple and blackberry pie. I tried a bit. The pastry was horrid. Vanessa left most of it.

Patio is in the most unremarkable street, close to the southern end of the Shepherd's Bush Shopping Market – which I used to own in my days as a landlord. It's comfortable, old-fashioned and Polish. It has a spick and span look with white tablecloths, and the customers were like I used to see in Hampstead: intellectuals. Quiet, nice-looking Ewa Michalik and her husband Kaz, who own it, have the air of well-turned-out Eastern Europeans who really care. The food demonstrates this. I had herrings with sour cream, red borscht and a sausage called cabamos for starters; then veal à la cracova, a rump of veal with a wine-cream sauce. For dessert I had nice fluffy cheesecake and a pancake filled with vanilla and rum.

I wanted a quick repast near my house, so the Princess (Paola Lombard) and I entered **Patisserie Valerie** in Kensington, part of the posh chain of cake-sellers with tables attached. Other branches include Belgravia, Soho and Marylebone.

I ordered eggs benedict on toasted muffins with smoked salmon and hollandaise sauce. The waiter, very smartly dressed in a striped waistcoat, diamond-patterned tie and white apron, asked, 'To drink?' I opted for a strawberry and banana smoothie. I do those rather well at home. Then I decided to add Toulouse sausages, so I went to the counter and ordered some.

A sober-looking gent at the next table said, 'I thought you normally wrote about

Cont'd
more exciting places than this.' 'Sometimes I do and sometimes I don't,' I replied, adding, 'I guess this is exciting to some people.'

My sausages were excellent. I got two muffin things and they were very good, too. It's a real quality serving. Unfortunately a bit cramped at the table, otherwise it would all be superb.

A very nice, rich woman, Gael Boglione, bought a mansion in Petersham. Then she bought (or possibly hubby Francesco did) the surrounding fields. Then she had an idea! 'I'll put a nursery there!' Not a place for kiddy-widdies to scream and shout. A greenhouse, where people buy plants and ornaments.

Then Gael, or possibly Francesco, thought up another wheeze. 'We'll open a cafe at one end of the greenhouse!' So there appeared rickety chairs, simple country-style tables and – hey presto! – a place to eat. Not all the time. Just lunch, or morning and afternoon tea.

Then either Gael or Francesco made a terrible mistake. They employed the rudest restaurant manager I've ever come across in my life. And I've lived a few decades and met many.

I'll put that out of my mind and give judgement on the **Petersham Nurseries Cafe** unbiased by the horror of the conversation I endured. Let's mark it on a scale of one to 10, 10 being the best. They say if you buy a house the three most important things are location, location and location. On that the PNC warrants a weak three, unless you live in Richmond or Petersham – in which case it's a strong eight!

Now we'll mark it on the comfort. If you like rickety-dickety, a nine. If you don't, a weak four. Service: seven. Food comes out best. A strong eight.

Gael may have fallen down on the restaurant manager, but she triumphed on the chef. Skye Gyngell is a superb cook, with a wonderfully simple style, offering fresh, Winner-type food. There was delicious home-made lemonade on the table. I started with shaved, raw English asparagus with celery and anchovy vinaigrette. Then I had roasted wild salmon with garlic shoots and sauce vert. Very good. I finished with strawberries and ginger pudding, which was historic.

The place must be gruesome in bad weather and in winter. I can't believe it makes money. As for Skye Gyngell, she's bound to move on. The minute I hear where, I'll rush to support her. I recently returned. The food is still superb.

One of my favourite restaurants in the world is La Petite Maison in the old part of Nice. It's run by an industrious, very welcoming French lady, Nicole Rubi. It has a boisterous, casual atmosphere. They specialise in truffles with almost everything. The food is amazing. Now an English version of **La Petite Maison** has opened in the staid

Cont'd

surroundings of a Mayfair mews. I saw no similarity between this and the French one. The low-ceilinged room is full of hard surfaces. This makes conversation virtually impossible. I chose a table near the door to cut down on neighbours. It was still noisy beyond belief.

It's famous for truffles but all the dishes with truffles were off. I ask you? Madness. I started with onion tart. This was five strips of what looked like British Airways canapés. Quite pleasant but not nearly as good as the onion tart I had at Brasserie St Quentin recently. Then I had the speciality main course, whole roast black leg chicken. It was rather dry. I had far better roast chicken from my butcher, H G Walter, at home two days later, cooked by my receptionist Dinah. The desserts were vanilla crème brûlée and dark chocolate tart with orange cream. They were all right, not spectacular.

This is, apparently, a very popular place. But unlike another of Arjun Waney's restaurants, Zuma – also deafeningly noisy but with spectacular food – what's on offer at La Petite Maison is ordinary.

Finchley Road is not a place I've ever dined in. I'm highly suspicious of the Hampstead area as far as restaurants go. **Philpott's Mezzaluna** is in a particularly barren part of Finchley Road. It's north of Hendon Way and before it reaches the bustle of Golders Green. I recall a bingo hall being on that stretch once. But I never visited it.

The dining room has black ceiling fans, rather strange prints on the wall, one of a body, one of a red splurge and one, above my head, of a prisoner in Bergen County sheriff's office. There are some rather tacky Venetian masks hanging through an arch and a tiled floor. I would not call it an elegant space.

Alex Ross, the co-owner – his partner David Philpott is the chef – gave me their card. This was black type on dark red. I've never seen anything so ridiculous. You couldn't read the address at all.

We got leek and potato soup with parmesan oil as a freebie starter. It was pleasant. I chose a starter of crisp mackerel, rocket, pistachio, anchovy and paprika. By the time it arrived I'd forgotten what I'd ordered. Geraldine said: 'What's that you're eating, mackerel?' I said: 'Yes, it probably is.' It was also pleasant. No more no less.

Then I had grilled Dover sole on the bone. This was very succulent, nice and with a lovely texture. It was served hot, which is more than my fish was at the Connaught. Also very tasty little potatoes. I'd have liked some butter to put on them but they only had olive oil on the table.

The waitresses, all with black hair, were dressed head to toe in black. I wondered if they had to dye their hair to match the costumes.

I hate Charlotte Street. It runs north of, and at right angles to, Oxford Street, which is the wrong end. Not that Oxford Street has a right end. I hate Oxford Street too. I only have one happy memory of Charlotte Street, which was in the mid-1950s. I went to a movie location there one night to meet, supposedly, the most difficult and unpleasant actor ever – Rex Harrison. Like many people with fearsome reputations he was absolutely charming and asked me to dinner with his co-star and future wife, Kay Kendall.

For some 50 years since, I've steered clear of Charlotte Street, despite it, from time to time, housing well-respected restaurants. It was my friend Jeremy Thomas who lured me back. Jeremy is one of Britain's brightest movie producers. I suggested lunch at **Pied à Terre**, a place near his office in the aforementioned and horrid Charlotte Street.

The set lunch menu was £26.50 for three courses, plus the so-called 'optional' service charge of 12.5%. I ordered black truffle and white bean soup from the set menu, then steamed and roasted saddle of rabbit, tortellini of confit leg, braised lentils and red wine sauce. It was all very good, as was my dessert of mandarin parfait with lemon curd, meringues and blood orange sauce. Even the pre-dessert freebie of mango coulis and coconut foam was excellent.

It was only when I got home to the civilisation of Holland Park and looked up Pied à Terre in the Michelin guide that I realised it was one of the only four restaurants in London and nine in the United Kingdom with two Michelin stars. If I'd known, I'd have appeared more in awe of the proceedings.

I also realised it was the restaurant famous, or notorious, according to how you view these things, where Tom Aikens, current super-hot Chelsea restaurateur and chef, once did something naughty in the kitchen. How naughty depends on which account you believe. The newspapers accused him of branding a member of his staff with a red-hot kitchen implement. His wife, Laura, in the wonderful television programme *Trouble at the Top* that featured Tom, said, in a cautionary voice, 'Don't talk about it, Tom, you only tapped him.'

It's a miracle there's not a mass murder in every restaurant kitchen every night. The pressure these people are under to turn out immaculate, plate-decorated food from lunchtime to late at night plus coming in early to prepare – all in horrific heat and noise – is enough to make them totally demented. I like to think I do my bit in that direction. It's nice to make a contribution, isn't it?

I'd heard all sorts of stories about **Planet Hollywood** being the greatest success and then collapsing into failure, but it's now back. The London Planet Hollywood has a heaving atmosphere and is unbelievably full. The vanilla milkshake got the world record for slow service, but was very good when it arrived, even though the straw was a bit too thin. Owner Robert Earl guided me, pointing out Whoopi Goldberg and Demi

Cont'd

Moore's favourite, which is called Chicken Crunch. There were blackened shrimps, nachos with chicken barbecue sauce and two types of cheese, and for a main course ribeye steak with sauce béarnaise and French fries. The dessert was various ice creams, chocolate brownies, chocolate cake and a particularly good bread pudding with whisky sauce. If I could get this sort of excellent snack food, without all the noise and the hustle and bustle, I'd eat there frequently.

There are restaurants you pass, year after year, but which you never enter. So I was pleased when the actress Kathleen Breck invited me to lunch at **Poissonnerie de l'Avenue**, Chelsea, a restaurant I have ignored all my life. Kathleen was the lead in my film *West 11* in 1962. She went on to better things – she quit acting, found a handsome and rich husband (the famous screenwriter Allan Scott) and settled down to a delightful life.

When I entered the premises I thought they looked extraordinarily dull. I had impressed upon Miss Breck the importance of having a large table well enough away from other diners. Kathleen had done well. At the next table Mary Quant turned up, so it was a really 1960s reunion! The food was okay. I had langoustines, Kathleen had field mushrooms with polenta. We both had the grilled sole.

I later suggested Vanessa went there for dinner with me. This time I started with some smallish fried sardines – good, not spectacular – followed by adequate salmon fishcakes.

It's not great and I am not going to put the Poissonnerie on my regular list because of its ambience.

I must admit a great liking for Polish cooking. I don't think it's because my mother was born in Poland as, sadly, she never cooked the local dishes. I do recall with great pleasure a few trips to a very strange building in King Street, Hammersmith, which looks like a seedy government office. In fact it houses the Polish Social and Cultural Association and a Polish restaurant open to the public called Lowizanka (now re-named **Polish Centre Restaurant**). It has quite extraordinarily good food at very low prices – so cheap that I ordered three main courses just to have the pleasure of tasting each. Unfortunately the waitress was extremely snooty about it as she tried, with difficulty, to fit them all on the table.

River disaster

The least enjoyable restaurant evening of my life was at Sir Terence Conran's **Le Pont De La Tour**. I was the guest of an American music supremo; Chris Wright, the chairman of Chrysalis Records, was with us. An evening of tepid food, of unremarkable quality, and poor service was rounded off with a remarkable performance by one of the most unrepentant managers I have ever come across. One guest wasn't served until everyone else had virtually finished a course. My fish came without any vegetables; it tasted old and tired. We'd ordered coffee and after a while I saw two young waiters staring in confusion at a tray with cups on it. I suspected they couldn't work out which was decaffeinated and which wasn't. After a while, I looked again. They were still staring. Eventually they took a chance and served it. 'This coffee's cold,' murmured my quiet American host. I shot up.

The manager, resplendent in evening dress, was way down the restaurant. I walked over. He saw me coming and headed for the cash-desk. 'Excuse me,' I said. He seemed to ignore me. That was a mistake. 'Excuse me,' I said again, a bit louder. He kept walking. 'Excuse me!' I yelled. When I yell you can hear it 60 miles away. He turned. 'We're having a terrible time at our table,' I said with venom. 'I suggest you come and deal with it.'

He followed me back. I pointed out that the coffee was cold and asked could he get some more. Things were not going well and one guest mentioned my fish. This clearly upset the manager. 'What was that?' 'It's not important,' I said. 'Let's just have some hot coffee.' But that was a forlorn hope; the manager wanted to know 'what was wrong' there and then. Oh dear, I thought. I told him my fish had been solid and unfresh. He protested at length about how fresh everything was. Always. Inevitably.

The wife of our host, trying to calm things, said how nice the place usually was, what famous rock stars she'd brought, but how tonight we'd all thought there had been a collapse of service and quality.

'I shall go to the kitchen and discuss this,' said the manager, walking off with all the neurosis of Basil Fawlty. He returned with a delivery note. 'That proves the fish was fresh this morning,' he said. 'Ah well, perhaps it was overcooked,' I said.

The manager stormed off again, returning to whisper in my ear: 'The chef was very satisfied with your fish.' 'Well, he didn't have to eat it,' I replied.

I wrote to Sir Terence, detailing how a distressing meal had been turned into a remarkably unpleasant evening by the quite extraordinary antics of his manager. Unlike other restaurateurs I've written to, Sir Terence replied sarcastically: 'Thank you for your film script, I shall certainly investigate the situation.' I did not hear from him further.

P.S. I later became great friends with Terence Conran.

Il Portico is time-warped in the 1960s, but the food has stayed fresh and pleasant. It's uncomfortable, very family-run by the offspring of Pino Chiavarini, the founder, and his wife. I am only prepared to sit in one of the booths and then I insist the next one be kept empty. I have visited it on and off since 1969, usually for al dente spaghetti with tomato sauce, but there is a varied menu and the service couldn't be better.

P.S. I no longer go much. My staff tell me it's too expensive.

If you go south from Sloane Square and turn left, there are lots of chi-chi antique shops, Lord Linley's furniture showroom, and then on the left is Ebury Street with a French bistro, **La Poule au Pot**, that looks like it was designed for a 1950s MGM movie. You expect Gene Kelly to tap dance by. He wasn't there when I visited for lunch.

It's as if the set decorator went mad. There are hanging baskets with wheat, dried flowers and grapes coming from them. The only things missing were human heads from the tumbrel. Some of the wooden tables have cloths. Ours did, but it was also covered with two pieces of brown paper.

Geraldine ordered ratatouille to start followed by grilled salmon with sauce béarnaise. I chose onion soup from the £18.75 set lunch and then rabbit with mustard sauce.

My soup was fine. My rabbit arrived in a large copper pot. There were also petit pois with onions, bacon, more ratatouille and pommes boulangère. The rabbit was bionic. I mean enormous. It was the sort of rabbit you might have seen in the 1950s horror film the *Attack of the Killer Rabbits*. That's where gargantuan rabbits attacked America, sweeping skyscrapers aside with their paws, trampling on tanks and other weaponry brought up to do them in and then biting off the troops' heads and spitting them out into the streets. You didn't see that movie? It was absolutely marvellous.

The rabbit, oversized as it undoubtedly was, remained very good. The sauce was pleasant, so were the vegetables. Geraldine liked her salmon and thought the béarnaise was superb. If it wasn't for the crashing of waiters it would have been a peaceful meal.

My tarte tartin was robust. Nowhere near the standard of the ones I used to love when Marco Pierre White cooked in the kitchen of the Hyde Park hotel, but not unpleasant.

I now offer you a useless piece of information: the restaurant has been here since 1962. It's pretty good really if you like that sort of thing, everyone looking very pleasant French. Personally I can take it or leave it, but Geraldine assures me she's going back. Bet she doesn't.

Quo Vadis in Dean Street, Soho, is fantastically good in every way. Food, ambience, service. For years it was a dump. Then my friend Joseph Ettedgui bought it from Marco Pierre White and promptly sold it on to Sam and Eddie Hart. Sam and Eddie are stars.

When I visited with Geraldine, Sam seated us at a nice table with a view of the room: bright, modern pictures, mirrored walls, very buzzy. 'Very swish-looking people here,' said Geraldine. Do you think she meant me?

I said to Sam: 'I presume you're too grand to take an order.' He promptly produced a pad. I said, 'Madame will have green salad to start, then poached egg with artichoke and hollandaise sauce. For me [I'm the low end of the market], brown shrimps on toast followed by veal sweetbreads and tartare sauce.' Sam assured me the chips were made on the premises so I added chips and fresh peas.

The food was absolutely marvellous. Including very good bread and butter. The home-made chips were the best I've had in London. The fresh peas were historic.

I finished with treacle tart, usually a total letdown. Theirs was soft, hot and actually tasted of treacle. It came with clotted cream.

I liked Quo Vadis so much we went again with musician Chris Rea and his lovely wife Joan. This time I started with whitebait. A repeat of veal sweetbreads and rum baba to finish. Great texture, tasty, perfect. Joan had crab linguine, which she described as stunning, and a magnificent lemon tart. Everything was sensational.

I've come across a restaurant that deserves the greatest praise. It is superb, outstanding, incredible and – most importantly – quadruple historic. It's **Racine** in Brompton Road. It is a jolly bistro-type place. It was recommended by my friend Lord Andrew Lloyd-Webber, who knows a great deal more about food than me. Who doesn't?

I've been to Racine many times and the food is always fantastic. Tasty, not too messed about, original, delicious. On my first visit I noted how excellent the bread was. That's always a good sign. I had deep-fried brain with sauce gribiche, then I had ox tongue, sauerkraut, beetroot and horseradish purée. The fried brain was delicious. The tongue was perfectly cooked and they gave me a spoon for the sauce, which was useful because it was marvellous.

When I went with Michael Caine I had roes on toast to start plus some herring and pepper steak. It was perfectly prepared and professionally presented. Michael said it was the best steak he'd ever had. He also commented, correctly, that the customers looked bright and interesting. Which is extremely rare these days.

The only slight disappointment was the dessert on my first outing. It was a Mont Blanc. I consider myself a world expert on Mont Blanc. I could do *Mastermind* on it. The chestnut was a little too tart, although it was in lovely squiggles as it used to be at Fortnum & Mason. They once did the best Mont Blanc ever. The base of Racine's meringue had become a bit clingy. I'd rate their Mont Blanc 'just good'.

Bhatia Vineet was the first Indian chef to get a Michelin star. This glory was tarnished by his boss, Claudio Pulze, banishing him to ugly premises in a strange part of Kensington High Street. So Vineet sensibly left to open his own, elegant restaurant in a small townhouse near Sloane Square, called **Rasoi Vineet Bhatia**.

On the ground floor are two dining rooms, upstairs can house private parties. The look is extremely pleasing. Pastel shades, Indian artefacts framed as pictures, bells hanging from the metal struts of an observatory roof. Vineet's wife did the décor. She usually manages the restaurant but was noticeably absent when I visited. 'Probably terrified,' explained Vineet. He smiles a lot and has great charm. Rare for people in the totally misnamed hospitality business.

We started with what I guess were small, round poppadoms. Three containers of brightly coloured accoutrements to go with them were in a long china bowl. All delicious. By the time we'd finished we didn't need anything else. Cuppa tea and the bill would have done me.

Instead we got a seafood platter, a duck platter and a tandoori paneer. Don't ask me what it all consisted of. Find someone who knows about food. It was above historic. Really delicate flavouring. Beautifully prepared. But only the start of foodie world 'shock and awe'.

Then came ginger and chilli lobster, grilled red mullet, prawns poached in coconut, tandoori chicken breast, Kashmiri lamb and accompaniments of mustard-tempered vegetables, tarka dal (whatever that is!), kachumber raita, trio of breads, old Uncle Tom Cobleigh and all. Everything was so sensational I just kept eating. It's a miracle I didn't blow up, blasting little pieces of Winner over the other diners.

Indian desserts are usually beyond belief frightful. But I had rose petal and vanilla, pistachio and coriander, and mango ice-cream. Also masala tea and lime ice-cream.

To finish me off I had Indian petit fours. This meal was, without doubt one, of the great food experiences, even though I was so stuffed I could hardly walk.

I know of no kinder or more generous person than John Cleese. I met him in Barbados in 1984. For our first dinner he shaved off most of his black moustaches, leaving a bit in the middle so he looked like Hitler. He's since assailed me with the most disgracefully racist remarks, often in public or after-dinner speeches. I find them extremely amusing, although some observers have been shocked. My favourite John-remark came as we walked along the sands in Barbados, our feet in the sparkling sea, past flowering bushes full of colour, with birds tweeting in the clear blue sky. John said, 'You know, Michael, there must be more to life than this.'

Now he's just completed a lengthy and bitter divorce. His ex-wife, Alyce Faye Eichelberger, told me on a previous spat, when she'd hired solicitor Fiona Shackleton, 'John doesn't know what's going to hit him. I'll take him for every penny.' She kept her word. When John and Alyce parted, John said to me, 'This is going to be a friendly and quick divorce.' I responded, 'What planet are you on? It'll be horrific.' John had settled amicably, minus lawyers, with two previous wives, remaining friendly with both of them. He expected it would be the same with Alyce. Boy, did he have a wrong number. He's been deeply hurt by Alyce and her and her lawyer's tactics.

The result is extraordinary. John and Alyce were married for 15 years. She lived in a council flat when they met. There are no dependent children. Yet she's getting millions of dollars. In cash and assets Alyce ends up far richer than John himself. As he put it, 'What I find so unfair is that if we both died today, her children would get much more than mine.' On top of that Alyce gets a further $1million a year for seven years. If ever there was a case for pre-nuptial agreements, this is it. Court papers finalising this bizarre settlement only went before the judge a few days ago. John commented, 'Think what Alyce might have got if she'd been a good wife.'

One evening, I went with John, my adorable fiancée Geraldine and my lovely PA Ruby Snape to dinner at the **Red Fort**, an Indian restaurant in Soho. As Westminster council no longer tow away cars and I can't deal with the phone-in meter paying system, I park my car on the yellow lines and pay the £60 penalty. Geraldine is kindly holding my ticket. I find them too heavy to carry. The Red Fort is fairly minimalist. Yellowish walls, banquettes, a new bar. John thought of it because the Pythons had a meeting there before starting their movie *Life of Brian*. Eric Idle suggested the title 'Jesus Christ – Lust for Glory'.

We commenced with spicy poppadoms, which I don't normally like. They were excellent. The plain ones were fine too, the chapatis the best I've ever had. 'John's lamb was too hot,' I dictated. 'A bit hot but very good,' corrected John. 'You put it aside,' I persisted. 'It was my shrimp he put aside,' explained Geraldine. 'If you're eating something hot and you switch to something subtle you can't taste it,' said John feigning patience. 'I can't taste anything anyway,' I said. There's a sign in the toilet: 'Anyone caught taking or distributing drugs will be banned'. Not the police called. Just banned from eating curry. That'll teach 'em to distribute drugs. John asked Ruby about me, 'What's he like?' 'He's so bad tempered,' Ruby replied. 'I'm used to it. I get a bit disconcerted when he's not.' My main course was Hyderabadi bhuna gosht, Hardwick skewer lamb with ginger, garlic, coriander and red chilli. We all liked everything. John went back recently and liked it again.

It was towards the end of my stay at the London Clinic that I decided to try **Reubens** in Baker Street. I expected nothing. I received some of the tastiest, best food I've ever eaten. My super-sleuths Geraldine and Dinah went to get the grub. They were fascinated to see Jewish men in skullcaps decorated with silver and gold.

As you enter there's a big counter with, among other things, fresh chips, which both Geraldine and Dinah found irresistible. There are tables without cloths, but downstairs tables are fully laid in an elegant way.

In spite of the fact that the food is close to historic I can't see you rushing off to Reubens. Nor do I hold that against you. I've never been there myself. Like you, I'm a creature of habit. I'd rather eat tired sea bass on a bed of exhausted spinach with the 'in' crowd at some mediocre Chelsea or West End venue. That makes us feel comfortable. Better than going to some odd place on the west side of Baker Street and being surrounded by strange men in funny hats.

Reubens is light years ahead of the other restaurants serving this sort of Middle European food of the diaspora. For example, there's a thing called chicken soup with matzo balls. You can get this at the Wolseley. I've had it on many occasions at many places. The matzo balls are always too hard. At Reubens they're soft, flaky and delicious. All their soups were outstanding.

I had a stuffed cabbage with sauce that was one of the most memorable excellent tastes ever. Their smoked salmon sandwiches on rye bread with lettuce are simply the best. I was amazed my beefburger was so good, because Reubens is kosher. I've always understood kosher meat, while being religiously pure, is not too tasty. This beefburger was. The salt beef is moist and of great quality. Even better than Selfridges. Then they do memorable sauté potatoes with onions, and latkes beyond belief. A latke is a fried potato pancake. They're often slightly below nauseous. Reubens' ones were near perfect.

Normally, Jewish desserts are an unmitigated disaster. Cloying, heavy and simply inedible. I've never had better apple strudel than the one from Reubens. They even do a lockshen pudding (usually horrid, horrid, horrid), which I think is made from some sort of vermicelli. Currants were in there, too. I thought: 'I'll never eat this.' I finished the lot.

I do recommend you go there. Reubens has an enormous menu of almost everything you could want. To my knowledge, none of it, thankfully, served on a bed of spinach. And the chips? They're to die for. Be brave. Give it a try.

I like Gary Rhodes, his haircut and his attitude. I warm to the fact that he looks like an overgrown version of the Bisto kid from those old adverts. I also can't remember Gary ever saying anything stupid to the press, which makes him practically unique among chefs. On a recent Saturday I ventured to **Rhodes W1 Brasserie** at the Cumberland hotel on Oxford Street where Gary recently took over the dining room.

The duty restaurant manager, Anna Kowalczyk, was in charge that day at Gary's glossy cafeteria. 'The fine dining room is closed for Saturday lunch,' she explained. If there's one thing I hate (and believe me, there's more than one) it's the phrase 'fine dining'. What a pretentious, suburban, pathetic grouping of words that is. It implies stupid, tiny portions, interminably served and not worth eating anyway.

We settled in the very spacious, practical in the best way, eating place for lesser mortals. As a poor boy from Willesden that certainly includes me. The first arrival, on a shiny table with no cloth, was the bread. It was warm and wonderful. The brown granary bread with seeds was spectacularly good. I was shaken but not stirred. They also had Evian water, which is classy.

Geraldine started with pressed duck foie gras served with chicory and pear salad and apple jelly. She loved it. I tried some, it was excellent. Made even better because I'd persuaded them to turn off the horrific piped music. I had lightly smoked mackerel rillette on soft potato with cucumber and dill, spring onion and radish salad. Very acceptable.

Then I had deep-fried breadcrumbed fillets of plaice with a superb shallot and caper mayonnaise and some rather disappointing home-made chunky-cut chips. If you're going to serve home-made chips, Gary, get someone who knows how to do them. These were soggy on the inside and chewy on the outside as if they'd been kept in a heater too long. My rocket and parmesan salad was fine and the fried fish definitely good. Geraldine had a 'perfectly cooked' piece of tuna. Her view of the chips was more favourable than mine.

My almond cake dessert with steeped blackberries and apple sorbet was absolutely historic. Then I tried iced orange and espresso parfait with coffee syrup. This was also superb, well above what you'd expect in a glorified canteen.

Gary, I don't know what your fine dining is like. But your simple shopper's lunch menu is a triumph.

Charles Saatchi said: 'Let's have dinner.' I was expecting to go to his house in Belgravia, which boasts a staggering collection of modern art, none of which I understand. Instead Charles invited us to the **Rib Room at The Carlton Tower Hotel**, a regular haunt of Mr S and the delightful Nigella Lawson.

The room has brightened up since I was there many years ago. Everywhere you look you see people working in white outfits. It's either a lunatic asylum or a restaurant. The assembled, amusing group was: Charles and Nigella, Geraldine and me, Matthew Norman (witty columnist), his wife Rebecca (ditto), Charles Elton (TV producer) and Lucy (his wife).

'Would you like my recommendation?' said Charles Saatchi. 'Prawn cocktail.' I'm easily led. I ordered it – and a sirloin steak. The cocktail was spectacularly good. A marvellous 50s dish, soft, large prawns, nice sauce and crisp lettuce. Just as well as it was the only food I'd see for over an hour. 'You couldn't call the service nippy here,' I complained.

When the meat eventually arrived, I looked at everyone else's plate and observed, 'I haven't got a potato. Why haven't I got a potato?'

'Would you please get Mr Winner a potato?' Nigella asked sweetly. The waiter looked baffled. Eventually I got one. The vegetables and butter arrived later. To say the service is terrible at the Rib Room is a gross understatement.

Cont'd

'How was your potato?' asked Matthew. 'It was fine,' I answered. 'It didn't look crispy on the outside,' said Nigella. She was right. It wasn't top class. But the meat was very good, if you can survive long enough to get it.

The distinguished chef Richard Corrigan is a genius because he agrees with me. In a magazine article Richard said: 'The customer isn't just king, he's emperor.' It's okay, Richard, I'll settle for king. He went on: 'You'd be amazed how often restaurateurs overlook their customers – or even insult them or simply rob them. You have to get the right staff. I look for people who are happy to be themselves. At home with the concept of service.'

Having decided he was a bright lad, I set off to be treated like an emperor at **Richard Corrigan at Lindsay House** in Soho. Richard greeted me in exemplary fashion and showed me round. The ground floor, where we sat, is simple. Like a room in a private house. Richard is the only chef I've met without his name embroidered on his tunic. Luckily he told me who he was, otherwise I'd never have known.

He specially got Evian water in for me in an art deco silver-plated decanter. I ordered crubeens (pig's trotters) with Jabugo ham and woodland sorrel followed by West Cork beef, bone marrow, prune and caramelised onions. *The Independent* called Richard 'a genius with flavour'. 'Another reason he's good is he's actually here,' said Paola. A lot of named chefs are seldom in their restaurants, which I find appalling.

We got a freebie starter – two spoons, one with fresh mackerel tartare, one with sturgeon caviar, smoked sturgeon and cucumber, plus some croquettes of I know not what and a small glass of tomato soup. Very nice. By now I felt I'd eaten enough. A vanilla ice and a cuppa tea and I'd be finished. Instead I got my pig's trotters, which were little savoury croquettes.

Then my main course of beef arrived. All very good. But when you add the homemade bread and organic butter, I'd scoffed too much. This didn't stop me asking for all the desserts, including blackcurrant soufflé with lemon curd and ripple ice cream.

I hate Soho. My chauffeur Jim, outside with the Rolls Phantom V, said he had strange propositions from men and women. Richard should move to Holland Park. There are large premises going on the corner of my street. Although it says 'bar use', Richard's Irish, so he could charm them into letting it be a restaurant. Then I could walk down the road and be treated like an emperor. More than I get at home.

Richoux in Piccadilly is part of a chain of olde-worlde French-type coffee shops. It's an attractively designed place; bit twee. Geraldine thought it needed an aspidistra and a string orchestra.

The manager is a tall, thin woman with black hair called Iwona, dressed in all-over black. She looks exactly like Morticia Addams of the Addams family.

The menu read 'fresh orange juice'. 'You don't have fresh orange juice, do you?' I asked. 'No,' was the waiter's reply. 'It's fresh, but it's not freshly squeezed.' We all know what that means. Delivered in a plastic container housing who knows what.

When I asked if the fish had been delivered that morning, always tricky on a Monday, the waiter went to the kitchen, returned and assured me it had been. Maybe in senility I'm becoming gullible, but I believed him.

I started with French onion soup (acceptable to good); Geraldine had prawn and avocado cocktail. She liked it. Being common as muck, I ordered 'traditional home-made fish and chips served with mushy peas and a lemon wedge'. The haddock was fine. The mushy peas totally cold. The chips were bought in, but they are at the Wolseley, Ivy, Caprice and most places. They were okay.

For dessert I got a waffle with ice cream and maple syrup. Waffles are not easy. This one was historically awful. Clammy, soggy, no crispness. I did like the decor though. Art nouveau meets Dracula.

The only place in England offering a really spendid British Sunday lunch is the **Ritz** hotel in Piccadilly. It is one of the last of the grand hotels that's not been messed about or largely destroyed. Its interiors remain as they were when it was built in 1906.

The main entrance has been moved from Piccadilly, where horse-drawn carriages would visit in more elegant times, to Arlington Street round the corner. There it sports the best doormen in the world. Attentive, cheerful and old school.

The only problem I have with the Ritz is the absurd dress code. This does not produce an elegant clientele. Particularly on Sundays, when it's a 'special event' place. People turn up from the suburbs to celebrate Granny's birthday. Penge must be empty. I'm sure they're all marvellous human beings, but wear total rubbish.

Ever willing to obey rules, I donned a Brioni double-breasted jacket, a silk tie from Sulka & Co, handmade Savile Row trousers and scuffed black suede shoes. I was sartorial perfection.

The Princess (Paola Lombard) and I entered the marvellous hall and walked past the grandly designed tea room to be greeted by Simon Girling, restaurant manager of the finest dining room in London. The tables look beautiful, the view to the garden and Green Park is fine. A pianist tinkled *Some Enchanted Evening*, even though it was lunchtime.

Seven types of bread were presented in a vast basket and then served on a little silver tray. It was exemplary, fresh and tasty. We started lunch with a freebie tomato gazpacho, avocado mousse with a piece a fresh crab, a parmesan crisp and topped with beluga caviar. I followed with the best asparagus ever, while Princess had a confit of beetroot with biscotti and roquefort and horseradish cream, lentil dressing.

I was greatly, massively, enormously looking forward to a rib of beef from the trolley. Instead there was a roll of sirloin. I was shattered. It was nice beef, but not a patch of the texture, look, quality and taste of a good rib.

The Yorkshire pudding was perfect, the veg terrific. To top it all the soufflé potatoes were triple, if not quadruple, even five-truble, historic. These are blown up, fried bags of potato. Only the Ritz chef, John Williams, does them in the whole of England.

For dessert I had an excellent Rothschild soufflé, with candied fruit and a little Grande Marnier. Princess had a great mango and lemon sorbet.

Although it let me down dreadfully in one area, it remains overall superb.

They say when buying property only three things matter: location, location and location. If so, the **River Café** is a dead duck. It's located in a strange part of Hammersmith, which is itself a strange part of London. It's more or less impossible to find.

You might imagine if it's called the River Café it would be on the river. In all the years I've been going there I've never seen a stream, a trickle or an ooze, let alone a river. What you do see from the restaurant, even from seats outside, is a sort of sunken lawn. At the end of this space is a wall. I'm assured the Thames lurks behind it. It could equally as well be a motorway, railway lines or a car park.

If you can (a) find the place and (b) get over your disappointment at not seeing a river, you will be spectacularly rewarded. The restaurant is brilliantly designed with great simplicity and the food is superb. Every dish is near-perfect. I have never had a bad course. It's unquestionably the most reliable good grub to be had in London.

It's Italian food, often prepared by the owners, Lady Ruth ('call me Ruthie') Rogers and her partner, Rose Gray. I had bruschetta, followed by wood-baked sardine fillet layered with pine nuts, chilli and lemon zest. Then tagliatelle 'hand-cut pasta with first-of-the-season basil, lemon and parmesan', two Coca-Colas (most unlike me) and, for dessert, their chocolate nemesis, one of the great choccie-puds of the world.

On previous visits I've had marvellous Anjou pigeon, lamb, calf's liver – you name it, they do it brilliantly. There's no doubt Ruthie and Rose can cook Italian better than most Italians.

A lot of people complain it's too expensive. I don't agree. For real quality you have to up the ante a bob or two.

P.S. The River Café has re-opened after 'tarting up'. Its new design incorporates the whole kitchen. It's a delight. You see a wood-burning oven, counters, bars. It gives it great perspective and distance where there used to be just a white wall. There's no better restaurant design anywhere.

The room at **Roast** in Southwark is absolutely beautiful. It's got tall windows overlooking the Victorian wrought iron of Borough Market, a place many restaurateurs buy from. Another window reveals St Paul's Cathedral. It's on two levels, wooden floors, a view of the kitchen. There's lots of space between good-sized tables. It's owned by Iqbal Wahhab who has the Cinnamon Club in Westminster, which I hated beyond belief.

The menu's very sensible, full of English dishes, simply described. Paola observed, 'For once someone's got roast chicken on a Sunday lunch menu.' I had a starter of Cornish crab cake with chickweed and cooked salad cream. It was excellent. Paola had Shropshire blue cheese with Cox apple salad, very nice.

Her main course was roast Banham chicken with Ayrshire bacon and bread sauce with root vegetable mash and potato mash. She wasn't mad about the chicken. I had roast 28-day-aged Scottish fore-rib of beef with Yorkshire pudding, curly cabbage and house-cooked chips. The Yorkshire was useless. The chips were okay but not a patch on those at Heston Blumenthal's Hind Head in Bray. The beef was moderate.

For dessert I had rhubarb and hazelnut crumble with custard. It was brilliant, possibly historic. Paola spooned away my custard and declared it superb. She asked, 'Why don't they call my clementine water ice a sorbet?' I said, 'Because it's an English restaurant and there's too much French influence around anyway.' We both thought the ice water incredibly good.

My friends David and Wendy chose a restaurant in Charlotte Street called **Roka** for our soirée. Roka is a good restaurant. Very good. But as David observed: 'It's the sort of place you wouldn't rush back to.' Roka is owned by Zuma, the ever-so-chic (and absurdly noisy) place in Knightsbridge. It's the cafe version.

The menu card is ridiculous. It's very stiff plastic. So stiff you can't open it more than 45 degrees and then you have to fight to keep it open. I ripped out the paper pages in the middle.

Dishes are under headings such as chu-maki, roka dishes, robata sakana and many more. David said: 'Shall I order lots of things?' I asked: 'Do I trust you? Do you know what you're doing?' David said: 'Tell me at the end of the meal.' 'That could be too late,' I advised. 'You've got to tell me what I get because I won't know what it is.' 'I'll give you a copy of the bill. You can look at it when I've paid,' offered David.

He did give me the bill. It came to £247.60. It included edamame (raw beans), kim chi – no idea what that is, couldn't find it on the menu – egg roll, king crab hotpot, rock shrimp (particularly delicious), onion rings in breadcrumbs, crispy prawn maki, salmon hand roll, tiger prawns, quail marinated in plum wine and red miso, lamb cutlets, sashimi, chicken skewers. I could go on. It was all absolutely fabulous, to quote my friend Joanna Lumley.

My tape-recorded notes are odder than usual. Here's a sample: 'A cold roll. It's like a square thing. We're now hearing this thing is called something completely different. It's an egg omelette with a fish stock. We've had tuna and now we've got tuna on white things.'

After I decided I was totally full up a lobster appeared. I managed to force some down before ordering a dark chocolate and nougat pudding with plum wine ice cream. Geraldine said: 'I'll have some of his.' I don't want to share my desserts. 'Give her a whole portion,' I said magnanimously as a person not paying the bill.

Here's a quiz for you. What London restaurant, which has been going since 1798, was frequented by Charles Dickens, William Makepeace Thackeray, HG Wells, Evelyn Waugh, Clark Gable, Laurence Olivier and Graham Greene?

Not got it? Here's a clue. John Betjeman, when poet laureate, described the ground-floor room interior as a 'unique and irreplaceable part of literary and theatrical London'. No, it's not Moishe's fish and chip shop in Golders Green Road. That's a really stupid suggestion. It's **Rules** in Maiden Lane, situated behind the Adelphi theatre.

Geraldine accompanied me on my first visit to Rules on a recent Saturday lunchtime. I looked in vain for a major literary figure (there being no mirrors, I couldn't see myself) or even a movie star or theatrical knight. Only a few bedraggled tourists sitting in what is indeed a stunningly preserved interior. Mind you, not preserved from 1798. The stuffed birds, stags' heads with antlers and profusion of oil paintings and old prints look more Victorian to me.

We were met at the door by a man who might have been wearing a frock coat and who exuded old-fashioned charm. I said: 'I've never been here before.' He replied: 'I've been here for ever.' This turned out to be 19 years. He was Terry Wood, the maitre d'.

We settled at a table with a stuffed pheasant on a ledge above who was facing the doorway. So I had an uninterrupted view of its arse. The waitress said the mineral water was Irish. 'Do you just have that one?' I asked. 'Or from the Thames,' was the reply. 'Great sense of humour here,' I dictated into my machine. When the water arrived it turned out to be Scottish, not Irish. It was called Speyside Glenlivet premium Scottish quality. Not bad, not good, I noted.

It's an old-fashioned English menu. 'Have you got any grouse today?' I asked Terry. 'I haven't, it's not in season yet,' he responded, thus putting me in my place. Some melba toast and white bread arrived. The white bread was beyond belief horrific. Chewy, sagging, horrible, horrible, horrible. One of my previous employers, the wonderful Italian producer Dino De Laurentiis, told me: 'You can always judge a restaurant by the bread.' In that case Rules was stone dead.

Geraldine ordered foie gras terrine with smoked duck, rillettes and elderflower jelly, followed by hot wild Tay salmon with sorrel, morel mushrooms and roasted shallots. I took from 'to-day's specials' stilton and watercress soup and then cottage pie with melted Montgomery cheddar.

My soup was British Rail 1953, which is no great insult as 1953 was a good year for British Rail soup. My shepherd's pie was okay, not as good as one I got at home a few days later. Geraldine greatly enjoyed her salmon. For dessert I chose golden treacle sponge pudding with warm vanilla custard. It came also with clotted cream. It was pleasant but, as always, there wasn't enough golden treacle. I usually ask for extra in a jug, but on this occasion I forgot.

The service was very slow. The gap between starter and main course went on for ever. They advertise post-theatre suppers. 'Just as well they don't do pre-theatre supper,' I remarked, 'if they did no one would get there until the intermission.'

On the menu it said: 'Complimentary soft drinks served, if you have a car and driver waiting for you. Please inform your waiter.' I forgot to do that. Could have saved a bob or two on the mineral water. I guess it won't make a significant difference to my financial postion.

Let me say straight away, **St Alban** is absolutely superb. It has the charm of the 1950s at its best. The banquettes and chairs are in green, purple or deep red. They curve gently through a wide space. The tables are well spaced apart, the acoustics perfect. It's one of the few places in London where you can hear even the most soft-spoken guest.

None of this surprises as its creators are Jeremy King and Chris Corbin, unquestionably the best restaurateurs I've ever come across. They took over Le Caprice in 1981, going on to re-create the Ivy and J Sheekey. They sold the lot. Then came back triumphantly with the Wolseley. With St Alban in Regent Street they've done it again.

On this visit every dish was perfect. I started with Iberian jabugo ham with home-made pickles. I've had this three times before. It's sensational. Dinah had deep-fried soft shell crab with tarragon mayonnaise. I tried one and then another. Totally historic.

Our main course was sea bass 'a la plancha' with turnip. It was above excellent. In the 1950s it used to be grilled sole all the time. Now it's sea bass, with or without plancha. It's usually overcooked and has the taste of having spent far too long in the deep freeze. This was tender, soft and succulent. Previously I've tasted their slow-roasted black pig with turnip tops. Geraldine particularly liked their charcoal-grilled duck breast.

I've never had an even slightly dodgy course at St Alban. My dessert on this visit was lemon cream with pomegranate sorbet. As a dessert-lover I was ecstatic.

I haven't mentioned the chef because his name's not on the menu and I really don't want to contribute to the birth of another verbose TV 'star' – the word star these days being attached to any passing nonentity. I grew up and worked with stars, real ones such as Brando, Mitchum, Burt Lancaster, Sophia Loren. They had immense talent and were known throughout the world. Today most so-called stars are known only in their own toilet.

Talking of which, St Alban has the most glamorous toilets in London. Make it a part of your journey there to visit them. Which brings us to the final item I've not mentioned: service.

I apologise for going on about how great everything is at St Alban. But it is. The service is no exception. All the waiters, wine waiters, commis waiters, doormen, dishwashers and assorted dog catchers are utterly charming, helpful and above all speedy. This doesn't surprise me as they're under the control of general manager Mitchell Everard, who left the Ivy to be with Chris and Jeremy.

If I had to eat at one place for the rest of my life it would either be the Wolseley or St Alban. After serious consideration I'd choose St Alban because the tables are bigger. I think you'll have gathered by now – I'm a fan.

Jeremy King and Chris Corbin are too clever to have a failure, but St Alban in Regent Street hasn't been as financially successful as some other ventures. St Alban opened in December 2006. Food then, and now, is superb. Simple, impeccable. 'What you need,' I told Chris and Jeremy, to the point of total tedium, 'is a bar and a piano.' They smiled and ignored me. When I go there now they put a tiny grand piano on my table.

Go to St Alban anyway. It's good. I went back recently with that great movie actor Ernest Borgnine. They still need a piano. Otherwise, it's great.

I undertake arduous journeys beset with danger so you can read my tales of restaurant life. I intended to go to St John in EC1, who won an award or two and sounded interesting. But St John was closed. Obviously in EC1 they don't go out for lunch on Sundays. So instead we went to its poor companion, **St John Bread and Wine** in Commercial Street E1, the heart of the East End.

I'd spoken twice to the lady manager. Once to book a table and secondly to ask if it could please not be a small table. We were met on arrival by a ferocious woman. A smile to her would have been like a silver cross to a vampire. 'Do you have a reservation?' she asked coldly. No sense of greeting or hospitality. 'I've spoken to you twice this morning already,' I stuttered. This impressed Mrs Dracula not at all.

Now let this be clear: I care not one jot whether the manager, Esther Harding, recognised me. I look in the mirror and frequently don't recognise myself. But I do think any customer (we are, after all, paying her wages) is entitled to some warmth of greeting.

Keeping an eye on Mrs Dracula throughout my stay, I noticed her lack of welcoming smile was habitual. Everyone was greeted with po-faced, charmless attitude.

This was particularly odd because all the other staff were cheerful; smiling, and pleasant. Our waitress, a delightful girl named Kate Mullinger, greeted me with, 'We've only got Hildon water. You don't like Hildon do you, darling?'

'I hate it,' I replied.

'Would you like eau du tap?' suggested Kate. I put up with Hildon.

It's a very pleasant canteen-like place. There's a printed menu and a blackboard, which had written on it beetroot with nettle soup, braised Lowestoft kippers, langoustines and mayonnaise and greengage crumble.

Kate pointed out they only had a few servings of blackboard items. 'Keep a greengage crumble,' I said speedily. She also advised there were only three portions of langoustines. 'We'll both have langoustines as a starter,' I announced.

I decided to have old spot and chicory pork belly as my main course. Geraldine chose puff ball bacon and watercress and some large mushroom, I also asked for a small cup of beetroot soup. And a green salad, because it looked so good on the next table. Everything was absolutely superb. Congratulations to the duty sous-chef, Lee Kiernan.

There was a long delay between the first and second course. Geraldine suggested, 'Let's try and be sociable by discussing books and theatre.' Boy, did she have a wrong number.

I don't know why they've got wonderful places like this in the East End, whereas in elegant areas such as Holland Park, High Street Kensington and their environs there are the biggest load of useless, naff eating places you could imagine. Why can't Fergus Henderson, owner of this and St John, open up where I live? Much as I admire him, I can't be bothered with that horrid drive eastwards.

Salloos was very popular in the late 60s and early 70s and looks like it. There is something very run down about it. Time has passed it by. The guests looked like they were minor salesmen taking a meal-time off from a conference. There's a wonderful elderly Egyptian, Hassan, with white hair, who says 'Yes, sir', emphasising the 'sir' as if he was in the army, every time you give him a food order.

The food wasn't bad. Georgina was given a burnt poppadum. She had mulligatawny soup and then a chicken shish-kebab. I did as I was told by Hassan and had chicken karahi, a speciality from the Khyber, of diced de-boned chicken cooked with spices, tomatoes, chopped ginger and green chillies. Various other stuff came a bit late, such as chickpeas and vegetables. All in all it was extremely pleasant. If they spend a fortune redecorating they might get the glitterati in. On the other hand they might not.

Restaurant critics tend to dismiss **San Lorenzo**. Ridiculous. It's extremely good. The home-made pasta – and even the bought-in spaghetti – are marvellous. Paola's parents were born in Italy. She's a great cook and she thinks San Lorenzo is like mama's cooking.

Watching the owner, Mara, aged – well, shall we say not young – working the room and checking on every detail is to observe one of the greatest restaurant professionals. Her chocolate ice cream is definitely historic. The best ever by a long way.

The good fellas

I exclude anyone who is Italian from my general displeasure with hospitality in the catering industry. The Italians are natural experts at being genuinely charming hosts. They make you feel at ease and wanted, unlike many English restaurant employees who make you feel edgy and unwanted. This bonhomie, if I may mix languages, is never more evident than at **Scalini**, a popular place in Knightsbridge. I've always considered it too noisy for one of delicate disposition, but I risked it one Saturday lunch. I was greeted by a jovial man with a large moustache, Valerio Calzolari. Then I met another senior person, Michel Lengui. 'Valerio is the owner, more or less,' he said when I tried to establish the pecking order. 'I'm the deputy manager.' I walked round a bit, finally settling for the table Valerio originally suggested, in the corner of the main room. It's all very bright and cheerful.

Papardelle with prosciutto, peas and meatballs was the speciality of the day. Miss Lid and I opted for that. A nice selection of focaccia, parmesan squares and bruschetta was speedily plonked on the table. I admired a fine view of the police station opposite. Then Michel brought 'English calamari, they're the best in the world, from the south coast, Portland Bill.' He put some pork spare ribs on the same plate. Everything so far was superb.

I watched a very good-looking Dover sole served to the table opposite. It made me seek my main course. 'He's taking hours to put it on the table because of you,' said Valerio, indicating a man at the serving table. 'He's trying to be French. Italian food should be thrown on the plate.' It was a good, flat, robust pasta. Nice sauce. A Barolo Bersano wine was produced.

They did a particularly thorough job of crumbing down (clearing the mess off the tablecloth) and then put a new tablecloth on top anyway. The dessert trolley bumped its way through the crowded restaurant. Apple flan, fruit flan, a strawberry cheesecake, sacher torte, tiramisu. By 17 minutes to 2 things were slowing down. Miss Lid chose an apple pie hours ago, I thought. All they've got to do is cut it and bring it.

'They're putting it in the oven,' said Valerio. 'I didn't ask for it to go in the oven,' I huffed. When the dessert came, I thought the chocolate cake was good, the apple pie with raisins better. And I had to admit that they were quite right to heat it.

Valerio arrived and said to Miss Lid: 'Here's your cappuccino.' 'She didn't order a cappuccino,' I thought angrily. Valerio then tipped it all over her. But it wasn't real coffee, it was a plastic fake. Good gag that. I like a bit of knockabout comedy.

Scott's in Mayfair is a triumph. I'm particularly pleased for Richard Caring that his first solo creation is just about perfect. I've hated all the previous versions that occupied the same space. Richard has a 14-seat bar with a lavish centrepiece display of shellfish. Deep red banquettes and chairs surround the bar. At the back there's a more formal 29-seat area with tablecloths.

Cont'd

Not wishing to rise above my station I chose a table in the bar area with a good view of who was coming in and out. I noted two distinguished members of the royal family (as opposed to the dopey, lightweight ones) soon came to the next table.

The food at Scott's is fantastic. Its chef, Kevin Grattan, was at Le Caprice. I started with 'wood pigeon on toast with hedgehog mushroom'. Perfectly done slices of pigeon breast, great texture, a triumph. Geraldine and Dinah had sea fish cocktail. My main course was scampi provançale with fennel pilaf. Outstanding.

For dessert dark chocolate and blood orange soufflé. The soft interior chocolate mingled with the taste of cake-like surround. There was clotted cream and a cherry sauce. I've never had better.

The room is under the expert control of suave Matthew Hobbs. The only thing I found slightly disconcerting was the clientele. Nearly all businessmen in suits. Personally I like to see slightly deranged people in casual clothing. At lunch I fulfilled this role. But good as the food is, I'm not available every day.

At **Sheekey's**, near Leicester Square, the food is totally superb, beautifully cooked, a wonderful menu, all seafood and puddings. The service is as good as you could get. But there is a problem for us space-lovers. Sheekey's is not so much a restaurant as four separate corridors with tables and chairs. Plus a 'crush bar' so narrow that if you put a couple of people in it, you could define 'crush' for ever. I had as large a table for two as you can get, but it was still so dinky that when a waiter brought the main course and the veg plates I was in a panic. 'Let's take away the bread basket...' Nevertheless, I'm sure Sheekey's will be a success. I certainly hope so.

P.S. Although Christopher Corbin and Jeremy King have sold out and it's now owned by Richard Caring, it's still good. And he's opened another bar.

My friend Roger Moore was feeling like a bit of Japanese, so he suggested **Shogun**, buried behind the Britannia hotel in Mayfair. This was once terribly fashionable, largely with people in the music business. I had been there with a rock star, but so long ago I had no real memory of it. Shogun is entered through a small door in what looks like the back of an ill-designed council block. You descend into a cellar of indeterminate style, reminiscent of French existentialism in the 1950s. Edith Piaf could have sung there, or Juliette Gréco. In fact, it was full of Japanese – I suppose a good sign.

We waited a very long time for a waitress to pay us any attention. I've never mastered chopsticks, or had any interest in them, as they impede the progress of food to the gullet, so I asked for a spoon and fork for my sushi. I then had tempura fish with tempura sauce. Excellent. Rog had chicken teriyaki with soya beans. He liked that. My girlfriend had salmon grilled with sake sauce, and uttered rare words of praise: 'Lovely meal.'

Cont'd

Rog looked round the room. 'You look good in this light,' he said to me. 'But then, anyone looks good in this light, even Darth Vader, sitting behind you.' He indicated a squat figure of a Japanese warrior in armour lodged by the wall.

In my search for a good English Sunday lunch, unrewarding since the destruction of the Dorchester Grill – and the 'upgrading' of other great hotels by dear Mr Ramsay – I took the advice of a mass-market restaurateur and booked **Simpson's-in-the-Strand**.

The room at Simpson's is marvellous. Comfortable booths clothed in Victorian-type fabric. Lovely wood panelling. Classy wall candelabra and chandeliers. They have two trolleys, one for the beef and one for lamb. The trolleys are the same as when it became a restaurant in 1848. Ladies were not allowed in until 1983.

Disraeli, Gladstone and Charles Dickens dined here when it was a club. They don't have a menu because they're proudly British. They have a 'bill of fare'. There's no chef, he's a 'master cook'.

The service, under restaurant manager Stuart Bloomfield, was superb. Everything was on the table in seconds. The bread was moderate at best, the potted shrimps well below moderate.

The master cook, Paul Muddiman, was giving carving lessons in an upstairs room. He eventually came to our table and then sat down. 'Bloody liberty!' I thought. He was very jack-the-lad, telling us where he sourced the meat and generally playing the role of food provider supreme.

It took for ever for the main course to arrive as they were making fresh Yorkshire pudding for me. Other places manage it in normal time. The beef and lamb were absolutely stunning. As good as you could possibly want. Brilliant. The two elderly 'trolley men' were a delight. The vegetables were a total disaster. Everything was overcooked. The oil taste stayed in your mouth like a disease. My bubble and squeak was actively revolting. The mashed potatoes were ghastly.

The desserts improved things a bit. My treacle pudding was light, excellent, well-made, exemplary texture. The syrup was perfect and there was a lot of it. I asked for cream but got custard. It was very good, anyway. The bread and butter pudding was a joke. It was hard slices of aged toast, greasy and tough, sitting in horrid yellow stuff.

As we left Stuart asked how I'd liked it. 'Marvellous meat, superb treacle sponge,' I replied diplomatically. 'What about the rest?' asked Stuart. 'Vegetables beyond belief disgusting,' I said.

Instead of being jack-the-lad teaching carving upstairs the master cook should be in his kitchen teaching the staff how to cook vegetables. That's if he knows, which I doubt.

There was a lot of 'oohing' and 'aahing' when it was said a man from north London invested £15 million in a Mayfair house to turn it into a restaurant complex called **Sketch**. The poshest restaurant there, the Lecture Room, had steaks at £84 each. They may be more now. I went once. It was quite nice, but diminished by too much pomp and circumstance. The French chef, Pierre Gagnaire, lurked somewhere behind the food. The Lecture Room rose to just one Michelin star.

A downstairs area that was a bar is now called Glade. It opens only for lunch. My friend, ace photographer Terry O'Neill, was already there when I arrived on the dot of 1. They'd given us two tables put together so that we had a lot of space. That was intelligent. The room is quite glamorous. Pink walls with squiggled flowers. Mirrors revolve high up showing you who's dining where.

I ordered eggs en cocotte served with peppered gambas, serrano ham and smoked milk. That's a dotty menu description. I'm not surprised a recent Lloyds TSB survey showed a quarter of people quizzed didn't know any of the items on a sophisticated menu. Terry and I opted for a main course of smoked haddock, creamed désirée potatoes with olive oil, gordal green olives. I hate olives. Also steamed vegetables.

My starter was very good. My main course was a bit like my starter. I'd chosen carelessly. I often do that. The haddock could have been hotter. The plate was just warm. Other than tepid temperature, it was quite pleasant.

There were only three desserts: petits gateaux; fruit salad with blueberry and olive oil cake; or three flavours of ice cream – vanilla, lemon verbena and walnut. 'Bring the lot, I'll sort it out,' I said.

The desserts looked good. 'He's an inventive chef. I'll tell you that,' said Terry. He's a wonderful human being. But if there's any group I wouldn't trust on food it's photographers. They've got even less of a palate than food critics. And that's saying something.

The desserts were okay. The ice cream was strange. It was very soft with no discernable flavour. 'It's sort of an under-taste which you don't often get in ice cream,' advised Terry. 'I couldn't find the over-taste,' I responded.

It was a pleasant meal. 'And not expensive,' said Terry. 'How do we know? We haven't got the bill yet,' I responded. It turned out to be £75.38 for two. I call that expensive.

'How can you judge a restaurant properly?' people ask me. 'When you go in everyone does their best; you get special attention.' Oh yes? Then how come I was served these dreadful, burnt fish cakes at **Snows on the Green**? My host, someone terribly important at Polygram, couldn't believe it. 'I can understand me getting burnt food,' he said, 'but you?! It's like they're taking the mickey!' I sawed away at the hardened edges of my

Cont'd

lunch and then gave up. Snows had been recommended to me by various celebrities. It's a cafe-like place on a hideous main road near Shepherd's Bush, very noisy, no tablecloths. In the cause of learning how common folk live, I was having the set lunch. I had started with linguine with pesto that was so uninteresting I left most of it. Then came the fish cakes with spinach and chips, and then the worst pear and almond tart I have ever eaten. The pastry was heavy, the taste like mass catering at its worst, the texture clogging.

Occasionally I lunch in the chairman's suite at Sotheby's, but when Henry Wyndham, their immeasurably affable European chairman, asked me this time, he said: 'Would you rather we eat in our café?' 'Much rather,' I said. I prefer a bit of bustle. **Sotheby's Café** is adjacent to the corridor as you enter the building, so there's a lot of lobby activity.

I went in the Sunday before our date and faxed Henry a Winner-drawn plan showing the exact table I wished to sit at. We were due to meet at 1pm. After a bit of chitchat, with Henry mentioning very fashionable names, he said: 'Let's order. I always have the lobster club sandwich. It's legendary.' And, in case I didn't get the drift, he added: 'It's incredibly good.' So we all asked for it. It was invented by Sotheby's former chairman, the American Alfred Taubman, and comes in a brioche. I was looking forward to it.

At exactly 1.03pm the waiter returned. 'We have no lobster sandwiches left,' he announced. 'What a dump!' I thought. 'They have a tiny menu and before lunch has even started for most people, they've run out of the best thing.'

Then the restaurant manager, Ken Hall, appeared and said: 'For you, we're not out of them.' He told us they're so popular that people order their lobster club sandwiches in advance. I suggest that anyone planning to eat at Sotheby's Café phones Ken six months ahead and orders the lobster sandwich. It's ridiculous.

My chilled spinach soup with yoghurt was fine. The lobster sandwich was, indeed, deliciously special. I felt sorry for diners who couldn't get one. Henry had changed to quail and I tried a bit. Perfectly pleasant.

The situation of the café is particularly interesting with bulky men in overalls walking past carrying furniture. 'I like the stuff coming in,' said Henry Wyndham. 'Means we've got something to sell. Something to look forward to.' At one point three small tables, a commode and four large pots went in right to left. Henry was practically orgasmic.

For dessert I had baked vanilla cheesecake with fresh apricots. That was excellent. Henry had toffee-apple ice cream on shortbread. He said he loved it, but then 'he would, wouldn't he', as Mandy Rice-Davies once brilliantly remarked.

It was an extremely amusing and pleasing lunch. Afterwards, we admired a

Degas bronze of a dancer. It later sold for £8m. If people say to me, 'You're rich.' I say, 'No, I'm not.' When I can afford knick-knacks like the Degas, I will be.

The Sanderson, one of Ian Schrager's hotels, is in a horrible street in the middle of the wholesale dress business. The building looks like a block of flats in Kazakhstan. There was nowhere to park and the doormen didn't help. They never left the revolving door. So I parked in a bay reserved for diplomats. The lobby is turgid beyond belief. It's an amalgam of the worst of 1950s furnishings, together with some scrap-iron chairs and a kitsch empire-style chair with gilded swans. The restaurant, called **Spoon**, is hideous. A totally soulless place for transient people. White sort-of-leather chairs, canteenish, with dreadful, middle-of-the-road plonky piped music, the type you used to hear in cinemas. Spoon is the concept of three-Michelin-star chef Alain Ducasse. To climax the disaster, I got a parking ticket.

I commend **The Square** in Mayfair. I've been there a lot. The chef and co-owner, Philip Howard, is charming and a master of the gas ring. He has two Michelin stars to prove it. I'm sure they found his cinnamon doughnuts stratospheric. On my first visit to The Square I rated the doughnuts – or 'beigne' as they call them – totally top-of-the-line historic. I ate mine. Then I nicked them from both of my guests. They were so delicious that I asked to take some with me. Thus, I left with six doughnuts in a see-through bag. I gave one to my PA, Margaret, and ate the rest myself.

The Square does proper food, too. The service is exemplary. If you're planning a special night, or just want to pig out, you couldn't do better.

I used to be a regular at **Sticky Fingers** when it was owned by Bill Wyman, once bass guitarist with the Rolling Stones. Bill was a terrific restaurateur.

The hotdogs and hamburgers were exquisite, the fried chicken wings a rare treat, the strawberry milkshake historic, the potato skins with cheese, bacon and sour cream a delight. I still recall the chilli con carne with immense affection. The chocolate iced yoghurt was supremely delicious.

Sadly, Sticky Fingers minus Bill is a shadow of its former self. He sold it to Maxwell's restaurants. I'll say one thing for them – and only one – they greatly improved the look of the place. They brightened it up, put mirrors on the ridiculously lowered ceilings, added some red neon strip lighting and spaced the tables so I could actually hear what Geraldine had to say.

I was distressed that many of my old-time favourites were no longer available. The strawberry milkshake had dropped from historic to just okay. There was no chilli con carne. Hotdogs were only on the kiddies' menu.

I had a hamburger with American cheese and a fried egg plus tomato, plus salad and a slice of pickled cucumber. Oh, and chips. The burger was very feeble, not a patch on what it was before.

I finished with a waffle with maple syrup and vanilla ice cream. If this was real maple syrup it was a ghastly variety. The waffle itself was soggy, no crispness, really awful.

Under Bill's rule, I gave the burgers the Winner's Dinners Best Hamburger award. Why not buy the place back, Bill? I have been back a few times recently and things have greatly improved.

Tamarind in Mayfair is a disaster. It is the most ghastly room I have ever seen. Golders Green minimalism would be a kind way to describe it. A works canteen with horrid gold pillars in the middle, no sign of humanity and 1950s-type office chairs with over-curved hard backs which kept bashing my arms. Things did not improve when I was told they only had spicy poppadoms, the ones that look like they've got mumps. I much prefer the old-fashioned large potato-crisp-appearance type. We waited for ever for our main course, and this at lunch time with only five other tables occupied. After looking at the room for 50 minutes, and having great difficulty in getting any service from anyone, by the time the food came I was ready to kill.

Teatro in Shaftesbury Avenue is another of those ever-so-chics that seem to open every day. It is not for actors, even though an actress is one of the owners. It's very grand and seriously designed. You go up metallic stairs to a rather dark members' lounge. The restaurant is fairly minimalist, inhabited by uninteresting people. Except for us. I started with duck foie gras served over poached rhubarb. It was extremely good. Then I had roast breast of squab glazed with fresh dates served with root vegetables. I had great difficulty finding any vegetables. It was a bit tough, not bad, nice gravy, but they'd failed to give me any mashed potatoes, so Michael Grade's sister Anita Land, sitting next to me, gave me some of hers. I thought the service was slow. I noticed many tables had only men sitting at them. Cellular phones have to be left at reception – an idea that should be widely adopted.

I think the National Theatre does a terrific job. Not only are the productions invariably excellent, but they've managed to take an awful building, which looks like an unfinished car park, and jolly it up no end with musicians, exhibitions, bookshops, stalls and three places serving food and drink. I've only eaten once in the main restaurant, the **Terrace Cafe**, and it was dire beyond belief. I am told it has improved, but I'm not about to find out. The other two are cafeterias, both rather good.

As I frequently arrive early, being punctilious to a fault, it is then that I grab a snack from the Lyttleton buffet. Often I am put off by the queue. But I have invented a way

Cont'd

to get to the front without offending people. A lady with two children was at the cash desk with her tray, just about to pay. I went up to her. 'Excuse me,' I said. 'You have won tonight's prize. I am going to pay for your food. You can have anything else that you want, and I'll have a coffee and a piece of carrot cake.' Thus I got served without delay, for £7.50 extra. Perhaps I should wait until someone comes along with just a lemonade – but that would spoil the fun.

I've always had a soft spot for the InterContinental hotel in Hamilton Place, Mayfair. It used to have (and still may) a marvellous coffee bar that served very good snack food.

Since my last visit the hotel has had a makeover. The lobby didn't look that different to me. Pleasant in a practical, hotel sort of way. Turn right for the main restaurant called **Theo Randall**. Theo was a chef, for 17 years, at the River Café, one of my all-time favourite places. He left to set up on his own at the InterContinental.

When I first entered the room I quite liked it. Perspectives with pillars. But it soon began to depress me greatly. Everything seemed to be dark brown. The walls, the pillars, the furniture. There's a low ceiling and it's in the basement. I began to think I was in a coffin. In the brown gloom (Count Dracula would love it) there's seating for 120 people. I reckoned there were only 16 diners for Sunday lunch.

The food was very good indeed. My starter of scallops with chilli, parsley, capers, Swiss chard and lentils was piquant and delicious. My main course of Anjou pigeon, with the crispiest of bacon, was good as I've ever eaten. The fried zucchini had a perfect light batter. Memorable. Geraldine's fish stew was sensational. For dessert she had chocolate cake without flour, I had Amalfi lemon tart. Both were totally superb.

Theo Randall himself is a delight. 'You'd expect someone like him would be able to find something like a bistro with an awning coming down,' said Geraldine. She's right. The River Café, a lesson in simple, friendly design, undoubtedly cost a mini-fraction of what some twit spent redecorating Theo's restaurant. Save up for the awning will you, Theo. Then I'll become a regular. Is that a threat, I wonder, or a promise?

I took Michael Edwards, a very nice, efficient travel agent, to **Timo**, not far from JK Rowling's townhouse off Kensington High Street. It's a long, narrow restaurant but perfectly pleasant. Nicely done out with simple brown and beige chairs and a wooden floor.

I was reading the set menu, three courses £18 plus 12.5% service, when Sir David Frost walked in. He announced, 'I do like this place, it's near my office.' 'Now Frost is here we're all taking notice of him,' I observed.

Michael ordered vegetarian timbale gratinated with smoked mozzarella and then 'grilled chicken paillard served with roast potatoes and salad'. I went for spaghetti with bacon, onion, chilli and fresh tomatoes followed by boar stew with fried polenta.

My staff had said the service was slow. It was slow. Very slow. 'We came in at 10 to 1. We must have ordered by 1. It's now 25 past and we haven't got anything!' I moaned to my guest. Eventually came a very big starter portion of spaghetti. 'I can't eat all that,' I announced. But it was so good I did. Michael said his vegetable stuff was excellent.

Michael commented, 'My chicken lacks flavour.' 'Chicken nearly always lacks flavour,' I responded. My boar stew was superb, very tasty, very tender. 'Wild boar,' said Michael. It's good he remembers things. He's in the travel industry. At least he'll get the right tickets for the right people.

I went on a reconnaissance to Elystan Street, Chelsea, looking for a restaurant called **Tom Aikens**. This was recommended to Sir Michael Caine by someone who'd never been there. I have considerable fear of the unknown. Would the tables be spaced well apart? Would it be an amenable atmosphere? These matters require advance enlightenment.

I discovered Tom Aikens and, with some difficulty, the way in. A charming lady, Laura Aikens, greeted me. I revealed my mission was to investigate pending a possible visitation from Sir Michael and myself. Laura and I toured the tables. I suggested one. She capped it with another. Laura explained the restaurant was full when we wanted to come, but she'd sort it out for us. This is the charisma of Michael Caine. If it were just me I'd be left, most properly, in the street.

A few days later I arrived at 7.45pm for our 8pm date. The world has two time zones. Most people's and Michael Caine's. Michael is courteous and marvellously punctual. I've never known him late for a professional or social engagement in 40 years. Michael and Shakira arrived. Five minutes early. We proceeded to a corner table.

Tom Aikens is one of the new hot chefs. He worked in a restaurant somewhere. I should know but I've forgotten. Then he spent three years looking for premises of his own.

Michael and I ordered roast langoustine with cocoa beans and braised chicken. We followed with braised pig's head with pork belly, stuffed trotter, celeriac and some purée or other! You can see this is a seriously posh menu. Not the sort of thing I want every day. But nice for a treat. The rosemary bread was exceptionally good. The freebie duck mousse was lovely. The langoustines really superb. The pig's trotter was shrouded in something that resembled pasta.

The service was like lightning. Possibly they wanted to get rid of us to use the table again. I failed to make taped comment on the pig's trotter. This may not be a totally positive sign.

After our wonderfully lavish dinner Michael and I ordered Fernet-Branca because a waiter arrived and gave it to me. 'That's for Sir Michael,' I said. 'Now where's mine?'

Tom's Deli & Cafe in Notting Hill is not any old joint. It's owned by Sir Terence Conran's son, is extremely buzzy and exceptionally good. There's a site going in Kensington High Street near the junction with my road. I wish Tom would open there. Travelling two miles to Westbourne Grove is quite exhausting.

They'd kept a booth for me, my assistant Dinah and Princess. I was told they weren't licensed so I should descend to the basement deli to buy the wine. At my request the waitress went down. They've got a wonderful menu. I'd like to try everything. But they should increase the size of the booths by 50%.

Princess ordered a mix of fresh grapefruit and orange juice. They do it there and then. I had orange juice. We all chose the smoky roast tomato, aubergine and chickpea soup.

'Delicious, isn't it?' Princess said. I'd describe it as robust. The soup was remarkable. I dictated, 'If I knew anything about food I could describe this. It's really very, very good.' 'Very Italian,' added Princess.

I'd ordered parmesan-encrusted chicken with potato gratin and green beans and, to taste, boboti (minced lamb) with salad. They were fine.

For dessert I went berserk. I served myself a piece of lemon crunch cake, chocolate biscuit cake, carrot and pineapple cake, and stem ginger cake. All this held up a man waiting for a fruit flapjack. 'Had 'em before?' I asked. He assured me he had and they were superb. This inspired me to add a raspberry meringue to my overflowing plate. I found Princess's pancakes a bit heavy. She added a lot of maple syrup. Dinah had red berry and frangipane tart. That, we agreed, was the best.

When I went to an excellent Knightsbridge Italian place, **Toto**, I was greeted by the dreaded words: 'Who are you with?' As I was on my own at the time, this seemed a fairly pointless remark. 'Nobody,' I said. The door official repeated his question. 'Roger Moore,' I replied. 'It's that table in the corner,' I was told gracelessly. A short time later, Roger himself arrived, fuming. He, too, had been asked who he was with. 'I'm Roger Moore,' he responded. The man thought for a moment. 'Ah, you're with Roger Moore,' he said. 'That's his table in the corner.' This is not what I call a grand start to an evening. I shall not go there again until I am assured there is a sympathetic greeter on the premises.

Tramp's Gold

I could not be described as a devotee of **Tramp**, the discotheque that remains endlessly in fashion, but I have had some marvellous times there, the greatest being the night I was dining with Robert Mitchum in Claridge's, and we saw Jack Lemmon at another table. We all got together for coffee and Jack said to me: 'Can you get us into Tramp?' 'Of course,' I said. 'They know me well, I've been a member since 1970!' So I presented myself at the desk, flanked by Jack and Bob. The two receptionists looked up ferociously. 'Michael Winner,' I announced. 'He's not here,' said a receptionist, quick as a flash. 'Come on, Bob,' I said, 'Follow me,' and we walked off down the stairs into the smoke-filled, dusty atmosphere. Jack Lemmon had been drinking a bit. Jack is the best drunk ever. Nothing malicious comes out; he's just unbelievably funny. The comedy performance he put on, his eyes swivelling as each new girl came in dressed in less than the one before, is a great treasure that I hold in my memory. Bob Mitchum had just come out of the Betty Ford clinic, so he sat, very sober – a wonderful, benign presence.

P.S. *A few years ago, Tramp was bought by some Scots group headed by a very nice chap called Kevin Doyle. Johnny, who was boss of the club, is no longer there. I went once after he'd left. Rude, chaotic staff. Tramp's day is done.*

In the old days, before the American West became cluttered with freeways and skyscrapers, they'd say, 'Go west, young man.' I went west recently. Stuck in traffic outside the Olympia I pined for the open plains and cursed my decision to visit **La Trompette**.

Eventually we turned left down a neat suburban street and there it was. I wouldn't say this part of London has become gentrified. More middle-class-ified. La Trompette was surprisingly pleasant. A very nice room indeed, tables spaced well apart, parquet floor, simple, one wall all glass, looking onto mini shops and boutiques. There's a little hedge outside allowing a row of tables on the pavement.

Three breads were offered: black olive, white, and walnut and raisin. I chose the latter. It was good. Not great. I ordered boudin blanc as a starter. They had to tell me what it was. It's a lightly spiced French sausage of pork shoulder and chicken meat. It came with madeira sauce, sautéed spinach and pistachio nuts. It was absolutely marvellous. Just as well because my next two courses were, in order of consumption, awful and not very good.

My main course was fresh pasta with field mushrooms, white onion purée, artichokes, pine nuts and beurre noisette. Why it took 14 words to describe this miserable plate of ravioli I do not understand. The taste was meat-flavoured cotton wool. That's only three words, but let them suffice. For dessert my lime and lemon sorbet didn't speak to me at all.

Truc Vert, an all-day restaurant in Mayfair, is the favourite of Terry O'Neill, the enduringly excellent photographer. Philip Kingsley, who has a local 'save your hair' establishment, and John Gold, the supremo of Tramp.

Truc Vert is French for green thing. It's spacious with a high ceiling and a bar. The piped music was too loud.

I asked the waitress for her name and she wrote Marketta on the table. I asked where she came from. 'The Czech Republic,' she said, adding: 'Do you want my phone number as well?' 'Okay, write your phone number down,' I suggested encouragingly. She didn't.

I ordered spiced crab cakes with watercress and tartare sauce to start. The crab cakes were phenomenal. 'The value for money here is unbelievable,' advised Terry. My crab cakes were £7.25. Reasonable. I tried the freshly made pumpkin and broccoli broth. That was very good too. My main course of Toulouse sausages with braised cabbage, red onion, tomato and harissa was all right. I'm not sure I like Toulouse sausages.

The owner is a pleasant man from New Zealand, Russell Cameron. He said they made all their cakes and bread on the premises.

'Nice feeling in this place,' observed Doug. This is true. Marketta came with the bill. I offered her £20. 'For this will you give me your phone number?' I asked. 'No,' said Marketta smiling, 'give me yours.'

At the northern end of Marylebone High Street, an area I always considered bleak and uninhabitable, I was suddenly dropped like a mutant from outer space. During my stay in the London Clinic I had to ask locals where the unbelievably lovely and helpful Geraldine and my long-time assistant Dinah could forage for sustenance.

Malcolm Miller, the urbane chief executive of the clinic, strongly recommended **2 Veneti** in nearby Wigmore Street. I had no idea people ate in Wigmore Street. I thought they just drove through it. Nor was I totally convinced Malcolm Miller was the best judge of food.

I phoned and spoke to the co-owner of 2 Veneti, Simon Piovesan. He and his partner, Stephan Frassoni, opened in 2006 with chef Luca Conti. Simon was extremely cheerful and hospitable. So armed with Tupperware containers and very posh insulated bags, Geraldine and Dinah set forth into uncharted waters. They loved the look of 2 Veneti. It's got a mixture of brick walls, some plastered, with photos of old Italy, wood floors, good linen tableclothes.

When they dined there (after they'd served me, of course) they reported no trouble in hearing every word they said. I'm surprised either of them stopped talking long enough to hear anything.

The food was undoubtedly and surprisingly excellent.

As the partners come from Venice they have starters such as Venetian creamed salted cod with potato purée and polenta croutons. I didn't have that.

Also grilled vegetables with warm buffalo mozzarella. I didn't have that either. Geraldine and Dinah did and said it was perfection.

I had home-made short pasta with venison in Amarone wine ragout. Outstanding. Geraldine had risotto with asparagus and scallops. She was very impressed. I wasn't offered this because it was the dish of the day and not read out to me as I lingered in the clinic. I did have calf's liver with green beans, sweet onion and Marsala sauce. As tender, well-cooked and good as anyone could wish for. My dessert was millefeuille, poached pear and mini strudel. The strudel was superb pastry, flaky, genuinely memorable.

There's no question 2 Veneti serves superior Italian food. Would I return through those mind-numbing streets when I'm back home? I'm not sure. But for locals living in those sombre Marylebone buildings, 2 Veneti is a shining light.

202 in Westbourne Grove is in Nicole Farhi's clothing-cum-furniture shop. It's got great bustle, irregular old tables, a counter and, at Sunday lunch, a large queue of locals who know what's good for them.

202 is a snacky place. Not grand. But highly useful. You can have poached salmon, piquillo pepper, spring onion and watercress salad, hot salt beef sandwich on rye with mustard and pickles, moussaka and more, all of which looked worth trying. Paola ordered fresh orange juice. I said to Andy Howard, the very good restaurant manager: 'When were these oranges squeezed?' 'In about a minute,' he replied.

Their two specials were sweet potato soup with coriander and spinach and ricotta ravioli. We ordered French toast with crispy bacon, maple syrup and hash brown potatoes. We also drank superb home-made lemonade.

Paola said: 'This place is fantastic. We've got comfort and tasty food with no pomp and circumstance.' The portions were enormous. We were going to share fish and chips with mushy peas but there was so much on our plates we went straight to apple and peach crumble.

'Where's it made?' I asked Andy. 'Here,' he replied. 'What's the ice cream?' I asked. 'Vanilla,' he said. 'That's made here, too.' The crumble was robust, very big, a lot of crumble, ice cream on top. Each portion could easily have served two people.

My friend Robert Earl, of Planet Hollywood, has opened a large casino called Fifty in a historic building at the top of St James's. It has all been beautifully decked out with a nightclub and an Asian restaurant called **V** downstairs. The supervising chef is Jean-Georges Vongerichten, who's very significant in New York.

I started with egg caviar, which apparently JG is famous for. Caviar and some whipped up stuff in an eggshell. Very good. Then I had a first-rate old-fashioned Dover sole meunière. This used to be everywhere. But it's been replaced by sea bass on a bed of spinach. Just as you never see shrimp cocktail with pink sauce and lettuce. And what happened to those meat loaves with an egg through the middle? I adored them.

Villandry is the most wonderful-looking place. You enter a food store that is full of highly attractive goodies – bread, pizzas, cakes, everything. The next two rooms are called the charcuterie bar, which offers a great selection of salami and other sausages. There are some dining tables, but the real restaurant is one room further on. There we had a terrific meal in very pleasing surroundings.

I started with gratin of macaroni cheese with crispy lardons. It was presented in a copper pan. It may sound silly to go ballistic over macaroni cheese, and I don't know what they did to it, but it was historic. Geraldine had dressed Dorset crab and avocado salad. She adored it.

My main course, chicken paillard, was fine. Geraldine had organic salmon. It was a good colour, juicy. It looked absolutely perfect.

The accompanying veggies were beyond belief. I'd asked if the chips were bought in. I was assured they were hand cut in the kitchen and then fried with parmesan and truffle oil. They were as good in their own way as the ones Heston Blumenthal used to serve at the Fat Duck. The carrots (I mean, there's a boring vegetable, I bet carrots even bore each other) were out of this world. Cut in strips. Cumin and honey had been added. That turned them from boring to great. Then there were parmesan-fried courgettes with chilli relish. Fantastic.

This left dessert. The sticky toffee pudding could not be bettered. It wasn't cloying or heavy as they usually are. And the toffee sauce was sensational.

Where I live, Holland Park, is a restaurant catastrophe area. It could be saved by Philip Howard of the Square in Mayfair. He's a two star Michelin chef I greatly admire. He makes the best cinnamon doughnuts in the world. Philip's taken over a ghastly restaurant in Abingdon Road which never had anyone in it, except me when I wrote a review of total condemnation. Philip intends to re-open this in late October under a new name.

In the meantime, a few doors away, there's a delightful little place called **W8 Catering**. It has a counter full of salad, chilli chicken, baked cod with pancetta, chicken korma, pasta bolognaise and some delicious looking desserts. It's for local workers to buy takeaway food or eat at bar seats. In the back and on the pavement are a few tables.

The boss is Fiona Gooley, an ex air hostess married to Mike Gooley, who owns and founded the travel agency Trailfinders. Fiona caters for his staff who all get free meals. That alone accounts for 2000 lunches a week. 'I had to marry him to get the contract,' explained Fiona cheerfully.

Mike is ex SAS and looks it. When he joined Geraldine and me for lunch I expected him to come through the window on a rope and chuck CS gas all over the place, followed by a burst of machine gun fire. What are a few dead staff and customers between friends? Instead he sat meekly at a pavement table.

'The council kept telling us to remove the tables because they were obstructing the footpath,' explained Fiona. There are only two of them. I didn't notice any pedestrians inconvenienced. With outstanding logic, which typifies the Kensington and Chelsea council, they then decided that if Fiona paid them £720 a year just to apply for a licence, they might decide the tables weren't obstructing anyone and she could keep them outside. That for a mere five days a week licence.

Mike drives an Aston Martin. I'm always suspicious of cars like that, having had a Ferrari which spent more time in garage repair shops than it did with me. It was always going wrong. 'The Aston's four years old and it's finally working properly,' said Mike. At this point a wasp appeared. 'You're in the SAS, deal with it,' I said to Mike. I had chill con-carne and then beef meatballs with feta cheese. Both very nice. They'll be even better in winter when they're kept on a hot plate in the area used for salad in summer. Then they won't be re-heated in the microwave.

The desserts were beyond belief historic. The apple crumble, made, as is everything, daily in their kitchen, was the best I've ever eaten. Then there was a giant fairy cake. It looked like a mushroom with pink icing and big white spots on top. Texture and taste of the cake: superb. Icing: perfect. This is an oasis in the culinary desert of Abingdon Road and its environs. When Philip Howard comes there could be two. That makes it oases, doesn't it? Who cares? Just get some good food near my house. I'm too old to travel.

I wanted to go to Arbutus in Soho. But when I looked at a photo of their restaurant it all seemed to be little tables where one person has their back to the wall, the other looks at the wall. I can't take that. Then I found they had a sister restaurant, **Wild Honey** in Mayfair. The owner-manager, Will Smith, promised me a booth. It's a nice panelled room. Anthony Demetre is the co-owner and 'in' chef.

I started with braised pig's head, caramelised onions and potato purée. It was square. Didn't look like a pig's head. Quite tasty. Not mind-blowing.

My main course was massively recommended. 'It'll melt in your mouth,' said Will. It was French limousin veal, soft polenta with parmesan. 'I'll have anything but polenta,' I said, 'marbles, toilet rolls, anything.' I settled for mashed potato. A pleasant dish. Veal is always tasteless.

Things went stratospheric with their treacle tart. It actually tasted of treacle, which is rare. It was light. Historic.

I was making a commercial in Wandsworth, directing one of my favourite people: me. **Willie Gunn** was recommended for a quick lunch as we had to be back – both of us, actor and director – within the hour. I expected nothing. The restaurant itself was pleasant. Plain, wooden floors, tables spaced well apart. It started remarkably well – my goat's cheese soufflé came like a small upside-down pot, nicely crisp on the outside. Vanessa's eggs benedict were on a particularly excellent muffin: very fresh, not soggy. Perhaps this would turn out to be a real find. My main course was braised oxtail, flageolet beans and mash. It alone could convince anyone that banning meat on the bone was a terrific idea. Vanessa had ravioli; she left most of it. She liked her pot of chocolate for dessert. I hated my steamed apricot pudding with crème anglaise. But I give Willie Gunn high marks for the charm of its owners, Giles Cunliffe and Duncan Turner.

Sometimes I really want to give a restaurant a favourable review. Thus it was as I entered **Wiltons** in London's St James's. This is a place that, for decades, produced the best food I've ever eaten. Under Jimmy Marks, who died in 1976, everything was quadruple historic.

It stayed good with a marvellous restaurant manager, Robin Gundry. Then he died of cancer. A horrid woman, Margaret Levin, took over and things began to slide. They brought in a chef from the Connaught, Jerome Ponchelle, who started messing things up. Instead of serving the best and freshest simple English food he went in for ginger and lemon grass. He mucked things about. They were worse than before. But I live in hope.

There's now a different restaurant manager, James Grant, from the Rib Room at the Carlton Tower. Not a glorious recommendation.

I sat in a booth decorated with two ghastly, cheap-looking prints. They'd have suited a corridor in the Marriott Newcastle – if there is a Marriott in Newcastle! Wiltons used to have real watercolours and oils beautifully framed.

We had very good Colchester oysters to start, we being Dinah May, my receptionist, and I. Geraldine was in Paris. My next course was fried plaice, always historic at Wiltons. Now it was extremely dreary. It didn't taste fresh. Wiltons' plaice used to be juicy and fresh-tasting because Jimmy Marks wouldn't even keep fish in the fridge overnight. Madame Prunier, who had a restaurant nearby, would collect all his unsold fish around 11pm and sell it the next day to her clients.

My plaice was not moist. As for the chips, supposedly hand cut in Wiltons' kitchen, they were thin and utterly uniform in size as if sliced by a machine. They were no good anyway.

Dinah had dressed crab. She said: 'It's very poor.' Even the melba toast was too thin and spindly. Wiltons used to have slightly rough, rather tasty melba toast. A considerable achievement.

I've eaten at Wiltons since I was six. It saddens me to see it sink into mediocrity. It's a shadow of its former self. And that's an insult to shadows.

When I visited Portobello Road one Saturday, I went into a restaurant called the **Wine Factory**, a narrow buzzy place offering Lurex-bright pictures of ships and castles for sale. 'The restaurant's full,' I said, looking round. 'Who can I pay to leave?' I was introduced to Dee Bliss, the manageress. 'Tell that man,' I said, pointing to a couple sitting next to my friend Didier Milinaire, 'that if he leaves in five minutes his meal is free.' 'You can't do that to people,' said Dee. 'I do it all the time,' I replied (a slight exaggeration, although it usually works). This man looked ferocious, so I decided to wait. Didier offered us a piece of his garlic bread as we squashed in beside him, his girlfriend Lesley Burton and their two friends. Then, thank God, the man at the table I was waiting for left. I ordered a four seasons pizza. First I was given grilled vegetables with what had been described as a hot chilli sauce. It was so strong that, after one mouthful, I was dying. I gulped water. The pizza was pretty good and my hot toffee cake perfectly pleasant.

I don't usually go out to lunch. I have a one-course meal at home that takes less than 10 minutes to eat. I start on the dot of 1pm. The phone always goes. I don't answer it. I greatly believe in my great friend Robert Mitchum's dictum: 'Why should any bum with 10 cents be allowed to intrude on my life?'

On Saturday I do go out. Johnny Gold, who used to own Tramp discotheque, recently visited from Nassau, where he now lives. He suggested he, Terry and I should have lunch at Brinkley's on Hollywood Road in Fulham. So I took my Suzuki Grand Vitara on a rare lunchtime outing and luckily found a meter right outside. Not much use really because Brinkley's was shut.

But then Johnny appeared from the **Wine Gallery** next door where he and Terry were waiting. The Wine Gallery (same owner, John Brinkley) is open for lunch. It's narrow, there's a bar, wooden tables in the front area, no tablecloths and paper napkins.

The menu was mercifully simple. Cottage pie, house lamb burger, penne, pork and leek sausages, home-made fishcakes and so on. 'I'll have prawn cocktail and then cottage pie with peas,' I said to the waitress. The cocktail was nice: shrimp on top, avocado underneath. Johnny's goat's cheese salad looked very colourful. My individual cottage pie came in a very hot bowl. 'From the microwave?' I wondered. I also got a bowl of peas. I added some Lea & Perrins sauce. 'It's not terrible,' I announced. 'It's not going to win an award, but it's very tasty.'

Johnny had vanilla ice cream with chocolate sauce. I had a brownie with ice cream and chocolate sauce. It was fine. Not historic, not bad.

I've been around the block a few times but never seen any restaurant operation as successful and excellent as that mounted by Jeremy King and Christopher Corbin.

I remember El Cubano, 'the' 1950s place in the Brompton Road with rare tropical birds in cages. The Caprice in the 1950s where, before it sank, we gathered in evening dress after theatrical first nights. The Trattoria Terraza in Soho in the 1960s… I could go on listing fashionable restaurants that came and went. Some famous ones are teetering on the edge, their suppliers demanding cash on delivery after being unpaid for months.

For readers in the Outer Hebrides I'll explain that King and Corbin took over, and made historic, Le Caprice in 1981, the Ivy in 1990 and J Sheekey in 1998. They offered marvellous comfort food, devoid of plate decoration, attracting glitterati and gawpers in unprecedented numbers.

For reasons I don't understand K&C sold in 1998 to Luke Johnson of the Belgo group. Luke behaved with admirable restraint and let the Ivy, Caprice and Sheekey managers run things much as before, minus the personal charm of King and Corbin dispensed walking round the tables. They are true gentlemen. A rarity, indeed. Many restaurateurs think because they dress like gentlemen, they are gentlemen. This is not so.

Their new venture is the **Wolseley**. It's one of London's most stunning rooms. A 1920s high vaulted ceiling, exquisite chinoiserie designs and fantastic chandeliers dripping mini period lampposts. In 1922 it was a Wolseley car showroom. Barclays took over and added the tasteful glitter.

The Wolseley is unquestionably the most important new place for decades. I've seen it battle ragged service, erratic food and the traumatic departure of one of its founding partners. In spite of inevitable early-day wobbles I've always enjoyed going there.

My regard for it rises on each occasion. I think it's the greatest room in London and one of the best in the world. The place is phenomenally popular. Over 1,200 reservation requests a day.

Let's deal with some of the food I've greatly enjoyed. The Irish stew is historic; the crab fishcakes superb; the foie gras on toast a delight; the dressed crab remarkable; the caviar omelette wonderful; the cassoulet de Toulouse incredible; the Vacherin mont blanc – chestnut, meringue and ice cream – superb.

In conclusion I'd like, very strongly indeed, to recommend the Wolseley. I think it's the best overall dining experience in London. In fact I'll go further. It's the second best dining experience in the world. The first is downstairs at Harry's Bar in Venice.

All things spice

When I tried **Yatra**, in Dover Street, Mayfair, I thought: 'Good, another Indian place for my list.' We entered a bar overfull of screaming people. I pushed through nervously to a strange room. One half had diners sitting close to floor level: the other half, where I sat, had normal-height tables with black tablecloths. A very charming man, Sonu P Lalvani, opened Yatra. He'd never run restaurants before. He told me Yatra is a Sanskrit word meaning sacred pilgrimage or spiritual journey. All I can say is that it was a very heavily booked pilgrimage in the bar. So much so that I told Sonu I couldn't sit and listen to that din. So he kindly sent them down to the basement.

My napkin was served on a red cushion, so if your head dropped toward the table, the cushion softened your fall. Sonu recommended a starter of chicken mince flavoured with galangal and kaffir lime, and moulded on a crab claw. I took one bite of it, choked, and my eyes watered. I coughed and they rushed extra water to me. I couldn't speak it was so spicy. 'I've got water, I'm half-dead, but I'm all right!' I gasped when able to mutter. Miss Lid pointed out my starter only had one pepper-like mark by it on the menu. 'Some of them had three peppers,' she explained. If anyone lives after a three-pepper marked item, I'd like to hear about it. But I did drink a milkshake-type thing called a mango lassi. That was exceptionally pleasant. Miss Lid started with a Yatra salad, which is a grilled Parmesan tower with tiger prawns. She said nothing, which is rare.

My main course was a mixed grill of tandoori prawns, chicken, lamb and 'everything else', I dictated. It could have fed a family of six. It was what I'd call 'glumpy'. Not terrible, not worth coming back for. Miss Lid had chicken with coconut sauce and rice pancake.

My dessert was called Khekachelo's passion. It was mango-based. It had no good texture or taste. Sonu explained it was made by a very young man. That is no excuse. Miss Lid's dessert looked like runny yoghurt with nuts in it. Having finished, she said: 'It was good. All that I chose was good.' But as she often says what she chooses is good and, according to her, she always chooses the best, this did not weigh very heavily with me.

I was not pleased with Yatra and this distresses me, because Sonu and his wife, Liah, are lovely people. They've gone from supplying catering equipment into the quagmire of restaurant ownership. I hope they do very well. I shall revisit in a year's time. If they're still open.

P.S. *They are.*

Zafferano is a comfortable restaurant in Knightsbridge. It's been struck from my list. Enzo Cassini, the maitre d', was okay in the relaxed atmosphere of Château Eza in the south of France, but here, well I won't tell you what's gone on, but it's shambolic to say the least. I never like to go into a room that isn't well managed and Zafferano isn't. A friend of mine asked why his was the only table without bread, and witty Enzo said: 'We're sending out to Marks & Spencer for it!' The superb Giorgio Locatelli was the chef. He ain't now.

I've been going to **Zia Teresa** in Hans Road, opposite the west side of Harrods, on and off for over 40 years. It still looks like the archetypal Italian restaurant of the mid-1950s. Taking a trip down memory lane, I recently attended with Dinah May, whom you may recall is my chief receptionist. She hails from the Wirral, so on the few occasions I am munificent enough to take her out, she looks forward to eating well. On this occasion she was disappointed. Zia Teresa was never posh. But it used to be robust, cheerful and with very pleasant food. I started by asking for one of my favourites: spaghetti with meatballs. The manager, said: 'We don't do them any more.' 'Why not?' I asked. 'People stopped ordering them,' he said. We were recommended asparagus. It was very thin, tasteless and coated with melted cheese. The finger bowls were optimistic. You'd have had to prise the asparagus from the cheese and it was so stringy it would have flopped over if you tried to pick it up. My breadcrumbed veal was tough and of no taste. The tomato sauce with the spaghetti was just a pasty mush with a strange, tangy flavour. The coup de grâce was Dinah's Dover sole, which smelled strongly of fish. Fish should not smell of fish. This usually means it's not fresh.

Everything was a disaster, except for a cheerful waitress called Irene Rodriguez.

P.S. Zia Teresa been taken over by a man who has a totally terrible restaurant in Marylebone called Getti.

Zuma, arguably the most 'in' place in London is hidden in a back street off Knightsbridge. There were so many bouncers at the door I thought I'd never get in. I'm glad I did because it's a strikingly well-designed restaurant. The bar is rough stone with masses of bottles above. The ceiling looks like a cellar, with ducts and black vents. There's another bar in light brown and black seats, a wooden wall of reclaimed slabs, another with crisscross wood. A massive mish-mash, but it works superbly.

Russell Norman gave me his card. He's the general manager. 'I'm in charge of hearts and minds,' he explained. I felt like asking for the person in charge of stomachs.

Here's a canter through my food: raw sea bass with truffle oil dressing and soya sauce; seared beef with an oriental dressing; fried soft-shell crab on a bed of mizuma salad; edamame – a green soya bean; Japanese tiger prawns with a yuzu dressing; chicken spatchcock – which is marinated in barley miso with a ginger cheese, garlic, shallots and another soya sauce; tempura; aubergine with a soya bean paste; vegetable skewers; sushi; and finally fried lobster balls, which were triple historic. All the food was superb to brilliant.

I waited too long for my dark chocolate pudding with raspberry centre. Russell said: 'The pastry chef is a craftsman, you can't rush him.' Oh yeah! Put me in the kitchen, I'll rush him.

There was also confusion as to which was the almond ice-cream. It was all worth it, because the desserts were truly remarkable. That's rare for a Japanese-type restaurant.

The only problem with Zuma was the noise. I was with David and Wendy, the odd couple from St John's Wood. Everyone's peculiar up there. I usually rely on Wendy, a New Yorker, to provide humorous lines. She was sitting opposite me and I couldn't hear a word she said.

WINNIE AT GORDON RAMSAY (ON A RARE DAY WHEN GORDON COOKED!)

WINNIE
IN DICK
MACKS.
IN DINGLE

← GUINNESS

UK & IRELAND
England

At a cafe-looking basement in Bath called, quite descriptively, the **Hole in the Wall**, I had some excellent food. From the three-course lunch menu at £11.50, I chose sweet pea soup, which was country-delicious, and pan-fried Cornish haddock with fresh samphire – soft and lovely, with a real taste. My dessert of iced armagnac, prune and hazelnut ice cream was disappointing, but Vanessa's cinnamon biscuit of rhubarb and apple with elderflower custard was historic. Overall, wonderful food and unbelievable value.

Hunstrete House near Bath is 'an 18th-century manor house set in 92 acres of deer park, woodland and exquisite gardens', none of which I could see because it was night. The service was a delight, very friendly and together. The gem of the evening was a bottle of Haut Brion 1961 at £275 inc. VAT. What?! I hear you say! Well, the same bottle is £790 inc. VAT and service at Chez Nico, and I recently bought some in auction for £391.12 a bottle. So £275 is a gift. 'Could you wrap a dozen up for me?' I asked the wine waiter. But they didn't.

P.S. This is now owned by Von Essen hotels. A very classy group! They've spent a lot on it!

I had seen **Menzies Flitwick Manor**, a country hotel in Bedfordshire, in a guide book. It being a sunny day and, as it was only an hour away off the M1, I thought I'd have a go. I phoned up. 'Do you serve tea?' I asked the manageress. 'If guests want tea, we do it,' she said. 'Suppose I want tea and I'm not a guest?' I asked. 'We'll start baking,' she replied. Later, we arrived on a gravel terrace overlooking fields and a 600-year-old cedar of Lebanon. The sandwiches were not a good start. A lot of them, not terrible, just failing in spectacular. Then came the cakes. Enough for a party of 12. Shortbread, chocolate biscuit (amazing looking with choccy cream oozing out from a 'sandwich'), strawberry feuilleté, fruit cake, banana strudel, profiteroles, scones, a large bowl of cream, home-made strawberry jam. The ginger cake was masterful; scones tip-top. I attempted, in the cause of duty, to try everything, but even I was defeated. I don't know how the Flitwick chef does proper meals, but his tea ranks with the greats.

In my desperate hunt for a good English Sunday lunch I ventured into our idyllic countryside to see what the strange people who live out of London eat. We stopped at the **Black Horse** in Ireland. Not Ireland, Ireland. Ireland, Bedfordshire.

The Black Horse is run by dad Jim Campbell (who wasn't there) and son Darren. He was very pleasant. The room was pleasant. I was pleasant. Princess was, as ever, phenomenal.

They had fantastic pieces of wonderful, warm bread. I dipped it in something which looked like olive oil with pesto. 'The bread is made here,' said the waitress, adding very loudly, 'everything is home-made.' 'She obviously thinks I'm stone deaf,' I whispered to Princess.

Princess had French onion soup, which was definitely good. I had mussels in a sort of sauce. I liked them. Princess enjoyed her cod. My pork had an enormous amount of crackling with it and stuffing. The pork didn't taste of much but the roast potatoes were excellent. There were enormous amounts of cabbage, beans, mange tout – all beautifully cooked. The crumble was superb though I got custard not cream, which I'd ordered. 'This really is a very good place,' I observed.

When I presented Darren with my American Express card, which doesn't have chip and pin, he put it in a funny little machine and said, 'Would you press the green button?' I did. Then he said, 'Would you press the red button?' 'This is mechanic's work,' I observed.

The BBC invited me to be interviewed at Ascot – on the occasion of the King George VI and Queen Elizabeth Stakes. Word got out I was coming and the Duke and Duchess of Devonshire asked me to dine with them in the **Ascot Authority Luncheon Room**. Investigation uncovered the necessity of a tie. I demurred, then gave in. Immaculately dressed, I duly turned up.

I was seated on the right of the duchess, known to her confidantes (and me) as Amanda. I'd been dreading the lunch. I'm not very good with strangers, even aristocrats. But Amanda was so delightful, when I review duchesses she'll get the highest possible mark – a strong 10.

The food was pretty good. We started with poached Maine lobster, foie gras and pea shoot salad, warm Canadian lobster and morel cappuccino. My morel soup didn't arrive. 'Can we have another one of these?' requested the duchess, feeling my discomfort at missing any sustenance.

The people seated next to the duchess and me hadn't arrived. So the duchess said, 'If you want to eat this, you can,' as she passed me the absentee's plate. Being well mannered to a fault I scooped half of it onto her plate.

The main course – lamb with beans, baby fennel and other bits and pieces – was fine as was the dessert of chocolate mousse with raspberries.

Unfortunately I told the interviewer I'd been lunching with the Duke and Duchess of Westminster. There's another place I won't be able to go back to.

Sitting pretty

It's a serious menu. You can tell the **Fat Duck** means business because of all the posh French words. The bread was ghastly: cold, nasty texture. Augurs ill, I thought. I started with lasagne of langoustines, pig's trotter and truffles. Excellent, memorable. Vanessa had escabèche of mackerel, carrots and saffron. She hated it. Didn't worry me: I ate her portion. Then I had fillet of venison, gateau of potato with époisses, confit of chestnut and shallot, sauce poivrade. I have no idea what all that meant, but it was definitely good.

For dessert I ordered chocolate coulant with ice cream, which I was told was an Italian meringue mixed with sweet pastry. It's put inside a cake mould, frozen ganache of chocolate is forced into the centre, then it's covered and baked in the oven. It was one of the great chocolate puddings of all time. Even Vanessa liked it; she nicked as much as she could. She also enjoyed her apple crumble, so the meal ended on a high note.

Heston Blumenthal, the owner-chef, turned up. His culinary experience seemed limited. He met Marco Pierre White while working briefly at Le Manoir and then did a couple of weeks in the Canteen. Whatever – it did him proud. He made good. He's a nice young man if ever there was one.

On my next visit I enjoyed one of the best lunches I've ever eaten. I noted that the guests were posher than when I first came. Michelin has given it three stars. What's particularly good about Heston Blumenthal's cooking is that he takes British nouvelle cuisine, which is getting very tired, and does new, inventive and tasty things with it. The food sounds over-elaborate and it was a bit that way on my previous visit. Good, but experimentally fussy. Now, it's cleaner and more refined.

The Fat Duck staff cleared the plates with amazing speed, which I like. Perhaps they were trying to get rid of me, as, with my usual insouciance, I'd booked only an hour before arrival.

Heston Blumenthal is an amazingly talented chef. At a recent lunch the food was utterly historic. The addition of seven freebie bits and pieces between courses was a bit much. However, a small, foamy 'milkshake' of green tea and lime sour was one of the greatest tastes ever. I could have done without potato lime jelly and maple syrup being fed into my mouth on a teaspoon by the waiter. I may be incontinent, but I like to pretend I retain my faculties.

P.S. Heston is now rightly rated a culinary legend.

I used to lunch regularly at the bar of Wheeler's in Soho in the 1950s, sitting next to Francis Bacon and Lucian Freud. Fascinating though they both were, the main objects of my attention were the luscious bosoms of the girl behind the bar, Carole Walsh. I was mesmerised.

Ronnie Emmanuel got closer to Carole's bosoms than I did. He married her. Carole and Ronnie now run, with their children Michael and Elaine, the **French Horn** at Sonning-on-Thames. It has no Michelin stars; gets a miserable two rosettes out of five in the AA Restaurant Guide; isn't even mentioned in *The Good Food Guide*. But it's one of the best restaurants ever. The so-called professionals are idiots. Follow only me.

It's an extremely beautiful 1850s house with sloping lawns and flowerbeds that lead down to weeping willows and the Thames. It's a small hotel as well as a superb restaurant. Aylesbury ducks roast on an open-fire spit as you enter. I always have that. You get a whole, crisp-skinned duck carved at a side table. Not some ridiculous nouvelle cuisine strips of semi-raw duck, which are now in vogue among those with supposed taste.

I had fantastic fried scampi from the Orkney Isles. The vegetables were marvellous. To finish, I scoffed miraculous bread-and-butter pudding with custard. This is old-style good-quality food, very 1950s. The decade that produced the best fare this country's ever offered.

The Emmanuel family are superb hosts. Service is immaculate, quiet, professional. Sonning village is picturesque. The French Horn setting is idyllic. The ambience a delight. The food fantastic.

Mustard ice cream or bacon-and-egg ice cream alarms purists like me. What's wrong with vanilla or chocolate? If you must experiment, why not deliver a straw-berry ice cream that tastes of strawberries and not chemical flavour? But Heston Blumenthal, Britain's latest three-Michelin-starred chef, is into new flavours.

Now Heston has excelled himself. He bought the pub almost beside his Fat Duck in Bray in Berkshire called the **Hind's Head**. There they serve the best pub food in the world. This is the sort of restaurant I dream of finding but, even though I'm in my dotage, have never found before.

A very charming restaurant manager, Susan Proctor, offered various tables. We opted for a large alcove in the bar – the site of the reception desk when it was a hotel. Now there are no bedrooms. The attic-type room above will soon be in ye olde English pub style and house extra tables.

I advise dumping the sign that, above a low arch to the toilet, announces 'Caution – duck or grouse'. Other than that, and the disgusting use of paper napkins, the Hind's Head is close to perfect. Perfect, in case you're wondering, is above historic.

My guests were Chris Rea, musician supreme, and his exceptionally marvellous wife, Joan. They hadn't arrived so I ordered potted shrimps with watercress salad and toast. Chris looked startled to see me already eating when he was only 10 minutes late. I eat lunch at one o' clock regardless.

Then I had oxtail and kidney pudding with red cabbage, bacon and triple-cooked chips. Everything was fantastic. But the chips were super-stratospheric incredible. They also offered 'fries' at £2.50. The triple cooked chips are £4.

'Chris, these three-times-cooked chips are beyond belief,' I enthused. If you can't go bonkers about chips, what else is there? 'I like the other one's better,' responded Chris dismissively. 'They're bought in! They come pre-sliced in packets!' I said in horror. He's a sweet fellow, Chris Rea, and immensely talented. But he comes from Middlesbrough. Say no more.

Geraldine had rabbit and bacon terrine with watercress salad followed by roast cod with champ and parsley sauce. It was all above sensational.

I scoffed treacle tart with milk ice cream. 'Definitely one of the best treacle tarts I've ever eaten,' I dictated.

Flock to the Hind's Head. You'll love it. If you don't, sue me. See if I care.

Sir Michael Parkinson (that fellow wot used to be on TV) owns a pub called the **Royal Oak** in Paley Street in Berkshire. Nick, Michael's amiable and able son, runs the place, which is beautifully designed by Lady Mary Parkinson.

The food is fantastic, super-historic, brilliant beyond belief. I ate as good a meal as has ever passed my ruby lips. This place is more than a must. It's a major-super-duper must. Miss it at your peril.

I started with Scotch egg made with tangy sausage meat and containing a soft-boiled quail's egg in the middle. Total perfection. Then I had lamb's kidneys with scrambled duck's eggs. I'm brilliant at scrambled eggs. Ava Gardner told me my way (geddit?) was exactly how Frank did them. That's Sinatra, not Spencer. The Royal Oak chef, Dominic Chapman, a genius for sure, is even better than me with the egg whisk. The kidneys were succulent, delicious, adorable.

There followed roast English partridge very nicely sliced and cut up, on a bed of runner beans. The gravy was unbeatable and the chips – well I can only say they're the best chips you'll ever get. Totally amazing. It's something to do with boiling them and frying them three times. The taste is mind-blowing.

I finished off with bread and butter pudding (the best ever) and quince and blackberry crumble – well up to the perfect standard I was getting used to. I've never had a better meal than this in my life. This is what cooking should be. Superb ingredients, simple, done with stratospheric skill. If I was giving out Michelin stars Dominic Chapman would have 5.681.

Everyone else at the table, including Sir Michael and Lady Parkinson, thought the food exemplary. Well, the Parkinsons would, wouldn't they? I later recommended the Royal Oak to my friends Sir Michael and Lady Caine, Sir Roger and Lady Moore and multi-Oscar winning songwriter Leslie Bricusse and his ex-actress wife Evie.

Bit of a problem when I visited with them. It was a disaster. The whole thing had fallen to pieces. Beyond belief awful. I can just see Parky's face reading this. Calm down, dear, it's only a bad taste joke. Things were impeccably fantastic as ever.

The **Vineyard at Stockcross**, near Newbury in Berkshire, is naff, naff, naff. It's a case, as Dick Emery used to say, of, 'Oooh you are awful, but I like you.' The building is odd, the decorations are odd, the chairs are odd, everything is odd. The best decorative feature is framed reviews of the hotel and restaurant hanging on the walls of the stairway. Some of the comments are quite terrible. 'We've got some real stinkers up there,' admitted the immensely charming manager, Andrew McKenzie. That's clever. Only a finicky person like me reads them.

The Vineyard is highly regarded. At least by a dodgy magazine, *Caterer and Hotelkeeper*, admired by some in the misnamed 'hospitality industry'. It gave the Vineyard's cook, John Campbell, the chef of the year award and Andrew the 2008 hotelier of the year award. That's somewhere below the Jewish Blind School white bar third class. I give the Vineyard the Winner 'very good' award. Not historic. Not super-historic. But 'very good' isn't bad, is it?

All its staff are marvellous. Genuinely friendly, efficient and hospitable. The restaurant has two Michelin stars. I've never eaten there. Little details like that don't stop me giving an incisive review of the food.

The reason I've never scoffed anything except breakfast and tea is that I stay when visiting my friends Lord and Lady Lloyd-Webber. I eat main meals with the aristocracy.

On my last visit I advised John Campbell, 'I'm going to order two breakfasts from the lunch or dinner menus.' I had among other things that I've forgotten, a vanilla soufflé, scrambled duck eggs with black pudding, truffles with something (they were fantastic), fresh crayfish, various biscuits, cookies and shortbreads (incredible), the afore-mentioned kippers and some chips. Everything was excellent. Go there with confidence and good cheer.

I had a superb meal in the private room at the **Waterside Inn** for Nico Ladenis's 60th birthday, but on my next visit, oh dear. In order of horrible: dreary bread, a canapé of duck rillettes that would have been at home on British Airways and a bellini that tasted of soap and wasn't cold (and then I had to face the empty, dirty glasses for ever until a waiter took one away, leaving the other for ages more). The table was so small the plate of the person opposite (very famous, but I won't give you the name) nearly touched mine. The freebie starter – tomato bavarois, cucumber and tapenade croutonne – was bland and the sauce tasted of mass-produced ketchup. My first course of salmon was okay, no more, and Vanessa's of eggs in a sauce and pastry was actively nasty, the pastry being soggy and tasteless. My kidneys main course was all right, but my guests

Cont'd

had duck that was chewy and had skin like rubber. The dessert, millefeuille de nougatine au melon de cavaillon glace vanille, was just unbelievable! Soggy, over-ripe, odd-tasting melon, between layers of tasteless crisp brown stuff.

In order to have the honour of eating this rubbish I had been instructed not to wear jeans. I didn't, but faced fellow diners in jeans, with denim shirts and without jackets. This is one of only two three-star Michelin restaurants in England, and the menu says 'Discover the delights of these exceptional dishes' (always suspect). What is Michel Roux's excuse for serving this quality of food?

My Cliveden re-birth

Under a previous owner, John Tam, **Cliveden** was the worst. Dust on every surface, diabolical food, grossly mismanaged, an example of how a hotel should not be. Pity, because it's a glamorous stately home, once the scene of debauched parties involving Christine Keeler and married war minister John Profumo. Their scandalous affair helped bring down the MacMillan government in the 1960s. When I visited under Mr Tam's mismanagement I got dirty champagne glasses, cutlery missing for breakfast and a chain of disasters. Mr Tam, realising he was going to get a terrible review, banned me. Whereupon the *Daily Mail* went down and ran a story across two pages headed 'At last Michael Winner gets it right.' They found even more wrong with Cliveden than I did.

Luckily Mr Tam disappeared and the place was taken over by Andrew Davis of von Essen hotels. It is now immaculate. The food in the two restaurants I visited was exemplary. The setting is magnificent. The staff were friendly and efficient. I was in the best accommodation, the Lady Astor suite, which is large and elegant with an enormous terrace. It's much used by couples who've had their wedding at Cliveden, for their first night of marital bliss. Or otherwise. We even had tea served by our very own butler on a 1916 boat as it cruised up the river Thames. That's available for all guests. Whereas it used to be my 'no-no' of all time, I can now thoroughly recommend Cliveden.

I cruised into Beaconsfield like the shark in *Jaws* looking for its next victim. It was getting near lunchtime. Then I spotted **Gilbey's** in Old Amersham, Buckinghamshire. Old house, little flagstoned courtyard in the sun with wrought-iron tables and chairs. This was to be it! The bread was excellent. Vanessa had sweet pepper and tomato soup, good but certainly not hot. I had spinach and dolcelatte tart with a fresh herb salsa. Pleasant, if unremarkable. Main course for me was grilled cod fillet served on a pancake filled with radicchio leaves, with a goat's cheese and basil salsa. The basil salsa turned out to be exactly the same green gunge as the herb salsa in my first course.

Cont'd

Otherwise, it was pretty good. I was not unhappy. I also had an uninterrupted view of the A404, which I do not remember having seen before. 'The chef recommends a crème brûlée and the lemon tart,' said Miss Charlotte Gilbey, who served us. We had them both, and they were good to excellent. Stephen Spooner, the young chef, was dragged out. 'What did you think? he asked nervously. 'Fine, a few quibbles,' I said. 'What quibbles?' 'Soup was cold,' I muttered. He asked no more.

The **Old Red Lion Inn**, at Great Brickhill in Buckinghamshire, looked quaint. Inside there were photos of Joanna Lumley, Jeremy Beadle, David Jason and Mick Jagger. This was clearly a glitterati area. I sat at the bar and surveyed the menu, then ordered a 'Lion's Feast: two rashers of bacon, sausage, tomato, burger, two eggs, mushrooms, baked beans and chips. £6.25.' It was as adventurous as anything else on the menu. Vanessa ordered a ploughman's lunch. In came my robust plate of food. Very basic, very British. Perfectly all right. The chips were very chunky. 'Home-made?' I asked. 'Not home-made, just excellent,' said Andrew McCollin, the landlord. I poured tomato ketchup on my fry-up. I enjoyed it. The atmosphere was particularly relaxed and understated. All exceptionally pleasant.

There used to be only one restaurant in Bridge Street, Cambridge. It served Indian food. Every Friday in the mid-fifties I'd dine there with George Webb, a wonderfully ebullient cockney who owned the specialist Rex cinema, and his manager Leslie Halliwell who became a famous writer of books on movies.

At the Cambridge Union Society I recently delivered a light-hearted talk: My Life in Movies and Other Places. The Union President, Adam Bott, led me along Bridge Street, now wall-to-wall restaurants, to **Brasserie Chez Gérard** for dinner with a group of students.

I ordered 'gravadlax, slow-cured salmon with dill and a mustard and cucumber sauce'. It was over-salty, dry, awful. The aftertaste was ghastly beyond belief. I followed with 'merguez sausages, three authentic spicy Moroccan lamb and beef sausages simply grilled and served with frites and minted yoghurt'. It read better than it tasted. Accompanying it were very tired green leaves.

The first course arrived nearly an hour after being ordered. A student, Chris, didn't get his lemonade. For his main course he got fries instead of mashed potatoes. The bread, dry and weary, came after the first course. It's normally before. At the other end of the proceedings, service had been so slow, there was no time for dessert. Everything, except the company, was below mediocre.

Gowned and out

Why on earth should anyone buy a Cambridge University master of arts gown with a white-lined hood? Thus I mused while unwrapping the one I'd ordered from Ede & Ravenscroft of Trumpington Street, Cambridge. Perhaps I'd wear it to greet dinner guests. Unlikely: I've only given three dinner parties in the past 27 years. It rested on the sofa in my study until – knock me down with a feather – a few days later I received an invitation from the master and fellows of **Downing College, Cambridge**, inviting me to their commemoration feast. 'Dress black tie, gowns with scarlet decoration may be worn' was hand-written on the bottom. Gown or no gown, this was not for me.

Invitations usually get put on the left of my desk. There they lie, soon covered with further ephemera, forgotten and unanswered. I wrote to Professor David King MA, ScD, FRS, Master, pointing out he really didn't want me. 'I ask to see the seating plan, know exactly who is on the table, be told who's placed either side of me and opposite, have the right to make changes. All this is far too much for a man of your stature, so I'll say thank you no, and hope to meet another time.' Professor King graciously replied that I was seated on his right-hand side, he would send me a top table plan and a thumbnail sketch of everyone on it, and let me do as I wished. Now it became: how to get the helicopter in? I liked the idea of returning, for the first time since I came down in 1955, in some style and with a bit of noise. Mrs Professor King told my copter man that we could land on the college lawn; others had done so before. But this was not to be. Apparently the 'others' were royalty. Royal flights are okay; plebs like me, decreed the Civil Aviation Authority, had to land on a nearby rugby pitch. And I thought we lived in a democracy.

There was more trouble. I was doing a BBC television show just before the 20-minute flight from Battersea. So I took my evening dress and other paraphernalia into the lavatory of the heliport for a quick change. It was unimportant I'd forgotten cuff links. But my evening-dress trousers were not on the hanger. Oh well, I would appear immaculately dressed from the waist up. Below, there would be the considerable contrast of a pair of jeans. Nobody cared, even though I took the trouble to point out in my speech that this was not a protest, but an error, for which I apologised.

To describe any meal in a Cambridge dining hall as a 'feast' would, I thought, require a stretch of normal meaning. But my Cambridge dictionary called it 'a meal with very good food or a large meal for many people'. Since there were 140 guests and a six-course menu in which the word 'dessert' strangely meant cheese and biscuits, I suppose we qualified. I was particularly pleased that by the end of our correspondence the master was signing himself 'Dave'. Most unlike my dour tutor, Mr Norman, who referred to me, in student days, as 'Winner', and endlessly told me I spent far too much time watching films and working on the university newspaper. But then my headmaster at

school lectured me on how the Warner Bros gangster movies, now cine-
mathèque classics, would result in my growing up disturbed. Sit down the
reader who said, 'He was right'.

Fronted by an ornate, silver bowl 'from the Long Range Rifle Club', we started
with terrine de légumes: fair to middling. Went on to filet de bar grillé au safran:
very good indeed, first-rate sauce. Then a sorbet; I like sorbets. Thus to the main
course, suprême de faisan châtelaine. Perfectly acceptable, but a bit dry. The
carrots were historic. At this point I realised I was the only one at the table who
was eating. Many others had not been served. I think it's essential to commence
while the food is hot, regardless. I turned to the master. 'Start, David, because
I'm the only one,' I said. 'Right,' said Dave, and started eating. College masters
have certainly improved since my day. The only time I met Sir Lionel Whitby,
Downing's boss in 1954, was when he hauled me up for taking the porter's
bicycle and leaving it at the Varsity newspaper office. Sir Lionel sent me down
for two weeks. Yah boo, Sir L. I've got the best seat in the house. I'm about to
reply on behalf of the guests. I even scoffed the poire macaron au coulis de
fraises. That's more than you ever gave me.

The **Cambridge Garden House Moat House** used to be the Garden House hotel, a lovely
old building on the River Cam. Sadly it burnt down and was replaced by a functional
brick edifice. The sort of place where you see people in the lift, poshed up for a
wedding, holding balloons.

My junior suite (a bedroom with added furniture) overlooked the river, fields, cows
and old buildings. Only a contortionist could get onto the tiny balcony, where there
was no room to stand anyway. In one corner the wallpaper was peeling and damp
stained the ceiling. There was a tea-making facility, something I'm not used to. I put
mineral water in the kettle and knocked up a tea-bag-based cuppa.

There was no ventilation fan in the bathroom. A sign read: 'When taking a shower,
please close the door as the steam may be liable to set off the fire alarm.' There was a
good supply of towels and other bathroom stuff. The breakfast was fine. It's not the
sort of hotel I'm used to, but so what.

I can't believe **Midsummer House** in Cambridge has two Michelin stars. I normally
admire the Michelin Guide. Now I'm sceptical.

I'll deal first with two excellent aspects of Midsummer House. The room, like a
greenhouse extension, is extremely pleasant. It faces Midsummer Common. This didn't
help on the night I went. There was a funfair with louts throwing bottles.

Tables are well spaced so it lacks noise pollution. Thus Geraldine could easily hear
me complaining about the food. We started with very ordinary bread (brought rather
late) and ghastly Hildon water. Then we got a couple of freebies: a green tea and lime

Cont'd

frothy thing and 'a cucumber julie topped with smoked salmon and a cappuccino dubarry', I dictated on the tape. These were unexceptional but pleasant.

I was recommended 'ravioli with quails, Savoy cabbage purée, roasted grapes'. There were four grapes placed carefully at the edges of the plate, then a green mush, then two bits of quail and in the middle the quail ravioli with a mushroom on top. 'The plate decoration is really effortful,' I dictated. The pasta was tough.

Then I had another recommended item: 'tronçon of turbot with cep risotto, mushroom biscuit cep foam'. The risotto formed a square. The fish was tasteless and solid. My dessert of rhubarb and custard had no substance. The rhubarb was just mush.

At the end the guest book was presented. I wrote: 'I enjoyed myself.' This is true. Regardless of the food I did enjoy myself. But I'm certainly not going back.

I dropped in for lunch at a picture-postcard thatched cottage, the **Pink Geranium** in Melbourn, Cambridgeshire. It's owned by Lawrence and Sally Champion. He was restaurant manager on my first visit to the dreaded Midsummer House in Cambridge years ago.

The setting is typically lovely English country cottage with a garden full of roses and other flowers and opposite a church. Not surprisingly, in view of its name, the cottage was painted pink.

I ordered a parfait of foie gras and chicken livers with fig chutney. Apart from some rather weird jazz coming through it was a very pleasant place. The home-made tomato and parmesan bread was good. So was the foie gras. I finished it and forgot to eat the chutney. So I started eating my lettuce leaves with the chutney. Geraldine said, 'It's horrific,' referring to my table manners. She says this frequently. I'm used to it. 'Just an ordinary day in Winnerland,' I said cheerfully.

The Yorkshire pudding was very good indeed. My roast beef was on a bed of spinach. I hate spinach in beds or any other form. The beef was thick cut and very chewy. Geraldine said her fillet of brill was seriously good. My roast potatoes were a long way off good. They didn't have a crisp exterior.

I finished with griottine cherry and almond Bakewell tart with mascarpone ice cream. I'm a world expert on Bakewell tart. My dessert was not a Bakewell tart. It was like an almond cake with cherries in it. But it was very, very good.

The AA Restaurant Guide gives **Chester Crabwell Manor** hotel two rosettes and says, 'slick skills are in evidence, creating detailed dishes and daring flavour combinations'. It describes a 'quality environment'. I suggest AA inspectors are blind and have had their taste buds surgically removed. This is the tackiest hotel with an appallingly run restaurant serving the worst imaginable fodder.

I hardly know where to start, but I'll manage. The banisters were painted in white gloss and ingrained with dirt. There was a hook where a picture once hung, with horrid marks where the picture had been. There was an odd smell. The suite comprised the two most garish rooms I've ever been in. The lounge had a sofa, a couple of small chairs, a tiny, low round table and a dead plant. The bedroom had no bedside lights. You had to get out of bed to switch the lights, all of which glared mercilessly. As did the ones in the sitting room.

The dining room was crass and tacky. Chintz curtains and a green carpet with red and white stars. I'd been autobiography-signing all day and had to leave early the next morning, so I said to the head waiter: 'I'd like to get in and out quickly please.' 'Not a problem, sir,' replied Andrew Wilbraham.

The three-course set menu was £35 per person ex service. Add 12.5% gratuity and that's £39.37. High if they were capable. Grotesque as they were not.

My first course, described on the pompously headed 'Menu du Marché', was 'prestorine of ham shank and truffle, coarse mustard dressing'. It was like a dreary slice of meat pie at a catered lunch for 800 people. Accompanying it were some tired leaves and a sun-dried tomato, which tasted like a pickle gone wrong.

The main course 'pan roast loin of pork, boulangère potatoes, tomato provençal, crackling, port jus' was a slab of hard, atrocious pork, nothing crackling anywhere near it, with soggy potatoes. I left almost all of it.

The desserts included 'espresso and caramelised hazelnut bavrois (sic)'. After being given the menu we were left in a room devoid of staff. 'Wave the napkin over your head,' suggested Geraldine. 'There's no one to see it!' I said, getting up to go outside. There was Andrew 'not a problem' Wilbraham standing in a small corridor by the restaurant entrance. He was staring into space.

I said quietly, 'I told you I wished to get through speedily. I've been given a dessert menu and abandoned. There are no staff in the restaurant and you're standing in a corridor from where you can see nothing at all. Do you think this is doing your job properly?'

That got the dessert served. The plate was decorated like a touring version of *Waitrose Food Illustrated*. It tasted as if it came from a newsagent's fridge.

Breakfast was a nightmare. The table was too small for the tray. Cutlery missing. Food awful.

Rampsbeck Country House hotel, on Ullswater in Cumbria, is a modest-priced place. Ullswater is a particularly beautiful lake. The surrounding countryside is magnificent. The Rampsbeck public room decoration defies description. Blobs, badly mixed colours. Ghastly.

They finished redecorating a couple of weeks ago but left the dining room untouched. A pity, because it's one of the most hideous rooms ever. Various types of wall brackets, ludicrous standing lamps, cheap-looking, horrid carpet with yellow diamonds on it. Lovely view of the lake, somewhat diminished by the intrusion of dreary parked cars.

The food was up and down. My prune and walnut bread was better than I've had in any London restaurant. Historic. My chicken terrine was very good. Exceedingly fresh,

Cont'd

didn't taste as if it had hung around. The brioche with it was terrific. Geraldine's salad delighted her.

Then everything collapsed. Geraldine said her turbot was too dry. My roast beef was the worst I've ever tried to eat, so tough I couldn't cut it even with a serrated knife. The carrots were good. So were the parsnips. The Yorkshire pudding was atrocious. The roast potatoes were not great. Geraldine's chocolate mousse was too solid. My apple and banana rösti with toffee apple ice cream was well below average.

The service, largely from the charming general manager, Marion Gibb, was superb. The chef, Andrew McGeorge, should do better. I found it odd that, faced with a plate of uneaten roast beef and Yorkshire pudding, the waiter asked, 'Did you enjoy your main course?' Why did he think I left most of it?

When I first tried to visit **Sharrow Bay**, a hotel on Lake Ullswater in Cumbria, I was refused entry. The two gay owners, Francis Coulson (chef) and Brian Sack (general manager), were terrified of me. Years later, I applied again. Sadly by then Francis had died. But the once-frightened Brian Sack and I became friends.

Brian told me he was leaving Sharrow Bay and his house to the hotel's managing director, Nigel Lightburn, whom he jokingly referred to as his 'illegitimate son'. 'He'll look after Sharrow Bay and keep it as Francis and I want it always to be,' he said.

Not long after Nigel inherited the hotel he flogged it to Andrew Davis of the Von Essen hotel group and retired to Brian's magnificent house on the lake.

So I wondered: will it all have collapsed? It hadn't. Sharrow Bay is fantastic. The food is historic. The wonderful kitsch decor and knick-knacks remain as they were. The views of the lake are breathtaking. All the staff are delightful. You'll gather I like it.

Sharrow Bay has a well-deserved Michelin star. The food is simple, tasty, memorable. The chefs are Colin Akrigg and Mark Teasdale, both tutored by Francis Coulson. Some of the stuff I enjoyed ('stuff' may not be a sophisticated description, but so what?) included a stunning soufflé of stilton, spinach and roast onion; roast breast of quail with truffle fettuccine and wild mushroom sauce; breast of Gressingham duckling with creamed savoury cabbage, black pudding, glazed apple and sage sauce.

The puddings (love puddings) were headed by 'Francis Coulson's famous and original sticky toffee sponge served with cream'. The best sticky toffee sponge pudding I've ever had.

In our room were incredible shortbread, toffees, fudge plus more. It was a marvellous experience.

Beau Gidleigh

What I like about Devon is that it's not the home counties. You feel you really are somewhere else. You can drive for miles and not see very much. In fact, a great deal of the time you can see nothing at all, except high hedgerows that tower over the one-track lanes. Set in the heart of it all is **Gidleigh Park**, a deservedly famous hotel with a Michelin two-star restaurant.

I'd been wanting to visit for a while. When a gap appeared in their regular bookings, I got one room for £460 a night, including full breakfast and dinner. It was a nice room, but the one next door was better because it had a balcony. I was able to check this out as they don't give you keys at Gidleigh Park, on the assumption that everyone is unbelievably honest. Even in Devon this strikes me as optimistic.

The hotel is a fake Tudor 1920s Surrey-style mansion. There's a stream outside and it's all pleasantly well worn, with weeds (or were they flowers?) peeping out between cracks in the paving stones. Cat's hair is spread over the armchairs. This upset Georgina because she got her black trouser suit messed up. A couple from New York tried to strike up a conversation, but I decided against it. Then I learned it was George Shearing and his wife.

We started with a superb Devon tea. Best scones ever, great clotted cream, wonderful home-made jam, historic biscuits and pleasant sandwiches that were overfilled. The banana cake was poor, the chocolate cake just good. You sit on a lovely terrace overlooking the view.

The general manager, Catherine Endacott, was totally devoted. She walked quickly, with purpose. The hotel was obviously her life. 'We don't reserve seats in the dining room,' she advised. 'That's all right, Catherine,' I said. 'I'll go now and leave a bar of soap and an old shoe on the table to show it's occupied.' 'Don't worry,' said Catherine. 'I'll fix it.' I pointed helpfully to the table I wanted fixed.

The room literature advised that she and the chef, Michael Caines, owned the hotel. 'Catherine's not a proprietor and Caines isn't either,' said Paul later. 'But it's in your guest book,' I said. 'I didn't proofread it,' said Paul. Shortly thereafter I met Michael Caines. 'Why are you giving me a left-handed handshake?' I asked rather tartly. 'Because I lost my right arm in a car accident last year,' he explained. That shut me up. They certainly did a wonderful matching job on the false arm.

There were two small dining rooms at Gidleigh. The guests talked in hushed whispers. The service was efficient but impersonal. I missed someone greeting and checking up on things, like Peter Crome does at Chewton Glen. This lack of human touch may have been because Mrs Henderson (the owner's wife) was laid up with a bad leg and the restaurant manager was on holiday. The food was good; not up to the level of Gordon Ramsay, but commendable.

Sizzling good

We'd decided to forego a posh dinner at Chewton Glen and take our chances. Vanessa had requested a brief walk by the sea. Now, we proceeded along the coast, but the only inn that served food on that stretch stopped at 8.30pm and that was the time. So I cruised down the main drag to Highcliffe, Dorset.

'There's something!' I exclaimed, jamming my foot on the brake. There was a screech of tyres behind. Two young men in a Jeep yelled something deeply unpleasant. 'Entirely my fault,' I said. 'I'm so sorry, I'm a terrible driver.' I say that a great deal, so I'm rather good at it. Then I continued down the street.

There it was: Erties Fish and Chips. Large gold letters standing out from a bright red background with four lights extending over them. Next door was a Methodist church. 'No Parking. Private Property' it said of the area in front. I pulled into a gap labelled 'Reserved for Organist'.

We walked into Erties. A stand-up wooden sign in old-fashioned lettering read 'Wait here to be seated'. A waitress showed us a table for two; I sat at one for eight. The large, plastic-covered menu confused me. A blackboard announced **Bertie's** evening specials (the B was missing outside): tuna steak or rock, £5.75, lemon sole, halibut steak, skate wing, large haddock with chips, £5.95. I was baffled. 'Is the owner in?' I asked the waitress. 'Yes, Rob's upstairs,' she told me. 'What's he doing there?' I asked. 'Watching the telly,' she replied. Seemed a pity to disturb him, so I walked into the kitchen.

A chef opened metal drawers revealing frozen cod. 'That's not on the board,' I said. 'Outside, the catch of the day's the special stuff; cod's a regular thing,' the chef explained. 'Anyway, it's all frozen, except the skate.'

It was a tough choice: beef and onion pie, steak and kidney pasties for £1.20, black-pudding fritters 40p, fish cake burgers 99p. 'Do you make them here?' I yelled. 'Yes,' said the chef. 'I'll have one and some cod, chips and mushy peas.' Vanessa ordered the rock.

My cod had that too-long frozen taste, but Vanessa's rock was first-rate. We both had two enormous pieces, enough for a group. The chips were superb, made on the premises. 'We get through two and a half tons of potatoes a week,' obliged the chef. The mushy peas were good too. I had trouble pouring the vinegar. 'It helps if you take the top off,' said Vanessa.

I went to another kitchen to examine a syrup sponge, melancholy in a refrigerator. I ordered it together with some New Forest ice cream. It arrived microwave hot. I only ate the syrupy bits on the outside of the sponge and the ice cream. I liked it, but Vanessa said it tasted of spray cream that comes out of a tin. She's much fussier than me. We rounded it off with cups of Assam and Kenyan Ty-Phoo tea.

P.S. The ownership has changed, but it's still excellent.

We'd turned down Sunday lunch at Chewton Glen – beignets of cod cooked in beer batter, roast strip-loin Black Aberdeen Angus served with Yorkshire pudding, and much more – and had walked to Highcliffe on the sweeping Christchurch Bay. On the fringe of the car park were two stalls, one for ice cream and the other offering sausage sandwiches, hot dogs, fried-egg sandwiches and the like. 'I'll have a jumbo frankfurter hot dog,' I said. 'With or without onions?' asked **Linda Attrell** from her caravan-type booth. 'With,' I replied. I filled it with tomato ketchup. It was a nice hot dog. Not as good as Nathan's in New York, but very serviceable. I then had a sausage sandwich – two bits of white bread with two pork sausages sliced in between. I filled that with mustard. That completed, I chose a whippy soft ice cream. Tacky, no real quality, but a splendid experience.

Oscar's, at the Royal Bath hotel in Bournemouth, is a corridor-like restaurant over-looking trees and the road outside. It features a photo of Oscar Wilde, who supposedly used to go there. Wilde would have had a seizure at the sight of the wallpaper. It was one of the most awful meals I have ever eaten. Don't tell me food is getting better in England. No French or Italian hotel in a place the size of Bournemouth would dare offer anything like it. Vanessa's cream of broccoli soup was so sweet even I found it impossible to take. I had tough, stringy Parma ham and mushy figs. A small white loaf was unexceptional in the extreme. I went on to grey mullet presented with a roast-tomato confit. It did not taste fresh – too long in the deep-freeze or fridge. Vanessa had cod fillet and potato mash with parsley and lemon sauce. Dull to awful. To finish, a millefeuille of chocolate filled with fresh cream and strawberries – beyond belief horrid. But the staff were all very pleasant, and it wasn't their fault that the food was dreary.

I drove down tiny little roads with passing places, to Cranborne in Dorset. This looked sleepy. There was a pub called **The Sheaf of Arrows**. A sign read: 'The Sheaf of Arrows, en suite accommodation, real ales, skittle alley, function room, outside bars, home cooked country fayre, hot and cold food now served.' The 'home cooked country fayre' line attracted me.

We walked in. The bar was empty. A man called Andrew Ranger – 'as in Lone', he explained – greeted us. He started to light the real log fire. 'Are you the chef?' I asked. 'We've got a cook. Everything is made on the premises,' said Andrew. I asked him for advice. 'I'm a bit partial to the curry,' he said, 'curry's nice.' It was on the blackboard: 'Chicken madras curry with pilau rice, poppadom and mango chutney £5.95. I ordered it. Geraldine asked for the ham, double egg and chips.

They served Malvern water, which is excellent. I had a Coca-Cola. It was all going extremely well until my curry arrived. The chicken was mushy, quite horrible. The rice was awful, the poppadom flopped about like a lettuce, the mango chutney was cloying. I left nearly everything.

Cont'd

I thought to myself: 'The food is unspeakable. I can't possibly say that's any good. But all the people are lovely. Very polite, genuinely hospitable.' Even though the pub was more or less empty you could imagine it being a really social place when it got going.

I don't eat in Dorset very often. 'Who does?' I said to myself as I drove across the Hampshire border into the sleepy seaside town of Mudeford. I like these little adventures. The **Ship in Distress** pub had been recommended by Peter Crome, then of Chewton Glen.

We entered through the back door into a cluttered restaurant painted light blue. The walls and shelves are filled with an enormous selection of pictures and knick-knacks. The place was nice. So were the guests. Locals, dressed up for Sunday dinner.

Georgina ordered a small Mudeford dressed crab salad followed by pan-fried monkfish with lardons, pied bleu mushrooms and herbs in a white wine butter sauce. I, being a poor boy from Willesden, chose cod and chips. I did go all posh by having moules to start. These were accompanied by five packs of Handy Freshener. 'I like this place,' observed Georgina. 'It's unpretentious.' I stifled a burp. Something I don't always do.

Remarkably, all six desserts on offer were made on the premises. Georgina pronounced her peach tatin 'excellent'. I scored my pear and almond tart as good-plus. The lemon posset was very fine indeed. Then I waited for a chocolate brownie that had been forgotten in all the excitement. It arrived with honeycomb ice cream and chocolate sauce. It was pleasant; not quite chocolately enough, but very acceptable. The desserts were honest and not grossly refined, but they worked well.

Vanessa wanted a weekend in the country, so I picked **Stock Hill House**, in Dorset, at random from the Ronay Guide because it was in an area I didn't know. The guide said: 'Arrive in time for afternoon tea, which is splendid.' I did and it wasn't. All we got with the excellent tea was a swiss roll, a chocolate cake and an apricot tart, and they were unexceptional.

The accommodation was a bit off, too. I'd asked for a suite; in future I must remember to ask for a view, suite or not. We got a strangely furnished, comfortable suite, a bit away from the Victorian house, with tiny windows and outside views of asphalt yards and cars. It was like living in a car park. Ronay describes this as 'the sumptuous Robin's Nest suite'. It had chintz curtains one side and striped the other, one of the hundreds of animalia, a Chinese dog, on the floor and a very well-stocked bathroom.

The service at Stock Hill is unbeatable. We asked for an iron and Vanessa's dress was ironed for her in five minutes. I asked for a razor and three came over in seconds. Peter and Nita Hauser – he from Austria, she from Walthamstow – are as nice a couple as you could meet. They certainly care.

Thankfully, the food at dinner perked up no end. The canapés were beautifully done. My mango and chicken ballotine starter was three large pieces of chicken with mango in the middle, all right but too much. The cream of lovage and sweet-water crayfish soup was historic. We'd seen the crayfish moving in a bucket a short time before. The main course of Aga-roasted duckling breast in cassis and blackcurrants was good. The vegetables, all home-grown, were tip-top. The food in general is charmingly robust.

The next morning Peter showed me round the herb and vegetable garden (not at its best this year through lack of rain). He called out and dozens of his chickens jumped on to perches to cluck back! So there's always fresh eggs.

The place is typical of the massively over-decorated style that pervades English, privately owned, small hotels. According to your taste, it's either delightfully eccentric or totally bizarre. The Hausers are avid collectors and the place is awash with carved animals, bronzes, an absolute mishmash of different period and coffee tables, furniture and mirrors, all interesting, but certainly not 'antiques of the highest standard', as the Ronay says. But then Ronay is as erratic a book as you can get.

It was a very pleasant stay and, yes, I can recommend Stock Hill House. The most magical moments were after dinner. I suddenly heard the sound of a zither. An Austrian record, I thought. But no, there in the lobby Peter was plucking expertly at a 100-year-old zither while two Japanese children watched enchanted.

At my request he played *The Third Man* theme, my favourite film and my favourite film music. Exceptionally well performed too. Now, there's not many hotels where you get that!

In Durham, Palace Green is one of the major sights of the world. It's staggering. At one end is the massive 11th-century cathedral, rightly described in the guidebook as 'one of the great architectural experiences in Europe'. The other side is the castle, also 11th century, now housing Durham's University College. In between is a large green surrounded by old buildings dating back to the 15th century.

One of them, the **Almshouses Café**, was rebuilt in 1666. Gilly and Eric Marrion own that. It has a door leading to the adjacent dining room of the university students' union, the debating society. Eric and Gilly cater for special dinners when highly distinguished guest speakers, such as me, are asked to perform.

The food that came through the door from the Almshouses Café to the union's big dining table – seating 14 people – was most acceptable. I think we had some sort of soup to start. If we didn't, too bad. We definitely had excellent venison in orange and red wine. There was a bowl of mashed-up sweet potatoes, which was totally sensational. I kept serving myself more. We finished with a lemon tart. It was fine without being historic. The surroundings were historic. That's enough historic for one evening.

On my little trips, I make rare journeys into the unknown. I cruised through Lymington, Hampshire. We'd travelled a bit and it was getting cold, so Peelers Bistro [now called **Egans**] would have to be it. Wooden floors, wooden chairs, painted beams, pink walls, candles and an overpowering air of quiet, good behaviour. I'll soon put a stop to that, I thought. I sauntered, unannounced, into the kitchen. The chef looked concerned. He assured me, most charmingly, that his fish was very fresh indeed. In the dining room I chose supreme of turbot served with white wine and prawn sauce, £17.95 excluding service. With service, that was £20 for a main course. Not cheap. To start I got some mushy, overripe melon. Vanessa had gazpacho, which was 'fine'. There followed a very long wait indeed for the main course, possibly a world record. My turbot had a pink sauce in front and a yellow sauce at the back. It was perfectly pleasant. Vanessa pronounced her tomato salad and goat's cheese 'very good' – and she's not easy to please.

I was staying in the presidential suite of the absurdly named **Durham Marriott Hotel Royal County**. I'd describe the accommodation as modest but not bad. They brought tea and cellophane-wrapped biscuits with no napkins. The breakfast came on time but was pretty awful. The bacon was tough, the scrambled eggs had been tipped out of a cone and left too long to dry, the hash brown potatoes also seemed to have stood about and were far too chewy. From our windows we had a clear view of the cathedral, the castle and Bhs.

The **Daylesford Farm Shop** near Kingham in Gloucestershire is owned by my friend Lady Carole Bamford who lives round there. Her husband does something strange with earth-moving vehicles. They have by far the best house in Barbados.

This is a fantastic shop. It's got everything – garden stuff, flowers, a tea service area, an interior restaurant. It sells almond croissants, organic pain au chocolat, organic apricot Danish, salads, all sorts of meat. I'm told you can get Daylesford Farm produce in Selfridges.

My friend the distinguished interior decorator Richard Hanlon is normally highly reliable when recommending Cotswold restaurants. He assured me the **Kings Arms** in Stow-in-the-Wold was excellent. It wasn't.

It's an inn with rooms in the main square of a quaint little town. The background music was Dean Martin. If you must have piped music Dean's the best person to pipe. The restaurant is on the first floor. Olde Worlde with some ghastly modern paintings and a large cluster of wine racks. Richard explained: 'You go and see the wine and choose what you want. It's quite fun.' 'I can't imagine anything less fun,' I thought.

We were greeted by an over-chummy Australian waiter. My first course was Oddington asparagus, poached egg and parmesan. The asparagus was vastly undercooked.

Richard said: 'Breast of duck's very good.' Wrong again, Richard. It was horrific. Tough, chewy slices that were beyond belief awful. Paola had roast turbot, which was absurdly overcooked. It was dry and flaky. 'This is a seriously horrible meal,' I observed.

We entered the place at 1pm. 'It's now 11 minutes to 3 and we haven't even got our desserts,' I commented, 'we're only trying to have a three-course meal!' I kept looking at the door through which the food was coming, in the hope someone would appear with mine.

Eventually we received Carole's rhubarb crumble, Carole being a customer. The rhubarb was apparently from her garden. This bordered on historic. Paola's white chocolate tart and raspberries was also terrific. Richard had meringue. That was tip-top too. So we ended on a high note.

The Lords of the Manor, in Upper Slaughter, Gloucestershire, is a 17th-century rectory with endless additions in Cotswold stone and done up inside in an acceptably twee style, in which chintz figures heavily. Not only were the curtains chintz and the modern brass four-poster bed heavy with chintz, but the bath had a chintz pelmet on top and a chintz curtain at one side. I wondered if you could curtain yourself off while bathing, but it appeared the chintz there was purely decorative.

One window overlooked the wondrous sight of English countryside, rolling hills and a lake; the other had an uninterrupted view of my Ferrari. I have been waiting years for a TV or print journalist to ask me, 'What was your greatest mistake in life?' to which I would reply, 'Buying a Ferrari.' But nobody's asked me.

The restaurant gets one star in the Michelin, but nothing in the Ronay. It's somewhere between the two. The room is pleasant. My soupe de poisson was surprisingly good for land-locked Gloucestershire and would have been better if I'd dared add the garlic, but for the sake of my guest Sarah, a beautiful and posh English actress, I did not.

We both greatly enjoyed the freebie pre-starter. It was parfait of foie gras infused with lemon thyme, buttered brioche and an apple and grape cardamom chutney! My main course was assiette of pork. Sarah thought her cod baked with mustard with tagliatelle and basil sauce okay, but not more. For dessert, I ordered one orange sorbet between us. It came, surprisingly, on an unbelievably delicious rich chocolate slice. So we ate it anyway.

Breakfast was a pleasant meal, and the staff were exceptional. All in all, it's a smashing place.

We flew to **Lower Slaughter Manor** in Gloucestershire for lunch. Very posh. They had Evian water in a jug. I ate blue cheese pannacotta, yellow pepper coulis and crisp brown bread, followed by a venison and hare pie topped with potato purée, and finished with summer pudding. All excellent.

It's a bit out of the way, unless you live in Broughton Poggs, Gloucestershire, in which case it's just down the road. I refer to the **Swan** at Southrop. The Swan is an old pub that inside is pleasingly modern and jolly. The co-owner is Graham Williams, ex-general manager of Bibendum on the Fulham Road.

My English asparagus with balsamic vinegar and parmesan was terrific. Then I had some marvellous roast pork with a lot of extra crackling. Paola had the same. The bread was crispy and very good indeed.

Paola liked the décor because it was simple and bright. 'It's full of character,' she said. 'I don't like old and grubby.' 'What are you doing with me then?' I asked.

To pass the time I ran my hand along a window ledge. 'You could definitely improve the dusting here,' I said to Graham.

To finish I had a historic apple and sultana crumble and custard. Then I tried the ice cream. That was great, too. The chef is James Parkinson. He deserves mammoth applause. That's if mammoths can clap.

My introduction to the **Wyck Hill House** was poor. It was raining. I opened the boot of the Ferrari. The porter stood inside in the warm hall watching through a glass-panelled door. I went moderately bananas. 'Dare I say,' I announced in a loud voice, 'that the purpose of being a porter is to help the guests, not stand idly by.' Thus the fellow was inspired to action. Our room was pleasant but odd, saved by a wonderful view of sweeping Gloucestershire countryside, and some very comfortable chairs and a sofa. The bathroom was appallingly small. The public rooms have a nice, not-done-up feel about them. Service at lunch was leisurely – it took 40 minutes for the first course to arrive. Vanessa's cream of asparagus soup was good, but coldish; her chicken was all right. My roast beef and Yorkshire was okay at best. The wine waiter poured the Château Beychevelle without offering it for tasting, dropping blobs of it on the table as he did so. My chocolate brownies were sickly sweet and didn't taste of chocolate. Wyck Hill House is nice, but erratic. I've stayed in better country hotels, but this place is certainly not offensive.

The problem with **Chewton Glen**, a deservedly famous hotel in Hampshire, can be summed up in two words: Peter Crome. He haunts the place. Peter was in charge for nine years. When he left six years ago I stopped going. He was the best hotel manager ever. Amazingly efficient, great charm and sense of humour, unique, irreplaceable. Now replaced. So are the old owners, a lovely couple called Brigitte and Martin Skan. New proprietor is Ian Livingstone, a real estate developer. Andrew Stembridge, Crome's successor, is very pleasant.

The restaurant had a Michelin star under Crome. That's gone. It's not as good as it was. Chef is Luke Matthews. The bread was horrific, cold, clammy, tough; the menu unexciting. I missed the historic double-baked Emmenthal soufflé. The set dinner, including coffee, petit fours and service, was £65. The back of the menu listed extra courses. Nobody directed us to them, or to desserts that took 20 minutes. Normally they're pointed out early on.

The freebie pea and mint soup was brilliant, my lobster cocktail clumsy with strange mayonnaise. I left most of it. I asked for more lemon. Never got it. Geraldine thought her crab starter was great, 'Not in my book,' I said, having tasted it. 'It's too refined for you,' was her response. 'The crab seemed old,' I continued. 'Hope it got a birthday card from the Queen before it died.' My main course fish was a bit overcooked. Not terrible, but far from great. The panettone bread and butter pudding was too moist. English bread and butter pud is better. On the way out we passed a lonely grand piano. 'You had a pianist before,' I observed to Andrew Stembridge. 'He got past his best,' was the reply. 'Why not get another one? It's better than piped music,' I advised.

Chewton Glen's still nice. Their set tea was absolutely superb. The hotel's been tarted up. Adequately, except for the nauseous deep purple dining room. It used to be cheerful yellow. The breakfast waiter greeted me with 'Good morning, Mr Winter'. This doesn't indicate a tight ship. To Andrew Stembridge's credit, he removed Peter Crome's 'no jeans' rule. Bit late for me as I now wear pyjamas.

The Mill at Gordleton, a restaurant in Lymington, Hampshire, is owned by Liz and Andy Cottingham. Inside it looks like a 1940s roadhouse. Outside is a pond with ducks.

Some hot and excellent rolls were offered. Andy took our order. I started with pâté of fresh chicken livers with mixed leaves, toasted brioche and apple chutney. I dictated: 'Very, very nice. Delicate taste. Interesting.' I followed with rump of Welsh lamb marinated in provençal herbs with garlic, spinach leaves and a rich lamb gravy. There were three enormous pieces of lamb and a lot of veg. It was pleasant.

Geraldine started with a trio of salmon: warm poached, oak-smoked and marinated. 'This is just scrumptious,' she said. She went on to seared scallops and roast loin of cod. She liked that too.

I ended with sticky toffee pudding with walnuts, banana ice cream and coffee sauce. I expected it to be white but it was dark brown. I don't like that colour. It puts me off. The pudding was adequate.

Let me recommend **Lainston House** near Winchester: excellent food, beautifully decorated 17th-century house, with super-attentive staff.

Nomansland is not a First World War no-go area, it's a village on the edge of the New Forest. The **Restaurant and Bistro Les Mirabelles**, next to the Nomansland Methodist church, was recommended to me by Martin Skaan, the owner of Chewton Glen. It is very Provençal, with hops wreathed around arches and a French doll on every table. Claude Laage, the co-owner with fellow Frenchman Eric Nicolas, explained this is 'instead of flowers, which you have to change every week'. Very French, that. There was a very posh, large menu, as well as a blackboard menu headed 'Pigs', with a picture of a pig on top. The wine list offered a substantial selection of half bottles, which is excellent and rare.

My pastry basket with scallops in it was genuinely tasty, with a nice sauce. Vanessa's John Dory was not on the bone. Fish always tastes less interesting filleted, unless it's fried. Hers tasted of very little, and was accompanied by a sort of raspberry sauce. For dessert I had a fondant au chocolat, which was a very good hot chocolate mousse, runny on the inside, crisp on the surface, sitting in a sea of creamy custard.

Lord Montagu of Beaulieu recommended I visit the **Thatched Cottage** in Brockenhurst, Hampshire. Rambling roses up the wall, baskets brimful to overflowing with flowers. We arrived at 12.40pm, announced by the shouts of a driver enraged that I had turned into the parking area without signalling. 'That's a man in a hurry,' said Robert Matysik, a member of the family that owns the place. 'I'm such a terrible driver, I'm used to it,' I responded cheerfully. We wandered into the restaurant, all very twee and olde worlde. I turned my attention to the open-plan kitchen, where a basket of small sausage rolls attracted my eye. I took one. This was definitely the best sausage roll I have ever eaten. It was made of New Forest venison, still warm from the oven. I grabbed another.

Then we sat down to eat. There were three home-made breads on offer – not very good and none of them warm. Definitely a minus. An iced blueberry soup was served as a freebie starter with my old friend the venison sausage roll, except now the roll was cold and not the better for it. I had excellent smoked venison for a first course. My main course of lamb wrapped in a rösti of potato, leek and garlic was only fair. The dessert shot things up the scale again. My cup of cappuccino came with a handle of meringue and whipped cream on top. I had two more at the table and three with coffee in the lounge.

Instead of driving to The Ivy for Saturday lunch, Vanessa redirected me to the **Alford Arms** in Frithsden. It was very pretty. White stucco, on the edge of a charming Hertfordshire village. Excellent countryside. Trestle tables outside were too communal and too uncomfortable for one in my delicate condition: I think the medical term is egomania. Inside I surveyed the menu. For a starter I chose roast ham, bubble-and-squeak hollandaise and poached egg. Then I had the fish cake, followed by bread-and-butter pudding, which was nice. The warm chocolate brownie was very good too, crisp outside and then runny in the middle. I would describe the food as robust to highly pleasant – good Middle England fodder.

The **Auberge du Lac** near Welwyn in Hertfordshire is like a little house with statues and tables outside and a nice view including, not surprisingly, a lake. All slightly spoiled by a clubhouse opposite. 'Apparently it's Nick Faldo's golf thing,' informed Paola. 'Pull it down,' I suggested. The weather wasn't good enough to eat outside, but the interior is quietly elegant.

The Auberge is very pleasant with a delightfully genteel clientele. It's all quintessentially British, so it was no surprise to learn it's owned by a German company based in Hong Kong. There must be something left in England owned by the English, although sometimes I doubt it.

The chef, Phil Thompson, took over when Jean-Christophe Novelli was fired, or not fired, according to who you believe. The set lunch was £28.50 for three courses, including two glasses of wine per person, plus 10% service. Shortly after my visit they raised it £1, surely reckoning that if I'd been there it must be worth more.

After I'd declined Hildon water and been saved by Evian, they gave us really excellent canapés. A smoked salmon croissant, parmesan cheese straws and fromage blanc mousse. I greatly liked them.

We both chose pan-seared smoked salmon, jersey royals and watercress salad with vanilla mayonnaise. It was grossly substantial for a starter, but they like a lot for their money in the suburbs. Or the stockbroker belt. Or whatever areas housing strange people are called.

There was a choice of five breads: bacon and onion, walnut and raisin, sunflower, mascarpone and chive. Main course was pan-roast fillet of haddock with sautéed greens, brown shrimps and white wine cream. Separately we ordered mashed potatoes, spring carrots and green beans. It was beautifully and speedily presented, not overdressed.

Paola had fresh fruit, artistically laid out, for dessert. I had Grand Marnier parfait with chocolate tart and oranges in caramel. The tart was totally superb. Close to historic.

'The tables are well spaced apart,' I observed to Paola. 'You can certainly hear yourself talk. It's very important when I eat I can hear myself talk, because I always say such interesting things.' 'Yes, you like the sound of your own voice,' added Paola. 'You are your own favourite subject.' I felt like responding, 'Name a better one,' but modestly forbade.

Then we got eight petit fours. Paola took the biggest, chocolate with raspberry on top. I had a chocolate toffee one. 'Delicious,' observed Paola. 'They're really fresh.' It was all good.

The excellent service sadly collapsed at the end. I dropped my napkin on the floor as I was drinking my mint tea. They picked it up, and didn't replace it. So I had to wipe my lips with my fingers. This is very vulgar, but certainly not the last vulgar thing I'll do in my life.

In my opinion (the one that counts) we British can boast of two gargantuan gastronomic achievements. One is the traditional English tea with crumpets, scones, fairy cakes, thinly sliced sandwiches et al.

Our other fantastic contribution is the Great British Fry-Up. Using every inch of my skill I can, on a rare day, get the following ingredients onto a plate in good order: fried eggs, grilled tomatoes, fried bread, sausages, baked beans, mushrooms, crispy bacon. When I'm asked what my last meal should be (and, amazingly, I frequently am) I reply, 'The great British fry-up.' Never mind your Gordon Ramsay and your plates decorated with moronic squiggles. GBFU beats them all.

At the **Bird in Hand** pub in Gosmore, a delightful Hertfordshire village, they gave me a nice table in the window facing a fireplace, which, being summer, was unlit. Leslie Hendry, the co-owner, serves; his wife Carol cooks. The menu offered home-made steak and kidney pie, chicken and mushroom pie, liver and bacon with mash. Desserts included spotted dick, treacle pudding and chocolate sponge. My sort of menu. Then I spotted the egg, bacon, sausage and beans.

'I'd rather have a jacket potato instead of chips,' I said. Paola chipped in (geddit?) with, 'You can't have a jacket potato with a fry-up because you dunk the chips in the egg.' Thus spoke a true expert. It was all splendidly robust.

To finish I had treacle pudding with custard and Billy Boy, a local ice cream. The bill was only £18.20. I gave them £25 because everyone was so pleasant.

In Ayot St Lawrence in Hertfordshire I drove the short distance to the 14th-century **Brocket Arms**. A nice girl behind the bar said, 'You can only have baguettes. The kitchen's overstretched.'

I strolled into the kitchen. Two men were working and a very pretty girl, who looked 10 years old, was taking plates out. 'Good morning,' I said, 'I'm Michael Winner.' With these magic words Toby Wingfield-Digby, the boss, agreed to let me have proper food.

On a counter were two stews with filo pastry on top. 'I'll have one of those,' I said. Toby advised one was venison, one steak and kidney. The 'waitress', Bethany, was the daughter of Colin who was helping Toby.

We went into a lovely garden and sat in the sun on a bench near a flowering cherry tree. My pie or stew (whichever) arrived with boiled potatoes and peas. The venison was delicious. Tender with a lovely sauce. Very good vegetables.

I returned to the kitchen where Toby recommended home-made apple crumble with ice cream. A lady with a turban, Sandra, was helping out. It was a delightfully unpretentious family atmosphere. The crumble was terrific.

I do end up in strange places. It maybe pushing it to call the **Bull of Cottered** strange. But then I'm used to Kensington High Street. This bull is in Hertfordshire, near Buntingford. I went for lunch one Saturday. Pubs, restaurants and hotels outside London usually don't offer Saturday lunch. That's bizarre. The

Bull is open seven days a week. I mention that in case you get lost and end up at Cottered. If you do you'll get a perfectly good meal.

The Bull itself is a straightforward English pub with a highly ambitious menu. I can't be bothered to detail it because that would take for ever. It's the sort of menu you might find in Mayfair. Being a poor boy from Willesden I kept things simple.

I ordered French onion soup with a cheese crouton followed by a home-made beefburger with mature cheddar and bacon. The soup was fine, very French. My hamburger was a bit too well done. I should have asked for it to be rare. But it was okay and the new potatoes with it were superb.

I went mad and ordered four desserts. A sticky date cake, a 'luxury' bread and butter pudding, an apple and raspberry crumble, a vanilla ice cream and a chocolate chip ice cream. I only ate a bit of each dessert. The date cake was best because it's very difficult to do and theirs was perfect. All the rest was good.

As I left Darren, the boss, said, 'In the evenings cloth napkins come out.' 'It wouldn't have killed you to bring one out for me,' I responded. 'I had to put up with a ghastly red paper thing.'

Dropping into a pub called the **Fox and Hounds** in Barley, Hertfordshire, I watched, riveted, as a plate of pork with Yorkshire pudding went by, left to right. 'Do you serve Yorkshire pudding with lamb?' I asked Caroline Cox, the landlady. She said: 'Yes, it goes with everything.' So the reader who wrote in and said I was common because I had Yorkshire pudding with lamb is a twit. I'm common because I come from Willesden. What other reason is needed? It was a very nice pub.

I phoned Martin Roberts, the boss at the ivy-covered **Greyhound Inn** in the pretty Hertfordshire village of Aldbury. 'We're coming to lunch,' I said. 'Six of us.' Stating things as fact is a good way of getting what you want. Mr Roberts was unconcerned. 'We're used to hundreds on Sunday,' he said. That did not augur well.

On arrival we were shown to a wooden table in a front room overlooking the village, with a bookcase and an old fireplace. The first thing I tasted was someone else's duck pâté. It was admirable. Nice texture. The bread was good, even though the butter was in foil. I had potato wedges with a chilli and garlic dip. The potatoes reminded me of World War II when food was food and not chemical twaddle. My lamb was the most generous portion I've ever seen, set around a large bone. It was every bit as good as the meat from my butcher, R Allen of Mount Street, or at Claridge's or The Dorchester. Home-made chips appeared for me, with some really old-fashioned, lovely cauliflower cheese and robust carrots and beans. Treacle tart was like schooldays: thick, not heavy on finesse, but tip-top. All this is pretty remarkable for a pub. 'In high season we do 2,500 customers a week,' said Martin. 'We've pushed about 300 meals through today so far.' It is rare that quantity and quality go hand in hand.

P.S. Martin Roberts has now left, but I understand it's still good.

In 1941 my family moved to Hitchin in Hertfordshire. Hitchin was a pleasant town then, as it is today. There are some nice old houses. Down the cobbled street off the attractive main square is **Just 32**. Unsurprisingly at No 32.

Just 32 is oak-beamed and olde worlde. The manager, Lockman Uddim, is exemplary. He told me the place was built in 1600. It's a pleasing room, hoop chairs, wooden floor, yellow cloths. Every table adorned by a sunflower.

Paola ordered roasted sea bass. She liked it. 'I'll have the slowly pan-fried duck breast with dauphinoise potatoes and a red compote port dressing,' I announced. 'Any preference how you'd like that cooked, sir?' asked Lockman. 'I don't want it pink. Pink duck doesn't amuse me,' I advised.

I started with corn and lemongrass soup served with sesame seed puff and finished with coriander oil. 'This soup would be a credit to any restaurant anywhere,' I dictated into my tape. It could have been a bit hotter. The duck was overcooked. Probably because I'd asked for it that way by mistake. The sauce was good. The carrots and cauliflower tasted like the real, chemical-free veg I ate during the war.

They had rum baba with roast peaches in syrup and chantilly cream, made on the premises. That's an old-fashioned dessert. It was fine.

The first time I ever wrote about food in the *Sunday Times* I listed 10 restaurant 'Winners'. One was the Loch Fyne Oyster Bar near Inveraray, on the west coast of Scotland. I'd been filming there and met the owner. Johnny Noble. Mr Noble inhabited a mansion, which I nearly used as a location.

I'll never forget his kitchen. It was filthy beyond belief. I can still see the mould, the old food, the unwashed plates and cutlery. He personally made me a cup of tea. The bravest thing I ever did in my life was to drink it. Johnny has been, for many years, in the great restaurant in the sky. I hope he's not in charge of hygiene.

There are 23 **Loch Fyne** restaurants owned by a company no longer related to Mr Noble's original, except they get most of their produce from the Loch Fyne suppliers. The oysters apparently are delivered three times a week. We went to a Loch Fyne restaurant in Barnet.

I chose 'Loch Fyne Ashet Bradan Rost Bradan Orach smoked salmon and gravadlax'. Followed by a pair of Loch Fyne kippers. Well, if they're good enough for John Prescott, they're good enough for me. The kippers were excellent. The Bradan Rost smoked salmon was too chewy for me. The rest was good.

Geraldine ordered 'hot and cold shellfish platter with whole crab or whole lobster'. She chose crab (£25.95) as opposed to lobster (£34.95). They've obviously got a bob or two, these people who live in Barnet. She got an enormous portion of fish and shellfish on a multi-storey plate holder. She said, 'It must be for two.' She loved the fish but wasn't happy with the mayonnaise. 'It's ready made,' she complained, 'in France it's all fresh.' I felt it indiscreet to point out this was Barnet. Which ain't France by a long way.

I was awakened at 7.15am by loud moaning and groaning. Not a companion with food poisoning, but something in the pipes. There was whistling, then a rumble, a sound like an old tugboat motor dying, high wind noises. This was at the **Pendley Manor Hotel**, Tring, Hertfordshire, described in the brochure as 'a setting which speaks of tranquillity'. The peak of non-tranquillity continued until 7.50am, then subsided, but for the next hour strange noises came back, as if a monster, now caged, was trying to fight his way out. Forced to rise, I read the brochure further: The hotel (built in 1872) had been 'transformed to its former glory, allowing guests to enjoy once more the distinguished elegance and beauty of the Victorian era'. Breakfast was ordered at 9.09am and arrived at 9.14am. A world record for a cooked breakfast. I thought it was pretty good. Nine pats of unwrapped butter, a small but nice portion of egg, sausage, tomato and mushrooms, and orange juice they assured me was fresh. The general manager, Mr Michael Tadros, was charming and very apologetic about my being disturbed. Well, it wasn't his fault. Craydown Ltd, who own the hotel, obviously thought Victorian plumbing carried its own elegance.

Letchworth, Hertfordshire was one of the first garden cities, well designed, tree-lined avenues, splendid architecture. I returned to Letchworth recently. Like all British cities, it had not improved. There were the usual chain restaurants – a Pizza Hut here, something else unappetising there. We settled on **Simmons Bakers** in Eastcheap. In the front a sales counter, at the back a café. Very pleasant really. Flowers on the tables, black hooped chairs, imitation Victorian marble-topped tables.

It was a very friendly restaurant. People kept wandering over and chatting and asking for autographs. At the counter I ordered: 'Two fried eggs, bacon, a jacket potato . . . ' 'All on the same plate?' asked Lisa Chamberlain, a delightful Saturday assistant, still at school. 'I haven't finished yet,' I said, 'and some baked beans all on the same plate. I'll have sausages as well. If you can't get it on one plate I'll have two.' While ordering I took a chocolate-coated doughnut and ate that. Absolutely splendid. Incomparably better than the ones at Gordon Ramsay's Boxwood Café.

The staff were all efficient, cheerful and charming. A lesson to the legions of snotty restaurant employees in London. Everything about the food was excellent. The eggs were cooked correctly, the sausages were tasty. If this place was near my house I'd go there frequently. My staff would be ecstatic. Simmons has a number of these venues throughout Hertfordshire. What must I pay the Simmons people to open in Holland Park, I wonder?

I could easily compose a blistering review of **Sopwell House and Country Club** in St Albans. I won't, because it does a very good job for people who want that sort of thing. Plus the owner, Abraham Bejerano, is a great rarity: a charming Israeli.

Cont'd

Sopwell House is a messed-about building, once the home of Lord Mountbatten. The England football team often stay there. I recognised the place when a soccer scandal was rampant and TV commentators stood outside the entrance recounting its development. The corridors offer framed and signed football shirts. Outside, the gardens are beautifully kept.

The main hotel restaurant, Magnolia, offers brass rails, globe lights, lanterns, candelabra, a bright white statue of a Grecian woman holding an urn and a saucer, trellis work, plants, the kitchen sink. They exhibited a 'Concept of the Kitchen' dinner menu. I had chunky chicken livers, which were okay, then a dried-up, cloying Dover sole. It took forever to get a dessert menu and then to get the dessert. Their sticky toffee pudding wasn't hot and didn't taste of toffee.

Breakfast took far too long to come. But, most intelligently, they'd put the saucer over the espresso cup to keep it hot. I'd specifically asked for marmalade. I got six jars of confiture. None was marmalade.

The sign on an old building read: 'Inn **Wellington** village pub dining AD 1352.' It's in Welwyn village, which is very pretty. Not like the rubbish they've put up in the new town.

The Wellington menu included beef and Guinness pie, cod and chips, fish pie, lamb shank in red wine and rosemary and many other excellent-sounding dishes. I chose a starter of crispy dipping mushrooms, deep-fried, served with a chilli sauce and home-made yoghurt and dill dip. Princess ordered baked asparagus parcel with tomato and basil topped with glazed goat's cheese served with crisp herb salad. I ordered grilled Scotch fillet steak with chunky chips, spring vegetables and béarnaise sauce for my main course.

As the supremely efficient waitress, Janet Chance, wrote everything down we got exactly what we ordered. Unlike many times in posh restaurants, before I insisted on a pad being produced, when we certainly did not.

The Wellington portions were enormous. Big enough for three people at least. But very good. The vegetables were perfect. The bubble and squeak exemplary. With my steak I got 10 enormous chunky chips. Three would have been enough. But they beat the chips at most West End restaurants by a long way. Those are usually bought in, pre-sliced. For dessert I had treacle tart (good, but not enough treacle taste) and a double chocolate brownie with mint choc ice cream. This was not a brownie. It was a first class chocolate pudding with a soft interior.

Princess observed: 'It's like you've been round to a friend for Sunday lunch.' That's a considerable, and well-deserved, compliment.

At the Ramada Jarvis hotel in Harbour Parade, Ramsgate, you look out on to a bleak harbour. In my modest suite there were two TV sets, one in the tiny sitting area, one opposite the bed. Only the bedroom one worked. The curtains were manipulated by hand.

It's a hideous modern building on the seafront. My suite was called Sundown. Since it was pitch black outside this seemed reasonably appropriate.

In the Ramada dining room the menu was very posh, too much so for a simple hotel. But the food wasn't bad at all. I had roast loin of pork stuffed with black pudding. The duchess potatoes with it were amazing. This now called the **Kent International Hotel**.

The dining room had one glass wall revealing the swimming pool. A fat woman in a red striped bathing costume was walking about. This rather put me off. But not as much as the fat lady would have been if she'd been in the dining room watching me walk round the pool.

Wilmslow Road in Manchester is known as 'the curry mile' because it's so full of Indian restaurants. Locals claim 500 of them line the street. I was taken to one, **Lal Qila**, which offers the standard decor for Indian restaurants in England: white tablecloths with a yellow cloth over them, simple chairs, a patterned Indian carpet and much fake greenery. I greatly liked the food. It reminded me of the tasty meals served at an Indian restaurant I frequented in Cambridge when I was a student.

I get letters saying, 'You don't go up north enough.' Perhaps you want me at the North Pole, never to return. Instead I recently visited Manchester.

Much as I'd rather not recall it, we must deal with lunch at the **Lowry** hotel. The people attending it were lovely. The food, ugh, ugh, ugh. The soup, described as 'creamed leak (sic) and sweet potato with cinnamon toast and chives' was the best part of a miserable meal. Not terrible. The main course was memorably unpleasant.

Dessert was described on the menu as 'mulled wine posset with poached pear and raisin shortbread'. It was like a tired mousse. Then came petit fours that were down to standard.

The menu announced, 'Food comes first, then morals – Bertolt Brecht.' Bertie obviously hadn't eaten at the Lowry hotel.

In Manchester, on a tour to meet the people, I stayed at the **Meridien Victoria & Albert**. This is a delightfully froufrou, overdecorated oddity with rooms named after Granada TV series. My suite was the Wealth of the Windsors, which I was told had something to do with *Brideshead Revisited*. The shower curtain had great swags and curls on it, as if designed for a grand ballroom. I was particularly impressed with Simon Murphy, the deputy manager, who'd obviously been told to watch my every move. He was cheery and hospitable.

Rochdale borders the north of Manchester. **Nutters** is set in grounds of considerable beauty. As we arrived Rodney Nutter, in evening dress at 12.15pm – well, he's restaurant manager – got out of a personalised number-plated 4x4.

Nutters is in a lovely 18th-century gothic mansion once owned by the grandfather of the late attorney-general Hartley Shawcross. Now Rodney's son Andrew, who's been on TV (who in catering hasn't?), is the chef.

The starters were little welsh rarebits, the best I've ever eaten, plus other bits and pieces including large smoked salmon canapés. I liked my scallops but the black pudding was in such thin slivers I couldn't taste it. And it was the black pudding that led me to place the order. The dessert was new-season plums with walnut crumble and port syrup. A very decent meal.

At **Yang Sing** in Manchester I thought the food was tasty, though it was all a bit gooey for Vanessa. I tried a roast pigeon, which appeared on my plate with a dummy white swan. Even the pigeon head was sitting there staring at me. With it was a mustard sauce and a spicy sauce. I had Peking-style dumplings, asparagus in a Sichuan sauce, bean curd with two sauces, prawns and scallops with a light saffron sauce, spicy nut dumplings, corn dumplings, spring onion in a pancake and more. This was one of my few dinners ever in Manchester – pleasing, I hope, for those who think I solely haunt the effete and overstylised south.

The **Trattoria Sorrento**, in Teddington High Street, Middlesex, is a downmarket cousin of the Trattoria Terraza group, which first made me aware of Italian restaurants in the early 1960s. Chianti bottles hung from the ceiling; there were deer antlers, pink tablecloths and, behind us, a mural of Italy. On the menu were things you never see any more: egg mayonnaise, avocado vinegarette (sic) and prawn cocktail. There was a list of 'Today's specials' on the menu and another on a blackboard. They were both different. My starter sardines were mediocre, tasteless and looked peculiar. The heads, almost parted from the body, seemed to be in agony. My main course trout came without lemon. It was perfectly cooked, but I didn't like it. The service was excellent.

On my next visit to Teddington, I was surprised to see my review, much blown up, displayed on the window of the Trattoria Sorrento. On closer reading, I realised they'd doctored the article to make it favourable. A letter to the local trading standards officer had the piece down in seconds. But I have to admire their cheek. Nice to know they thought people would care what I'd written.

Sausage rolls are extremely difficult. They're one of my favourites. Where can you get a good sausage roll these days? At **Byfords** in Holt, a small town in Norfolk. It's a long way to go for a sausage roll.

Byfords is large and quaint. It serves food, cakes, flapjacks. Attached to it is a shop selling much the same; above it, luxurious rooms are let at £130 a night. There's an exposed brick wall. A massive pile of logs for the real fireplace was stacked next to my bay window table. A mouth-watering display of cakes rested on the wide window ledge. The home-made bread was superb. So was my aromatic crispy duck soup. I thought Duck Soup was just the name of a Marx Brothers movie. I tried a vanilla milkshake. 'Rather thin,' I dictated into my tape. I tried a Bakewell tart. Poor. Then a Victoria sponge. Not good at all, very clammy. Paola was having cheese on toast with apple and mint chutney. I ate some. It was fantastic. The banana bread was very good too. I was beginning to feel rather bloated. So we left.

When I arrived at **Fishes** restaurant in Burnham Market, Norfolk a sign on the door read: 'Fishes restaurant is looking for an enthusiastic, amiable, confident person with a passion for good food and wine to join our front-of-house team.' I thought of applying but decided I didn't measure up.

It's a pleasant room – two rooms, actually – the one we were in had a log fire and bookshelves. It looked out on to the quaint village street. Matthew and Caroline Owsley-Brown own it. He cooks, she does front of house.

On the menu was tandoori porbeagle shark, pilau rice, kachumba raita, mango chutney and poppadom, mash and one vegetable. I ordered that. I was assured everything was freshly made on the premises.

Paola started with sardine becca ficcu, slow-roast tomato and salad. I had Norfolk smoked eel, foie gras and piquillo, pepper terrine, chilli salt and toasted brioche. The brioche came in a napkin. There were red bloodstains on it going through all the folds.

The restaurant manager, Neil Foster, came over. 'It's Caroline's blood,' he explained helpfully. 'She cut her finger.' 'At least she's the owner,' I said. 'You're not serving blood from a stranger. It's as you promise: 'made fresh on the premises'.' Caroline was very apologetic. 'Never mind,' I said consolingly, 'if you're O rhesus negative I could have a transfusion.' My starter, with or without blood was superb. I tried Paola's sardine thing and it was very tasty indeed. My tandoori shark was terrific.

Paola remarked how friendly everyone was from the beginning and what a difference it made. 'Particularly commendable as Caroline was suffering from blood loss,' I observed.

It's difficult, though not impossible, to criticise a hotel when the staff are so welcoming as they are at the **Hoste Arms** in Burnham Market, Norfolk. It's massively to the credit of the owners, Paul Whittome and his wife, Jeanne. I've never come across people who so genuinely put 'hospitality' into the absurdly named 'hospitality industry'.

Now down to basics. My suite was beyond belief bizarre. It was called the Penthouse. Yet it was on a low second floor with other rooms adjacent. The only thing sky high about it was the price – £396 a night. This in a glorified pub in a 'quaint' village. I was in the Zulu wing. Honestly. You couldn't make it up. Apparently Jeanne had connections with Zululand.

The room featured lumpish lamps with ghastly oversized lampshades fringed with exotic fur and feathers; endless prints of African animals on fabrics and walls; six bright red things, which resembled straw hats, fixed to the wall; and a peculiar framed shield-like collage of animal skins. This is not a hotel where the animal rights people should hold their convention.

The bathroom had second-rate products in it and not many of them. The sinks were awful pudding basins with taps you had to operate like the joystick of an aeroplane. The bathroom windows were – if you'll excuse the word in a refined newspaper – at genital level. So if you mistakenly wandered about naked (in my case not a pretty sight!) people in the car park saw all.

Breakfast was a disaster. The coffee was tepid so we sent it back. The croissants were the most horrible I've ever tasted.

The staff were vastly efficient. I was brushing my teeth one morning and heard a clonk. A gold cap rolled down the plughole. The hotel returned it to me in a neat white envelope within half an hour.

I'm happy to say Sunday lunch was terrific. The roast beef and Yorkshire pudding were excellent. For dessert I had a trio of apple crumble, milkshake and mousse. It was a delight.

I've had some terrible meals in my life, but none so ridiculous and overpriced as at the **Devonshire Arms** in Bolton Abbey, North Yorkshire. Pity, really, because in general I liked the hotel. The owners, Stoker and Amanda, Duke and Duchess of Devonshire, are splendid people whom I consider friends. Although now that may not be reciprocated.

The 'refined' restaurant (their brochure's description) is called the Burlington. The set three-course dinner is £58. Coffee is £5 extra. Add the 'optional' 12.5% service charge and it becomes £70.88. In the Yorkshire Dales, where rent is two sheep and a goat.

I started with clammy, heavy and tired roast veal sweetbread, onion purée, pig's trotter croquette. It was very chewy; been somewhere too long. Before the Burlington sweetbread we had white mush, bitter confit of tomatoes, olives and 'tomato air'. Put that in your pipe and smoke it.

My main course was dry turbot. Dreadful. The service was slow to ludicrous until I complained. Then it was slow to slow. For dessert I had apple mousse in pastry with frothy stuff around it. Tasted of nothing. As for it being 'chic' (as per the brochure), I was about the only man wearing a jacket.

The Devonshire Arms has a brasserie with a sensible menu. Smoked haddock, roast duck, Devonshire burger, vanilla cheesecake. Should have dined there.

The hotel, set in stunning countryside, was a coaching inn 350 years ago. The staff are superb, a credit to the managing director, Iain Shelton, and general manager, Brian van Oosten. My suite was delightful. Breakfast bacon, egg and sausage arrived without salt or pepper but were extremely good. Afternoon tea was excellent, including a little cake called a financier, which had taste and texture so perfect I'll remember it for ever.

For atmosphere, it's hard to beat Guilian Alonzi's **Harbour Bar**, a 1950s American-style diner in Scarborough. The customers are local tear-aways and wonderful old ladies. The ice cream is the best I ever had.

Guidebooks had produced two dreadful overnight places in Tadcaster and I had no reason to think the **Hazlewood Castle hotel** would be any better. It's a castle first mentioned in the Domesday Book.

The public rooms are pleasing and understated. The suite was excellent. Bit chintzy, but I don't mind that. There were no face flannels in the bathroom, but two packets of Smarties on the pillows. I like Smarties.

The dining room is called 1086. It was grotesque. Quite unlike the restrained elegance of the rest of the hotel. Black tables without cloths, upright chairs, a bar with low hanging lights, pink bar stools, beige sofas – a total mess.

The restaurant manager, Simon Chiu, took our order and repeated it twice to be sure he got it right. That's clever. The canapés were terrific, fried veggies I believe, also a pleasing dip of asparagus and truffle oil and marvellous, spindly cheese straws.

I asked to see the hotel's general manager and a chef turned up. He introduced himself as John Benson-Smith. He said: 'I'm everything. I'm equivalent of the chef-patron.'

The food was absolutely splendid. Stupidly (thus maintaining my normal stance) I ordered squab pigeon with foie gras and sweet potato to start and then roast partridge with puy lentils, cannelloni and red wine sauce to follow. Silly that. They're quite similar small birds that get shot a lot. Portions were enormous: 'Each one big enough for 23 people,' I dictated on my tape. But everything was superb.

'Excuse me!' I shouted downstairs to the receptionist. 'There are two people in the lounge here without a drink. Can you tell me what year they arrived?' At this the manager, who had been having a long conversation about wine with a customer and ignoring me, came running. After that the service was good. I was at the

Cont'd
Langley Castle, a tarted-up 14th-century pile in Langley-on-Tyne, Northumberland. The North is peopled by delightful residents, but the food is generally Langley Castle-style. Grandly described hors d'oeuvres were six bowls of dried-up sausage and tinned beans, followed, believe it or not, by a heavy sorbet. The duck was over-cooked strips, the apple tart so solid you needed a power drill to break the pastry. When the charming, efficient young waitress said, 'I hope you enjoyed your meal, sir.' I replied, honestly, 'The service was excellent.'

Slaley Hall, a hotel in Hexham, Northumberland, is a disaster. It's the most appallingly decorated place I've ever been in. My sort-of suite – I say 'sort-of' because there's a lounge area and a wall that only partly divides it from the bedroom – had a bath in the middle of the sitting area underneath a window. There was ample room for the bath to replace a ridiculous double shower out of which water trickled. Were they under instructions to save water? At £300 a night, the ability to clean oneself properly should be thrown in.

The room was all dark and gloomy. A variety of dreary tartans, floor coverings, wall coverings – every piece of furniture seemed to be different, vying for awfulness. There's a saying: 'It had everything but the kitchen sink.' My room had the kitchen sink, in the form of this lunatic bath. It also had a putter, a plastic 'dustpan' and golf balls to knock in. You could leap out of the bath and play naked putting.

Dinner was down to standard. So was the dining room. Another edifice of gloom. Dark blinds one-third down, covering a lovely view of the countryside. Dark walls, enormous vulgar chairs, with immensely high backs and tassels, dwarfed the tables. Glass-paintings lit so dimly you couldn't see what they pictured. And the coup de grace – dreadful piped music.

I was told the bread had been freshly made by the pastry chef. So what? It was mediocre. My asparagus was hardly cooked at all, would have been better in a salad. The hollandaise sauce tasted bitter. The home-made chips were squashy. My calves' liver was unbelievably soft and gooey. The Northumbrian bacon was the only good thing and there was only a tiny bit of that. My dessert of Tate & Lyle treacle sponge had the tiniest bit of treacle on top of white stodge. The hotel manager, Neal Crocker, was superb. Pity he hasn't got anything worth managing.

The **Angel** pub in the picturesque Cotswold town of Burford, Oxfordshire, is a pleasant old place. It's opposite what was once a shop owned by an Austrian who sold Nazi memorabilia.

The dining area of the pub is Ikea-style. All modern tables. I chose Shetland queen

Cont'd

scallops with niçoise salad, shellfish sauce and then roast fore-rib of Scottish beef with Yorkshire pudding and red wine gravy. Geraldine enjoyed pork with good crackling. The roast potatoes were excellent, although not as good as Sir Michael Caine's. Then I ordered summer pudding with berry compote. Instead of mascarpone ice cream I asked for vanilla. Summer pudding: good. Ice cream: exceptionally good.

My mob visited the **Chequers Inn** at Fingest, in Oxfordshire, for Sunday lunch when on a location recce. It's a pretty place – the dining room is pink with oak beans, dried hops and wheelback chairs with padded seats. I chose the honeydew melon gondola, which had a 1950s look – sliced with a bit of orange bent over a stick topped by a glacé cherry. The soup was pea and mint, 'like posh mushy peas'. The beef and Yorkshire pud came swimming in gravy; the carrots and beans were overdone. It's a nice enough place – not a high rating on the Sunday lunch score, but not a disaster.

The general twee atmosphere at the **Malmaison** hotel in Oxford extended to my comfortable suite. In the bathroom there was Help the Paw Vitamin-Rich Hand Cream and Snoozers Are Losers Energy Patches.

Lunch was in the basement. Terrible piped music. A waitress's T-shirt read, 'Your plaice or mine'. It's that sort of hotel. 'All the ingredients come from within a 30-mile radius of the hotel,' said the general manager Stephen Woodhouse.

My cheese tart was brilliant. The duck a bit heavy. They should have gone beyond their 30-mile radius and found a better duck. Summing up: okay meal, extremely efficient general manager, over-egged but pleasant hotel.

'I'm a control freak,' said Raymond Blanc, boss of **Le Manoir de Quat' Saisons** near Oxford. 'I do everything. Everything in the hotel.' Le Manoir is an immense credit to Raymond. It's a beautifully run hotel, set in lovely grounds and with a two-Michelin-starred restaurant.

There's no dress code in Raymond's dining room. Here's some of the superb food I stuffed down. A starter of braised veal sweetbreads, cauliflower purée, wild mushrooms and truffles. Then grouse in a blackberry and red wine sauce. They were both delicious. And multi-historic pommes soufflés. My dessert was ice orgeat parfait and lemon confit in fine biscuit leaves, warm cherries.

There was a mini disaster with the tea. I asked for mint tea, fresh green mint leaves in hot water. Their leaves looked dried. It was apparently peppermint tea. 'It's the most pungent leaf you can get,' explained Raymond. That may be, but I didn't order it.

The day before for dinner I had a confit of foie gras with rhubarb compote and a toasted ginger brioche, then a delicious pigeon baked in a salt crust. All the food was fantastic.

The restaurant staff I saw were the gloomiest bunch ever to haunt a dining room. That's amazing as Raymond is effusive and cheerful. He went round tables smiling at everyone.

On a guided tour of his gardens and greenhouses, he greeted all the guests we passed. His reception staff smile. Why can't the restaurant people?

Reading that I was going to the **Mason Arms** in South Leigh, as guest of my friend the television writer Laurence Marks, Robert Warner of Woodstock, Oxfordshire, wrote to me, saying: 'You will either love it . . . or loathe it.' I loathed it. It was the most extraordinary meal I've ever had. Not because of the food, but because of the bizarre behaviour of the 'host', Gerry Stonhill, and his waiter, Roger Castel.

The pub itself is vastly, but not unpleasantly, overdecorated. There are photos, plates, prints, books, stuffed birds, carefully placed cigar boxes and, pretentiously laid out on a table, 'every armagnac from 1919 to 1993,' explained Marks.

The whole meal was ruined by constant, pathetic repartee from Gerry or Mr Castel. I came to have lunch with my friend Laurence Marks, a quiet-spoken gent who's always interesting. Not to participate in buffoon dialogue with the staff. The problem with Gerry is someone obviously told him he was a character and he believed them. That was a mistake.

Fat of the land

The B4027 runs north off the M40, shortly before you reach a hideous roundabout on the outskirts of Oxford. It is the sort of road I always feel greatly relieved to come upon; it smacks of the past, when tracks wobbled about between fields and occasional little villages.

It was about 1pm – lunchtime. I had made no reservations. We passed a ramshackle farm: barns with corrugated-iron roofs, cracked concrete courtyards and a sign saying '**Royal Oak Farm**: Teas'. 'It said light lunches, too,' said Vanessa. 'Let's try it,' I suggested.

I crossed a courtyard beset with fountains and strange garden ornaments of girls sitting on poles, and walked into the farm shop. I ventured through an open door that led to a concrete path through a back-garden area full of animals, many with pens named after them. There were African pygmy goats: Baldrick, born in March 1995, Capricorn, and many more. A large number of ducks, cockerels, pigs and other animalia abounded.

At the end of the path was a hut. In it were four tables, with four chairs round each and, at the rear, an opening to a kitchen. Nobody was there, but one of the tables was full of home-made cakes and biscuits that looked highly attractive. I walked back into the shop and the farmer's wife, Nathalie Soames, appeared. She offered an enormous array of home-made soups. I checked that one, at least, had no meat stock, Vanessa being almost vegetarian, and established that there were various quiches and ploughman's lunch. Drooling over the cakes, I assured Vanessa it would be terrific.

Vanessa's lentil and thyme soup would have graced any Michelin-starred establishment, as would my leek and orange. Bethany, the chef's three-year-old daughter, established herself. She had already told us which table to sit at.

'I have tea the same as my daddy,' she announced. 'I don't have sugar, I only have milk.' I accepted this fact. 'Are those scones?' I asked. 'Yes,' said Bethany. 'Are those more scones?' I continued, pointing to brown and white bags on the table. 'No, those are goat and chicken food, because people buy them to feed the animals.'

Bethany asked for apple juice and occasionally said loudly: 'Where is my apple juice?' Then she went to a full yell, 'Mummy, get my apple juice!' followed by: 'Is it coming, mummy?' When it did, she bashed the table to show exactly where she wanted it. This kid could take over any time I have a week off.

I had chosen a tomato, cheese and onion quiche; Vanessa had a ploughman's lunch. Both came with fresh salad. Mrs Soames offered salad dressing of mustard and garlic, spicy herb, Californian tomato, roasted garlic and mayonnaise, or salad cream. Not bad for a hut off a B road. The quiche was terrific and the cakes amazing. I'd tried a lemon and lime cookie before lunch. Now I had a chocolate fudge slice, some coffee sponge and a chocolate-orange chip shortbread. I started on the chocolate fudge slice, which was hard to cut, but unbelievably delicious. They all were. I was tempted to have meringue and clotted cream, with maybe a bit of pear and butterscotch flan, but narrowly chose against it.

Bethany was having lettuce and ham. 'And I want tea,' she added. 'I'll wait for my daddy to get it.' Then, after a brief silence: 'I've got a big shirt on today.'

I walked through the garden, where they serve teas and lunches on less rainy days, to see five ducks ganging up on another duck. They held it down and pecked at its face. *Death Wish* in animal land. When I came back, Mrs Soames explained it was an attempt to mate, and told me the cockerels also think they're ducks, so they 'tread' the ducks as well. Life on the land is riveting.

This place is a real find. If you want a meal that tastes like food, and not like over-mucked-about plate decoration, get out your road map – the nearest town is Headington, Oxfordshire. And bring me back a chocolate fudge slice, will you?

Knight club

It was on a Sunday film reconnaissance that my production designer suggested the **Sir Charles Napier** near Chinnor in Oxfordshire. I rang up. The owner, a nice lady called Julie Griffiths, said: 'We'll squeeze you in. How many will you be?' 'Six,' I replied, thinking this would cause a problem. It did. Julie could only manage two.

On a recent Sunday, years later, I booked with her daughter, the equally charming Caroline. I told my neighbour, the lyricist Don Black, that I was going. He said: 'You won't like it. The tables are very close together.' On the way I phoned again. 'Are the tables close together?' I asked. 'Not yours,' said Caroline. 'We're not that silly.'

We arrived at a pebbly car park to find the flintstone and brick inn next to a tacky housing estate. Julie showed us to a nice table by the window, facing a paved terrace and guests' cars. I was introduced to Caroline's husband, Chris, who does the wines. Chris said he wouldn't offer me the normal wines by the glass, he'd bring a special bottle and finish it himself later as a treat. 'I want you to try it,' he said, 'because it's quite an eclectic choice.' 'Don't give me a test, I'm useless,' I pleaded. It was a very smooth Hamilton Russell, South African Pinot Noir 1998. Chris altered his description of it to 'capricious'.

I ordered casserole of snails à la catalane. Why, I don't know. You have to be a twit to order a typical Spanish dish at an English pub in the middle of Oxfordshire. To compound my silliness I ordered a main course of bouillabaisse with saffron potatoes. Why didn't I order English stuff like roast pork with crackling (which I love), or roast beef, or even braised oxtail? I soon wished I had. There was a very dead bit of toast stuck in the middle of my starter. The snails were small, rubbery and of no taste whatsoever. The surrounding chopped-up veggies were quite nice. The bouillabaisse was poor. The white fish was all right but uninteresting, the sauce or soup with it was of no taste I've ever associated with bouillabaisse. Dull in the extreme.

Miss Lid enjoyed (though was not crazy about) both her starter of timbale of crab with lemon juice and her main course of pan-fried scallops with celeriac and truffle ravioli. She also praised her fresh orange juice.

The desserts were very good indeed. Miss Lid had hot date cake with toffee sauce. I thought it was terrific. Not overfancy, solid, lovely taste and texture. My pithivier of almonds and dried fruit had good flaky pastry and was a pleasant experience. There were no silly red squiggle decorations around the plate. Just two excellent, solid desserts deserving top marks.

The other diners were very nice people. There was a good atmosphere. Guests are obviously deeply loyal to the Sir Charles Napier. They were concerned I should write well of it. I liked them all, even though I feel compelled to write as I find.

Country ways

They were kind enough to put a large white cross on the croquet lawn at **Ston Easton Park**, Somerset, so my helicopter pilot could see it and not deposit me at the wrong hotel. I took this transport (50 minutes instead of two-and-a-half-hours) because there was a rail strike and I assumed the roads would be packed. As it happens, they weren't, and I looked down on fast-moving traffic some £1,500 the poorer.

The manager, Mr Kevin Marchant, came to greet us with a member of staff. As the luggage was being taken upstairs I caught sight of tea laid out on a round table, circling a bowl of flowers, in the highly impressive Georgian lounge. This was too much for me. I immediately started eating. I am normally a pig, but on this occasion I excelled myself. There were egg mayonnaise and cucumber sandwiches, carrot cake and coffee cake, éclairs and meringues, fruit cake and ginger cake, scones and a great deal more. Every item was utterly exceptional in its quality. The Earl Grey was served in a splendid room in first-rate crockery.

Ston Easton is an architectural gem dating from the mid-18th century. When I had tea the next day with its admirably hands-on owners, Peter and Christine Smedley, they explained they'd bought it from Sir William Rees-Mogg. 'Didn't know he had that sort of money,' I muttered, stuffing down a bakewell tart. Apparently he got it in wrecked condition, sold it on to the Smedleys who lived there, then 'as needs must' they opened it as a hotel in 1982. It is superbly decorated, in unison and with great taste, although my bathroom was terrible. Not only was it small, it looked like every item had come from a warehouse sale on a bad day. They've had a number of famous people to stay. 'Terry Wogan and Larry Hagman,' said Christine helpfully, 'and Cary Grant.' 'Before he died, of course,' added her husband, Peter.

Dinner, I'm sorry to say, was less impressive than the tea. We had home-made courgette and dill soup, which was all right. But the Dover sole, oddly served with slices of hot grapefruit on it, had definitely died of exhaustion after being on a lengthy diet. However, I greatly enjoyed (or should I say endured!) the gems of conversation from other tables. 'Was it under British mandate at the time?' 'Oh yes, very peaceful, a lot of Palestinians and very few Jews.' The lime sorbet was good and the room was elegant, but I'd call the food English-boring. This has now been taken over by Von Essen hotels. It is very good.

There are times, if things do not go absolutely splendidly, when it is better to give people A for effort than severe castigation. Such a moment occurred when I visited, of all places, Sheffield. **The Old Vicarage** is, as one might guess from the name, the old (1846) residence of the Vicar of Ridgeway. It is done out in a diluted version of northern overkill with just too many colours and bits and pieces abounding.

Cont'd

The first real surprise was finding a bowl of soft fruit in the lavatory – above the wash-basin, next to the pot-pourri, in a white china basket were raspberries, strawberries and gooseberries. I touched them to check they were real. I wondered if other people prodding them had done so before or after washing their hands, so I didn't eat any.

The owner and chef of this much-cared-for establishment is Mrs Tessa Bramley. She was just genuinely and unbelievably nice. So were her handsome son, Andrew, and his lovely fiancée, Justine, who run the dining room. Oh dear, I thought, I shall feel awful if I write a word of criticism about this place. But then came the canapés. Dinner after that ranged from very good to adequate to awful. Things did look up a bit with an exceptional dessert of baked chocolate pudding with hot fudge sauce and English custard.

Given the bird

A nice group met the helicopter as it landed on the lawn by **Dovecliff Hall**, a hotel outside Burton-on-Trent. They were the owners, Brian Moore and his wife Jeanne and their son Nick. 'I never thought the day would come when Michael Winner came up here to Staffordshire to this hotel,' said Jeanne. 'I never thought it would happen.' 'All good things come to an end,' I responded.

In the lobby, a delightful old lady was playing the piano. She looked as if she came from a 1950s movie with Joyce Grenfell and Alastair Sim. The whole place had that black-and-white atmosphere of times sadly gone by. Amazingly, Mary Green had not been brought in just to play for me. There was a wedding and she was the icing on the cake. Brian explained that after he'd spent 30 years in the family engineering business making taps and dies, his children fancied catering. Well, let's face it, taps and dies are not everybody's idea of a laugh. So he bought a couple of restaurants and then this pleasant country-house hotel.

Our room was very cheerful. Views of gardens and grounds, not over-tarted-up. They had the taps the wrong way round on the washbasin, hot on the right. To make it worse, the 'label' had come off, so I nearly scalded myself. Lunch was in a conservatory. I chose 'rillettes of pork-belly pork cooked in its own juices, shredded set and served with pickled vegetables'. It took longer to read than to eat. It was fine. For my main course I had baked supreme of chicken carved on to an asparagus sauce. Vanessa thought her sea bass was very good. My chicken was all right but ordinary. The veg were excellent.

The pastry chef, Mrs Samantha Dowie, came and told me how to make a chilled praline parfait served with a raspberry coulis. It was splendid to eat, but I never understand recipes. That's why we have chefs – to do the menial work.

We went for a walk by a river, not too strenuous, of course, and back for tea. Very fresh sandwiches, real old-English tea with scones, chocolate cake and strawberry tart. The next day daughter Tania was there. She'd been off duty. For some reason, Mary was still tinkling away. 'Do you just play the piano?' I asked. 'I have an electric organ as well,' said Mary. It was extremely delightful, the whole thing. Another world, really. Went back to normal when I left.

P.S. Now owned by Von Essen hotels. I like them. I visited. All went well.

It was windy and pouring with rain in Sutton, Surrey. Geraldine and I, umbrellas rampant, battled our way to **Finnigans**. It looked like your standard fish and chip place. A long, silver counter, then a few stairs up to a dining area. We proceeded in an orderly fashion to a table.

My pot of tea arrived. It was excellent. Very British. The bread and butter were fine, too. The cod arrived. It was superb. Moist, very good light batter, also pickled cucumbers and onions, excellent mushy peas. I ordered syrup sponge. The sponge was light, there was a pleasing taste of syrup. I dropped some on my shirt. Always a good sign.

I chose Michel's in Ripley, Surrey from a food guide. It's in a nice building that the owner, Michel Albina, assured me was a mixture of early Georgian and Queen Anne.

I ordered 'mixed leaves salad served with crispy Parma ham topped with poached skate with blackcurrant dressing', followed by 'pan-fried rib of beef served with vegetables in Yorkshire pudding finished with tomato coulis'. Geraldine chose the salad followed by 'papillote of salmon served with julienne vegetables scented with tarragon'.

The bread, made with molasses, honey and cumin, was truly excellent. The salad was tasteless, the blackcurrant dressing a mere decorative smear on the plate. The beef was okay. But the Yorkshire pudding was historic. For dessert I had 'cold lemon soufflé with pistachio custard'. It wasn't a soufflé, more a bland sort of mousse.

Michel's is perfectly all right as a pleasant local eating-place. The room is likeable and Michel Albina and his wife Dorothy – she's from Liverpool – are superb and caring hosts. The restaurant is now called **Drake's**.

Around lunchtime we were in New Malden. 'Now for a dreadful meal,' I muttered. 'It could be very good. We'll go to a pub and have some nice shepherd's pie,' said Geraldine, in her role of Little Mary Sunshine. 'I can't remember when I last saw shepherd's pie in a pub,' I sighed.

Geraldine spotted the **Royal Oak** in Coombe Road. A notice outside read: 'Family Lunch.' A Union Jack was waving from an intricately detailed Edwardian building. 'It looks quite dreadful to me,' I said into my tape recorder, 'but I'm going to risk it.'

It was very busy. 'If you wait at the bar, I'll get you a table in 10 minutes,' said the manager, Sean Doyle. 'I don't wait,' I said. Then I spotted an old lady on a banquette with a younger lady opposite. They had two spare places. 'Could we please join you?' I asked, politely as ever. And then, when the ladies said they'd be delighted, I added: 'It's very kind of you.'

The younger one, Lindy, was lunching with her mum, who's blind. Mum lives nearby in Wimbledon village. 'She can't eat any foreign food and this is typically English,' explained Lindy. Sunday lunch consisted of roast beef, chicken, lamb or vegetarian option. I chose lamb, Geraldine the chicken.

We got truly superb Yorkshire pudding with both the chicken and the lamb. The roast potatoes were very good. The cabbage, peas and carrots okay. So was the lamb. It was a perfectly respectable meal. So my dire predictions were wrong. That makes a change.

At the **Stepping Stones** pub in Westhumble, Surrey the whole area seemed deserted, yet we entered a packed bar and restaurant area. 'Where did all these people come from?' I wondered. I must have been bemused because I ordered a draught Guinness. Don't think I've ever done that before. I enjoyed it immensely. I peered over the bar into the kitchen at what seemed a highly efficient organisation. Plates were passing by. The food looked terrific.

I was hypnotised by some long sausages. 'They're from James Harris, a butcher in Reigate,' said the owner, Sharon Normington. With her husband, Roger, she was doing a lot of work. 'You want steak and kidney pie,' advised Sharon. 'I was about to order the sausage,' I said. 'You can have sausages everywhere,' said Sharon with finality. I ordered a sausage as well. Geraldine ordered home-made fish pie. We got an old-fashioned prawn salad with pink sauce and salad. It was very good.

The steak and kidney pie was enormous. It had excellent pastry on top. I dictated: 'As steak and kidney pie goes this is historic. Very good gravy, very good steak, soft and tasty kidney.' But the sausage beat it. I've never had such superb sausage ever. It came with a bread roll and butter. The sausage was really light and tasty. Later, I congratulated Mr Harris the butcher. He said Judi Dench was one of his customers.

There's a notice saying, 'The management reserves the right to refuse admittance to those unsuitably dressed – sleeveless vests, muddy shorts or shirts, etc.' Lucky I got by, really.

sweet potato (they rather pretentiously don't use capital letters) in Reigate, Surrey is a simple place with wooden tables and 1950s-type chairs. Tara Unwin is the welcoming co-owner. Her husband Carn does the cooking. A large menu included a selection of sausages and mash. I chose 'ostrich steak served with a red wine cappuccino on a bed of dauphinoise potatoes with roasted vegetables'.

'This ostrich steak is seriously horrible,' I dictated into my tape recorder. 'I can't quite make out what it tastes like. But certainly nothing like I've ever eaten before or will ever eat again.' As we left, Tara assured me ostrich was really popular. Carn added: 'It's quite a strong flavour, isn't it.' I remained silent.

I had an excellent lunch at the **Thai Elephant** in Richmond-upon-Thames. It was a set meal and the silence that came over us as we ate was a sign of the excellence of the food. Chicken satay, fish cakes, spring rolls and deep-fried prawns in pastry.

I've never understood people who think it amusing to have a restaurant on the side. I'd find it horrible to worry about staff, food and ridiculous customers like me.

A man I greatly admire is Peter Wood, the founder of Direct Line insurance and now the boss of esure and First Alternative. Peter sensibly uses me to sell his policies on television. Even he's not immune to 'I must have a restaurant' madness. He opened one near his office in Reigate, Surrey called **Tony Tobin@The Dining Room**. Peter's partner is the host and chef, Tony Tobin who worked with Nico Ladenis. He's on TV in *Ready Steady Cook*.

Our table, in a pleasant first-floor room, was by a window overlooking a church. My first course was 'seared kangaroo salad, crushed peanuts, crispy garlic and shallots'. It was extremely pleasant. The salad was exceptional.

Then I had 'crispy aromatic duck, pineapple chutney, mustard mash'. The duck was like all other crispy ducks, very tasty. The mashed potato, with whatever they'd added, was exceptional. I recall it with great pleasure.

For dessert I chose 'cherry Bakewell tart, warm cherry compote, softly whipped cream'. The Bakewell tart was not real Bakewell tart but it was superb. It was more like a slice of cake. I'd like to place a regular order. The rest was fine.

Tony Tobin is highly pleasant. Nevertheless, I judge every restaurant by one simple maxim: if it was near my house, would I go? Yes, I would.

Shere is a picture-postcard village in Surrey. It has a small village green and a lovely church, with two rows of quaint houses and shops peeking at it. On the other side of the triangle is an historic old building called the **White Horse Inn**. Outside it are wooden benches, tables and some stocks where I once photographed Marlon Brando, his head through the centre, his hands in the holes left and right. Inside, we were placed by an old open fireplace. It took an extraordinarily long time for our food to arrive. My Thai-spiced chicken breast came with McCain-type chips, a salad and some hot red sauce. It was quite dreadful. We waited endlessly for desserts. It was all so slow we got the bill and fled without getting our desserts at all.

At **Bella Italia Pasta** in Brighton, after eating a historically bad pizza, I waited so long for coffee that I went to the restaurant next door, got some and brought it back. This greatly amused Lia Williams, star of my film *Dirty Weekend*, but made the waiters glummer than before.

Cont'd

When I first stayed at the **Copthorne Hotel Newcastle**, I had a wonderful, memorably large room with an enormous, canopied bed and a window overlooking the river Tyne and a marvellous iron bridge. The next visit I found they'd divided things up into two smaller rooms with a worse view. There was very 1950s yellow-diamond wallpaper and a tacky three-piece suite. It all looked gloomy. But in the morning a delicious, enormous fry-up English breakfast arrived 18 minutes after being ordered, which I thought was good. And we had a delicious lunch in a room called The Bar, decorated with oars and boating stuff. The fish was exceptionally fine and fresh, one of the nicest bits of fried fish I've every eaten. The batter was superb. The mushy peas were good, but tepid. I only ate one chip.

I went for lunch in Newcastle at **Jesmond Dene House**, a hotel co-owned by Terry Laybourne. Terry used to be chef-owner of 21 Queen Street, a local Michelin-starred restaurant.

It's a rather odd 1827 building. Terry explained it had been a naughty girls' school. I've known a few of those in my time. Delightful people. Added to Terry's 1827 house were bizarre structures of thick Swedish bare wood and glass. Typical ghastly northern taste. Exceptionally nice people, the northerners. No idea about clothes, buildings, hairstyles, anything. The dining room had a red wall and a grey wall. Typical northern idea of decoration. The chairs were orange rattan. They swivelled like an office chair. I like that. Gives you something to do.

I ordered confit of duck foie gras, pickled figs and young leaves, followed by roast loin of Aberdeen Angus beef, young vegetables (everything's described as 'young' here) and Yorkshire pudding. 'Get that moving – I don't want to wait for hours,' I instructed the waiter.

The food was okay. Nowhere near the quality that Terry produced when he was in the kitchen. The beef was cut too thin. The roast potatoes looked very odd. They were awful. But the Yorkshire pudding was very good.

The **Spicy Grill** is a very small place in a terrace of small places overlooking the wall of a motorway overpass. This is quite a rough part of Birmingham. Locals told me gangs run around shooting each other. Most of the shops have signs in Arabic. Some appear African.

The Spicy Grill boasts four pink metal tables with a blue surround. They're attached to the chairs by a metal pole and they're all screwed to the floor. No chance of nicking them without a bit of equipment. On the right is the counter with food laid out. Behind it a grill and two microwave ovens. At the back, a soft drink dispenser. Posh isn't it?

Lamb and chicken turned on the spit. I ordered some katlama. It's like naan bread, with lamb or chicken added. Also two vegetable samosas, a sort of veggie burger.

Cont'd

The samosas were exceedingly spicy. My chicken balti turned out to be lamb balti. But it was very nice anyway. It was so hot I could have done with some rice to go with it. The chef, Mohammed Akram, came over. He suggested I try his onion bhaji, which he deep-fried in front of my eyes. It was excellent.

When I left, my local Rolls-Royce driver said: 'This is a bad area.' They all seemed very nice people to me.

We got to the Tudor, plus fake Victorian Tudor, plus fake 1992 Tudor **Gravetye Manor** near East Grinstead in good time for Sunday lunch. It's a beautiful spot. The dining room is elegantly panelled with a Victorian gothic fireplace and offers 'Gravetye Manor Spring Water from the spring which has served the manor since 1598'. Since the alternative was Hildon, which is awful, I tried the Manor water. It was adequate. I also ordered an £80 half-bottle of 1988 Mission-Haut-Brion. They had a large selection of half-bottles. That's unusual.

The canapés were totally historic. The bread was warm and excellent. We got a superb freebie tempura of soft-shell crab with crab and mango salad. The asparagus starter was correctly cooked, but crisper than I like it. The chef was having a day off. 'Why?' I asked.

Georgina had ordered a leg of duck dish from the set menu and got breast of duck from the à la carte. This happens when people don't write orders down and don't check them carefully. She was disappointed. 'That was not very together,' she said. The duck was good but not sensational. My roast beef was fine. The Yorkshire pudding fell in the final furlong. The roast potatoes weren't that crisp. What I'd call 'restaurant roast'. Georgina had ordered trio of chocolate tarts for dessert. My coffee cake was stodgy; my carrot cake was pleasant.

The other diners were wonderfully subdued. You could hear yourself talk. It was, in general, a very pleasant experience.

In Chichester they had a Michael Winner day at their film festival. I was early for my own talk, so we nipped into **Woodies Wine Bar & Brasserie**, where I ate one of the best summer puddings ever, with an excellent cappuccino. There was a lot of space, it was comfortable, friendly, well designed, and the waitress was charming. The more serious food coming from the kitchen looked terrific. Can I have a Woodies in Kensington please?

Leeds is gloomy, unkempt, a place to stay away from. I was at the **Malmaison** hotel, which is in a converted warehouse. It's over-chic, rather camp. The corridors are black cloth. Everything is sombre. Its only suite was dark, nasty and with a view of hideous office buildings. The sitting room was tiny. We asked to move to other accommodation that the general manager, Grant McKenzie, had offered. This was a modest, bright room with a lovely view overlooking an old iron bridge, a canal and warehouses.

The Malmaison lift offers a recorded voice announcing the floors in French. 'Troisième étage,' it said. How naff can you get? The plastic room key read, 'Stick with me, I'll open the door for you.' The laundry bag, 'Dirty clothes and thoughts in here.' The cotton bud container, 'Get an earful of these little beauties.' Oh dear.

The dinner food was okay. Geraldine loved her caramelised onion soup. I had salad of confit suckling pig. Very pleasant. Then rabbit pie. The rabbit over-shredded but tasty. The pastry hard, ghastly.

If you have to go to Leeds, I guess the Malmaison is as good as anywhere. Grant was superb. He's only 26. He deserves to be running a major hotel.

I parked outside the United Church in Warminster, Wiltshire. It was lunchtime. **Jacqueline's** restaurant and tea rooms looked all right to me. 'The best tea rooms in the West Country. Mark and Jacqui are pleased to welcome you to Jacqueline's,' was printed on the menu. Nice place, clientele even more decrepit than me.

The specials included onion soup with cheese and croutons, fresh melon, coq au vin, fish and prawn mornay. They also offered a lot of baked potatoes and baguettes. I got a baked potato with Longbridge Deverill smoked trout and cream cheese. My potato tasted good but the skin wasn't crisp enough. The salad and fish with it were fine. I also had the onion soup, which was excellent.

Mark referred me to a grand display of cakes, many of which he'd made. I settled for a flapjack, which was moist and very good. But not as good as the one I had at Salisbury Cathedral. That was the best ever. If you go there try the cathedral self-service place – it's terrific.

When I came out of the Lacock Abbeyin Wiltshire, it was past lunchtime. I eat on the dot of one. It was 1.40pm by the time I was in the pretty village street of Lacock, despoiled only by plebeian cars littered everywhere. Near the church was a little old stone-and-beamed house with a back garden serving refreshments. We sat under an apple tree. A bee was trapped in the sugar bowl. I ordered a pot of tea and a 'warm cheese and olive round' for £4. It was like a savoury scone with a lot of nice, crisp salad and spicy home-made chutney. I also had teacakes, which were very large and as good as I've ever eaten, and a cup of tea. Miss Lid the Third had delicious fresh vegetable soup. The bill, ex gratuity, was £12.35. It included very fine lemonade. The service was excellent. I went into the kitchen to congratulate the owner, but Margaret M Vaughn was having an operation. The place is called '**King John's Hunting Lodge**. Tea rooms and guest house'. It's a credit to the nation.

This charming manor

I didn't intend to visit **Lucknam Park** in Wiltshire. I phoned at four o'clock on Friday. The general manager was apologetic. 'We can only do a room in the courtyard,' she said. 'The best suites are in the main building.' 'Ask someone there to leave,' I suggested. 'I can't do that,' said the GM. 'They're already in.' 'Tell them it's a health hazard,' I advised. 'The helicopter lands 11am tomorrow.'

We glided along a few feet above the lawns, past a fine avenue of beech trees, to land in front of the lovely Georgian manor house. I think Lucknam Park is a find. Tastefully decorated, elegant, very beautiful setting and nice countryside around it.

We were shown to a lovely suite in the main building. Exhausted by the 40-minute flight, we sat on the terrace and were provided coffee and biscuits, but no napkins – even though one of the biscuits was chocolate and sticky.

For dinner, I had terrine of baby leeks and langoustine, a boring, triangular slice. I asked for crispy duck but got pink sliced duck, which was actually very good; so was its own confit of puy lentils and a hermitage sauce. Miss Lid greatly praised her salmon. The poached peach was fine.

Breakfast was excellent. I particularly admired the way the hotel bosses worked the room that early in the morning. I asked if the kipper was fresh or deep-frozen. The restaurant manager thought about that for a while. 'You've just said everything, haven't you?' I observed.

Entering the **Manor House Hotel** from the picture-postcard village of Castle Combe, Wiltshire you pass a wooden painted sign reading: 'Exclusivity has never been so affordable.' That's a laugh!

My room – I repeat room, not a suite – was £690 an night. Nor was it remotely exclusive. It was bizarre. The hotel is very old, stone Tudor. The room could have been beautiful but had been over-messed-about to a ludicrous degree. The four-poster bed, not against the wall, was raised on a dais. What's the point of that? Net curtains could be closed around it by a remote control, which supposedly did everything – lights, gadgets, served drinks, sang opera, wiped your forehead. You needed a degree in advanced electronics to work it. Even Geraldine, who's good with such things, couldn't find out how to turn off the reading lights, so we twisted them away from us for sleeping.

The bed's net curtains were bordered in endless glass-drop beads. So were the window curtains and all the pelmets. How tacky can you get? Five steep steps led to a low-ceilinged attic bathroom with permanently dim lighting. It had a flat-screen TV facing the bath – but no tissues. I've never been in a hotel, even the tackiest places I sometimes visit when on movie locations, that doesn't put a box of tissues in the bathroom.

Never mind, perhaps for £690 a night, which included breakfast and dinner for two, the food would save the day. It didn't. Things started well. Tea on the lawn was exemplary. Very fresh sandwiches, Earl Grey tea with a strainer for me and another for Geraldine.

At dinner my pâté was all right. It was followed, oddly, by a very average passion fruit sorbet. I'd asked for the duck strips to be well done. They tasted of very little, but they weren't horrible. They appeared on the dreaded bed of spinach. My dessert was disgusting. It was a chocolate mousse-type thing, sickly beyond belief.

At breakfast, although I was told the orange juice had been squeezed in the kitchen, I doubt if it had been squeezed that morning. I timed my wait for a kipper to 25 minutes, then said to a waitress: 'Could you please find out where my kipper is?' 'It's coming,' she replied dismissively. That sort of answer sums up inadequacy.

I asked the restaurant manager to check in the kitchen, otherwise I'd leave without it. He returned to say: 'It's coming in one minute.' We all know a restaurant minute is not the same as anyone else's. In fact it arrived three minutes 20 seconds later, meaning it had taken nearly half an hour. It was, I say in fairness, extremely good.

I was endeared to the **Tollgate Inn** at Holt, near Melksham in Wiltshire. A sign said, 'Please note we do not accept children under the age of 10.' I'd have raised it to 12.

The Tollgate is a typically pretty English inn set in a typically pretty English village, the whole thing brought down a peg or two by the arrival of me. The place is owned by Alison Ward-Baptiste and Alexander Venables. He cooks, she does front of house.

I went into the kitchen. Alex had cut all the fat off the beef. 'We're going to throw it away,' he explained. 'Keep it. Crisp it up for me,' I suggested. It's ridiculous they cut all the fat off beef these days. It's an integral part of a beef-eating experience. They fry the fat very well for me at the Ritz and the Dorchester. Unfortunately, after three attempts, Alex's fat remained soggy. I can't work out why. His beef was good. But I must stop ordering beef when I'm out. It's never a patch on what I eat at home from R Allen of Mount Street.

The veggies at the Tollgate, in particular the cabbage, were superb. My starter, 'ragout of fried lamb's sweetbreads, bacon and mushrooms', was terrific. The sauce was delicious. Geraldine had 'home-cured gravadlax'. She liked it.

We were in a first-floor room with oil paintings, prints, dark beams and garlic hanging from a nearby mirror. Perhaps they thought I was a vampire and would be scared away. They got a major demerit for Hildon Water and paper napkins. 'With everything so posh, you should have cloth ones,' I told Alison.

Geraldine's main course of calf's liver, Wiltshire bacon and red wine juice was fine. My sticky toffee pudding with butterscotch sauce and vanilla ice cream was okay. But it was a bit low on sauce, so got rather dry.

Affairs of the heart

I drove down a leafy Wiltshire lane to the **White Hart Inn** at Ford. They'd reserved a table in the dining room. I promptly changed it for a larger, round table, then decided I didn't like it. I checked the tables in front of the inn, then walked across the road to the river, beside which were tables with wooden benches. We walked back to the tables in front of the inn, on into the dining room, and then out the back where there were some more tables. But they overlooked a car park and an air-conditioning unit. So we looked at all the areas again. It was the biggest walkabout ever to choose a Winner table.

I finally decided to eat by the river. Large flower baskets hung behind me from the hotel part of the building. 'Is all this made here?' I asked, surveying the menu. 'We don't buy anything in,' I was told. I ordered spicy lamb curry with spinach and saffron, served with rice and dressed salad. Miss Lid (the real Lady in Danger) asked for braised chicken in white wine with garlic cream and sweet peppers, again served with rice and dressed salad. Shortly thereafter, Miss Lid, who is no pushover, said: 'My chicken is perfect.' Then, 'Very good.' Then, 'Very well prepared.' My lamb curry was excellent.

'Who does the desserts?' I asked, regarding a suspiciously large menu selection. 'They're all made here except for the treacle tart and apple and raspberry crumble. They're bought in,' I was told. In the cause of exploration I had the banoffie pie and the lemon cheesecake. The pie was robust, nice taste, filled with bananas. The lemon cheesecake very liquid. Both good. Overall, a pleasant experience.

Nobody in their right mind stays in Birmingham. So I chose **Brockencote Hall** hotel, which is nearby. It's a beautiful building, which the owners claim dates back 300 years. That means there may be stone somewhere from 1700. It's set in 70 acres of glorious parkland. More importantly, it's very classy, owned by lovely people, Alison Petitjean and her hubby Joseph, who used to be the chef.

The bedroom (they have no suites; build one for me in case I return) had 18th-century-type French wallpaper, lovely prints, dried flowers in an old fireplace. The dining room is exquisitely furnished with tasteful chandeliers and wall brackets, nice view over the gardens.

The food was fine. Not historic, but very acceptable. I started with Périgord duck foie gras, armagnac and salt flour. The waiter on delivering it, recited what it was. That's really irritating. Pompous nonsense. I ordered the stuff. It wasn't so long ago I'd forgotten. I don't need some twit telling me what the food is. I can see it. It's in front of me.

My main course was fillet of Brixham plaice, compote of onions, broad beans, girolle mushrooms and almond oil. 'It was pleasant,' I dictated onto my tape.

I dictated my opinion of the entire meal and everything surrounding it. Geraldine said, 'The fact I have to sit here and listen to this is unbelievable.' I dictated that onto my tape too.

Buckland Manor is a beautiful hotel, some of it 13th century, near Broadway in Worcestershire. Buckland 'village' is a lane with a few houses, no post office, no pub – and the hotel. The suite was delightful, understated, nice architectural prints, leaded windows, a view of fields, gardens and sheep. The bathroom was immaculately done in inlaid wood. Very posh.

The food was less satisfactory. At dinner I felt I was in an old people's residential home. The canapés were glumpy and heavy. Bread was awful. My melon was cut up in tiny little pieces with a dried fig, some strawberries and poor-quality ham. After the starter we got melon and Grand Marnier sorbet. Pretentious. For the main course I had Dover sole. The mashed potatoes with it were cold. I then ordered pain perdu served with wine-poached pear and citrus sabayon. It was nasty. A highly unsuccessful dessert. I tried a jelly petit four. It was ghastly.

Paola was distressed there were no crackers, celery or walnuts with her cheese. 'The coffee's absolutely awful,' she said, after taking a sip. And pushed her cup away.

Scotland

We arrived at the **Malmaison** hotel in Glasgow around 11 o'clock at night. Although the people at the desk could see me coming, no attempt was made to get our luggage until I said: 'Porters off duty, are they?' We were shown a duplex suite. It was a nightmare, 1950s decor gone seriously wrong. The bedroom, if you can call it that, was up a spiral staircase. It was a cramped ledge with just room for a bed, a tea-maker, a kettle and a cupboard. The bathroom and toilet were below and equally small. I measured the downstairs lounge area. It was about 12ft 2in by 11ft 8in. Outside the windows was a large office building, lit up and occupied at midnight.

In the morning, I went to the dining room. The menu advertised 'freshly squeezed orange and grapefruit juice'. 'Does that mean you cut the oranges in half here and squeeze them in the hotel?' I asked. 'No,' said the waitress. Eventually, after a lifetime of negotiation, they provided me with freshly squeezed orange juice, which they promised on the menu anyway. For lunch, I asked for a pizza romano with two fried eggs on it. 'Seriously?' said the waitress as if this were the height of culinary ignorance. 'Yes,' I said. 'No problem,' she responded. I had to ask three times for a cappuccino, eventually walking the few paces to the machine to help myself.

While staying at Sharrow Bay on Lake Ullswater I was banned from Sunday lunch as they had 75 people booked. I cast my fate to the winds. Nothing looked enticing restaurant-wise in nearby Penrith, so I set off for Gretna Green, racing up the A7 in my

Cont'd

rented Audi sports car, hair a-blowing. After a while, I dropped into the Lynebank Coffee Shop in Westlinton. 'Is this Scotland?' I enquired of the owner. 'No, it's England,' he said. 'Will it become Scotland?' I asked, meaning the road further on. 'Never,' he said. Then he came outside and pointed me in the direction I was going anyway.

We journeyed until I came across a pretty blonde girl of about 16, sitting on a wall. 'Is this Gretna Green?' I asked. 'Yes,' she replied. 'Where is it?' I said, confused. 'There,' she explained, pointing to what looked like a garden centre on the other side of the road. It was a kind of visitor complex with a souvenir shop. The museum offered the complicated history of Lord Hardwicke's marriage laws. On display was the anvil where people used to be wed.

Nearby is the **Old Smithy Restaurant**, a barn-like place with self-service counters. I took a steak pie and a bit of cottage pie, with some vegetables and gravy. All was rather tasty for a cafeteria. The manageress, Jane Van Nuil, came over. 'My staff are trying to work out if you're a lookalike or the real thing,' she stated. I assured her I was as real as Michael Winner could be.

Highland fling

Vanessa wanted to see a tree. I don't know how the word Scotland got in, but suddenly it was a typical Winner excursion. 'I'll think about the private jet – is £9,000 the best you can do?' 'Take the helicopter from Inverness to **Inverlochy Castle** and back. £1,300! That's bloody high!' I had found Inverlochy Castle in a guide book; it said the room rate was £276 per night. On Thursday, I phoned. 'Have you got a cancellation for the weekend?' A voice said: 'Yes, as a matter of fact we have.' It turned out to be Michael Leonard, the general manager. 'I'll take it,' I said. 'What's the name?' said Mr Leonard. 'Michael Winner.' There was a pause. 'The Michael Winner?' he asked. 'Afraid so,' I replied. Another pause. 'Maybe I shouldn't have said we had a cancellation.' 'Too late now,' I said cheerfully. 'Ah well,' said Mr Leonard, uncertainly, 'we like a challenge.'

I decided the jet, at £9,000 for two nights, was a bit over the top, so I ended up on the British Airways shuttle. Mistake, that. The helicopter was next to it when we landed on Saturday morning, and a dramatic flight ensued over Loch Ness through varied weather from bright sun, to rain, to light cloud, to black cloud. There were great mountains sweeping down to rivers and lakes. I'd never seen the Highlands before. We landed on the lawn a few feet from the Victorian pile that is Inverlochy. Not so much a castle, more a wonderful, 19th-century fantasy of Ye Olde Britain. Mr Leonard was there to show us up to a very large room (upgraded from a small room when I'd first phoned) that had a lovely three-window bay with views over lochs (lakes), bens (mountains) and glens (valleys), only slightly diminished by a paper mill in the distance standing up from the town of Fort William.

The shower was ridiculous. It was above the end of the bath that slopes down, and trying to stand under it was like climbing a slippery hill. At what turned out to be £600 a night, a proper shower would be reasonable. There was ample room to take the lobby outside the bathroom and ... oh, never mind. In the bedroom were prints; one, with the inscription 'Throat', showed two fighting cocks with one holding the other. The next, 'Death', showing the victor standing on the vanquished's dead body. Very jolly.

The hotel lounge was comfortably regal with a real log fire. The main hall was a period Disneyland with Venetian chandeliers, cherubs on the ceiling, old-style British chairs and a chess set laid out on a table. It all worked rather well. Mr Leonard came as I checked out the dining room. 'I'll sit there!' I announced, showing him the table in the centre bay window. 'I fear that's taken by a regular visitor,' said Mr Leonard bravely. 'We think this is the nicest table.' He indicated one at the side bay window. 'It has the best view.' 'Not for the person sitting looking at the wall,' I remarked, dourly. I alternated tables. 'King Haakon of Norway gave the tables and chairs to the present owner,' advised Mr Leonard, going on to tell me that Charlie Chaplin, King Hussein and Mel Gibson were among those who had stayed.

The food, knocked up by a young Michelin-starred chef, Simon Haigh, was mostly extremely good. Ballotine of foie gras with smoked apple purée, very fresh salmon, later amazingly fresh and juicy lobsters, raspberry crème brûlée. Only two mini-disasters.

I checked the vegetable soup (adequate) for Vanessa, who's vegetarian, and they said it had a meat stock. So we asked for a salad two hours in advance. When it arrived it was full of bacon! And the morning Loch Fyne kippers were very tired. Later, Simon took exception to my criticising them. 'It's a Mallaig kipper and it came in Friday.' 'Mr Leonard said it came in Wednesday,' I said. 'What does he know, he doesn't order them!' said Simon. As Mr Leonard was standing next to him, I thought that rather brave. 'I would not have called the kipper juicy,' I continued. Mr Haigh defended his kipper to the death. Nice chap, though.

After that we turned to important matters, like how he finds girlfriends in this distant part of the Highlands. Bit of walking, bit of helicoptering around, all very pleasant. Hotel service was exemplary. Coming back Monday morning, we were late to Inverness airport. 'Land beside the shuttle,' I instructed the pilot. 'Then it won't be able to take off and they'll have to let us on.' He did. Nothing like private planes, really. They're great fun. Except when you get the bill.

In Scotland we left Skibo Castle in our rented Land Rover. I drove down a tiny road by the side of Loch Shin – staggeringly beautiful. Then to Kinloch. Now Loch More was on our right. Then to Achfary, past Lock Stack, to Laxford

Bridge, left to Scourie and thus to Lairg. Hardly any cars to be seen. Highlands looking great.

The **Kylesku** hotel has views over Loch Glendhu. Little white-tipped waves, lovely hills and a tiny harbour, which used to have a ferry. The bar was empty except for Imelda Gilmour, who, with her husband Patrick, owns the place. A log stove offered flames and much warmth.

I chose cullen skink, a just-made, creamy, smoked haddock soup. Geraldine had freshly caught spiny tails, local squat lobsters. Then she ordered langoustines. As the restaurant wasn't busy Imelda shelled my langoustines. I wasn't put on this earth to shell fish, unwrap butter or unwrap sugar. What I was put on earth for, I will not get into.

Darren MacKay came in. He'd caught the superb langoustines I'd just eaten. Darren fishes in another loch and also in the sea. Most of his catch goes straight to a big wholesaler in Barcelona. But he keeps some back for local hotels.

As it was out of season they only had one home-made pudding, bread and butter. It was excellent. Very light with a lot of currants. I had it with ice cream. There was absolutely nothing to complain about regarding our lunch. It was memorable.

Lochinver's Larder in Lochinver looked dreadful from the outside. Frozen fish fingers if we're lucky, I thought. I entered with a heavy heart. The first room had a counter on the right. It was full of pies. My spirits rose. 'Do you make those here?' I asked. 'Yes,' said a nice girl. There were 16 different pies – from leek and mushroom to venison and cranberry to chicken curry. Above were rows of home-made cakes that looked amazing. We ate in a large room overlooking the loch, an old church, wonderful scenery. I had a steak and ale pie and a chicken, cheese and potato one. Both absolutely tip-top. Then I chose a chocolate fudge cake and a vanilla fudge cake. Totally, absolutely, incredibly historic. Touch of moisture, delicious icing, perfect. My only regret was that I couldn't go through the lemon cake, pineapple fruit tart, shortbread tarts, carrot cake, rhubarb and strawberry pie, banoffee pie and the home-made cherry cheesecake, to name but a few. I'd like to have eaten everything, but I'd done pretty well having two main courses, two desserts, a chocolate milkshake and coffee.

When I was young (around 1892) BBC radio always gave a shipping forecast after the news. A man in a sombre voice would pronounce on Easter Ross. I never expected to go there.

It was Peter Crome, the masterful boss of Skibo Castle, who booked lunch for me at the **Oystercatcher** in the main street of Portmahomack, Easter Ross. The toilets are labelled 'Honest Men' and 'Bonnie Lassies'. It's run by Gordon and Susan Robertson. For a modest place in a little port it has the most enormous menu. Everything from braised thistles in an onion and cream sauce on a split cheese scone to a Monte Cristo cigar for £35 to a massive selection of single malt whiskies.

I went native with 'chieftain's castle – a haggis turret raised on an isle of clapshot fortified with a golden lochan of Glenmorangie malt whisky'. Clapshot is potatoes and neeps mashed together, in case you didn't know. The haggis came from Dingwall, 30 miles away. It was the most enormous portion for a starter and sitting in a bowl of whisky. Geraldine had bouillabaisse. I tasted it. It was outstandingly good. 'Here we are in the middle of nowhere, with cheap, red holiday homes and the food is stunning,' I observed.

I decided to finish with a small slice of carrot cake and a small slice of chocolate cake. Both home-made. 'These are not small in anybody's language but yours,' I said jovially to Susan. The carrot cake was very good indeed. The icing was crowdie, from a local cheesemaker, Susan adding icing sugar, vanilla essence, butter and orange.

We went for a long walk along the coast. Amazingly, the locals knew who I was. It was a sunny day. Sheep were grazing. They ignored me.

Skibo Castle is best known as the location for Madonna's marriage. It's actually called **The Carnegie Club at Skibo Castle**. Non-members are allowed one visit before deciding whether to join. Nine hundred pounds a night for superb accommodation includes three glorious main meals plus tea, endless wine, golf, other sports and bagpipes.

Bagpipes are rampant at Skibo. One piped us in as we arrived. You're piped in to dinner. A bagpiper walks round the castle at 8 o'clock every morning in the belief that if you wake up to the sound of the pipes your day will be fulfilled. As I wandered off to the lavatory, I expected a bagpiper to wail me in.

Skibo is in the eastern Highlands in Sutherland, a wonderful, sparsely populated county. It's set among stunning countryside and incredibly main-tained to an exemplary standard of old-money luxury. 'I don't think I've been in anything so beautiful,' observed Geraldine. That's an impertinence. She's been in my house.

Skibo is maintained regardless of profit, which is greatly to the credit of the owners. They're even spending £250,000 restoring an Edwardian swimming pool. The castle was completed in 1902 for American steel billionaire Andrew Carnegie, after whom New York's Carnegie Hall was named. It's run by Peter Crome, ex of Chewton Glen. He's the greatest hotel manager in the world. By a long way. He has genuine, not unctuous, charm. He's the perfect host. Staff wear kilts and white socks with tassels. It's all very MGM circa 1952.

I'd been told dinner was promptly at 8. 'It's 8!' I said. 'Where's my dinner?' 'We might wait 'til five past occasionally. At 8.12pm the piper led us to the communal table. 'Good,' I thought. 'Food at last.'

The food in general was impeccable. Delicious local produce simply cooked by their young chef, Craig Rowland. But communal dining is not for me. Andrew Carnegie apparently chose a variety of people from all walks of life who might be interesting. He didn't rely on what rich tourist happened to be around that particular night.

After that I dined in a lovely lounge with a log fire – just Geraldine and me. The first night Peter Crome asked, 'Would you like to be piped to the table?' Since I was on a sofa five paces away I said, 'That won't be necessary, thank you.'

Our stay was fantastic. Memorably excellent. Skibo is unique. If you can get there, go. If you can't, phone Rent-a-Piper and have fun at home.

If I was the comedy version of an American tourist, I would call the **Old Station Restaurant** 'cute'. It is a genuine, working station: Spean Bridge, on the London Midland Scottish, now Scotrail, one stop before Fort William. It is everybody's idyllic picture-postcard station. Little overhanging, woodworked roof with flower baskets, lovely flowerbeds all around, a bridge to rolling fields and, on the other side, a village and majestic mountains. The tables are well spaced out, the murmur of Scots voices extremely pleasant. I started with honey and ginger soup, very tasty, real country stuff. Then I ate some duck breast with apricot and lemon sauce, very good. Carrots a bit overcooked, but they tasted of carrots; cabbage tip-top; nice roast potato with a crisp skin. Mashed potato with nutmeg, too! Mozart piped through as I had white chocolate cheesecake. If this restaurant was moved to Holland Park it would be a terrific local and I'd go there a lot.

David Smyrl got a bit worried when I rang him at the **Morefield Motel** in Ullapool. 'We're only a fast-food fresh lobster place,' he said. Chef's specials included half lobster grilled with garlic, and mussels served with a jacket potato and dressed salad. They were the best mussels I've ever eaten. Fat, juicy, not shrivelled like they usually are in London. Lobster good, potato very good. Vanessa had turbot. Fresh, excellent. As pleasant a meal as you could ask for.

Wales

Tempting fete

Betws-y-Coed is a quaint little town of grey stone houses with slate roofs, spread out along a single roadway, with a river running on one side with mountains behind. I parked the car and noticed across the road a **Women's Institute** fête at St Mary's Church. That's for me, I thought. There were some enormous evergreen trees with little stalls beneath them offering a bedside cabinet for £2, some Sainsbury's vacuum-cleaner bags and a 1955 road atlas of Great Britain.

Inside, the Church hall was full of marvellous things. A large table was stacked with home-made jams, cakes and pies. Nearby, Anne Knowles, wearing a red-striped apron, stood by a hot griddle. Anne is famous for her Welsh cakes (two for 30p), her drop scones and jams. I tried the cakes and scones with her strawberry jam – £1.80, and the best I've ever eaten. The cakes were totally, beyond belief, historic. This was a serious taste experience. I added a cup of tea and read the notice board. The Morris Beachy Singers from Texas, USA, were an imminent attraction; also advertised was Weight Watchers and a ceilidh and barbecue at 8pm at Cwmlanerch Farm. The WI president, Moya Panting, explained this was pronounced cayley and meant a dance.

Looking for further sustenance, I bought an onion, cheese and tomato pasty from the trestle table and persuaded Anne to heat it for me on her griddle. I don't care if you think I'm unsophisticated, I have never eaten anything better in my life. These ladies have extraordinary skill. Simple it may be, but the result is pure heaven. I still have some of Anne's strawberry jam left at home and it beats anything in that line I've ever bought.

A lady with short blonde hair, Charlotte Irley, came up and said was I there because I'd heard she'd played Sporty Spice in the local show. She made a fruit cake that was being raffled, iced with unbelievable skill by Elsie Oughton with beautiful flowers, leaves, sweetpeas, and a purple and pink ruff. A cake that would grace any shop in the world. I proceeded to buy five tickets for a pound from a tombola stall run by Marion Betteney and won a greeny-blue face flannel and two large bars of soap.

Later, Vanessa was in a shop. A lady who'd been at the Women's Institute fête came over and remarked, 'When I read Michael Winner I always thought he was full of his own self-importance. But he was absolutely lovely with those ladies.' If only I could meet everybody. I'd be the most loved man in the world.

The **Nantyffin Cider Mill Inn**, at Crickhowell, has a big restaurant in a barn, but that was too smart for me. They'd reserved a table in the bar with the common folk, rightly assuming I'd prefer it. This bar had a gas stove in it, whereas in the adjacent bar, for people even more common, they have a proper log-burning one. Vanessa asked for orange, avocado and mint salad followed by whole, warm cracked Cornish crab served with new potatoes and salad. I chose grilled langoustines with a herb-crumb coating and garlic butter followed by roast leg of Welsh lamb with roast potatoes and mint sauce. To drink we ordered Hedges Red Mountain Reserve 1992, 'probably the purest fruit we have ever tasted, a stunning array of flavours'. It was all right. Give me a Lafite '61 any day. The bread was very good. The first two courses were excellent. We finished with a superb bread-and-butter pudding. The bill for two was £122.50. Must've been the wine. At early-evening dinner you get three courses for £11.95. This is the sort of place that gives Welsh food a good name.

In a sweet little antique shop in a cobbled street in Hay-on-Wye, a dear, white-haired Welsh lady sat behind a desk surrounded by bric-a-brac. My eye was caught by a piece of white paper hiding a picture in a wooden frame. 'Do not lift this up if you are easily shocked,' was written on it. I lifted it at once. I was shocked. There were two people, in an old print, caught in flagrante, and in considerable detail. A few inches away another such picture, then another. It was all too much for me. Vanessa, also obviously deeply traumatised, suggested a cup of tea to calm us down. Opposite was **Oscars Bistro**, with a large display of cakes, flapjacks, vegetable tart, beef in beer, chicken and leek pie, sausage in red wine gravy, and so on. I took some chocolate cake, carrot cake, and date and walnut cake. The second two were very good. I also grabbed a flapjack, the old-fashioned kind, moist, delicious. 'Marvellous,' I said, my mouth full. I felt better.

Cymru hither

I've always considered the Welsh to be marvellous. Thus, I was particularly disappointed with the lack of warmth and wit at Llangoed Hall. But the chef, Ben Davies, did me a very good turn. He recommended a number of nearby restaurants. 'The **Griffin Inn** in the village serves good local food,' he said. I got the impression he meant 'good local' as a slight put-down, as opposed to the 'international' food that he served. I visited the Griffin Inn in Llyswen the next morning to check out the table situation.

There are places you enter that you feel at once are going to be good: something about the atmosphere, the owner, the position of everything around you. Seated by the fireplace were four ladies talking in the Welsh language. Heaven! What a wonderfully melodious, mellifluous sound it is. I'm all for the Welsh nationalists. Ban McDonald's and Marks & Spencer, get back to traditional Welsh names and shops. Let everyone speak in their native tongue. There's quite enough English spoken in England. I may not have quite got the nationalist platform spot-on, but who cares?

The landlord, Richard Stockton, showed me a nice corner table for that evening and we went on our day's excursion. That night, the Griffin had a warm, orderly feeling. A notice on the bar read: 'Eat British lamb: 50,000 foxes can't be wrong.' The menu described it as a 15th-century sporting inn – whatever that was. Flowers were on every table in the small, low-beamed dining room. We had an excellent fresh brown roll. I listened for some Welsh language, but the diners seemed to be speaking posh English. Pam Morgan was identified as the lady with the most refined voice. 'She can speak Welsh,' whispered Richard. 'But she spent a lot of time in Hong Kong.'

All the food was historic-plus. It was as good a dinner as I've ever eaten. Apparently, people drive from miles around to come here. I'm not surprised. I had hot smoked salmon to start, like a little filet. With glanwye sauce. Amazing!

Then roast haunch of wild venison on a shallot ragout in red-wine sauce. Venison can be tricky. This was superb. Vanessa and I emptied our plates with total enjoyment. Service was smart and speedy, Richard's wife, Diana, helping out like a good 'un.

The best was left to last. The hot treacle tart had just the right thick, treacly taste, wonderfully moist texture, great pastry. Very fine crème anglaise with it. The lemon mousse was supreme. As I was on a diet I left some of the treacle tart. That pained me.

Wye bother

Sir Bernard Ashley, husband of the late Laura, owned **Llangoed Hall** in Llyswen, Wales. 'It has always been my ambition,' he writes in the brochure, 'to find a country-house hotel that would successfully re-create the atmosphere of an Edwardian house party. Here, guests would arrive, tired from their travels and the workaday world, to be greeted and cared for by their hosts as if they were indeed guests and not people simply renting rooms and patronising the restaurant. When you arrive there is no reception desk, no-one demanding a hostage credit card, just friendly staff to take your coat and carry your bags.' Boy, is that a joke.

My helicopter landed at the time I'd told the general manager, Andrew Brockett, I would arrive. One hotel porter represented the 'friendly staff'. He alone could not take all the luggage, so the pilot, Philip Amadeus, grabbed some and we trekked into the hotel. There, nobody else greeted us. The porter led us to the room and left. I can't think when I last entered a hotel without the manager, or at least the receptionist, welcoming me.

We went to the deserted lounge for tea. The same aged porter told us there were sandwiches and cakes. We ordered those, plus Earl Grey tea. After a while, cakes arrived and tea that was not Earl Grey. No sandwiches. I went into the hall and found an English lady, who said she'd deal with it. The staff are almost exclusively not Welsh. Warmth is not high on their list. A recently frozen éclair was poor; the fruit cake was okay but bland; a shortbread biscuit superb.

Another couple entered and a young man took their order. Our correct tea came with unexceptional sandwiches, which were also cold, as if the bread had been in the fridge. The new arrivals got tea with cakes, sandwiches and scones with home-made jam and cream. 'I never got scones,' I said, peering at theirs. 'Well, you didn't ask for them,' said the man. 'Nor did you,' I replied. 'I heard you order. You asked for an assortment.' The gentleman kindly offered me one of his scones. I took a bit of it. It was the best I've ever eaten.

Llangoed Hall has an attractive, faded elegance and excellent Edwardian oil paintings and drawings. Wild flowers grow through the cracks in the stone steps leading to the lawn. The view of fields, sheep and hills is first-rate. Walk outside and you hear the roar of the nearby A470. Go further and you hit the noise of engines dealing with the septic tanks. Only when you reach the river Wye and the rapids after a small waterfall does that noise drown out the sound of traffic.

The restaurant, an elegant, yellow room, has a Michelin star. I would describe the staff as snooty. An atmosphere so restrained nobody dared talk above a whisper. 'Boring,' said Vanessa. My first course was salad of quail with sautéed scollop (sic), foie gras and balsamic dressing. You can have foie gras with quail or scallops. But quail and scallops – ugh! Individually, they were adequate. It was an enormous portion. Vanessa liked her three large pan-fried scallops. Next I had black Welsh beef and Vanessa had salmon. Both were all right, but the whole thing totally lacked finesse and imagination.

Dessert was stated to be strawberry millefeuille. Millefeuille is thin layers of puff pastry; it dates back to the late 19th century. This one dated back to June 1998. It had hard, sweet biscuits in two layers with strawberries and cream. It was awful. I left most of it.

Vanessa had some cotton trousers ironed, and I've never seen anything like it: great ridges and furrows – unwearable. The room was nice, the bathroom large, but the bath too small even for normal people.

At breakfast one of the two pots of home-made jam (very good) had a big blob of congealed, old jam on the side. I removed it with my finger and then had great difficulty dislodging it. Eventually, I rubbed it off under my chair. The service was very slow. Again, the atmosphere was frigid. If this is an Edwardian house party, thank God nobody asked me to any.

Andrew Brockett left me a letter saying: 'If I or any of my colleagues can help, please let us know.' Mr Brockett was only there for a fleeting moment on Sunday morning, having been absent on Friday and Saturday and again on Monday. When I left, I passed Sir Bernard Ashley coming in. 'You took my helicopter pad,' he said, smiling pleasantly.

The **Ty'n Rhos Country House and Restaurant** is a rather grand name for a modest, but beautifully situated, domestic dwelling near the village of Seion in Gwynedd. A three-course Sunday lunch with coffee was £14.95 excluding service. Vanessa ordered a crispy pancake filled with a ragù of avocado, tomato and spring onion to start and fillet of salmon infused with lime and coriander with a white wine sauce to follow. They were excellent. My twice-baked goat's cheese soufflé was just right: properly crisp on the outside, not soggy on the inside. Then I had pot roast shoulder of lamb with an onion marmalade, herb dumplings and a minted red wine sauce. Plus superb veg. All the food was close to historic. The desserts were good too: summer pudding, vanilla baked cheesecake, home-grown gooseberry and elderflower cobbler with vanilla custard, and caramel ice cream. All this served in a pleasant domestic setting in the middle of nowhere. Bit of a triumph really.

Ireland

Since my visit to **Dick Mack's**, I am totally hooked on draught Guinness. I'm arranging for a draught Guinness apparatus in my house. Dick Mack's is a wondrous pub in Green Lane, Dingle, Co Kerry, where the left-hand bar is for shoe repairs and the one on the right for drinks. It's totally period, with little booths and a mêlée of old rooms at the back. Grandpa started it in 1899 and it must have looked just the same then.

Dingle, on Ireland's west coast, is where David Lean made *Ryan's Daughter*. There I stayed in **Milltown House**, a white Victorian house with a white picket fence and lawns leading down to the waterside, expertly looked after by the smiling red-haired owner, Angela Gill. It was the best value ever – for £42, not the sort of bill I'm used to, we got a charmingly decorated and well-cared-for room with a stunning view over Dingle, the estuary and the hills. The breakfast orange juice was genuinely fresh-squeezed, the jam and the bread were home-made, there was a newly baked apple cake, and everything else, from griddle pancakes with maple syrup to eggs to sausages to bacon, was as good as you could hope for. I had Ballyhea kippers! If you want a far-flung gem, this is it!

P.S. There is now a new owner. The old one probably retired rich because of me!

While in Dublin I was recommended **Balzac**. The owner is a charming Irishman (show me one who isn't) called Louis Murray. The 18th-century room is exquisite. Large, beautifully mirrored, urns of flowers, marble pillars. Yet again I was haunted by totally discordant 'modern' jazz playing far too loudly. I said to the waitress, 'The music is very intrusive, could you ask the management to turn it down a bit?' I asked Geraldine, 'What do you think will happen?' 'They'll turn it up,' she said. Mercifully they didn't.

I started with fish soup. I liked it. Geraldine thought the rouille could have been 'more garlicky'. My scallops with minted french beans, orange and almonds were excellent. Geraldine had crab brûlée, which she described as 'wonderful'.

The service was slow, slow, slow. Possibly even slower. The music, still too audible, was going 'boom, boom, boom'. For dessert I had a superb savarin of rhubarb and custard. Geraldine, world expert on crème brûlée, rated Balzac's highly.

The petits fours were madeleines, little French orange cakes. 'I've never tasted anything like that, ever,' said Geraldine, who lived in Paris for years. They were warm and absolutely incredible. We finished off a large bowl. Definitely a meal worth eating.

An extraordinary thing happened at **Locks Restaurant** in Dublin. It offered roast loin of pork with prune and apricot stuffing. 'Does it have crackling?' I asked Teresa Carr, who co-owns the place with Kelvin Rynhart. Teresa checked with the chef. She returned and said, 'Yes.' I said, 'Terrific, I'll have the pork with a lot of extra crackling, please.'

When my pork arrived, the 'crackling' on top resembled thin chips or bits of fried orange peel. It tasted nothing like the real thing. The pork was dreary, not major at all. 'This crackling is absolutely pathetic,' I dictated into my tape. I expressed disappointment. Teresa explained, 'It's crisp pork belly.' Which is not the same. 'This is one of the worst examples of restaurant service ever and by a long way,' I dictated.

At Locks it was lunch destroyed. Never mind the hole in the ozone layer, war in Afghanistan, Al-Qaeda – this is serious.

Inside **Messrs Maguire**, housed in a lovely old 1808 building on the Liffey in Dublin, it's fantastic. Old carved bars with 19th-century carvings behind, carved wood and wrought-iron banisters – a lot of the building is listed. The rest came from old buildings or antique shops. On the first floor the large room was a delight. Another superbly carved bar, a fireplace, old bookcases, wonderful plaster cornices. Six tables well spaced apart, very comfortable leather chairs. Lovely, quietly spoken Irish people.

Maguire brew their own beers. I was offered extra stout, red Irish ale, Christmas beer aka yule log, a weiss beer and pilsner lager. 'The yule log is very strong,' advised Michael. 'I don't want to get drunk too quickly,' I replied. 'I'll have a glass of extra stout.' Soft, creamy, utterly memorable. I declined a tour of their brewery downstairs. I'll drink it. I don't care how it's manufactured.

I started with pea and ham soup. 'Made on our premises this morning,' announced Michael. It tasted like it. The brown crusty bread was exceptionally good. To follow I had a plate that would have filled three people. There was honey-glazed collar of bacon, with gravy in a bowl, fantastic mashed potatoes, roast potatoes, carrots, stuffing, cabbage and a bowl of parsley sauce. All totally excellent.

During World War II, I would often go with my father to the Savoy Grill. In those days meat was rationed, and not much was available anyway. Whenever Dad ordered chicken, he would ask the head waiter, 'It will be chicken, won't it? Not rabbit?', for it was not unknown to switch one for the other. Today at posh restaurants, the humble rabbit is enjoying its day. It comes dressed up in all sorts of guises. Jambonette de lapin aux girolles is how rabbit with wild mushrooms is presented at **Patrick Guilbaud**, a bit of French chic in Dublin. The lump of rounded rabbit tasted okay, but was not remotely memorable. The sliced potatoes that came with it were so hard on the outside that I had trouble cutting them, and gave up. Luckily, the bitter chocolate tart with pistachio ice cream was exceptional.

The Princess Grace suite in the **Shelbourne** hotel, Dublin is extremely elegant. I'm not, but I stay there in the hope something might rub off. The hotel itself is wonderful Georgian splendour. The main lounge is beautifully proportioned, lovely chandeliers, rotten paintings.

Its tea, beautifully served by Clair Swaine, wasn't much good either. A pianist plonked away like a reluctant child who'd rather be on the sports field. The sandwiches were below average, the scones heavy and cloying, the cakes dreadful.

Room service was great. Masses of scotch, soft drinks, strawberries, raspberries, blackberries, chocolates. You could just eat the freebies in the room and save on meals. The bathrobes had MRW and GLE embroidered in gold. We were apparently meant to keep them. So we did.

Although it's very grand the Shelbourne attracts a buzzy group of young Irish people who fill the bars and the lobby. All the staff were charming and efficient. But why, oh why, do they have dreadful, discordant piped music in the lobby and in their dining room, the Saddle Room?

When we dined in the Saddle Room, Geraldine and I had foie gras torchon, fig and mandarin compote and soda bread. I followed with grilled black sole. It was all very good, simple food. The chef, John Mooney, is not going for an A-level in plate decoration. He lets the food speak for itself. My sole didn't actually say anything but tasted great.

In **Thornton's**, a restaurant in the Fitzwilliam hotel facing St Stephen's Green in Dublin, there was awful, discordant, piped music, which I persuaded them to turn off.

They brought us a freebie of king scallops from Bear Island with a light truffle mousse. Then we waited for our first course. 'We should have had the main course by now,' I said, 'let alone the starter.' When my first course finally arrived Geraldine asked, 'What's that you've got?' I replied, 'It was so long ago I ordered it, I can't remember.'

My main course of roast goose confit, red cabbage, fondant potato and morel sauce was a disaster. A little pile of goose slices that were totally tasteless. I had a house-keeper who wore a terrible wig, but she did a whole roast goose that was magical. Thornton's was nouvelle cuisine gone mad. Itsy-bitsy nothing.

I had lemon tart, which was so light and fluffy it was hardly there at all. The meal was like the hotel – modern, dreary and not very distinguished.

My suite at the **Park Hotel** in Kenmare was as elegant and old-fashioned a hotel space as I've ever seen. There was an 1882, dog-eared, limited edition of the works of Charles Dickens, very charming antique furniture and mirrors, some pleasing oil paintings and, above an enormous double bed, a set of seven saucy Edwardian pin-up pictures in an arts and crafts frame. I wondered if they'd heard of my age and decided I needed help. The view from the suite's bay windows was spectacular – palm trees, sloping lawns, a tidal

Cont'd

estuary and rolling hills beyond. Guests were having tea on the lawn, so I joined them. It was the worst tea I have ever had in my life. The sandwiches were grossly indelicate, great lumps of white bread, with two sandwiches speared together with a toothpick! The cakes were unspeakable. Food at dinner was okay. They have a Michelin star, but the chef who got it for them has since left. To be fair, the hotel, in general, is definitely pleasant. I liked it. Put me in charge for a couple of weeks and maybe it would live up to its award.

Longueville House, in Mallow, is a beautiful 18th-century restaurant and hotel that's rather like someone's home: a bit faded, very tastefully furnished with lovely old mirrors and armchairs, a grey marble carved fireplace with a log fire, and beautiful views of rolling green hills from the tall Georgian windows. My friend Oliver Reed was a regular visitor here. For lunch we ordered vegetable broth made with vegetables from their garden, a pâté of spinach, pork polenta and tomato in a millefeuille. I also asked for smoked salmon with garden salad. The bread was excellent, the salmon outstanding. My dessert was biscuit glacé with strawberries. That was nice too.

Happy landings

The Concorde was late. Seventeen hours late, to be exact. We were half an hour from Heathrow at 9 o'clock when the dreaded announcement came. You could tell from the tone of the captain's voice, the second he started, that it was a downer. Apparently there were storms and landing in London was too dangerous. These storms were widespread and affected every airport in southern England. We would divert to Shannon.

In the lounge I was given a pint of draught Guinness by Michael Pemberton, who owns luxury hotels in Barbados. Our chauffeurs in London were being told the plane had landed because it had a faulty tyre. My Mr Fraser confirmed the wind had long died down and there were no storms. Someone else phoned and found London airport fully operational. Why, then, were a lot of very posh people in an airport lounge in Ireland?

Being highly sophisticated, I knew the answer. The storm had caused a back-log. Planes were having to circle Heathrow for an indefinite time. The Concorde had little fuel left after its trip from Barbados, so it would take on more. We were herded back to the plane and told we would leave at 10.30pm. Then the pilot returned with that disaster tone in his voice. The noise restriction at Heathrow came on at 11.30 and we weren't going to make it. 'British Airways representatives got the head of the British Airports Authority out of bed, but he still refused to lift the noise restriction.' Colouful I thought, but unlikely. I couldn't imagine some lower echelon executive dragging Sir John Egan from his rest to say: 'Winner's on the plane. For heaven's sake let it land!'

We were to spend the night in Ireland. A very bright man named Anthony Buckingham was madly working his cellular phone. Mr B is in fascinating things such as oil and diamonds. He travels widely to strange African countries. He is a man of the world. Like me, he has the sense to travel only with carry-on luggage, so he was ready to disembark pronto. First, we tried for private jets to rescue us. 'Count me in!' I said eagerly. But no, they could not guarantee getting back. Mr B's man in London then informed us that **Dromoland Castle** was the only place to stay. 'I'll book us in,' he said. 'They're asking is it Michael Winner as in Michael Winner,' he added.

Then he was besieged. 'Book for me, please,' said Lady Annabel Goldsmith in row 2 behind me. 'And for us,' said Lady Rayne from across the aisle. 'Us, too!' called Lord Feldman from further back. Mr Buckingham obliged, and by the time he and I were hotfooting through the airport, all had been done.

If you have to be stuck somewhere, Ireland is the best place. The people seemed to know every word I'd ever written. A highly intelligent race. Pat Keogh, a wonderfully ruddy-faced taxi driver, took us to Dromoland Castle, an impressive historic building facing a large lake. There, the senior assistant manager, Niall Rochford, was all charm and efficiency. I was led up a grand staircase past enormous portraits, including William, 4th Earl of Inchquin in the robes of the Order of the Bath by Sir Godfrey Kneller. There was a distinct smell of smoke; I later learnt they'd had a fire. Luckily, my room was smell-free and very clean, with nice Tudor-style wall hangings and an old-fashioned bathroom that worked perfectly. My hot chocolate and biscuits arrived quickly and with lovely crockery, cutlery and terrific napkins.

The next morning, breakfast was superb. Quite the best kipper I've ever eaten. 'Is it local?' I asked. 'From Donegal,' said the waiter. 'Is that local?' I continued. 'Quite local,' he said. The dining room was very grand: four marvellous chandeliers, more oil paintings, a sensational view of the lake and the lovely Irish countryside beyond. This hotel I can recommend to anyone. I found no failings at all.

Aha, but when I had arrived Niall told me all the suites were occupied. Was he speaking with forked tongue? 'Did you have a suite?' I asked Lady Rayne, opposite me on the plane. She dipped into her bag and gave me four Opal Fruits. 'I didn't say sweets, I asked if you had a suite at the hotel,' I said. 'No,' said Lady Rayne. I therefore confirm Dromoland Castle is a sensational place.

WINNIE IN EGYPT (liked it!)

WINNIE IN AUSTRIA

ABROAD

HAPPY PORTUGESE PEOPLE
SING TO WINNIE IN ARSÉNIO'S

" DEAR MR WINNER, WHAT
WAS THAT PLACE
YOU RECOMMENDED
IN MOROCCO..?"

" READ ON AND
FIND OUT."

AUSTRIA

We dropped into the **Café Konditorei Brunhumer** on our way from somewhere to somewhere. It's in a very pleasant town called Zell am See, down by a lake. The old-fashioned home-made Eastern European goulash soup was marvellous. Georgina checked that it was fresh and it certainly was. I took an iced cake that looked like a Christmas pudding with a layer of marzipan under the pink icing. I thought it was all extremely cheerful.

Café Mozart, in Vienna, was made famous in one of my all-time great movies, *The Third Man*. They actually brought us a glass of water with the coffee, which Chris Rea always says is essential. He's very surprised when no one else brings it. Unfortunately, the Café Mozart was not like it was in *The Third Man*. It's very modernised, although well run. Not a place you should seek out for its historical association.

The restaurant in the **Hotel Hubertus**, in Filsmoos a Dachstein, is called Hubertushof. It is run by Johanna and Deitmar Maier. Deitmar is like a very third-rate comedian, the Austrian version of Jack the Lad, even though he's a bit old for the role. You ask where the pigeon cames from and he says, 'St Marks Square, Venice'. He's a laugh a minute, is Deitmar. Above us was a cuckoo clock that kept chiming about every ten minutes, with cuckoos coming out. My rabbit ravioli covering was very tough and heavy. The main course was veal with brains and kidneys. I was not terribly impressed. It's a pity because Johanna is a very famous local cook and she was a very nice person.

The **Hotel Sacher**, in Salzburg, could do with a bit of renovation, but the Presidential Suite is at least large, even though the furniture is a bit odd and glumpy. Georgina said she thought it looked like a Communist Russian apartment. I found it quite pleasant, although having duvets instead of sheets and blankets is abominable in a first-class hotel. The main restaurant is panelled and features carved deer heads with real horns around the wall. The bouillon of beef with vegetables, semolina dumpling and liver dumpling was quite tasty, and the inevitable goose liver (very popular in Austria) arrived as a freebie starter with some poached pears. The Sacher is most famous because its Viennese hotel (far posher than the one in Salzburg) got involved in a court case over its chocolate cake, which went on for two years without a very clear result! I enjoyed the Sacher in Salzburg, in particular because of the General Manager, Mrs Elfi Kammerhofer, who is not only the first female hotel general manager I've ever met, she's also one of the most efficient and charming of all time.

The **Hotel Schloss Fuschl** is a very classy hotel on a lake near Salzburg, where people stay particularly for the music festival. If the weather's good you eat by the lake, or you sunbathe by the lake on sun-loungers. If it's not, as the manager Herbert Llaublichoer-Pichler said, they 'mass exit, speedily reorganise and bung everyone inside'. The butter came straight from the fridge, so you couldn't spread it. My smoked trout was large but unbelievably fresh and good, and Georgina said her soup was 'great'. I was getting a bit fed up with rich Austrian and German food, so I had spaghetti bolognese. That was actually very acceptable.

The **Restaurant Obauer**, in Werfen, is owned by the brothers Karl and Rudolf the chef. It gets 19 out of 20 in the Gault Millau Guide! They suggested we have six different courses, which is quite minor in Austria. Obviously they thought we weren't hungry! Georgina commented: 'I love the atmosphere.' It's brightly lit, with lots of flowers, and definitely cheerful. The food was excellent. Georgina said she'd like to take their card. I said: 'You're coming back, are you?' She replied, 'Definitely.' I guess she'll be passing through Werfen regularly. The service was extremely slow.

BELGIUM

Breydel de Coninck, just off the market square in Bruges, was packed for Sunday lunch, so I prostrated myself before Caroline Janssens, a statuesque blonde at the counter. Her husband, Fernand, is chef and owner. She led us upstairs to a table for six by an open window facing whitewashed walls and flower baskets. 'You may have to share,' said Lieve, the waitress. I looked so shocked that she thought better of it. I got some really incredible white, very cold beer made in Bruges. Miss Lid had fried scampi that were very tasty. I had moules in cream sauce, one of 11 sauce options. They were good, but not south-of-France good. The chips were absolutely sensational. Home-made. You very seldom find that today. The grand finale was a superb apple pie with whipped cream and ice cream. An enormous portion. Totally historic.

Pie in the sky

The 24-year-old American chef from the US ambassador's residence in Brussels declined to give an opinion on the three-star-Michelin food served at **De Karmeliet**. Timothy Byres sat there in a corner, with his wife Brianne. They were the only other lunchtime customers. He'd travelled to Bruges to sample the supposedly wonderful food. On the whole I found it awful.

We started off with drinks in a lovely atrium overlooking a small garden. The main restaurant was not so attractive. Yellow-washed walls and paintings ranging from nice to awful. No cohesion. There was piped music coming from black loudspeakers hanging in the corners of the room. Disgusting.

I started with roast langoustine and bits and pieces. Miss Lid had coulis of aubergine, tartare tomato and slices of mozzarella with goose liver. 'It doesn't mix, the taste, with the goose liver,' she said. I took some goose liver. It was excellent, went very well with my langoustine.

Miss Lid enjoyed her risotto greatly, but my chicken pie was unspeakable. The chicken was very light and lacking in texture. It resembled a mousse of man-made, or false, chicken. It tasted of nothing. It was one of the worst dishes I've ever been served. Also, I don't think the chef, Geert Van Hecke, should expect you to eat salad with the same knife and fork you've been eating hot chicken with.

Some petits fours arrived before the dessert. I ate a small éclair that tasted as if it had been in the fridge. The recommended pasta and cream dessert was memorably terrible. The pasta was very overdone and chewy, particularly at the edges where it was sort of caramelised. You had to work very hard to pull a piece off to eat. The finale was partly saved by some historic honey bread cakes. All this goes to show that three Michelin stars don't always mean much.

Flemish masters

It's always nice to stumble on something marvellous when you aren't expecting it. This particular stumble occurred in Bruges, which even out of season seemed to be full of English people. The restaurant has one Michelin star and is called **Den Gouden Harynck**. The owner, Philippe Serruys, found the name buried in the 17th-century house, indicating it was once a fishmonger's named The Golden Herring.

The restaurant is exceptionally attractive. Large tables, well spaced, very quietly speaking diners, a real log fire, a tiled floor, white walls. Marike, Mrs Serruys, wafts between the tables in a grey silk coat. It's all extremely civilised. Wish there was somewhere like it in London. Butter was not wrapped; a large square of it rested on the table. Real orange juice came quickly with a little carafe for me to mix it with champagne. I did and it frothed on to the tablecloth. Scallops marinated with truffle were a freebie.

I started with excellent langoustine grilled with basil and mozzarella, and then we had roast lobster in butter with a curry sauce. Everything was sensational. They gave me a bib for the lobster, which is useful, as hardly a meal passes without me spilling some of it on my shirt. I should have taken my bib home. The couscous with raisins was particularly tasty and I had more of it when they brought some extra curry sauce. To finish, I had millefeuille with gingerbread ice cream: Miss Lid had ice cream, hot chocolate sauce and cream.

They didn't make the mint tea with fresh mint, which was the only downer. Otherwise, this was all very memorable.

It's always wise to ask the best restaurateurs where they eat on their days off. Phillipe Serruys, owner-chef of Den Gouden Harynck (one Michelin star) said, 'Try **Heer Halewyn**. It's where the in-crowd of Bruges go.' Later he left a panic message at the hotel that I should take cash because they didn't accept credit cards. The Heer Halewyn is a small bistro-like room featuring brick walls with maps on them and a charcoal grill in front of a roaring log fire. Two old ladies sitting close to it were going redder and redder.

I'd eaten a lot of rich food, so the tasty grilled steak with jacket potato was most welcome. Miss Lid had an extremely good kebab. I started with a fine salad with cheese and walnuts and ended with vanilla ice cream with chocolate sauce. All very nice. The in-crowd of Bruges didn't look much like the group you see at San Lorenzo in London, which sports more plastic surgery per square foot than anywhere in the world. And superb, much under-rated food. But they were a wholesome lot.

I don't often take risks. I go regularly to the same places. So when I recently decided to spend a weekend away, the question was – where? I decided on Bruges. I'd last been there in 1956 when I made my first ever movie, a documentary entitled *This Is Belgium*. It rained a lot that summer, so it was finished off in East Grinstead. It made it into the *Guinness Book of Records*, as the only film about Belgium ever shot in Sussex.

My first problem was that there's no legendary hotel in Bruges. In the Michelin Guide it has one three-star restaurant and two one-stars, but the highest-rated hotel had two black towers (three is top) and was modern. I hate modern. Among one-tower hotels listed, two were coloured red. For those who understand the Michelin Guide (and I've never met anyone who does) red means Hôtels agréables. Neither place could offer much, but the **Relais Oud Huis Amsterdam** came up with a junior suite.

Bruges is easy to get to. You take a private Learjet from RAF Northolt and it's a half-hour flight to Ostend. The hotel was a 40-minute drive. It's a lovely 18th-century house on one of the beautiful canals. The junior suite was an attic with a high, pointed ceiling and four tiny windows looking on to rooftops; very gloomy, not much furniture. I phoned downstairs to an immensely charming 22-year-old girl, the only person in charge. 'Ilse, this is the worst room I've ever been given!' I said, trusting the message would get through. Ilse appeared, quite unworried, with a bunch of keys and showed us six other rooms, all of which were worse. The next day someone failed to turn up, so we moved to a real suite, pleasantly furnished with three large windows overlooking the canal.

CARIBBEAN

Some people would place **The Cliff** at, or near the top of, their list of favourite restaurants in Barbados. It sits overlooking the sea. It is owned by Brian Ward, whose family once had Treasure Beach hotel. I think it's over-rated. Run by pompous, arrogant staff. Last time I went my so-called New York-cut steak was three pieces of overcooked monstrosity.

Coral Reef, the best Barbadian hotel of the old days, is still nice. But I always notice how the beach there has diminished. Indeed the ravenous removal of the coral reef to sell in little pieces to tourists has played havoc with the yellow sands. Don't bother.

Daphne's, a London place opened by a casting director in the 60s, went down the tubes and then became very chic when Mogens Tholstrup took it over. Then it went into decline and is now attempting a comeback, having been bought out by the Belgo Group. They have licensed a version of it to the Tamarind Cove in Barbados. Daphne's looks like a Balinese hut built on the Legoland principle. Not dreadful but no particular charm. The service is dire. Food at best moderate.

Amazingly you can stay in Barbados and pay less than the £63,000 I gave Sandy Lane for my 28-day Christmas visit. If you wish to enjoy almost the same view, to swim in the same bay, pay a fraction of what I paid and be in a nice hotel, I suggest the **Almond Beach Club**.

If I lie on my padded blue sun-lounger in a key position near the beach bar of Sandy Lane, and in the centre of the sweeping, palm-fringed bay, and look to my right, I see, on the tip of the bay, the Almond Beach Club. It's a five-minute walk past private villas on soft, golden sand.

This has 161 rooms built around three swimming pools and a garden. Some of the rooms look directly on to the sea. No children are allowed, but its sister place, the Almond Beach Village, does allow children. This particular child (me) has never been there.

A couple could go now for two weeks to the Almond Beach Club, including return air fares from London, for £3,195 per person. This buys you all meals – as much food and drink as you can devour – as well as the subsidiary delights of fishing, water-skiing, snorkelling and sailing.

I went one lunch time and inspected thoroughly. They were offering soup, wrapped butter (not my favourite), two urns of vegetables, one of rice, separate tureens of lettuce, cucumbers, tomatoes, plus hot dogs, hamburgers, barbecued chicken and freshly cooked marlin. There were many desserts. There's also an à la carte menu in the all-in price.

They have another restaurant in the hotel called Enid's, where you have to book. There they celebrate 'the culinary heritage of our native Barbados'.

After 26 years of going every Christmas-New Year to Barbados I've at last found a great restaurant there. One that ranks with the finest in the world. The owner, John Chandler, responded indignantly, 'It isn't a restaurant, it's my home.' I said, 'John, any place that sells meals is a restaurant to me.'

John's home and/or restaurant is a beautiful plantation house originally built in 1635 in the middle of cane fields. You drive down a rutted track. It's Barbados as it used to be. The place is furnished with exquisite antiques, the table settings, napkins, everything is perfection. The gardens are alive with the sound of brightly coloured macaws in enormous cages. The whole thing is an experience of total delight.

John's wife, Rain, is co-conspirator. John's family came to Barbados in 1638 from Scotland. He and Rain are the finest example of old-school hospitality. We lounged in the garden, following in the sitsteps of Prince Harry, the Tony Blairs, Drew Barrymore, Helen Mirren et al. I had a pina colada, Geraldine rum punch in a shell. Terrific canapés.

At lunch, pumpkin, carrot and ginger or callaloo soup were served at the table. The rest is a Sunday buffet. Eighty-seven-year-old Betty Sheppard, splendidly dressed in satin, played the piano. I took red snapper pâté, swordfish and steamed flying fish with plantain as my starter. Followed by brilliant plantain fritters, peas and rice, chicken fricassee, macaroni pie, pepper pot in a big bowl, stewed pigeon with peas, corn soufflé and curried green bananas.

'All done to perfection,' I observed.

Desserts I tried, included, but were not limited to, bread and butter pudding with butter sauce, chocolate mousse, trifle, coconut baked sweets. 'I've eaten so much I'm going to burst,' observed Geraldine. I was stuffed speechless.

I nearly forgot to tell you the name of this amazing place. It's **Fisher Pond Great House**, St Thomas, Barbados. Only available to the public for Sunday lunch. During the week, if you're six or more, they open specially. That's no good for me. I haven't got five friends, so I'd never get in.

At **Groots** I enjoyed myself immensely. There's a big U-shaped bar full of people you'd never see at Sandy Lane and an opening to the dining area. This has enormous tables, well spaced apart. The decor is World War II Nissen hut. Diners are encouraged to write on the walls in black marker pens. I produced a masterful cartoon of me and a glowing Groots recommendation.

I ordered cod with chips and mushy peas, also mashed potatoes with steak and kidney pudding. Nothing is too much trouble for me in my role of food investigator. My shrimp cocktail was the old-fashioned kind with a pink sauce and crisp lettuce. It was very pleasant. The portions were enormous. I strongly recommend you eat, at the same time, cod and chips with steak and kidney pudding. I went from one to the other. The mushy peas were the best ever. Geraldine kept nicking them. The chips were cut on the premises from real potatoes, not bought in as they are at nearly every London restaurant. The cod was okay to good, the batter sensational. The steak and kidney excellent.

Hans then shot into restaurant stratosphere by delivering a fantastic treacle pudding. It had treacle on top that tasted of treacle, it was kind of settling into the pudding. It was really very, very good. The custard was superb, too.

If you go to Barbados, never mind all the restaurants trying to be clever. Visit Hans. Even though he did say to Geraldine, when I went for the car, 'If you want to escape, come here and have a drink.'

In old Barbados there are little wooden houses, market stalls by the beach, cane fields and an aura of better times. At the **Fishpot**, you sit right by the sea, in a 17th-century fort. It's also a 21-room hotel. It's tranquil. It's beautiful. It's what Caribbean life should be.

The superb restaurant manager is Barbadian as is their excellent chef. The service is wonderful. For lunch the Fishpot had fresh local lobsters, which is more than Sandy Lane could offer at the time. I started with a perfect pina colada followed by a mixed fish platter, including lobster, clams, sardines, smoked salmon. I had a tiny cup of its fish chowder to taste. Marvellous. Everything was so fresh.

My dessert was home-made apple pie and tasted like one. Geraldine had coconut crème brûlée, which was superb. The Fishpot is absolutely terrific.

The restaurant I visit most in Barbados is the **Lone Star**, owned by Christian Roberts. In 1967 he starred in *To Sir, with Love*, opposite Sidney Poitier and Lulu. The Lone Star displays old film stills and posters featuring Christian. A few years ago he fell out with his junior partner, Steve Cox. After a five-year battle (the legal system in Barbados is almost as slow as restaurant service) they settled, leaving Christian unencumbered proprietor.

Cont'd

The Lone Star is an attractive room, right on the sea. It's part of a small hotel with four superb suites. I've stayed there. I always sit by the sea, facing the long wooden staircase that leads to the reception desk, because I like watching people enter restaurants. Their body language is fascinating.

The food is cheap and cheerful. They've got shepherd's pie, jerk chicken roulade, rack of US lamb, fresh local lobster, blackened dolphinfish, cheeseburger and chips. All pretty good.

The service is efficient, the ambience lively. There's always a buzz. I could mention celebrities I've seen and taken there, but you'd moan I was name-dropping.

A Pavilion too far

Barbados has become a goyish Golders Green. In case you're not au fait with Yiddish-New York dialogue, this means Barbados has become a suburban housing estate largely inhabited by non-Jews. My friend Lord Glenconner says it's 'like the Costa Brava blown up bigger. Not prettier, just larger'. I used to travel from the airport through lovely sugar plantations, past coloured-hut villages, old stone sugar mills and on to the sparkling Caribbean Sea. Now you sit in endless traffic jams on tacky motorways, looking out at car showrooms and supermarkets. What are laughingly called villas stretch back from the coast, annihilating the landscape that attracted people to the island in the first place.

The St James's coastal area is still pretty. I reserved a house with three bedrooms, a large sitting room, terraces and a garden in the grounds of the **Royal Pavilion**. And two further rooms at the chic little Lone Star hotel nearby. I chose which hotel to sleep in each night.

I unpacked first at the Royal Pavilion, locally nicknamed the Pink Pavilion. This is the second grandest hotel in Barbados, set in beautiful grounds. Unfortunately, it suffers from a design fault, irreversible unless it's knocked down. It's so close to the beach that an 8ft sea wall stands in front of the ground-floor suites, giving the residents nil view. The beach is a thin strip backed by a boring residential block. But it does expand at one end and that's where I sat.

Service at the Royal Pavilion seemed diabolical. It took me 44 minutes in boiling sun to get a Sprite. Jan Schöningh, the general manager, was apologetic. 'I can assure you, Mr Winner,' he said, 'that I intend to spruce the place up. If you come back in three months, you won't have to wait 44 minutes for a Sprite.' 'I won't be here in three months, Jan,' I said. 'What about tomorrow?'

Thereafter, room availability and beach service improved immensely. Sometimes there were five beach attendants asking if I wanted anything – and then there'd be none. But they were all nice people, particularly Egbert, who traversed the paved walkways throwing an iced bucket nonchalantly in the air and catching it behind him. Until it fell and dented, as we all knew it would. I left Egbert my hotel freebies: a bottle of champagne and a strange glass ornament of hands doing something odd.

Dinner at the Royal Pavilion is famous for being terrible. The hotel itself is actually pleasant. But I never saw more than six people eating dinner. Even regular and devoted guests told me it was abysmal. They wouldn't eat there, so I didn't. Breakfast was extremely good and well-organised, in a pleasing room on the beach. I got genuine, freshly squeezed orange juice without much trouble. The staff were all a delight; the bacon was excellent. They even started bringing ice lollies round the beach, compliments of the management. The Royal Pavilion is run by Fairmont Hotels and the Canadian Pacific group, and it's well worth a visit. If you eat dinner there, tell me about it. I'm sure it will improve.

At last I've found someone who knows less about food than me. Not only less about food, but less about presentation, about how to treat people. In fact I've met the most awful example of the so-called 'hospitality industry' I've ever come across in 70 years of eating in the finest restaurants all over the world. Quite a non-achievement.

Stop. Don't get overexcited. 'Calm down dear.' It's only a chef. He's Grant MacPherson, culinary director and head chef of **Sandy Lane**, Barbados. He is far and away the worst choice of chef since Dermot Desmond so beautifully rebuilt and improved Sandy Lane. It's been the subject of a considerable makeover, largely successful.

MacPherson struts round the dining room, a carefully tended little triangle of white hair under his lower lip. One lady on the beach said, 'I'd like to rip it off.' I understand her angst. If you said anything to him that wasn't total praise he looked as if you'd vanished, and walked away. If I had £1 for every guest who said to me, 'Be sure to hammer that ghastly chef,' I'd be ... well, about £53 richer. Under Richard Ekkebus a couple of years ago the food was fantastic.

Grant MacPherson came from running 4,000-room casino hotels in Las Vegas. What has that to do with a small, luxury beach resort? One VIP guest said, 'When you cater for casino gamblers they never even know where they are, let alone what they've eaten or what time of day it is. There are no clocks.' MacPherson and Sandy Lane are a total mismatch.

The new general manager, Robert Logan, on the other hand, came from six years in charge of Raffles hotel, Rangoon. I liked him. If he can flex his muscles and not sink under the gargantuan ego of chef MacPherson I think he'll do well.

Some of the memorably awful food I ate includes pizzas with a soggy base; dreary sausage and mash; chewy, tasteless flank steak; feeble spare ribs; shepherd's pie, all potato, little meat; sweet and sour pork like school dinners at their worst; chicken curry with cashew nuts, soggy and grotesque. Some good food, but not, in my opinion, enough to satisfy many guests, paying for food alone Bd$181.50 (£66), and on Friday and Sunday Bd$302.50 (£110). So with drinks and coffee five days would be at least £80 a head, the other two days £130 a head. No wonder the well-heeled were moaning.

Isle be damned

My January experience of Barbados hotel life was dire. I chose what used to be a good little place, **Treasure Beach**. Their only supersuite, for a period out of peak season, cost a fortune per night, accommodation only.

Marilil Troulan in reservations wrote: 'We'll arrange for a taxi to meet Mr Winner at the airport.' My Mr Fraser replied snottily: 'At those prices a limousine is usually provided free of charge.' The manager said they'd send one, explaining: 'We are a very small property, no pomp or grandeur.' For what they were charging a night all-in, a bit of grandeur would be quite acceptable. When we arrived at one o'clock in the afternoon the suite wasn't ready. It had not been occupied the previous night. We waited glumly in the tiny lobby. Finally, I walked into the suite and sat on the balcony as they cleaned up.

The second night no service was provided at all. We came back from dinner to find the same mess as when we'd departed. I went bananas. The fourth night the same thing happened again. Unbelievable! They deducted one day's charge. I don't go for discounts, I go for service. It took 40 minutes to get tea and biscuits, and their biscuits were dry cheese crackers. It was all basically horrendous. Room service even sent paper napkins.

The restaurant wasn't bad. The excellent maitre d', John Douglin, looked, talked and laughed exactly like Frank Bruno. 'All the English guests say to me, "You know what I mean, Harry?"' said John. 'I don't even know who Harry is.' I had three lunches there. Pan-fried dolphinfish was good. So was the chef Jeffrey Hyland's bajan chicken; the seasoning was memorable. Vanessa liked her catch of the day, kingfish, with herbs and spices.

I called 'Hello!' loudly to get attention. A smiley, chubby Welsh lady at the next table, wearing a pink cruise-ship cap with Oriana on it, cried 'Hello' back. Her husband hated his Caesar salad. He said: 'It was just lettuce, very dull. Thank God for breakfast.' I had no sympathy at all. They weren't paying £1,200 a night, plus food and extras, for poor service and scant hotel facilities. But then, they were Welsh. They had more sense.

Peace of Caicos

It was like something out of a Fellini movie. There were these luxury beach huts facing white sand and the most turquoise blue sea you could imagine. Then staff erected a series of open-sided tents, placed long tables in them, and more servants filed down from the hotel carrying food on silver trays. Ensconced in this little area, which common folk like me could only gaze at from the wooden walkway that led to the beach, was Donatella Versace, her daughter, bodyguards in assorted colours, and selected friends, relatives and who knows what.

Thus was the scene at **Parrot Cay** in the Turks & Caicos Islands, where the sun beat down from a blue sky on to the recently planted palm trees and other flora, as Robert Earl, of Planet Hollywood fame, struggled to perfect his hotel in time for my arrival. Possibly he also took into account the other guests, none of whom Signora Versace deigned to move among. She stayed in her manor, we crawled over the hotel – although Vanessa nearly got to see her close-up in the gym, stopped only by a large black bodyguard, who said: 'Why are you carrying a camera?'

I had to be content with the sighting of a blonde lady accompanied by burly minders, walking in the distance from sea to hut-suites. Still, there was the very jolly and excellent New York playwright Wendy Wasserstein, currently working on the screenplay of the musical *Chicago*, and a beautiful American blonde, Amber Valletta, whom I was assured was the most famous model in the world. I'd never heard of her, but the last model I knew anything about was Jean Shrimpton. So call me stupid, I don't care.

In this part of the Caribbean, Cay means island and Parrot was changed from Pirate, possibly to stop guests at this highly posh resort thinking they were heading for Disneyland. It's an elegant place, set on a 1,000-acre private island some 20 minutes by pleasing boat ride from the main island of Providenciales, which you get to from England via Miami. The 56-room hotel is co-owned with Earl by Christina and V S Ong, who also have the superb Metropolitan and Halkin hotels in London.

We arrived to be picked up by golf buggies at the small pier, taken to an excellent colonial-style suite with a large balcony and thence poolside, with the sand and sea only a few yards away.

I'd like to tell you what I had for lunch, but as I started dictating into my tape recorder, which has taken over all natural functions of memory, Mr Earl snapped (very unlike him, he's usually super-cheerful): 'We're not going to have to listen to you talking into that at every meal, are we?' Never one to offend, I turned it off, and it never saw the sunlight again, poor thing. I did manage to sneak a few hand-written notes when Robert wasn't looking. They recall the food was very good. In particular a strawberry sorbet that was majorly historic, some lovely Thai beef curry, a delicious papillote of lobster tail with spiced balsamic rice, and a memorable supreme of duckling with poached pear in spiced red wine and honey.

As the place was new, I was given a mercifully short document from Alison Marshall Public Relations of New York, whomever she might be. It provided me with the names of the French chef, Franck Aubert, who got a Michelin star in

St Maxime, and the general manager, Michel Neutelings. I was very impressed with him. He pitched in and did things. He'd been at the K Club in Barbuda, much visited by Princess Di. My press release told me: 'His interests include scuba diving, boating and reading.' That's rather like listening to Miss World contestants telling you they want to help the poor. I've always wanted to read a press release saying someone terribly significant is 'interested in picking his nose, ironmongery and farting', but then I'm extremely childish and I don't suppose I ever will.

I can definitely recommend Parrot Cay. The plan is to build many houses on what is now virgin land, so get there before all that. There's a nearby place you go to by boat called Iguana Island, which has 4,000 iguanas on it, and that's all. It's fascinating, just like a midget version of Jurassic Park. My only problem at Parrot Cay was when I walked into the lovely, warm sea. And walked. And walked. About quarter of a mile later the water was still only up to my waist. Vanessa was able to swim under those conditions. But my athletic skills are not yet that well developed. Nor will they ever be.

P.S. The hotel has become a haven for movie stars and rock 'n' roll legends because it's on an island with no access for gawpers. It's still excellent.

I'm a long-time expert on **Ladera** in St Lucia and its restaurant, Dasheen, as I've visited for over 25 years. It looks down on the rainforest between the Pitons. Either side are the towering Pitons themselves. Ladera is a small hotel. Many of its rooms have only three walls. The fourth side is open, with a balcony looking down to a truly stunning view of the beautiful bay far below. Some rooms feature a two-tier splash pool with a waterfall connecting one pool and the other. It doesn't have much land attached to it – just a swimming pool, small gardens and a spectacular dining area.

The buffets, featuring an astonishing variety, are adjacent to historic. I had marvellous fish stew with swordfish, yams, green bananas, christophene and pumpkin. That sounds odd, doesn't it? Perhaps the veggies were separate. I seldom know what I'm eating. I did try the jerk pork, which is spicy pork steaks, and the Ladera cocoa, a chocolate mousse. I also had the delicious Caribbean minestrone.

The whole place is magical. I drove – atrociously as always – in my rented Jeep, over potholed roads, past the steaming volcano and then a sharp right, up a desperately steep incline, to a ferocious man in a guardhouse. Mercifully, he always recognises me.

In February 2005 a very classy local hotelier, Craig Barnard, bought the now-called **Jalousie Plantation** near Soufrière in St Lucia. He was financed by Roger Myers, a nice man from St John's Wood who had a restaurant chain in London and who now lives on St Lucia. Roger will spend millions upgrading the hotel.

I visited recently. Not much has yet been done. The rooms, mostly chalets, are being tarted up in clusters.

When I was there the bay was tranquil. Luxuriant Caribbean foliage dominates the view in all directions – unless you're looking out to sea in which case there's salt water. It's the most incredible spot. There are almond trees, coconut palms, red cedar and more.

The food is average. I had a nice dinner on the terrace with chilled breadfruit vichyssoise, corn soup, chef's salad, coconut and chicken salad and lobster. Lunch by the sea was mediocre.

Craig says his two-year plan will transform the place into one of the greatest hotels in the world.

The **Fish Pot** in Grand Case, St Martin, is run by Kristal from Macedonia with husband Jean-Marc from Normandy. Lovely salmon and cheese tartlet. The French onion soup was good. Snapper and mahi-mahi were excellent, with a real, French-tasting sauce. Desserts reasonable, but profiteroles, always tricky, were poor.

It seemed you couldn't just phone up and book **Mario's**, a much-praised restaurant in St Martin: it was full for ever. I decided to visit and apply my legendary charm. Mario's is in a hut on a canal overlooking a junkyard. Martyne Audet, the wife of chef Mario Tardis, sat at her computer fending off would-be eaters. After a bit of chat, Martyne agreed I could come that evening. At night the place looked very nice. Candles on shiny wood tables, the ripple of light on the water, sunflowers everywhere. Martyne had not succumbed to greed and packed people in. Tables were well spaced. She was a superb hostess and order-taker. The service was like lightning.

I tasted Vanessa's black bean soup. It was totally brilliant. But I could smell, with great clarity, my Maine steamed mussels in a tomato, Parmesan and fines herbes broth. They weren't nice. I had chosen the main course 'signature' dish of half duck, honey-garlic glazed and crisply roasted, served with caramelised onion, mashed potato and sweet-and-sour sauce. The duck was shiny white. I've never seen anything like it. The texture and taste were poor. Vanessa had grilled tuna accompanied by gnocchi in tomato sauce and blue cheese that was smeared over everything. It was an extraordinary dish. Dessert was crispy profiteroles with ice cream and chocolate sauce. Nice and gooey, rather like they served on TWA in the 1970s.

Saints be praised

I was apprehensive going to **La Samanna** for Christmas on the half-Dutch half-French island of St Martin in the Caribbean. While I greatly admire the Orient Express people who own La Samanna, I'd had a dreadful time at their hotel in Madeira.

My suite was terrific. Nicely furnished in 'modern French rustic'. Great view of a large bay unspoilt by any rubbish, the balcony wrapping round to the front of the hotel. Our first lunch, by the pool, was horrid. My salade niçoise was disgusting. The tuna looked like slices of steak and tasted nasty. It had green and red peppers, which I've never seen before in a niçoise; many of the regular ingredients were missing. Vanessa's Caesar salad included tomato and had a sharp, unpleasant taste.

As it was five hours later for us because of the time change, I ordered room-service dinner. The two fried eggs I'd asked for on my hamburger weren't there. The so-called fresh orange juice definitely wasn't. It tasted deeply unpleasant. I telephoned again. 'Are you seriously telling me this orange juice is fresh?' I said. 'Yes, it is,' came the reply. It was now 9pm – two in the morning my time. I rang for the manager, having kept one glass of orange muck, which I was quite prepared to carry to England and have analysed in a laboratory. I rang the chef. 'Is all your orange juice fresh?' I asked. There was a pause that spoke volumes. 'Would you like some?' he volunteered. 'Thank you,' I replied. The chef, with fresh orange juice, arrived at the same time as the manager. I asked, could I please not be treated as an idiot.

Life after that was very nice. Including the orange juice. The staff at La Samanna are basically superb. It's a very well-run, excellent, beautiful hotel. The food, for the Caribbean, where fresh supplies are rare, was good.

Security at the hotel entrance gate was slack, but I put a stop to that. Cruise-ship people and any wanderer with a rucksack seemed to get in, sit on guest beach loungers and generally bring down the tone. They reckoned without Winner the beach vigilante, this time superbly abetted by Mrs Martin Bandier, he the head of EMI in New York, she a hotel regular who told of the days when the manageress, Lynn Webber, would patrol the sands like a storm trooper, removing intruders. That's my kinda gal. The guests were great too. There was an English computer genius who's the chairman of Psion, and a host of highly robust New York music-business people headed by the renowned lawyer Allen Grubman. In his home town Mr Grubman has dishes named after him in posh restaurants. That's the American equivalent of a peerage.

I booked dinner at **La Santal**, in St Martin, a poshed-up hut overlooking the sea, tented in pink-and cream-striped, pleated silk. The lady at the desk was extremely snooty, and with the Muzak going the place felt like a Jewish wedding. I ordered a Corton Charlemagne Grand Cru. Then suddenly thought: 'I don't think the wine list showed the year of any vintage.' I went to the desk and looked. 'We don't put the vintage because the stock always changes,' said the snooty woman. 'So the price stays the same whether it's a good year or bad!' I exclaimed. Nobody cared. The head waiter assured me ours was 1994. The bread was terrible. I felt I was chewing gum. When the wine

Cont'd

came it was 1991, not 1994. The gazpacho was like nothing I've ever tasted: it could have been tomato soup with HP sauce added. I ordered chicken casserole and got roast chicken with a sauce. It was like chicken at a bar mitzvah for thousands of people. The soufflé ordered for dessert was sickly. I am the most sweet-toothed person in the world, but I couldn't eat that one. This was a grossly mediocre dinner.

EGYPT

Entranced by the rule of tum

Okay, we haven't had a quiz yet. What time do you think Miss Lucy, the belly dancer at the Nice Hilton, started her two-hour act the Friday I was in Cairo? Go on, guess. The answer is 4.30 in the morning! In Cairo nobody goes to sleep and the big stars are the belly dancers. Some people support Fifi Abdou at the Sheraton, some Miss Lucy, some Mona Said at the Meridien. We opted for dinner with Mona on the 15th floor at the oddly named **La Belle Epoque**, sporting a red menu with black silhouettes of a lady dancing with a monocled gent to a horn gramophone.

Mona was coming on early that night, 1.30am I was told. So I had a sleep, got up, and we presented ourselves in this enormous barn with a tired three-piece orchestra playing on a large stage. Some 20 people were lost in a room that seated 200. We got a table for six with a Japanese party of four on our right. It looked desperately sad. I ordered a glass of wine, but a bottle appeared. It was Omar Kayyam from the Egyptian Vineyards Company. Rather sweet, no great taste, but quite harmless. We had the inevitable and good general mix, with mezze to start. By the time we got to the sea bass, a few more people had come in. The traditional bread and butter pudding, om aly, was gone, and it was still like sitting in an aircraft hangar at the function that time forgot.

Then at 1am things started to move. The three weary musicians left the stage and a rather grand 15-piece orchestra appeared in black trousers and flowered shirts. An Egyptian singer, looking like a mafioso Tony Bennett (mind you, Tony Bennett looks like a mafioso Tony Bennett), started to sing 'Autumn Leaves'. An Egyptian wedding group clapped as the bride danced well and the groom danced nervously on the stage. Then the singer started on upbeat numbers. Lots more people came in, and it all began to get lively.

The singer exited to great applause. The room had filled up. It was a quarter to two. The belly dancer's own 43-piece orchestra came on with six singers! Suddenly it was all happening. To a cacophony of rhythm, yelling and clapping, the very ample Mona Said appeared, making a triumphal entrance through the tables, accompanied by six male dancers in long grey smocks waving sticks above their heads. This was it! The star had arrived! The act was extraordinary. Bit of large-belly movement, many bespangled costume changes from a Liz Hurley safety-pin outfit to yellow sequins galore. A lot of finger pointing at the audience accompanied by small, sexy moves. The whole thing a cross between a jolly auntie and a massively voluptuous siren. 'I bet you'd be scared if you were alone with her,' Vanessa volunteered. 'She'd envelop you.' 'I'd be terrified,' I admitted.

A few seconds later I was welcomed as the famous English film director, a microphone was thrust in my hand and I had to say a few words. Arabs who got up and danced at their tables as Mona tripped the heavy fantastic, grinned and waved at me. A second bottle of Egyptian wine came and went. Around 4.15 Mona finished to a tumultuous roar of appreciation. The box of tissues which she'd dipped into for two hours to wipe away the sweat was discreetly taken from the side of the stage. We went back to our hotel through the X-ray check, past the soldiers on guard and up to sleep. Gosh, I thought, as I nodded off – I wish they had events like that in London.

Enjoying the Nile rushes

'**D**on't eat anything,' I was told. 'If you must eat, then only oranges or eggs because they're covered with peel or shell. Take stomach pills, take antibiotics.' I had been asked to Egypt for the Cairo Film Festival. They were paying a tribute to Oliver Stone, Ismail Merchant, Nicolas Cage, Marsha Mason and me. A motley crew. If I was not to be shot by terrorists, it seemed I was to be food-poisoned. We arrived at Cairo airport at one in the morning and a bank official tried to swindle me on the exchange rate. The motorway into town had raised sentry boxes every so often, with soldiers armed with machine guns looking down on us. More soldiers round the hotel and massive security. What, I wondered, am I doing here?

After a few hours of nervousness, I ate everything and anything. It was mostly terrific, none of it gave me tummy trouble. I saw no terrorists, no mugging, no violence, just fascinating places and jolly nice people. So much for over-caution.

I went to the **Cairo Sheraton** for my first Egyptian meal in the city. A staple starter here is one of my all-time favourites, mezze. It's lots of things in bowls with a thick, plate-shaped bread to dip in. There's samboussek with spinach, shrimps, deep-fried brain, chicken wings, hummus, babaghanough, stuffed vine leaves, tabouleh, kobeba and more. I have no idea which bowl was which (well, I could just identify a shrimp), but it was all excellent. The main course was beef and veal with sauce and veg. Far better, I thought, than mass catering in England. There was an amazing cabaret of whirling dervishes, men with tambourines and castanets dressed in skirts. That they eventually peel off over their heads in layers while going round and round at an amazing speed. An orchestra of many strange instruments goes barmy in the background. Most diverting.

I can recommend **El Mashrabia** in a part of Cairo tourists don't normally go. A jolly starter of grape leaves with calf's trotter and an excellent follow-up of stuffed pigeon.

The **Gezira Sheraton** is not the sort of place I'm used to. Okay for normal people and commercial travellers. But there are no posh hotels in the centre of Cairo. It was efficient, with sweeping views over the Nile and the ugly high-rises that dominate the city. And on our one smog-free day we saw the pyramids from our balcony, nestling by the suburbs between a closer view of two other Sheraton hotels.

The **Mena House Oberoi Hotel** in Cairo, near the pyramids, is the only real luxury hotel Cairo has. It was built in 1869, and has since had more gilt added than even The Dorchester. But it's simply terrific. The rooms, the pool and the restaurants all have a spectacular view of the pyramids. I ate by the pool. Good tahina and an 'Arab mixed grill' with four singers and a band playing. The Mena House is where the first peace talks between Egypt and Israel took place. In 1943 it hosted a conference with Roosevelt, Churchill and Chiang Kai-Shek. 'They sat in the sun and decided not to decide anything,' said Hussein Marzouk, one of the philosophical managers, as he showed me round suites and rooms of unbelievable opulence.

The **Windsor Hotel** in Alfi Bey Street, Cairo, used to be a biggie, but the area got burned down in 1951 and it remains a total time warp in a city overtaken by ghastly modernity. Luxurious it isn't, but atmosphere it has in spades. I had a drink with the owner, Wafik Doss, who's had it since 1964. Wooden tub chairs, wooden stools at the bar, just like you imagine Egypt was when upper-class British were going beserk nicking everything they could from the pharaohs' tombs. In the old-fashioned lounge there were two English people reading the *Guardian*. They looked unbelievably miserable.

FRANCE
(including MONACO)

Brasserie Bofinger in La Bastille, in Paris, is a great art deco place where Monsieur Bofinger himself drew the first draught beer ever served in Paris in 1864. Very bustling, tall pillars, artistic marquetry. Wonderful onion soup and pot au feu of fish.

People say 'You must know Paris very well.' They assume anyone writing about food knows every restaurant in the capital of cuisine. I don't. Paris is so overcrowded, I seldom go there. When I do, I usually revisit places that have given me pleasure, regardless of what new three-star genius chef has emerged. I recently sought advice from the Ritz Hotel concierge, having told him I didn't want fancy food. He recommended **D'Chez Eux** in Avenue Lowendal. I was delighted with the result. D'Chez Eux is a rustic bistro with red-checked tablecloths, owned by a very courteous man, Jean-Pierre Court.

I had a 'cassoulet de les berges and marmite avec les confit de canard'. It was a superb stew. Out of a pot came chicken, duck, pork sausage, white beans, all put in a soup plate. It was enormous and delicious. Before that, I had 12 snails in a special plate, each bubbling in its own little crater. Georgina had pâté with pickled onions caramelised with raisins, lentils with garlic and ratatouille of mixed vegetables. Then came an enormous dessert trolley with chocolate mousse, oranges, mangoes, figs in a red wine sauce, all terrific. Then M Court brought some vanilla ice cream and plonked down a bowl of cookies. This place definitely goes on my 'must visit' list if ever I dare risk the Parisian traffic again. The French are the only people in the world who drive as stupidly as I do.

We helicoptered to Paris from Battersea heliport, landing close to the Eiffel Tower. An hour-and-a-half flight, very pleasant. In Paris, the traffic jams were horrendous. For dinner I had booked **Le Duc** in the Boulevard Raspail. This came highly recommended by Arrigo Cipriani, the owner of my favourite restaurant in the whole world, Harry's Bar in Venice. I found it horrific. Probably the worst meal of all time. Everything about it was nasty.

The room is hideous. The brown wood panelling looks tacky. There's over-bright, vulgar lighting, a purple spotted 'cheap-motel' carpet, garish leather banquettes and small wooden chairs. It resembled the dining cabin of a package-tour ocean liner. We were given a horrid table by the entrance to the kitchen.

I had fried whitebait that tasted of nothing and was rather soggy. Then I had moules marinière in a soup both odd and unpleasant. The moules looked plump and soft, but they were utterly tasteless. We waited for ever for the plates to be cleared. Then I had scampi, which were soft and flabby. This is usually a sign they've been frozen, which breaks down the texture. Or left about too long. Either way, they were awful.

I asked for rum baba for dessert. Three slices of sponge cake were produced. 'I'm going to get the rum,' said the waiter. He poured rum over the sponge. It was all highly indifferent. Nobody would give me the bill, so I got up and went to the desk. Start to walk out and you always get the bill. At the time it came to £105. Expensive for what it was. This is a place to avoid.

When I complained bitterly to Arrigo, he admitted that he hadn't been to Le Duc for 10 years.

Geraldine wanted to do something romantic for Valentine's Day. 'Let's watch the spin dryer,' I suggested. She responded, very clearly, we should dine at the famous George V hotel in Paris. I'm a poor boy from Willesden. Who am I to argue with a toff? Before you could say 'ridiculous', we were on an Augusta 109 helicopter for the 1 hour 20 minute flight from Battersea to a heliport near the Eiffel Tower.

The **Four Seasons George V** is a fantastic hotel. The lobby and even the corridors are sublimely elegant. The suite was the most beautiful I've ever had. Lovely oil paintings, tasteful furniture.

The Valentine's Day dinner, in the hotel's three-Michelin-starred restaurant, Le Cinq, offered nine-course menus headed 'Ladies' and 'Gentlemen'. There commenced a parade of tiny courses. Twenty-minute delays between each. Even Geraldine, who loved them all, said: 'I wouldn't mind if these bits and pieces came one after the other.' After an hour I was dying for the solidity of sausage, egg and chips. But to be fair, some of our dinner was superb. It wasn't the best three-Michelin-starred meal I've had. But it was good. I definitely enjoyed myself.

Dopey as it is, I always visit the **Lido** when I'm in Paris. There's something about a really old-fashioned, high-kicking cabaret show that I find most endearing. The absurdly camp costumes, the superb acrobats and jugglers, the inevitable spectacle flying on rails over your head – it's old-time show business. Seeing this in comfort and with a reasonable meal is quite enchanting. The menus vary from 'Touristique' at £80 to 'Passion' at £122, including half a bottle of champagne. The last time I was there, my sea bass starter was fine, and the lamb extremely good for a mass-catered place.

In Paris, the **Napoli Pizzeria** in the Rue de Rosiers, adjacent to the flea market in St-Ouen, is fantastic. Very jovial, great pizzas, pasta and other things. It's run with a terrific buzz by the brothers Salvatore and Antonio D'Allessandro. The flea market has become rather posh, so great bargains such as I've bought over the years are considerably less available.

I am beginning to think going to the **Plaza Athénée** in Paris is a bad habit. Like picking your nose or biting your fingernails. Recently I asked for a suite I'd had before, with a nice balcony overlooking the garden. When I got there I was shown into something different. I settled for a gloomy suite on the fifth. Actually, trouble had started earlier. 'Could I have a convertible rental car when I arrive at 8.30pm?' I asked Mr Cailotto of guest relations. 'No,' he said. It is relevant that my modest suite and the car together cost £1200 a day! For that you might reasonably expect service! 'Why can't I have the car at 8.30pm?' I asked Mr Cailotto. 'Because the Hertz office shuts at seven,' he said. Did I find anything good about the Plaza Athénée? Yes. The building's elegant. I only ate there once, then in the Relais Plaza, the snackier bit. It was good, even if Vanessa didn't get what she ordered. There was no waste basket in the bedroom and the TV handset didn't work. But it does have the Winner World Record for room service. The breakfast arrived 2 minutes and 51 seconds after I put the phone down from ordering it.

P.S. This is under new owners and is much better.

Putting out the Ritz

In 1980, I had Christmas lunch at the **Ritz Hotel** in Paris. I can still see the beautifully dressed old ladies, some alone, some with female companions, sitting in the grandest of rooms. A string orchestra played. Liveried waiters hovered with white gloves. It was like a Fellini movie. Sadly that dining room is gone. It was too big and too grand for today's Ritz. It's now subdivided and used for private receptions.

The Ritz is one of the very greatest hotels in the world. Every time I go through its revolving doors I see in my mind Princess Diana and Dodi Fayed leaving through the same door to take their last journey. Tourists still gather outside to be photographed in front of the impressive façade.

We were shown to a pleasant suite on the sixth floor. You could just about see the Eiffel Tower from the attic windows. It was beautifully furnished, but a bit gloomy. Frank Klein, the hotel's president, arranged for us to be moved to the Coco Chanel suite on the third floor. This was larger, lighter and quite exceptional. Everything about the Ritz is impeccable – the service, the bathrobes, the food, the ambience. Everyone is friendly and helpful.

My first excursion into a public room was for tea in the Bar Vendôme, the light meal and general snack place overlooking the hotel's central courtyard. I had French muffins. The sandwiches were in little bread éclairs. I recall them in England in the old days, named bridge rolls. Everything was good.

The restaurant, L'Espadon, is an attractive room with the ceiling painted as sky and clouds. I lunched there with Frank Klein. He's delightfully courteous and cheerful. My napkin had MW embroidered on it. I forgot to take it home. I had cream of white bean soup with a light foie gras flan, truffles and mushrooms. Then fillet of cod roasted with herbs and vinegar. It was all exceptional. A zucchini risotto came with my fish, and some sautéed potatoes that turned out to be mushrooms. Shows what I know about food. Georgina's main course was langoustine ravioli. She had prunes and chocolate ice cream for dessert, which she thought was wonderful. My layering of warm dark chocolate and coffee ice cream and a crisp rice cookie was fine, too.

In case you think I've lost all critical faculties, I'll relate one minor irritation. On Saturday afternoon, the concierge promised to put a road map in my suite. Come Sunday there was no road map, so we spent for ever Sellotaping the concierge's torn one to make it usable. A tiny thing, I agree. But when everything else is so splendid and efficient, a minor hiccup is magnified into a major burp, if you'll forgive my putting it that way.

I recently returned to **La Tour d'Argent** in Paris. The late Claude Terrail's place (now run by his son) offers a historic view of Notre Dame and the river Seine. The waiter assured me he'd remember everything without a pad. Checking, he said to me: 'You ordered foie gras.' I said: 'No, I didn't, I ordered lobster bisque.' A waiter at another table had a pad. Georgina said: 'We're only two people, we're not important enough for a pad.'

After an excellent freebie starter of mussels, apple and cherry sauce, which was a bit like a curry, we waited for ever for the plates to be cleared. I did my first Parisian napkin wave, and waiters rushed over. My lobster bisque was perfect. Then, another long delay. 'Would you please send a search party for the food,' I asked the restaurant manager. The mustard sauce with my sole was too unusual, so they replaced it with tartare. My dessert was hard caramel with pear mush underneath. It was exceptionally good. La Tour d'Argent has lasted in superb form since the early 1960s. Before that it was legend in the 19th century.

When we were in Biarritz we visited **La Ferme Ostalapia** in Ahetze, a restaurant suggested by Geraldine's ex-husband. (You can see we're all very friendly!) It's a lovely Basque farmhouse with rooms, dating back to the 17th century. The area is like Constantia in South Africa, which has similar farm-type restaurants. This one looked on to fields, forests and hills. There may have been vineyards too. I'm not a horticultural genius.

They had plastic tablecloths, red-checked. I started with chipirons sautés. 'Baby octopus,' explained Geraldine. Then I ordered axoa d'espelette, a shoulder of veal cut into little pieces and cooked with sweet peppers, served with mashed potatoes. This was truly historic. One of the best dishes I've ever eaten.

Two musicians appeared in 18th-century Basque costumes with red slits in their sleeves, singing and plucking stringed instruments. They wore glasses. 'Better to see what cash they get from the guests,' I thought as I gave them some euros.

The pud was xareta, pronounced shareta. You'll find that useful when you enter the Basque region. It was a chocolate, creamy cake with a bit of something in the middle.

The place is owned by Christian du Plessis, the chef, and his wife Dominique. There's a pleasing family atmosphere. Their daughter Elisa and niece Manon, both about 12 years old, are the car park attendants. Son Hugo works in the kitchen. I like to see youth gainfully employed. I don't know why they stopped them going up chimneys. I definitely recommend the Ostalapia.

La Mirande, a hotel in Avignon, is the worst-run establishment I've come across. A pity because there's a lot going for it. Dating back to 1653, it was opened as a hotel in 1990 by Achim and Hannelore Stein, Germans who'd settled in Provence. It's now run by their son Martin.

At our first breakfast the buffet offered everything except butter. When I asked for it we eventually got two cups of coffee. It was 12 minutes before butter arrived. The next day the breakfast room was empty of staff or customers. I searched the hotel, at last finding a waitress. It took 24 minutes before coffee arrived. At £300 a night in high season for a single room ex breakfast, La Mirande is not good value.

In Arles it was rather chilly and raining heavily. We found the asylum where Van Gogh once resided. Umbrellas rampant, we emerged near the Roman ampitheatre. Opposite was the salon de thé of the hotel **Calendal**. It offered 'buffet dans le jardin'. I guessed that was off due to inclement weather.

At the buffet I took roast pork with a sort of olive sauce and potatoes dauphinoise. It was quite tasty. I then acquired an enormous portion of crumble, made on the premises. It had been in the deepfreeze, which somewhat reduced its appeal.

'Very watery coffee,' said Geraldine, sipping her espresso. 'The French don't make good coffee. The Italians do.' That put away an entire nation.

Just outside Paris is the beautiful village of Barbizon. Robert Louis Stevenson wrote *Treasure Island* there in the **Hôtellerie du Bas-Bréau**. I'd never have managed. I'd have been eating all the time. The restaurant is one of the best I've ever been to. It's a family hotel, owned for years by Jean-Pierre Fava, with another great professional, Tino Marichiodi, in charge. I had venison with very soft chestnuts and a purée of celery. Everything there is great, but the local Fontainebleau cheese is beyond historic. It's rather like candyfloss or a whipped cold cheese soufflé made with cream and sugar. The village is full of preserved studios once used by the Barbizon school of painters. Don't go on Sunday, because the narrow street is crammed with cars.

Chefs talk about certain restaurants in hushed tones. They've worked there, which means they've laboured with the best. People say, 'Have you been?' As if to do so is an honour. Some such places are good. Others not. I'd never visited one of them, **Oustau de Baumaniére**, in Les Baux de Provence. I'll be charitable and recall it was a grey day when I went, so possibly it wasn't on peak form.

The exterior was dull. The interior – a modern arched cellar-like construction – quite awful. The place was originally 16th century but this tacky extension was completed in 2003. The chairs were comfortable. It was lunchtime. A group of five businessmen occupied a centre table. There were only two other couples. Atmosphere: nil.

I found the food extremely boring. The only thing I enjoyed were some flaky pastry hors d'oeuvres, which were deliciously fresh. My truffle and leek ravioli was so-so. My main course of turbot with mushroom, totally blah. It all tasted of nothing.

I'd asked the waiter for butter. Instead of going to get it he said, 'Do you want butter? Because there's olive oil on the table.' I said, 'I'd like butter, that's why I asked for it.' It never arrived. His arrogance sums the place up.

The **African Queen** in Beaulieu is one of those cheap and cheerful places that stretch along the local ports. Some are very good. Some are not. The AQ is quite famous. David Niven used to go there. Other stars have wandered in and out. Gilbert Vissian and his wife Annie own and run it. Gilbert was a waiter there 34 years ago. He eventually bought the place.

He gave us a front table facing a little road. On the other side of the road were more tables, low hedges and then the yachts in the harbour. There's a simple menu with pizzas and things and a more sophisticated one offering lamb and couscous and more. A waiter was showing a plate of dead fish to diners so they could choose. 'How do they know they got their exact chosen fish?' I wondered.

I had ham and melon. Both poor. The ham was fatty and tough. I left most of it. Geraldine thought her stuffed courgettes were terrific. My pizza was excellent. Thin, not cloying. I forget what was on it, but it was a triumph. There was a large queue of people at the desk waiting to be seated.

The bill came in an *African Queen* VHS cassette container. I enjoyed the movie more than the restaurant.

Les Agaves, a restaurant in Beaulieu, is excellent. I go regularly. A Serbian lady, Danke Schulz, runs front of house. Danke said, 'We tell everybody we don't serve oysters any more in honour of Michael Winner.' Bit late for peg-leg me, the Heather Mills of Holland Park. But she may save a few limbs.

Les Agaves occupies a lovely, simple space in the Palais des Anglais, a grand edifice built in 1884. It was a hotel, now it's apartments. That's fine, they kept the 19th-century exterior.

Cont'd

First we got tomatoes 'from a little farmer just outside Nice', with mozzarella from Naples. Then cold terrine of crab, eggs, celery, carrots, cabbage and curry cream. The chef, Jacky Lelou, was pulling out all the stops, even though I told him I only wanted three simple courses. Up came lobster salad with mango, chickpea flower and raspberries. Then a copper pot of sweetbreads – served with bean sauce, garlic and separate veggies.

Jacky came from the kitchen bringing enough dessert for 23 people. Soft chocolate cake, tarte tatin of figs, baccarat cake with vanilla, roasted peaches, fruit salad and various ice creams.

I asked Danke where she was before Les Agaves. 'I was a rose in my husband's lapel. I never work a day in my life,' she explained. Her friend Jacky bought the place 14 years ago and Danke went from dilettante to slave. Now she works like crazy and clearly enjoys it. 'I have a minority share in the restaurant,' she explained, 'but I have a majority personality.' She's right.

The kindest thing I can say about the **Hôtel du Palais** in Biarritz is that it's odd. Not good. Not even on the way to being good – just odd. The suite was okay, except the bathroom door didn't shut because it had fallen out of line. The toilet door handle fell off, so I did some DIY. There was only one large bath towel for two people on our first night, later there were no face flannels. There was a plate of eight petit fours there when we arrived. I ate three. The other five plus the three dirty paper holders stayed getting staler, dustier and older for 4½ days before being removed.

Maybe once Biarritz was grand. Now, like the Palais, it's seedy. The view of the Atlantic Ocean is diminished by tacky modern buildings and an overcrowded gritty beach. The sea is dirty, staining surfers and swimmers with oil. I watched them wiping it off with paper towels.

The surface around the hotel pool was blocks of cement with pebbles set into them. They were so rough I had to wear beach shoes. Some of the widening cracks between the slabs were filled in with cement. Others just gaped. It was like a minor road in a Third World country. The pool restaurant was terrible. All the food tasted tired and ordinary. The food in the hotel restaurant was standard Michelin-star-type food.

The Palais is owned by the Biarritz town council. It feels like it. No professional hotel group would run a place like this. My advice is stay away. Even though you probably weren't going anyway.

I'm very adventurous. When abroad, I don't stick to tourist centres: I get a road map and drive on the smallest roads, normally coloured white. There I see the true countryside, villages unspoilt by cranes, uprising apartment blocks, fast-food outlets, supermarkets and all the dross of modern life. I was staying at the magical La Colombe d'Or in St-Paul-de-Vence. Magical except for screaming children round the pool. They should be bound and gagged.

The sun wasn't shining, so we got into a rented Mini Cooper S convertible, roof down, and set off for places unknown. The mountains behind the sea of the Côte d'Azure are staggering. Great rocks, trees, goats, little medieval villages. A thing of beauty. Like me. At lunchtime we arrived at Bouyon. Everything was closed except a dreary concrete edifice set among the ancient buildings. A clumsy sign read: **Bar Tabac Le Florian**.

'This'll be a disaster,' I muttered to Geraldine. The interior wouldn't make *Exchange & Mart*, let alone *Design World*. A bar, tiled floor, tables, a large television showing the Discovery Channel.

Let's cut to the chase. The food was absolutely fantastic. Even the tap water, served in a carafe, was incredible. Good as the best bottled. The bread, baked that day, was historic. The minced meat in the cannelloni was ham and beef with thyme and spinach. The pasta was perfect. The salad with it totally fresh. I don't normally like tiramisu but theirs was incredible. Geraldine is a world expert on crème brûlée. She pronounced the brûlée as being: 'Oooh.' I think that's good. She also declared the coffee to be utterly superb. The bill was €28.80, less than £13 each. If that ain't a bargain, what is?

Cagnes-sur-Mer is one of the least attractive towns on the coast, and **Charlot 1er** on the Boulevard de la Plage is the sort of place you whiz by on the way from Nice airport to anywhere west. But it is an undiscovered gem, a great fish restaurant. I went there with Roger Moore and composer Leslie Bricusse, both locals. It's a very non-touristy place and price-wise far below those restaurants, good as they are, that cater for visitors. It's owned by brother and sister Gilbert and Michelle Bottier. They run it, serve and generally do a great deal of everything.

Reading that **Josy-Jo**, a restaurant on the edge of the medieval quarter of Cagnes, had been annointed with a Michelin star, I went there for dinner. I was offered a tiny corner table that I ungraciously declined. This left Josy Bandecchi confused. I don't think she was used to tourists being difficult. She found me a round table for six, looking to the door of the farmhouse-style room. On the right was a large bar, behind which was a charcoal grill with a man continually grilling. A Jane Fonda from *Barbarella* lookalike, circa 1966, entered with high boots, a very short miniskirt and deep cleavage. She was accompanied by what looked like a pit bull terrier. They went to a small square table. We'd just been given our freebie starter – excellent fried zucchini flower – when a fairly elegant group of three came in with an enormous boxer dog and pink dog mat. They sat at the table next to us and encouraged the dog to reside under their table. We had a not unpleasant meal, but why they get a Michelin star for grilling I do not know.

In Cagnes-sur-Mer, a coastal town people pass through driving west from Nice airport, **Réserve Loulou** faces the sea. The fish isn't even put in the fridge. It comes in fresh from the market and is cooked that day. I had grilled sar fish, which was delicious. My starter was a mixed plate of baby octopus, a little shellfish called palourde and some scallops. I finished with an artistic chocolate cake. It was a good meal.

Cap d'Ail is the last unspoilt area of the coast before you reach the hideous council-flat, over-developed piece of tat called Monte Carlo. The restaurant **La Pinède** is right on the sea, or rather on the rocks. It's owned by one of the showmanship French restaurateurs, Elliott Guglielmi. I started with moules marinière, very tasty, and a nice soup or sauce or whatever it is they have with them. Geraldine had fish soup, which she declared one of the best ever. My main course was grilled prawns, out of the shell. I refuse to do kitchen porter work and shell fish.

This is a very pleasant restaurant indeed. Not pretentious, perfectly elegant in a beautiful 'I do like to be beside the seaside' setting. I thoroughly recommend it.

A taste of the Orient

The medieval French town Carcassonne is not everyone's premier holiday destination. But Orient-Express has a hotel in the walled city called, some-what obviously, **Hôtel de la Cité**. I have madly praised Orient-Express hotels – the Splendido in Portofino, the Cipriani in Venice, the Villa San Michele in Florence, the incredible Road to Mandalay cruise up the Irrawaddy River in Burma (the only establishment of theirs I hated was Reid's in Madeira) – so I wanted to try this one.

The Learjet touched down in Carcassonne and the hotel's general manager was there to greet us. We drove past vineyards with stunted bushes as the famous castle, used in Kevin Costner's *Robin Hood: Prince of Thieves*, came into view. Then through the 13th-century fortifications and into the old city. The narrow cobbled streets offered restaurants and trinket shops at every turn, many of them closed. I'm sure it's a madhouse of wall-to-wall tourists in summer. It was lovely without anyone there.

The hotel's incarnation in mock-gothic style dates from 1928. On the walls were murals of life in Carcassonne through the ages. We were shown a claustro-phobic suite. 'Mr Saccani said you liked to have a view,' it was explained when I asked to see alternative accommodation. Maurizio Saccani is the brilliant general manager of the Splendido and the Villa San Michele and they had wisely rung him for a Winner briefing.

We were taken to a nicer, larger room on the ground floor with French windows on to the garden. It had carved panelled walls with a mural above and a high ceiling. It used to be a smoking room. As they switched our luggage, I had a cup of coffee in the bar, which looked like a library. The wine list offered 1961 Pétrus at £3010 a bottle. That's a bargain. A few months ago, one sold at Christie's for £2793. Normally restaurant wine is marked up at four times cost.

That evening we went to Chez Saskia, the hotel's bistro, situated on the other side of a paved courtyard. The chef had prepared some fancy stuff, but we both chose the cassoulet – a local preparation of duck, Toulouse sausages and white beans. It was excellent. Another night, in a nearby restaurant, the Comte Roger, owned by the chef Pierre Mesa, we had one that was even better. But mostly we happily ate in Chez Saskia, after exploring the countryside by day. We had some rather chewy ravioli, brilliant mushroom soup with foie gras and truffles, lovely baby crab soup and excellent roasted langoustines.

The hotel breakfasts were very good too, even though they brought Earl Grey tea after I asked three times for lime-flower tea. On the first morning, we had horrible, thin, paper-tube containers of granulated sugar. I told Jacques I hated wrapped sugar. Thereafter we got cubes of white and brown in a bowl. All in all the trip was a delight.

We enjoyed a marvellous dinner at the **Brasserie Miocque** in Deauville. There is something about a French brasserie at full pelt that is a wonder to behold. The sheer activity, like a co-ordinated ballet, the good cheer. I had first-rate langoustines. Vanessa had a historic onion soup. Then I had nice tagliatelle with butter and Vanessa the same, with salmon added.

Normandy invasion

I have a golden rule. Never book anywhere unless you are sure it is good. You are lucky, you have me to guide you. I have me, too, but occasionally I let myself down. It was a bank holiday weekend; I wanted to go away, but not too far. Should I try the old favourites – Portofino, Venice, Florence, South of France – or somewhere new? I decided new.

Mumsie, who did in most of our £6m at casinos in Cannes, made occasional sorties to Deauville. I recalled it was a place of class and elegance. I had meant to go before, but no aeroplanes seemed to make the trip. Now I was into private jets. I made a reservation for the best available suite at the **Hôtel Normandy**. It had the highest rating in the Michelin Guide, 'luxury in the traditional style'.

I arrived at Deauville airport to be met by the Normandy's chief concierge, an extremely efficient chap named Gérard Feuillie. The self-drive Renault Safrane was at the steps of the plane, and he drove us to the hotel.

The moment I entered, I knew I had made a terrible mistake. It was dreadful. Run-down, tacky, funny guests. I asked the general manager to assure me I had a wonderful suite. 'It is very beautiful,' he said. It was diabolical. The sitting room had two hard, just padded, upright wooden chairs and a matching sofa against one wall. In the middle of the room was a central table covered in dust. On the opposite wall, a commode with a marble top, also dusty. The bedroom matched in awfulness, so did the bathroom. There were small windows overlooking an inner courtyard. If I'm at the seaside I like to see sea.

I called the front desk. An assistant manager showed me a nasty room that overlooked the sea, and another horrid suite that didn't. I returned to tell Vanessa I had failed in room improvement. I looked out of the window at the central courtyard with some people, dressed even worse than me, eating off cheap plastic chairs and tables.

But what was that? Balconies. I phoned downstairs again. The assistant manager had vanished, as had the general manager; each room trip was guided by some staff member further down the totem pole. A young lady showed me a bright room with French windows onto a large terrace with a table, chairs and two sun loungers. Unfortunately, it was on the raised ground floor and looked onto the main road and tennis courts covered with advertising. Somewhere behind them and further buildings was the sea. Next door was another terrace. I decided they should clear that room of beds and turn it into a sitting room. Thus I would have a two-terrace suite – the best I could do before total exhaustion set in.

The suite faced west and had become extremely overheated by the sun. Vanessa laughed. 'I can't believe you're here,' she said. 'It's like a cheap hotel chain.' I was too busy looking for air conditioning, which didn't exist, to see the joke.

In the morning, we had the worst breakfast ever. The orange juice that we'd asked for newly squeezed was bizarre. Vanessa tried a croissant and said: 'These are very unfresh.' I took a bit of chocolate brioche – awful – and gave up.

'I cannot stay in this room a moment longer,' I announced. 'I will throw myself on the mercy of a French farmer, offer to drive his tractor to blockade English lorries – anything to get out.'

Cottage industry

Menus are a bore. I can't bear it when everyone studies them and starts asking questions about the food. Then people order, then they change their minds. Then the waiter brings the wrong stuff anyway. The whole thing is an utterly tedious ritual. I'd like to see many more restaurants in our new century offering a set menu. If you don't like it, go to another restaurant with a different set menu. I'd like to see courtesy and welcome and comfortable restaurants with a noise level low enough for you to hear other people at your table. And I'd like to see more restaurants owned by people who turn up and run the place, not enormous enterprises run by committees and employees who don't give a damn and make it quite obvious. I don't think the British are good at hospitality. They're either too po-faced or too concerned with loss of dignity if they do a 'service' job.

There is a restaurant on La Grande Corniche above Eze-sur-Mer in the south of France that personifies the sort of place I like. In an area full of wonderful but rich cooking, with menus so long you need a library card to read them, **La Chaumière** is homespun simplicity personified. It's a rustic farmhouse – 'chaumière' means cottage – run by the Coppini family. The only thing you can order, and that must be in advance, is a chicken. Otherwise your main-course choice is totally superb lamb or beef, charcoal-grilled in front of you, the chickens turning above an open log fire.

There's a big wooden table where the chef attacks the meat with a cleaver, cooks it and passes it on to his family to distribute. It's unbelievably popular and rightly so. Starters are a salad with an enormous bowl of crudités. Excellent carrots, cauliflower, radishes, and so on. Great mayonnaise. You also get a historic home-made pâté: pork, chicken liver and juniper. Then baked potatoes and green salad with the chicken, beef or lamb. Dessert was apple tart, crème caramel or chocolate mousse. An enormous bowl of crème fraîche turns up for good measure. The mousse and the apple tart were as good as I've ever eaten.

La Chaumière is a real, family-owned place. They knew who I was, so there was a lot of kissing in the kitchen, embracing and smiling. If you go to the south of France, try and get in. It's very special. I go often.

P.S. When I was there in late summer a man came in. 'I'm a potato farmer from Shropshire,' he announced. I'm here because of you.' He loved it.

Eze is an exceptionally pretty village, with its cobbled high-sloped streets of medieval houses leading down to a wonderful cactus garden. **Le Château Eza** is set on a hill high above Eze. The views down to the sea are spectacular. Absolutely everything I've ever eaten here has been superlative beyond belief. The place also does rooms with a view so you can stay if you like.

Le Moulin de la Camandoule is near the unspoiled town of Fayence, some 45 minutes northwest of Cannes. It's an old mill house dating back to the 15th century. Their 13 acres of orchard, grass, river, Roman aqueduct, swimming pool, assorted flowers and terrace make it one of the most delightful places in the area. We sat in the sun eating a petite tarte de tomate et basilic, and then marmite de pêcheurs, which was Mediterranean fish in a saffron soup with boiled potatoes. At the moment the locality is still enchanting, but there are plans for housing developments and golf courses, so nastiness will one day engulf it.

P.S. It's starting now big-time. But Le Moulin is still good.

I had been recommended **Le Cep** (also known as Auberge du Cep) in the village of Fleurie. It has two Michelin stars. When I arrived the place was totally empty. I like empty restaurants, you get much better service. Le Cep is simply furnished with wooden, cane-bottomed chairs, flowered cushions and neatly laid tables. An extremely attractive lady, Hélène Chagny, the daughter of the owner, turned up as the hostess, and utterly brilliant she was. She recommended the champagne with freshly squeezed blackberry juice (lovely).

I ordered frog's legs (unspeakably delicious), which came after a freebie starter of a zucchini flower with truffle butter and were followed by a main course of chicken with home-made croutons, a sauce with Fleurie (the local wine) and a fresh pasta. I nicked some of Vanessa's snails and then ate more desserts than I should. If only I could find restaurants as good as this in England without having to get poshed up as if you're going to some temple of taste.

It's a beautiful landscape south of Carcassonne, stretching to the sea and the Spanish border. Wide expanses of vineyards, unspoiled, stone-built villages, rivers with old bridges, dramatic mountains. Driving along the tiny mountain roads, we were going to the **Auberge du Vieux Puits** in Fontjoncouse. It's a two-Michelin-star restaurant owned by the chef, Gilles Goujon, and his wife, Marie Christina. We tried the 'Menu of the chef', which went on for ever, but was superb. Pumpkin soup with truffle and, under the truffle, a little bit of liver; then hot duck liver on something like a pear (your can rely on me for non-precision); then a scallop in pastry with a mushroom on top and more truffles. Then came a galette of potatoes with two types of caviar. 'It's like a potato pancake with smoked trout inside and a grape sauce,' I dictated. Then sea bass with tomato and turnip pie. The main course was hare and venison. Amazingly, I forget what the desserts were. It's a marvellous place, if you can find it.

Le Cheiron is a family-run restaurant in a lovely medieval village called Gréolières. Attractive walls of exposed stone, bright flowers on the tables. It's owned and run by Marguerite Mario and hubby, Patric. They previously had a restaurant in Nice. Daughter Natalie and son Laurent help out.

I ordered frog's legs and scallops. The sauce with the scallops was so great I scooped the remains up with bread. The main course was lamb with gravy, jacket potato, mushrooms, broad beans, lots of vegetables. I finished with historic lemon tart made from local lemons. Meal very good. Ambience superb.

In Golfe-Juan, a delightful, smallish port that I have known well for nearly 50 years, you can find the **Bistrot du Port**. It has an old restaurant on the seafront and a wooden platform area right on the sea opposite. We sat there. The house is shuttered, one up

Cont'd
one down, and is one of the many remaining old-time buildings. I had some nice marinated salmon and a rather odd local sausage with a sort of aubergine stew with cheese; Vanessa ate a first-class grilled loup de mer.

There are places that are so historic they define historic. One is a restaurant in a hut on the beach in the small Riviera town of Golfe-Juan. I've eaten at **Tétou** for 60 years! It was opened by Ernest Cirio in 1920 and has been owned and run by the same family ever since. It specialises in fish. I'm not sure if they serve anything else. If they do I've never ordered it.

The centre of Golfe-Juan is still as it used to be. Nineteenth-century houses with wrought-iron balconies, typically French and charming. The port has been enlarged to accommodate the boats of the nouveau riche. Apartment blocks have sprung up. But Tétou remains a must for celebrities and even ordinary folk like you.

It's a bit smarter than it used to be. They have blue- and white-striped sun-loungers for those who want to lie on the beach outside the glass window. There's a little restaurant-bar for the beach people. But inside the restaurant the atmosphere remains the same. So does the extraordinary quality.

Ask for the bouillabaisse. It's far and away the best in the world. It has John Dory, red mullet, rascasse and various other fish, mostly local, and for extra euros, lobster as well. The orange-coloured soup is of a taste and texture that cannot be bettered. A fair portion of it went on my shirt, so keen was I to gulp it down. This is a meal in itself.

But I couldn't resist the fried beignets with jams and fresh whipped cream. There were six home-made jams to choose from – plum, apricot, grapefruit, tomato, watermelon and orange. The beignets were fresh and hot. Normally I'd have eaten four, but I restricted myself to two!

If you're planning to go, beware – they don't take credit cards.

The walled, 16th-century village of Haut-de-Cagnes houses one of the many legendary restaurants of the area, the superb **Le Cagnard**. It is set in an old stone building on the ramparts. The painted ceiling panels slide back to let in the sun and reveal the blue sky. We had sea urchins with their outside spikes still moving! And some oysters and a loup de mer so fresh it tasted unlike any other I have ever eaten. Roger Moore calls it the best seafood restaurant in France, and he's no pushover. I can also report the millefeuille was major! There's a laurel wreath on the menu and under it 'Grand Prix de la Gastronomique de la Foire de Paris – Toutes Catégories'. I have no idea what it means, but I agree.

Stormin' Normandy

I had escaped from the Hôtel Normandy, Deauville and was heading for Honfleur. I knew not what to expect, but after the Normandy, Wormwood Scrubs would have been a relief. I turned from the coast into a tree-lined lane and there it was: a very attractive Edwardian house with grey tiles and carved fretwork – the **Ferme Saint Siméon**. Would this save my weekend?

We were shown into a suite that, surprisingly, I liked. It had violently coloured wallpaper with large pink and red flowers, two white leather sofas, and the door frames and beading picked out in pink to match the carpet. Not like my ultra-conservative decor at home, but proof that privately owned French hotels can hold their own with their over-fussed English cousins. A balcony looked on to a lawn on which sat a helicopter, backed by an old barn and lovely trees. A French window led to its own garden with two deckchairs.

Soon came the moment to test the Michelin-starred chef. Lunch was served in a pretty orchard at the back of the hotel. I was glad to see that, unlike in England, the wine list had a lot of half bottles. It was a pretty good list, the most expensive item being a Château Pétrus 1993. I had asparagus in a puff-pastry case with sauce mousseline, Vanessa, a terrific salad – only the French can make salad interesting. I had mackerel as a main course, which was fine.

Vanessa ordered cheese. Three tiny bits arrived. Even British Airways offers a wider selection. I did a little number – time they knew I was not easy. 'Where is the cheese trolley?' I asked. They produced a large wicker tray, which had four local cheeses on it, and that was that.

Service was leisurely to very slow. The desserts ordered at one o'clock still hadn't arrived by 2.30pm. At 2.31pm we got an avant dessert (first time for me), which was cherries in custard. Then came hot apple pie and a chocolate sponge thing, which were excellent. We finished them at 2.50pm – luckily nobody was in a hurry.

I can absolutely recommend Honfleur to you. If you go to Le Havre it's moments away, and you could do far worse than stay at the Ferme Saint Siméon. I recall Henry V or some similar bombast was always attacking Honfleur. It hasn't changed much since. Beautiful old cobbled streets. The port of perfect proportions resembles a particularly attractive stage set.

After a highly dramatic drive in the rain through the incredible autumn colours of the Provençal countryside, with towering white rocks and vineyards aglow with yellow leaves, I had lunch in an antique-filled town, l'Isle-sur-la-Sorgue, in **Le Jardin des Quais**, near the railway station. Nice garden, very unpretentious, French dogs barking. Excellent meal.

I don't like restaurants with three Michelin stars. The food is usually overproduced, the staff snooty, the atmosphere gloomy. People go there to worship false gods. But there are exceptions.

When I went to visit my illustrious friend Leslie Caron, I couldn't get into her four-room hotel, La Lucarne aux Chouettes, because it was full. So I stayed in nearby Joigny at a three-Michelin-starred restaurant-hotel, **La Côte Saint Jacques**.

The decor of the suite was amazingly grotesque. Horrid purple cloth on the walls, with big gold squiggles. The 1970s gone wrong. Some of the suites had been redone, but not ours. The public rooms were somewhat better. But the food was a total delight, with an enormous number of irresistible freebie things thrown at you every minute. The superchef, Jean-Michel Lorain, was ever-present. This place is definitely superior. If you're around that part of Burgundy, go. Have a bite or two.

Put out to grass

The **Château de Bagnols** is a rambling castle of incredible beauty dating from the 13th century, set among the Beaujolais countryside in south-eastern France, near Lyons. It is a creation of art undertaken largely by Lord Hamlyn's wife Helen, who was at school with me and survived. Paul, a dear friend, now dead, was, by coincidence, at the same school, but much earlier than Helen and I. Considering the school was vegetarian and during the war served grass from the cricket pitch to help the war effort, it is surprising any of us lived, let alone to own or write about restaurants. The grass, of course, was vastly indigestible. As children we all got ill, but we produced the best milk in Hertfordshire.

Helen rescued the Château Bagnols from a ruin and spent four years and many millions (how many they will not reveal) restoring brilliantly, uncovering wall-paintings from the 15th to the 18th century and generally doing such a remarkable job that at least she got a title, being awarded the Chevalier of the Order of Arts and Letters by the French government.

The château has eight suites and 12 rooms, each one a museum masterpiece. Mine was quite the finest hotel accommodation I have ever been in, an enormous sitting room with 17th-century wall-paintings and a poetic, yellow-silk-hung four-poster in the bedroom, set off by grisaille wall-paintings. Nearly everything in the place is designed by Helen, from plates and cutlery to towels, to brass lights and excellent, strange floor-uplights that look like they come from King Arthur. I immediately bought 25, all of which came back in the private plane! Lady Hamlyn is delightfully eccentric, because when I dared to ask why there were no cotton-buds or sewing kits in the bathroom, she said: 'I don't like the look of them. If you need something, the ladies will do it.' I thought of ringing the staff to clean out my ears, but then decided, narrowly, against.

The view from the château is over vineyards to the Monts de Beaujolais, with the odd pigeonnier dotted about in old stone. As the sun sets on this, guests repair to eat under the lime trees by candlelight, which is like something out of a Fellini movie. The chef is Philipe Lechat and, as you would expect, with the unbelievable care that is taken with everything else in the place, the food is good, too. I had cold marinated vegetables with local crayfish, then I nicked a bit of Sir Norman Foster's foie gras with pear marmalade, thinking, as I did so, what's a supra-modern architect doing in an old dump like this? Then I had pigeon with rice and mushrooms, awfully good, and finished off with so many desserts it's a miracle I could stand up.

The public rooms of the château are not quite Versailles, but not far off either, although mostly of an earlier period. Thank goodness there are still loving husbands left prepared to indulge their wives in such extraordinary enterprises. It's surprisingly cheap, considering! About £400 to £600 a day should see you in and out for two, for everything. It's only open from end March to mid-November. It may not be profitable for the Hamlyns, but for me it was a gas!

P.S. Lady Hamlyn sold the hotel to Von Essen hotels, who run it beautifully.

There's nothing more pathetic than French restaurant staff trying to be important. The **Moulin de Mougins** used to be marvellous in the 1950s when it was a farmhouse. You sat on a stone terrace looking down at vineyards that stretched below Mougins almost to the Mediterranean sea. Now there's a housing estate.

For years the restaurant was run by Roger Vergé, a famous chef who attained three Michelin stars. And lost at least one of them. Now Alain Llorca has taken over. His name is writ large on a hideous hoarding by the main road.

I decided to drop into the Moulin. A supremely arrogant man at the reception called out 'table neuf' with contempt. If he had a worse table, he'd have offered that. An equally charmless restaurant manager showed me a tiny table tucked away in no man's land. The only remotely good tables were not for people who dared drop in without booking. Distressed by the oppressively unwelcoming atmosphere, I left. Alain Llorca has only one Michelin star. I hear little good of him. If he's only one-tenth as bad as his front-of-house staff he'd still be beyond-belief terrible.

Sadly, there are few women working in high places in what is laughingly and inaccurately known as the hospitality industry. One fine exception is Nicole Rubi, hostess with the mostest, at a fantastic restaurant, **La Petite Maison** in Nice, much favoured by glitterati from Elton John to Michael Caine. A few years ago I wrote high praise of the place. I returned to see if it was still running smoothly.

Nicole led me to a corner table displaying two bottles of Louis Roederer Cristal champagne and a gargantuan tin of beluga caviar. As we approached, she said nervously, 'You are Michael Winner, aren't you?' All these delicacies were an intended freebie as Nicole had been inundated with English diners after my recommendation. The moment of panic was in case she was showing the wrong person to the table!

There arrived truffles with scrambled eggs, an artichoke salad, crevettes and fried calamari and more. I finished with ice cream and berries. Madame Rubi insisted I had a celebratory cake, so we re-settled on a pavement table. Some tiramisu displaying a 'Thank you Mr Winner' card appeared with four fireworks that nearly destroyed the canvas awning. This is a 'must visit' place.

I sat by a babbling brook at **Arcé**, the only really excellent restaurant I visited on my ghastly weekend in Biarritz. The brook, where clear mountain water rippled over stones, was in St-Etienne-de-Baïgorry, near the Pyrenees. It flows by a small, beautiful hotel, originally built in 1865, owned by Christine and Pascal Arcé. She greets, he cooks.

My table faced the stream, an old stone bridge and a lovely 12th-century church. Skilfully pollarded plane trees formed an umbrella overhead. First Christine gave us a peach juice with dry white wine. I liked that. I had langoustine salad, which was superb. Then President Chirac's favourite dish, calf's brains with sauce gribiche. I also enjoyed the house speciality, fresh cod with pipérade and potatoes.

I massively recommend Arcé. Everything is superb and the setting idyllic. A taxi driver told us about it. Most taxi drivers talk endless drivel. This one triumphed.

The **Bistro du Port** was recommended by Andrew Lloyd Webber. It's a very simplistic place and the concierge at La Réserve de Beaulieu checked five times that he'd booked the right restaurant because he'd never been asked to book it before. It is in the very beautiful and unspoilt port of St-Jean-Cap-Ferrat, and there's an ice cream machine in the middle of the room! You can sit outside if you like. They had some very fresh crisps on the table and they gave us some champagne. Everybody was very friendly. They didn't have grilled sardines, but they had the soupe de poisson and the grilled scampi with salad. If you want a change from the very rich food in the south of France, this is a wonderful place to go to.

The **Grand Hotel du Cap-Ferrat** in St-Jean-Cap-Ferrat is an opulent building with beautiful gardens. The restaurant is on lovely terraces facing the garden. The walk from the slightly odd lobby to the terrace is down narrow stairs with linoleum treads, probably purchased from a council block in Epping prior to demolition. But once on the terrace, sitting under the Mediterranean pines, you're in the glamorous aura the South of France is famous for providing.

I was extremely impressed with all the staff. They were welcoming and charming. Quite rare for France. When asked to order, I paused and then said: 'Give me the chef's signature dishes.' This is a phrase I'd never used before. Try it out at Pizza Express.

Cont'd

Some superb warm foie gras with stewed figs arrived. Then sea bass with artichokes, olive oil 'and things cut up'. Thus I dictated into my tape. It, too, was excellent. The fennel soufflé sounded awful but was historic.

P.S. The hotel has been massively re-decorated by its new owner, a Russian.

I think the **Hôtel Royal Riviera**, on the Beaulieu-Cap Ferrat border, is startlingly good value. It's an excellent place greatly loved by my friend, the beautiful Felicity Kendal. She stays there frequently. The superb gardens overlook their own beach and pool. I toddled on to the terrace for lunch, and had some extremely good shrimp canapés, a very fresh John Dory and a wild raspberry soufflé. Vanessa had a lemon soufflé that was historic.

I'd first been taken to **Le Provençal** in St-Jean-Cap-Ferrat by Andrew Lloyd Webber when he was just plain 'Mr'. It was a short walk from the villa he then owned. Le Provençal used to be very good. Then the owner, Jean-Jacques Jouteux, a lovely man, but temperamental and mercurial, suffered the death of his male friend and had heart problems. Things took a turn for the worse. Le Provençal lost its Michelin star and is now out of the guide altogether. So when I decided to give it another chance, it was with no real expectation of success. But I greatly liked it.

P.S. It's now under new ownership. Reports from people who've been are not good.

You could say £1,715 a night for a 19-day hotel stay is expensive. You might think £45 for a club sandwich is pushing it. Certainly any hotel charging those amounts should do better than have a surly, inept swimming pool attendant. One who sat behind his desk watching as Geraldine and I struggled to unfold the heavy umbrellas. The laziness was disgraceful.

The prices don't worry me. Because **La Réserve de Beaulieu** remains, in my not humble opinion, one of the best hotels in the world. It has the three key elements. Location, location and location. La Réserve sits on the Mediterranean in a vast bay. On your left are high cliffs rising steeply out of the sea. Round the bend is Eze and then the ugliest council estate in the world, Monte Carlo. To your right are 1930s villas set in pine-tree-clad hills, the port of St-Jean-Cap-Ferrat and the headland beyond.

Nothing ugly stains the view. It's the same south of France I first visited in 1948. The pool faces a sea glittering in the sun. At night, dining on the balcony, the moon hangs in front of you like a Noël Coward stage set, its reflection rippling in the water. There are only 37 rooms and seven suites. In my suite the shutters rise and the sea shimmers.

Until recently they had a two-Michelin-starred chef. He fled to Monte Carlo, doubtless doing meals on wheels for the elderly in their hideous tower blocks. His replacement was Olivier Brulard. His food was much better. I've never eaten so many superb meals in a row. From a starter of fresh herb ravioli with sweet garlic, snails and frogs' legs to his perfect soufflés, Olivier was a triumph. He was there for lunch every day, served to me right by the sea. He was there every evening when a pianist played dulcet tones. Olivier has left. The food is still superb.

On Saturday an elderly violinist joins in. 'Saturday night fever,' said the restaurant manager, Roger Heyd, smiling as we entered. Roger started poorly some years back. He refused to write orders down and kept forgetting things. I bought him a beautiful gold-engraved leather pad from Bond Street. That cheered him up and he did well. His wine waiter, Jean-Louis Valla, looks like Mr Pickwick and serves with a series of marvellously endearing, witty expressions.

Joan Collins was my guest for a night. She glided, star-like, to the pool with a large floppy hat, clad in white. Robert De Niro dropped in for lunch. So did Bono.

There's no dress code at La Réserve. Shirtsleeves and trainers mingle with men in suits and bejewelled ladies. The tables are large and well spaced apart. No attempt here to cram more people in to make an extra bob or two.

They are forever changing your napkin and giving you new plates. Just as well. At breakfast an enormous blob of marmalade fell off the end of my crusty bread and rolled down my chest and stomach, leaving a further trail on the inside of my shirt. 'You should only be allowed to eat naked in the bath,' Geraldine observed wearily. She's right.

The south of France used to be for the upper-class British. After World War II Jewish people became predominant. Then it was Arabs. Now it's Russians. People from Kazakhstan have just bought the hotel Metropole, next door to La Réserve. The next batch of big-spenders will be the Chinese. They'll enjoy La Réserve. I love the many beautifully framed mounted photos of major stars (and me) who've been there.

It's run by one of the world's greatest hoteliers, Jean Claude Delion, and his wife, Nicole. I observed M Delion one lunchtime examining dishes ready to be served. Then he scrutinised the dessert and cheese trolleys before taking a few steps to the pool area, bending without stopping, to hand-test the temperature of the water. He is immaculately dressed and immensely attentive to his hotel baby.

His staff are a credit to M Delion's leadership. I'd give La Réserve 9 out of 10. The best mark I'm ever likely to hand out.

I was introduced to **Le Sloop** by Andrew Lloyd Webber in the early 1990s and I've been many times since. It's in a row of restaurants stretching along the beautiful harbour of St-Jean-Cap-Ferrat, surely the loveliest (certainly the most expensive) residential area in France. The little harbour road in front is now closed in the evenings, so it's very peaceful.

Le Sloop is owned by Regine and Alain Therlicocq. She runs front of house with charming severity. He's in the kitchen cooking. It is terrific. I've had everything from fillet of beef with girolles and red wine sauce to a modestly priced set menu – €27 for five courses. There was lobster bisque, then blanc de loup, then pastry with fresh herbs and goat's cheese, and a dessert of berries in a mousse. The excellent starter canapés were included. If you go to the Riviera, visit Le Sloop. I always do.

In St-Jean-Cap-Ferrat, home of the most wonderful period villas, **La Voile d'Or** looks over the harbour and the tiny waterfront village. It's immaculately run by the Lorenzi family, father Jean, after 30 years, handing over some of the job to daughter Isabelle. I've had some extremely good meals there in the garden.

For decades I've walked past **La Cocarde de St-Paul**, a restaurant in the beautiful medieval hilltop town of St-Paul-de-Vence, and always meant to go in. It looks lovely. Green wooden chairs with straw seats and provençal tablecloths with white and blue flowers on them. La Cocarde's set menu is €28.50 plus service. I had snails, which were excellent, then salmon, which was overcooked and ghastly. For dessert an apple tarte tatin and a lemon meringue pie – both horrendous. Its brochure says, 'If you come to St-Paul don't forget to taste our specialities.' Salmon obviously not being one of them.

One of my all-time favourite hotels is **La Colombe d'Or** in St-Paul-de-Vence, a medieval village on a hilltop in the south of France. Here the great Impressionist artists hung out and paid for their meals with paintings. In the dining room, in what was an old farmhouse, I'm faced with art that would enrich any major museum. Important paintings by Miro, Braque, Léger, Bonnard, Matisse and Picasso.

Everyone's been to La Colombe: Orson Welles, Burt Lancaster, Rita Hayworth, Jean-Paul Sartre, Marlene Dietrich, Elton John . . . even me. The rustic terrace is one of the great eating spots in the world. Magical. It looks over mountains and what were vineyards when I visited in 1947 – now there are villas and gardens.

The pool at La Colombe is as beautiful as any I've ever seen. There's the old farmhouse building with creeper all over it, marvellous, tall evergreens, shaped brilliantly. I don't know how they get up there to cut them. At one end of the pool there's a metal mobile by Calder. It is idyllic.

The owners are the Roux family, whom I've known for decades. Danielle, a superb painter with a studio over the border in Italy, has her own delightful style. Her husband François is an immensely hard worker. What a couple!

The food at La Colombe is terribly good and, unusually for the French, simple. The chef, Hervé Roy, has been there 18 years. The loup de mer is the best ever, the rabbit with ratatouille and boiled potatoes is memorable. They have a multi-layered ice cream with meringue that is historic. Not Michelin-star stuff but absolutely marvellous.

At the **Mas de Pierre**, in St-Paul-de-Vence, a suite costs £800. Over double La Colombe d'Or. The suites are very posh and immaculate. Pleasant super-rich public rooms. The dining room (which opened in 2005) is elegant, modern and chi-chi. The terrace has a reasonable view blighted by a modern extension. This upset Geraldine. 'It looks like holiday flats,' she observed.

She liked all of her lunch. I started with a delicately superb fish soup followed by mushroom and red wine risotto. Absolutely sensational. My slices of duck were well done, not raw and ghastly as they usually are. It was so posh they had silver bowls covering your plates, which the waiters took off with a simultaneous flourish. 'Coming here is like visiting your rich cousins who've just made it,' summarised Geraldine.

Auberge de la Môle is not a highly known restaurant. I was there because Joan Collins, who lives in nearby St Tropez, had told me it was one of the best restaurants on the coast. Joan can be fussy, so it was essential to try it out. It's a homely place next to a painted church, quite large, with very good old travel and other 1900-ish posters on the walls. The food was extraordinarily good. We started with various terrines including (for £16 extra) the best foie gras I've ever had. Then I had some frogs' legs and after that the special – goat with pasta. It was delicious. I don't remember what the dessert was, but we got there at 1.30 and the meal didn't finish until 5.30! If you can ever find a map with Môle on it (which isn't easy), go there.

In St Tropez, I often eat at **Byblos**, for years the most fashionable hotel, set well back from the sea, with a nice pool to relax by.

Côte tales

I've never quite understood St Tropez. I visit it from time to time, usually driving through Cannes and then along the winding coast road where the rocks turn red and the architecture becomes less interesting, until eventually you hit the harbour of St Tropez. It's pleasant enough, without being spectacular, and surrounded by a warren of lanes stuffed with boutiques, remarkably offering shirts large enough for me to get into.

I was told about **Résidence de la Pinède** by Jean-Claude Delion, owner of the hotel and La Réserve de Beaulieu, when I was staying. Madame Nicole Delion runs La Pinède, leaving her husband miles away in Beaulieu. What effect did such parting have on their marriage, I wondered, before accepting it was absolutely none of my business. M Delion suggested I visit La Pinède. I discovered you could park a helicopter only a few feet from La Réserve de Beaulieu, although you needed permission from the mayor's office as it took two police officers to ensure tourists didn't get chopped to pieces by the rotor blades. You could also land in St Tropez, some 20 minutes away, very close by La Pinède. I decided a day trip would not be out of the question.

Résidence de la Pinède was built in 1952, with more of it added in 1970, in Provençal style. It has a beach, a pool and overlooks the harbour of St Tropez. It's very luxurious in a modern way. We were taken to a suite with a view of the courtyard and the sea.

We went downstairs for lunch, admiring a 400-year-old cypress tree, a number of pine trees ('pinède' means pine) and a bit of the hotel that is an 18th-century windmill, much tarted up. There's a large, stone terrace with white plastic chairs and yellow-striped cushions, a lawn, red geraniums, palm trees and, on two sides, stands the hotel with lots of balconies and those crinkly terracotta tiles.

I walked towards the table with the best view of St Tropez. The waiter said, 'There's a nice table over there,' pointing to one with no view at all. 'If you want to eat there, please do,' I said. 'I shall sit here.' 'I wonder if pine cones fall on your head,' said Vanessa looking up.

The Pinède has a Michelin star. We both ordered salade niçoise, then, for Vanessa, spaghetti with tomato sauce and, for me, tagliatelle à la carbonara. The freebie starter was a rosette of salmon and crayfish. We were hardly testing the chef, but it was all very good. We also had an excellent pre-dessert, a sun of chocolate with three wild strawberries decorating the rim. It was like a frozen chocolate truffle. Some time later, I recommended the place to a highly significant newspaper editor. He went to dinner there with a party of three and thought it totally superb.

Madame Delion told me she and her husband came there on holiday in 1985, liked it and bought the place. She was very elegant in a light blue blazer and dark blue trousers – or were they black? I can highly recommend La Pinède, it's less formal than the excellent La Réserve de Beaulieu. Madame Delion told me there were only 5,000 permanent residents of St Tropez, but in the summer there were 100,000. She added that the main nationality of her guests was Belgian. This is something you may have to put up with.

In St Tropez, the port is pleasant but vastly overcrowded with souvenir shops and quayside vendors. Behind it are streets full of boutiques, where I've bought many items of clothing. Surrounding the town are private beaches with sun loungers laid out in close proximity to each other. They offer a restaurant, a beach shop selling high-class designer stuff and a bar. My friend Willy De Bruyn, the only amusing Belgian in the world, took me to **Tahiti** beach restaurant, owned by his friend Felix Palmari. I said I'd like to eat my lunch with a view of the sea and the topless girls stretched out between the restaurant and the water. The chef recommended the Swiss beef entrecôte, so I ordered that. I'm easily led. I was given something special for the first course even though I'd ordered melon. This often happens. Nobody takes any notice of what I order. They insist on giving me something they consider significant. This was lobster done with avocado. Perfectly pleasant. What happened next is unclear. I had dictated into my tape: 'Mashed potato came with the beef with a sort of fried, thin layer of potato on top and this is even more amazing because Willy is from a suburb of Brussels. Willy is 59. I never believe anyone who has a 9 on their age anyway.' Bizarre. I think the tape must have jammed.

Jean Ducloux's **Restaurant Greuze** in Tournus is a slightly poshed-up family place, comfortable in every way and with food so good I wish it was located round the corner from me in Holland Park. I had champagne with fresh raspberry juice in it. Ask in London and see how often, if ever, you get fresh juice added to champagne other than orange juice! The food was described as 'traditional', whatever that means. They offered cheese set in a brioche so light it flew. On the continent they often start with an absolutely extraordinary bread offering, so good it sets you off wonderfully. In London you get eight sorts of drying-up rubbish and it takes half an hour while you're told what each one is, which doesn't matter anyway because it's all dull, whether it's with carrots, caraway seeds or whatever. I had a totally historic meal, and if I could read my notes on the menu I'd tell you what it was! I can just make out 'sorta game pie, beyond belief' and 'langoustines, delicious sauce'. Go there.

The Hostellerie Jérome in La Turbie is one of the best places I've ever eaten in. It has two Michelin stars, which sometimes means a lot and sometimes means little. It's up a cobbled alley in the old part of a hill town between Beaulieu and Monte Carlo. The owners are Bruno Cirino, the chef, and his wife Marian. She dresses in a simple, elegant style and boy, does she work. She doesn't order people about. She takes the orders, serves when necessary and is a grand but superb hostess. My friend, the ex three star Michelin chef, Nico Ladenis who moved to France, said Bruno was a bit tense. But he seemed reasonably jolly when dragged out of his kitchen for the obligatory photo. The Hostellerie Jérome is open nearly all the time including Christmas. It's worth a trip over just to go for lunch. Don't sit on the little balcony: the chairs are naff and the tables too small. But in the castle-like dining room it's very comfortable with marvellous acoustics. You can even hear people at your own table.

My freebie was a very delightful minced duck tartlet followed by scampi in a fish soup with a cheese topping. All the ingredients were superb. Then I ordered rognon de veau, a whole kidney roasted in its fat, perfumed with rosemary, mustard sauce, girolle mushrooms and potatoes. The waiter showed me the kidney before serving. It was absolutely enormous. It could have fed a family of ten. Then he took it away. 'Maybe he's giving it to a family of ten,' I thought. With it were wonderful potatoes mashed in a casing rather like duchesse potatoes but better. There were mushrooms and a terrific spinach purée. I had to leave a lot, it was so large. But historic.

On a later visit I had a starter of scampi with white beans and pan fried foie gras. It was as good a course as I've ever eaten anywhere. I made a note on my tape: 'Although this is very posh, there are off-the-tourist-bus people dining here. One table of French people has come in now. They're not off the bus. They're kind of Honda Civic.' This shows how I sit dictating ridiculous nonsense into my tape. Why are you nodding in agreement? You're reading it.

A little pizza place I discovered in the town of Vence is **Chez Guy**, Guy presumably being the aproned chap who throws the pizzas in the air, catches them after they've had a good twirl, and then puts them into a log-fired oven to bake. Everyone in the place was local except for us. We sat on rush chairs at check-tableclothed tables in a white stucco room with old beams above and windows looking out on to period buildings. The pizzas had built-in fried eggs in the middle. Quite delicious, unbelievably cheap and no-nonsense waitress service.

Leslie Caron has a little hotel in Villeneuve-sur-Yonne in Burgundy called **Auberge La Lucarne aux Chouettes**. It's a 17th-century warehouse where they used to make barrels and store wheat and wine, which was taken by barge to Paris. Leslie restored it. The place is enchanting. Right on the river and decorated with antiques. There are four rooms. In the dining room it's all tools to do with grapes and barrel-making. The set lunch is €26. Ridiculously low. The food is fantastic, simple, exemplary. I started with lobster salad, went on to pigeon. Geraldine had turbot. We finished with one of the best citron tarts of all time. If you're in the area go and eat.

Leslie Bricusse recommended **Avenue 31** in Monte Carlo. It's housed in one of the endless apartment blocks that shelter tax avoiders. Very modern, tubular lighting, wooden tables, no cloths. Like an Angus Steak House minus the red. No one there worth less than £50m. Leslie pointed to a long banquette table where he once saw the entire Monaco royal family.

Cont'd

I chose ravioli shrimps and zucchini followed by tempura fish and chips. The fried cod was unbelievably tender and juicy, the batter perfect. The dessert mille-feuille was historic. I was dictating my notes when Leslie returned from a visit. 'You can say the men's upstairs is solid gold, the walls, the loo, the vulgar lid, it's all solid gold.'

Roger Moore took me to an excellent restaurant in Monte Carlo, called **Chez Gianni**. It had a nice little garden at the back, although it was still heavily overlooked by high-rise flats. But the food was extremely good.

One of the world's great establishments is the **Hôtel de Paris** in Monte Carlo, a gloriously preserved edifice built in 1864 for gamblers at the adjacent casino. It looks over the main square of Monaco, one of the few unspoilt sights in this bizarre, grossly overbuilt town.

The Hôtel de Paris lobby is the greatest ever. Towering ceiling, wonderful big chandelier, wrought-iron stairs, art deco glass skylight. Like Buckingham Palace, only grander.

The back garden restaurant, Le Côté Jardin, is an oasis of peace. We sat on a terrace facing the lovely grounds and, on the other side of the bay, the royal palace. It has a buffet as good as you'll get. I like buffets. They save me from being in the hands of indolent waiters.

A few days later I returned to the Hôtel de Paris for lunch with Sir Roger and Lady Moore on the front terrace overlooking the square. This is run by Alain Ducasse. It's the exterior bit of his three-Michelin-star Louis XV restaurant. My only experience of Alain Ducassse was his dump at the Dorchester. Awful beyond belief. The Monaco branch was another thing altogether. We had the Jardin de Provence tasting menu that went on for ever, but was worth it. I can't remember exactly what I was doing but Geraldine said I was extremely uncouth. Roger agreed.

The only unspoilt parts of the French Riviera are Beaulieu-sur-Mer and St-Jean-Cap-Ferrat. There, even in the height of the season, you're in the France of the 1950s. Walk out of the elegant Réserve de Beaulieu, turn left and you stroll along by the sea with tall palms, lovely flower gardens and hardly any people.

Monte Carlo is another story. **La Piazza** is set between towering 'council flat' blocks, with roads, tunnels and underpasses all around it. It's a pleasant, tiled restaurant with pink tablecloths and murals of old Italy on the walls. Our group was me, Roger Moore, his lady friend, Kristina Tholstrup, her daughter, Christina Knudsen, a sparkling girl who finds properties and does interior decoration, and her jolly banker boyfriend, Nikolaj Albinus. There was also Miss Lid the First.

We started with some excellent crostini – tomatoes on toast to you. This was followed by babajuan, little pancakes of ricotta cheese and spinach in a pastry shell. 'You only get them in Monaco,' said Kristina. I find ordering extremely tiring. 'What am I having, Rog?' I asked. 'You're having seafood salad, then you're having loup de mer, branzino, sea bass,' said Roger, enunciating very clearly in case I didn't understand. This was the only time ever I had a jacket on and Rog didn't.

Very rudely for one so soigné, I said to Kristina: 'Can I taste a bit of that, please?' But I'd taken her ham with my fingers before she could answer. It was very good. My main course was fine. Later Christina, the daughter, said: 'I'll have some of your crème brûlée.' I said: 'You can have it all because I should really not be ordering it.' When I got the crème brûlée, I scoffed it down. 'My goodness, I've eaten it,' I said, realising it was a bit late. 'You ate so quickly I didn't like to interrupt you,' said Christina.

Roger Moore is a rare creation: a generous actor. He took me to **Rampoldi** in Monte Carlo, which is near the casino in a street called Avenue des Spélugues. It has a crowded cafe feel about it. Indeed, most of the tables were so close together that I said a silent prayer of thanks I was with a movie star so we got, at least, the most separated spot. Rampoldi is owned by an Italian named Luciano di Saro who's had it for 15 years; before that he worked with nightclub queen Regine. It was terribly chic and the food was the very best.

GERMANY

The **Residenz Heinz Winkler**, in Aschau im Chiemgau, is a three-Michelin-star restaurant, which apparently occasionally goes down to two stars and then gets put back to three. On my rating it would go down to nil. My main course was lamb baked in light bread with a little bit of parsley, served with herb sauce. The bread was rather like fried bread stuck round the lamb, which was indifferent anyway. The best thing you could say about this is that the tables are very large and far apart, in a rather flashy and over-decorated hotel restaurant. My dessert, which was apparently a signature dish of Mr Winkler, was four blobs of hard chocolate with soft chocolate inside. The chocolate balls were heavy and there was nothing special about the liquid stuff inside. Obviously the Michelin inspector was in a very good mood when he came here to give out ratings.

Movable feast

Dinkelsbühl is a staggeringly preserved medieval town on the 'Romantic Road', with cobbled streets, richly decorated step gabling, wonderfully ornamented half-timbered façades and so on, et cetera and the rest. Never mind all that, it was lunchtime. We had booked into the **Hotel Restaurant Eisenkrug**, a beautiful building in the old wine market. It looked fine, except it was totally deserted. It was exactly 1pm, which is when I said I'd arrive. Nobody anywhere. Like the wreck of the *Marie Celeste*, but not even a half-eaten sandwich. A man eventually came up from the basement in a white uniform. I asked if he was Martin Scharff, the chef-owner. He said something about being his brother and was highly offish, so we left.

A bit down the road was the **Café Extrablatt**, set in another exquisite old house with exterior dining in the autumn sun. I went inside and found a lady in Bavarian costume, and told her that I was sitting outside, I was terribly hungry and I wanted amazing service. It worked a treat. Everyone became terribly efficient and jovial. I had excellent Bavarian white sausage with pretzel and mustard; Vanessa had noodles with cheese.

Then a worried man in a chef's uniform walked by. It was Martin Scharff, looking for me. He had no idea who the rude man had been in his hotel. He had no brother. We'd finished our main courses, so Martin went back to his hotel to make the most incredible desserts, which he brought to the Café Extrablatt (they didn't mind – they're all pals in Dinkelsbühl). Vanessa's pud was strudel leaves filled with white chocolate mousse, strawberries and Franconian riesling ice; mine was cold plum soup with cottage cheese dumplings and white chocolate ginger ice cream.

Then Martin went to a friend who had a cart which seated 16 tourists and was drawn by two lovely horses. He negotiated for Vanessa and me to trot round town on it alone. You think that's naff? Good luck to you. I found it a delightful jaunt through an amazingly historical place. But then I'm unsophisticated. We're much nicer people.

Romance in the air

The Romantic Road – 'Germany's best-known holiday route' – runs from Würzburg to Füssen. To which I hear you saying, loudly and in unison: 'So what?' I, too, never considered Germany high on the romance calendar. But when I arrived at the **Gasthaus Schwarzer Adler** in Kraftshof, near Nuremberg, in the company of Miss V Perry and Mr and Mrs J Cleese (they have since had a divorce, not a nice one), a whiff of amour stirred in some strange part of my body. And Kraftshof is not even on the 'Romantic Road' – only adjacent to it.

The Schwarzer Adler is an old inn with a Michelin star, situated in a pretty

Bavarian village. Vastly comfortable, lots of room, posh without being overbearing, pleasing oil paintings, wattle walls. 'Nice big chairs,' said John, making the point that 'nine out of ten restaurant chairs in London are too small for anyone over six foot'. 'And me,' I chipped in.

We were given an aperitif of raspberries, blackberries, blueberries, a little bit of cassis and port, home-made raspberry schnapps, topped up with Franconian sparkling wine. Almost equal in excellence to the Bellinis at Harry's Bar in Venice.

The food is quite simply amazing. If you happen to be in Nuremberg – and I'm sure you drop by regularly – it's on offer about 20 minutes from the centre. I had mushrooms in herb sauce with dumplings to start. Brilliant. We considered three pork dishes, including saddle of piglet with smoked beer sauce and potato dumplings. 'Germany is not a good place to be a pig,' Mr Cleese mused. I had venison on savoy cabbage with a cassis sauce, Vanessa had skate, Alyce, lamb . . . Oh, it doesn't matter – it was all absolutely exquisite. The boss, Gunther Hertel, was 'on a journey', said his daughter, Tanya. So she and the others took charge. Waiters of great charm; daughter ditto.

In the picturesque Tiergärtnertorplatz in Nuremberg, John Cleese and I inspected and chose the exterior eating area of the **Belm Schlenkeria**. Nice red-checked tablecloths. I had ogled the enormous shoulders of pork people seemed to eat at every turn, enough to feed a family of six, but served for one person. I ordered that. Historic. John had chicken soup with dumplings, which I tried and it was excellent. He said: 'What we don't have in England now is a tradition of English regional cooking. This is what they would have served us here in the 1920s.'

The **Gasthaus Rottner** is a lovely German inn, 300 years old, much bedecked with hanging lanterns, deer heads and antlers. We had a superb meal. The wild duck was exceptional, very non-fatty. We declared it the best ever.

The **Grand** in Nuremberg is a solid, turn-of-the-century Meridien hotel opposite the railway station. I was assured that the small, dark suite I was ushered into was their very best. Mmmm. In general, it was efficient. I even grew to like it, although my first impression was of a hotel for upper-class travelling salesmen. The breakfast room was very well run by David Stern. I definitely love Bavarian sausage, and if you sat by the window you had an uninterrupted view of the old town, an awful lot of which someone had bombed.

The **Gasthof Rehwinkl** is a wonderful little guest house in Ramsau bei Berchtesgarden, which we hit by accident. The vegetable soup was real country stuff, thick and delicious, and the roast pork was some of the best I've ever had. Although it's only a very minor place in a small town near where Hitler once had his country lair, I was very impressed with it indeed.

We settled at little tables outside the **Hotel Meistertrunk** in Rothenburg. I showed the owner one of my Winner multi-language mini brochures printed for film festivals. It was its greatest and only failure. The owner looked positively hostile. Still, we sat in the medieval street in hot, late-autumn sun and got by on my renowned charm.

ITALY

Lido Azzurro in Amalfi is right on the sea. Lovely view. The available fish are displayed as you enter. The owner, Antonio Pisani, gave us warm prawns with rocket. They tasted fresh. Nothing hard or chewy about them. Then he threw spaghetti about in a pan next to the table. The sauce with it was great, the scampi perfect. Then more spaghetti with clams in white sauce. The local fish was pezzogna. The lemon sauce with it was fantastic. One of the best fish dishes ever. 'This man's a genius,' said Geraldine.

For dessert Antonio gave us a millefeuille of ricotta cheese, pastry and strawberry sauce. The wine accompanying this masterpiece was Furore, a local white. Terrific.

Get in your private jet, take a boat down the Amalfi coast – the roads are overcrowded and horrible – and go to Lido Azzuro di Antonio Pisani.

Don't bother to eat at **Da Gemma** in Amalfi. We suffered discordant jazz from loudspeakers. My 'red prawn on Amalfitan lemon risotto' was pretty good. After that 'traditional fish soup made according to the Da Gemma 1872 recipe'... 1872 was not a great year for fish soup. The bread was terrible. The lemon profiterole was gooey. A mediocre meal.

Danielle Roux, who runs the fabulous Colombe d'Or in St-Paul-de-Vence with her husband François, has a studio over the Italian border in Apricale. She said, 'Go to **Apricale da Delio**.' So I did. The restaurant is at the start of the steep climb to the main square of Apricale. Delio Viale cooks in the morning and then leaves it to his wife, Lella, while he runs front of house. The restaurant is not a thing of beauty, but one wall is glass looking onto staggering hills, valleys and old buildings, so it's pleasant.

Cont'd

Paola started with asparagus and potato lasagne. I tasted it and found it exceptionally good. My notes are peculiar – which is fairly normal. I dictated I was having 'stuffed rabbit breast with maro (typical local sauce)' to start and later referred to eating 'slices of lamb with a stuffing in the middle'. Lamb or rabbit, who cares? It tasted terrific!

I can say, with almost certainty, that my main course was 'young goat stewed with white beans from Pigna'. That was very good too. I can also tell you, for sure, that the cistern in the toilet was labelled 'Genius'. I may not know what I'm eating but I'm an expert on toilets.

There's no question, the **Grand Hotel Villa Serbelloni** in Bellagio, a delightfully unspoilt town on Lake Como, is absolutely superb. The hotel is both beautiful and beautifully run. It's a grand villa with painted ceilings, opened in 1872, built earlier.

The staff are exemplary. The service is perfection. The head sommelier is of the old school. Discreet and excellent. On my first visit our table was in the best position but was smaller than the tables either side. I considered swapping them over myself. Instead I said to the restaurant manager, 'Tomorrow night that table will be here for me, and this smaller table can go.' It happened.

The food is extraordinarily good. You eat dinner serenaded by a lovely string quartet. There's a view of the lake and the pre-Alpine mountains beyond. As darkness falls, lights twinkle in the little village of Cadenabbia opposite. It's one of the great sights of the world. I had steamed asparagus, poached egg and truffle, then wild duck cooked two ways with plums, foie gras and spinach leaves, then an excellent cheesecake.

The downstairs restaurant, which is strangely by the pool and with plastic chairs, has a Michelin star. The brilliant chef, Ettore Bocchia, produced historic food, including a beyond-belief dessert of ice cream made with liquid nitrogen. Great smoky billows of dry ice poured from the bowl as it was stirred. You expected a rock concert to break through.

Everything was great. I cannot recommend this hotel enough.

La Capannina could have been done out by a 1950s MGM set decorator. It's a typical family-owned place, tiled floor, wooden chairs with flowers painted on the back, flowers on the table. The owner is Antonio de Angelis, who looks like a professor from a minor university. He's helped by his American wife, Aurelia, who met him on vacation aged 16. Although it's full of Italians and very unpretentious, the signatures in the guest book include many glitterati. Vanessa and I shared sea bream covered in a light potato crust, which was excellent. I also had ravioli and grilled scampi. When I went

Cont'd

again I had baby calamari filled with cheese, courgette flowers from Antonio's garden and chips, which were cut by hand in the kitchen: rare these days. Although La Capannina has low ceilings and hard walls and was full, you could hear conversation quite easily. In London, with our overhyped screamers, it would have been a noise nightmare.

Feraglioni in Capri is in a lovely open area overlooking a field of yellow flowers (please check a horticultural calendar; they may not be out on your visit). There's a view of staggering bougainvillea and a lilac tree wrapping itself round the outside. Juliano Tortiello is the owner. English is not spoken. The pasta and veal were good, and they served Coca-Cola in an exemplary way: in a tall glass, not a namby-pamby thing, with large ice cubes right down to the bottom and a healthy half-slice of lemon. The Coca-Cola in Capri was a little thinner and sharper than in the UK. (There are very few writers who'd go to Capri and do a dissertation on Coca-Cola. More's the pity.)

Da Gemma, near the market square in Capri, was bustling: a straw or bamboo ceiling, pink; a large antipasti buffet in the middle. I had linguine with lobster, which was terrific. Before that, they plonked an enormous bowl of soup on the buffet. It was called a pasta fajolie, made with pasta and clams. It was highly memorable. I also tried an excellent pizza. For dessert, I got a superb lemon profiterole, then some limoncello, a marvellous Italian liqueur tasting like lemon. I keep some in the fridge at home.

At the **Quisisana**, a highly rated hotel, we were shown to a lovely suite with a roof terrace facing unparalleled views of wooded mountains, the old rooftops of Capri, the sea, the dramatic Faraglioni rocks and the hotel gardens. This terrace saved us. Because the alternative to sunbathing there would have been to sit by a rather naff swimming pool, with a modern fountain with the words 'I' and 'Quisi' with a drawn heart between them. There was no view from the pool and it was constricted in area and ambience. The adjoining restaurant, the Colombaia Grill, offered a half-hour wait for a pizza because the ovens were never heated up, a salade niçoise served once without tuna, and no sorbet because the fridge had broken down.

Breakfast was particularly disastrous. There were tiny plastic containers of Lurpak butter, disgraceful for a supposedly top-class hotel. The fruit salad was tinned. Beyond belief! There was a limited supply of croissants and jams, there were tea bags instead of proper tea with a strainer and the crockery was uninteresting. The sugar was wrapped when it should have been in a bowl.

All this is a pity, because in many ways the Quisisana is extremely likeable.

You could not find better staff. The chief concierge, Leone Manzo, operated Winner-management superbly and with immense charm. He's one of the greats of his profession. Dr Morgano was also impeccably hospitable.

The main dining room is garishly bright in the evening. They really must dim the lights and get some candles on the tables. The maitre d' was fine at our first dinner, but on the second ignored us completely. My veal was excellent. But the triumph was a historic rum baba with custard. Rum babas used to be common in England. They have, sadly, gone into decline.

On our second dinner the Bellini was memorably ghastly, my ravioli was uninteresting, but my local fish, la pezzogna, was as good as I've ever eaten. Apparently this fish lives 120 metres down and is caught one at a time. I had it baked in salt.

In spite of some disappointments, I greatly enjoyed the Quisisana. Capri was nice, too. It's the only place where I've seen convertible six-seater taxis. It's overcrowded, though. Full of Italians and others on day trips. The streets display endlesss famous-name boutiques. I think I arrived at least 20 years too late.

A charming restaurant in Cernobbio is **Trattoria del Vapore**. I had a nice bean and pasta soup, some decent small macaroni with tomato and basil, and a terrific zabaglione.

At the highly exclusive and expensive **Villa d'Este** hotel in Cernobbio on Lake Como, our suite had the most awful bilious green carpet and a bathroom so small it would have been demi-monde in a council flat. When I went down to breakfast the first morning and asked if the orange juice was fresh, I was told it wasn't! This at a bed and breakfast rate of £375 a night! They squeezed some when I insisted. The room service breakfasts arrived speedily, but they were the worst. A heavy croissant; butter in those tiny, ludicrous plastic and silver paper cartons that you get on British Airways; and the tea was not hot. The face flannels were not replaced two nights out of four. On the plus side, the chief concierge, Romano Scotti, is superb. The grounds and views are spectacular, and the hotel has an attractive old grandeur. We had dinner there as guests of the manager, a very nice chap called Marco Sorbellini. I had one of the best spaghetti dishes ever, with bottarga of mullet roe and fresh tomato. Okay mixed grilled fish, very good raspberry soufflé with a peach sauce. But one good dinner does not a hotel make.

P.S. *A new manager has taken over the hotel and assures me he's improving it. I wonder!*

If you're adventurous, find **Restaurant La Vigne** set among vineyards at Radda in Chianti. I once sent a Scotland Yard commissioner of police there and he got lost!

I used to like the terrace of **Villa Sangiovese** at Panzano in Chianti, but the owner shouted at me when I tried to show it to Vanessa. Can you imagine somebody shouting at me? Now that's a turnaround situation if ever there was one!

The **Ristorante Passerini** in Chiavenna was a venture into the unknown. The owner, Flaviano Passerini, looked like he bought his suits in Savile Row. The restaurant had big hooks hanging from the ceiling, presumably on which to string up customers who were a nuisance. I watched my Ps and Qs. There was a log fire, a 19th-century ormolu clock on the mantelpiece and really nice silver plates with little doilies in the middle. On the menu was a sketch of the owner and a woman. 'That's my wife Sandra. She's in the kitchen,' Flaviano explained.

There followed one of the best meals I've ever had. My starter of spaghetti with scampi was close to historic. I followed with fillet of beef in red wine sauce. The home-made cheese straws were superb. There was excellent bread with lots of dips. They were all great. I'd love to tell you what I had for dessert but I forgot to put it on my tape recorder. Make a detour, as they say. Go there.

Fausto Allegri, superb Guest Relations Manager of the Splendido, has some good recommendations and some bad recommendations. **The Lord Nelson Pub**, in Chiavari, was well below bad. Fausto must have had a mental blackout in recommending to us a fake English pub in an Italian seaside resort. There was dreadful muzak, a horrid view of large concrete slabs and the sea. The menu said it was 'A perfect combination of English aplomb, Italian fantasy and international professionalism to welcome the guests in a unique atmosphere'. It looked like a roadhouse in Essex. The meal was accompanied by the endless pinging of the microwave. I can't even bother to tell you what we had because I don't recommend you go there. But just in case you pass it, or Fausto recommends it to you, stay away.

I like set menus. I particularly like them when there's only one set of food available and the restaurant has been doing it for ever. The **Locanda dell'Isola Comacina**, on an island in Lake Como, has been doing the same set menu since 1947. I guess they must have got it right by now.

You can only get to Comacina by boat. There's a ferry from the tiny lakeside village of Masala or you come, as Geraldine and I did, while travelling on Lake Como. The owner is Benvenuto Puricelli. He had reserved a perfect table overlooking the pine-covered hills and Masala.

The food is fantastic. We started with a vegetable selection. All superb. Then prosciutto and bresaola. Then an incredible dish that I've never had before. A whole onion baked, so it turns out sweet. That was delicious. Plus warm beetroot. Followed by fresh trout grilled over charcoal. Then free-range chicken open and crushed and fried in an iron pot with oil and served with salad. Then from an enormous block, some parmigiano-reggiano cheese, followed by a dessert of oranges sliced at the table, with an ice cream called 'fior di vaniglia'.

At the end of the meal Benvenuto rings a cowbell to get attention, then tells the story of the island. This was in Italian so it meant nothing to me! It's all very touristy. But it works.

They shouldn't give Italians Michelin stars. It encourages bad habits. Italian cooking is simple and unfussed. Michelin-starred cooking is over-the-top show-off stuff. So as I drove through pouring rain to Erbusco (don't ask where that is – it's in Italy) I thought, 'Why am I bothering?' When I arrived my dismay increased.

The restaurant is called **Gualtiero Marchesi**. It's in the hotel L'Albereta. We were shown into a garish, long bar with two airport lounge-type tables. I asked at reception if the renowned two-Michelin-star chef was in. 'Yes,' was the reply.

We were shown into a bland dining room to a table facing an enormous photo of chefs in a kitchen. There were only two other customers. Gualtiero Marchesi himself appeared, a very charming elderly man. 'Do you want five portions?' he asked. 'No thanks, I get too full up,' I responded. 'Just two and a dolce.' Off he went.

Delicious freebies flew in. Fried mackerel with sweet and sour sauce. Then focaccia. The photo on the wall rose revealing a real kitchen, not with 18 chefs as in the picture, only six. I reckoned that was enough for four customers.

Aubergine cream, candied tomatoes and star anise croccante arrived. Then egg cream with ratatouille in egg shells. 'Very posh all this,' I dictated into my tape. We got a mushroom cream with spring onions in a champagne glass. Then we got marinated salmon with dill and a mustard and pear sauce. The main course was chicken in a white picnic basket. The chicken had butter in it. This used to be called chicken kiev. The excellent Italian chips were made on the premises. The dessert was chocolate biscuit with chocolate mousse and passion fruit sorbet. All the food was exemplary.

The San Villa Michele manager recommended a magical little lunch place near the Piazza Della Signoria called **Cantinetta Verrazzano**. They refused to serve Coca-Cola, but everything else was brilliant. No space left to tell you more – just note the name and go there. That's if you can push your way through the human throng in Florence's jam-packed streets.

There are people who say the 'new' **Four Seasons** hotel in Florence is better than the Villa San Michele. Rubbish. The Four Seasons is in a dreary area. It's a grand old palace, drearily done out like a standard-issue hotel. It's got a large garden but it seems the budget ran out when it came to buying flowers. Excellent staff and good food though.

Sir Michael and Lady Caine had never been to Florence. Out came private jet. In went the fabulous four. Destination: the **Villa San Michele**, once a 15th-century monastery, attributed to Michelangelo, now a fantastic hotel with views down hills, vineyards and villas to the town of Florence below.

I'd forgotten what a great hotel this is. The last time I went things were dented by the restaurant manager believing he could remember the order and frequently getting it wrong. This time Vittorio Dallo wrote everything down so we got what we expected. That helps.

Things were stratospheric foodwise. The Bellinis were perfect. Everything we ate on the trip: fresh homemade spaghetti with spring mushroom and summer truffle, duck liver terrine with pepper and puréed caramel apple, thinly sliced beef in a Brunello wine sauce with spinach and Tuscan beans, roast suckling pig, fried scampi . . . not one mouthful of food in six days was less than memorable. Top marks to chef Attilio di Fabrizio, hotel manager Luca Finardi and all who sail with them. If you believe in tranquillity, beauty and quality (a) read me, (b) go to Villa San Michele. This is not optional. It's a must.

At the 'wrong' end of the Ponte Vecchio is a lovely little restaurant called **Bibo**, in Santa Felicita. Pink tablecloths, black-hooped chairs. It was extremely efficient in a refreshing, non-fussy way. They behaved most properly and gave me a table for four. A quietly well-dressed Italian in a grey suit supervised all and shook my hand. He was the owner. Everything was excellent and inexpensive. The ravioli with ricotta cheese and spinach inside with a tomato, basil and cream sauce was tip-top. The lemon sorbet was soft, historic and the best ever. If you go to Florence, find it.

Faded glory

I have come to a highly important conclusion. I was not put on this earth to unwrap butter. I considered this as I looked at a number of small, silver-wrapped butter pats in my £700-a-night suite at the Grand Hotel Villa Cora in Florence. For that money, I expect the butter to be in nice little ringlets on a bowl, the bowl itself set in a larger bowl with ice in it. I also do not wish to unwrap sugar from paper sachets that give the appearance of British Rail, nor do I expect to see four large black chips in one of the cheap-looking plastic baths. It would be nice if the television were positioned facing the bed, and not the only two small chairs in the most enormous ballroom-like bedroom.

We got there by accident. It has the same Michelin rating as the Villa San Michele near Florence, and I couldn't get in that for two nights. The Grand Hotel Villa Cora is grand. Built by Baron Oppenheim in 1865, later lived in by the Empress Eugénie, widow of Napoleon III, its pure neo-classical style includes a great deal of rococo gilt and pillars, ceiling paintings (cherubs and doves doing odd things above my bed) and ornate rooms that look rather different from the brochure. The main lounge, beautifully furnished in the coloured pictures, had hardly any furniture in it at all. 'It lets in more light,' explained a hotel manager helpfully.

The dining room is ugly and in a windowless basement. It also smelled musty so I never ate there. The swimming pool is tacky-modern with, thrown in for bad measure, five little islands with poles on them and the flags of Japan, Europe, America, Germany and France. Since I was not attending a convention of the United Nations I didn't use the pool, either.

The breakfast orange juice was so bitter we couldn't drink it and the croissants were chewy. The staff were rather nice. The whole thing has great possibility but hardly any actuality.

You can sit in a 'best view' position at the **Rivoire Pasticceria** in the Piazza della Signoria in Florence, facing the old tower and statues including a copy of Michelangelo's David. Snacky, good quality, old-fashioned but at speed.

The next outing for Sir Michael Caine, his wife Shakira, me and my adorable fiancée was to Pisa and Lucca from our base at the hotel Villa San Michele near Florence. I was arrested in Pisa some years ago to the amusement of assorted English tourists. I'd driven my open convertible under the arch into the road by the leaning tower and duomo, which I knew was strictly a pedestrian area. The police escorted me to a nearby car park. For this trip I decided to take just the driver Lorenzo. I'd navigate to be sure we travelled the scenic route. 'Look Michael,' I said, laying a road map of Tuscany out on the Mercedes people carrier, 'they're good these maps, the villages of beauty are highlighted in yellow.' Sir Michael looked just a teensy bit sceptical. Lorenzo soon assured us the motorway was blocked. That suited me. We went off onto the smaller roads. I was trying to navigate. Not easy when the vehicle has tinted windows. Light doesn't exactly pour in. The scenery was not historic. 'I see we're doing a tour of the industrial estates,' observed Sir Michael. It was also taking a long time.

Our plan was to see Pisa, then take the short drive to Lucca where there's an amazing restaurant. 'I think we'd better head straight for Lucca,' I advised. Michael C looked out of the window. 'We know where to get a used car and a second hand lawnmower,' he commented, 'a couple of council estates on the right. We'll go there and get mugged.' I said, 'I assure you we're heading towards …' 'Oblivion,' observed Michael Caine. 'Thank God we're not on the scenic route otherwise we'd have to pop out every two minutes for Michael Winner to take a photo,' said Shakira. 'This route makes the motorway look interesting,' added her husband. We made it to Lucca, one of Italy's most stunning medieval towns. Just as Michael got to the door of the Cathedral it slammed shut and a voice said 'funeral.' We had lunch, walked around, but two hours later the cathedral was still closed. 'Perhaps someone got a deal on a block booking,' I suggested, 'eight corpses for the price of one.'

The **Bucadisantantantonio** in Lucca is a superb restaurant, go there. Michael had ravioli bolognaise, me spaghetti with white truffles followed by baby goat cooked on the spit, everything was excellent. Except for a baby at the next table throwing plastic toys onto the tiled floor. 'They follow me around,' I muttered, 'go from country to country just to annoy me.' However touristy it is the leaning tower, the duomo, basilica and baptistery in Pisa remain spectacular. I got a good photo of Michael seemingly holding up the tower. He was looking to buy a baseball cap. He reckons, not untruly, that wearing dark clothes and dark baseball cap he can stay fairly anonymous. Soon as someone recognises him he charges off before being swamped by a crowd. So I had Michael over there, miles ahead, Shakira looking elegant checking out things for sale, Geraldine seeing the sights. No one together. 'It's the tour group from hell.' I muttered, trying to keep everyone in sight. Still, we had a lovely time, later going to a market in Florence. At an adjacent shop Geraldine bought a leather fur-trimmed coat. 'Only she could spend £1,000 on a fur coat when it's 32 degrees,' commented Michael.

We did find two superb restaurants in Florence. At **La Giostra** we were served by the owner, disgustingly handsome Hapsburg Prince Anastasio Soldana. Giostra means carousel. That's where they kept it in the 17th century. There was a vaulted roof somewhat let down by tiny Christmas tree lights which went endlessly on and off. This distracted from a pleasant room with nice-looking people. The Prince had bangles going right up to his elbows. If he'd been one of those African women with rings round their necks to enlarge them he'd have been too tall for any room. Michael Caine said he was an extreme example of the cuddle factor, 'which is something you should have in every restaurant.' He's spot on, of course. Food included osso bucco, goat chop (amazingly tasty) with zucchini flowers and fried artichokes and donkey ham. Sorry about the donkey, marvellous ham. To finish I had semi freddo with raspberry sauce, Michael tiramisu. Both historic.

The other restaurant was recommended by Chris Rea's staggeringly lovely daughter Josephine who's been studying art in Florence for 8 years. Her paintings are magical. I promised her an exhibition. This was bustling **Santa Bevitore**. Very atmospheric. The carrot and fennel soup with golden shrimp was incredible, 'It's like nothing you've ever had in a restaurant anywhere' observed Michael. My dessert, a dome of white chocolate with lemon zest meringue and raspberry coulis, was great, too. The trip was a major success. With a very funny ending when the jet company's credit card was not accepted at the airport for the fuel. So we had to have a whip round to pay cash in order to get out. We're arranging for a week in Balham next. Can't wait.

The **Locanda San Vigilio** in Garda, on Lake Garda, is a 500-year-old small hotel and restaurant next to a grand villa, overlooking the beautiful lake. We came by boat from the hotel Villa Feltrinelli. The whole place is delightfully rustic. The owner, Count Guarienti Agostino, lives in the villa. Christine Weber explained, 'He comes maybe lunchtime, but for dinner, yes.' She and her husband Erich have helped the count run the restaurant for 25 years. Erich cooks and she serves.

We sat and looked at the autumn sun sparkling on the lake. I ordered cheese flan with white truffles and cream. Geraldine had the antipasto. They were both superb. Our plates were cleared as soon as we'd finished. Always a good sign.

I asked for spaghetti with lobster. I was given pincers. I called Christine over. 'You will not do that,' she said. 'You're quite right. Would you please do it somewhere in the background?' I wasn't going to start dissecting lobsters. It always goes wrong. The minute I see the finger bowl coming I don't want it. I want someone else to do it. I'm too delicate.

The lobster, beautifully shelled, was terrific. So was Geraldine's fish. My pudding, a chocolate sponge with vanilla sauce, was like blancmange. It was very, very good. Over coffee I read their brochure. Winston Churchill stayed there. So did Laurence Olivier and Vivien Leigh. It's an idyllic spot. You should go there. I will return.

La Tortuga, in Gargnano on Lake Garda, has a Michelin star. 'It's like a public toilet with bright lights on the end of squiggly things sticking up a mile,' I noted on my tape. Above me was a chandelier with orange, green, red and grey bulbs. 'This is one of the ugliest rooms I've ever seen.'

Geraldine said: 'Mother's in the kitchen and the two daughters are serving.' This may or may not have been true. 'If you're right daddy should be here giving the place a bit of oomph,' I observed. I ate a bit of bread, which was not good. Geraldine had a vegetable thing that looked like a pasty. She said it was delicious. I put on tape that 'mine was perfectly all right'. But as I failed to record what I was eating, and I've since forgotten, that was not entirely helpful. I received a pear tart. It was all mush. I couldn't wait to get out of this restaurant. So I paid and left.

From time to time 'new' hotels are talked about with great reverence and praise. Such is the case with the **Grand Hotel and Villa Feltrinelli** on Lake Garda. American Bob Burns sold his posh Regent group of hotels (it once included the Dorchester) and invested £24m in restoring a marvellous late 19th-century Italian villa, which had been commandeered and lived in by Mussolini. It has only 21 rooms.

The small, elegant dining room seats about 30 people. The hotel closes for five months from the end of October to April 1. So profit is unlikely. It's a labour of love. And it shows. It is staggeringly beautiful, set in eight acres of immaculately kept lakeside gardens. It is, in the truest sense of the word, a gem.

Unlike other hotel writers, who are nearly all given free accommodation and therefore praise everything, I paid. Therefore I can offer some gentle criticism. Why have sisal mats in my room? These are horrid on my feet. Why have the toilet in the bathroom when you've got masses of space to house it separately? Why put flower petals in the toilet basin at night? Why is piped music always on in the bedrooms, so if guests don't want it they have to turn it off?

Markus Odermatt, the Swiss manager of the Feltrinelli, is immensely charming, efficient and witty. Except he didn't give me the best room in the villa. That has a really large balcony overlooking the lake. I was in the next-door second-best room. Somewhat diminished by the most enormous magnolia tree right in front of my balcony, largely blocking the view of Lake Garda. Markus assured me it was Mussolini's favourite room and he liked it because the magnolia tree made him less visible to assassins.

The hotel chef is a young man, Stefano Baicco. His food is very good without being gasp-making. I had a nice white fish from the lake, thankfully not served on a bed of spinach, but with broccoli and a delicious sauce. I also enjoyed scampi and some special pigeon. Best of the puds was the home-made ice cream, admirably soft like Mr Whippy.

I particularly enjoyed the mural on my bedroom ceiling. It showed a topless woman holding a palm frond, then a decorative border, and on the other side a winged cherub strangling a distraught dragon. In the centre, in gothic style, were the words 'Ave Maria'. So my visit was not only highly luxurious, but of considerable religious significance as well.

We visited the **Lido** in Villa Gargnano on Lake Garda. It was out of season and completely empty. Appallingly overlit. Plastic chairs and blue-check tablecloths. Adriano Gramatica ran the deserted front of house. His mother, Maria, was in the kitchen.

Adriano said: 'We have wonderful vegetable soup.' We ordered it, followed by tortoloni with ricotta cheese and pumpkin. The soup was superb. A real home-made brew. I got so overexcited a fair amount of it went on my grey silk shirt. The pasta was utterly historic. For dessert I ordered chocolate cake with pear and a semi-freddo. The semi-freddo was thin slices of cold whatever, made with fresh cream, amaretto and egg yolk. It was absolutely incredible. Altogether brilliant.

Everyone was extremely pleasant and friendly as I entered the **Four Seasons** hotel in Milan. My junior suite (a bedroom with sofas and armchairs) had a lovely 18th-century mural on the ceiling. The hotel had filled the elegant space with fruit, flowers, gift champagne. I only ate breakfast there. That was spectacular.

Service, please!

'**Y**ou see what I mean,' said our driver. 'One of the most horrible sections of Milan, human-being containers.' We are passing working-class flats on our way from Lake Como to Milan's highest-rated Michelin restaurant, the two-starred **Il Luogo di Aimo e Nadia**. We'd been told to be there no later than 1.30pm. We arrived at one, rang the bell of a nice door in an ugly block and were buzzed in.

A man in a dark grey suit, white shirt, grey- and black-striped bow tie and glasses showed us to a back room with two other people in it. A larger front room to the right was empty and better. I walked into the front room, the bow-tied one indicated a good table and we sat. Then we sat some more. It was the start of the worst 15 minutes I have ever spent in a restaurant. We were totally ignored. Occasionally a chef could be seen walking in the distance. Occasionally, Mr Bow Tie walked in the distance. After seven minutes, I asked Bow Tie to come over.

'Excuse me,' I said. 'Is the maitre d' here?' 'maitre d'!' said Bow Tie as if I'd got off a tourist bus and was using a word of horror that he failed to understand. 'The restaurant manager then?' I continued. 'Restaurant manager?!' sneered BT and he walked off. Another four minutes went by. BT returned. 'The restaurant manager will be here in an hour,' he announced. Off he went yet again. I had seen enough of the beige rag-rolled walls, the black up-lights, a few trees and ferns, some nice pictures. When I spotted BT again, I called him over.

'This may be a surprise to you,' I said, 'but it is normal when entering a restaurant to be asked whether you want a drink, given a menu and then given some bread. It is not normal to be left sitting for 15 minutes.' A bit later he reappeared with some sparkling white wine 'I don't want that,' I said. A wine waiter in a red coat joined him. 'What do you want?' asked Bow Tie. 'Two mineral waters, one still, one fizzy,' I said. Let them know the big spenders have arrived. He went off and soon thereafter returned.

'The general manager and owner,' he introduced the chef I had seen in the distance, now with another, younger chef. Both wore tall, white hats. The boss was Aimo Morani. 'You're a chef, too, are you?' I asked the younger one. 'No,' he said in an American accent. 'I'm a photographer.' 'Then why are you dressed as a chef?' I enquired. It transpired that his name was Conrad Firestein, from New York. He married into the family and was helping out.

'Tell Aimo this is the most horrible time I have ever known in a restaurant,' I requested. I listed my complaints. They then sought the villain. They explained that Aimo's daughter Stefania was the manageress, but she was at the bank.

'It must have been Fabio,' said Conrad. 'He doesn't understand greeting, he's the wine waiter.' 'Then why didn't he offer me a drink?' I asked. Fabio was brought in. 'It's not him,' I said. Fabio grabbed my arm. 'Thank you,' he breathed.

'It's the man in the dark suit. I'm going to murder him,' I announced. 'Don't do that, he's my brother-in-law,' said Conrad. He turned to Aimo and mentioned the name Marco. 'I don't care if he's in the family or not,' I said. 'He's a total disaster.' Having made my point, we settled down to one of the best meals I have ever eaten.

Aimo, endearingly helpful, was now all attention. He showed us mushrooms, suggested this and that. His daughter, Stefania, wife of the dreaded Marco, turned up looking like Liza Minnelli and with the same forthright charm. I liked her. We were given red Barbaresco 1993, a pleasant wine. I had what I thought Aimo said was Hotten Hen in a sauce of raspberry vinegar marinated with sweet peppers. Sensational. Vanessa had fresh goat's cheese with a salad sprout and mushrooms. Then she had green lasagnette with nettles, watercress, tomatoes, ricotta cheese and basil. I had Italian lamb cooked in sweet grape juice with chickpeas and thyme pie. All was absolutely, totally brilliant. A crab hors d'oeuvre figured somewhere, bresaola – old cured beef in oil, a chestnut flower tart with pears, chocolate with cinnamon cream, some cheese from Val D'Aosta. Vanessa had hazelnut biscuits filled with whatever. It was superb.

Then Aimo's jolly wife, Nadia, appeared. They started the place 35 years ago after moving from Tuscany. This restaurant is absolutely great. Seek it out when you are in Milan. If you see Marco the son-in-law, tell him Winner thinks he's... Oh well, better not.

If you go to Milan and aren't asphyxiated by the worst traffic fume pollution I can ever recall (except for Mexico City) find the **Velo Bar**. Shiny tables, framed Martini posters, mirrors. Unpretentious. I saw nothing over €8 on the menu blackboard. This is not a price range I'm familiar with. We started with bruschetta. Also an Italian salad with anchovies. Then finely cut up octopus in a salad. Some farro grains arrived with a warm sauce and beans. Very, very good. Then penne with smoked cheese and meat. Then sea bass with thinly sliced courgettes. The dessert was a toasted cake-like bread with currants, topped with mascarpone cheese whipped with cream and sugar, plus a couple of strawberries. All done by hand in the kitchen. This is good home cooking, Italian-style.

Italian ruins

When I decided to show Miss Lid the Leaning Tower of Pisa, we decided to have lunch at **Il Bottaccio** in nearby Montignoso. On a scale of 1 to 10, this was a weak 3 – in spite of having had in residence luminaries ranging from Barbra Streisand to Eric Clapton. The immensely charming host and chef, Nino Mosca, exhibits photos of himself with them to prove it.

The dining room itself is a disaster. To sit among the beauties of Italy in what is no more than an enlarged garage or small aircraft hangar is a total waste of time. Five hideous, brown air-conditioning vents faced me. A large stage took up about a third of the room, covered in dirty grey material with a piano and a guitar. Four plant holders full of shopping-arcade flora faced a pool. Some dreadful modern sculpture added to the visual cacophony. There was what looked like a copy of a Kandinsky gone wrong on one wall and something equally horrid on another. Nino assured me that they were all of artistic magnitude and valuable. Not to me they weren't.

At Il Bottaccio there was a very large menu and very few people were lunching. 'This can't all be fresh,' I said. 'Eighty per cent of it is,' replied Nino. I started with four shrimps and a small portion of black rice. Quite nice. The piped music was Addams Family at its gloomiest. Miss Lid greatly liked her salad of greens and vegetables. There was then a long delay before my main course arrived. The lamb with a sauce and stuffed with spinach and kidneys surrounded by veggies looked nice. But the plate was cold and the appearance of the food was better than its taste. Miss Lid's penne con scampi with tomato sauce didn't go down too well. 'The edges of the pasta are cold,' she said. 'Because they put it on the plate and ponce about for half an hour before they bring it here.' That's esoteric food reviewing at its best. She added that the shrimps hadn't been shelled, so by the time you finished doing that all the pasta was cold anyway.

For dessert, I had what Nino assured me was his speciality, chocolate cake in the form of a triangle, standing upright. It was impossible to use your fork without laying it down. 'You've destroyed my piramide, my pyramid!' Nino expostulated. It was more like mousse on a vague pastry base and it tasted of coffee not chocolate. 'Mushy and very oversweet,' I dictated in order to inform the world. Miss Lid thought her sorbet and fruit salad very good.

The final note on to my tape was 'There's no question this is a terrible place, but made pleasant because of Nino, his attitude and personality.' Unfortunately that isn't enough.

Hot sun in mid-March. No sustenance. I was about to turn back when we made a left, as the Americans say, and ended up on the lakeshore in the village of Olmo. There I spotted an oasis. The **Gelataria Olmo** in the Piazza Ciceri had tables right on Lake Como with a view of lovely old buildings, distant mountains and ducks. Church bells were chiming. Geraldine had a very fresh salad with broad beans. I had a memorable pizza with tomato, shrimps, rucola and cheese. Followed by an almost perfect vanilla ice cream.

The **San Pietro** hotel rises from the rocks outside Positano. It's run very personally and immaculately by Virginia Cinque and her sons Carlo and Vito. There's a helicopter pad where I landed when I flew in from Capri. That'll be useful for you. The dining room and an enormous terrace are elegant and with unbeatable sea and coast views. It's a Michelin-starred restaurant.

Joy of joys, Virginia doesn't allow children unless they're over 10. Not surprising because when she showed me one of the best suites the bath had a full-sized eunuch with an enormous erection as a tap. For sensitive *Sunday Times* readers, Virginia's prepared to drape a union jack over the offending protrusion. That's what I call service.

Le Sirenuse is a fantastic hotel in Positano, on the coast and with an incredible view of the town, the sea and the Byzantine church. The hotel is a 17th-century villa owned by the Sersale family. They turned it into a hotel in 1951. Some incredible antiques, a sea-view dining room lit at night with 420 candles, a swimming pool and a lift where they change the mat so it gives you the day of the week. If you don't know what day it is, just push the button for the lift.

At lunch we looked out on to the island of Gallo Lungo, which Geraldine assured me is where Ulysses resisted the sirens. It's shaped like a woman. Rudolph Nureyev used to live there. Between us we had ham and melon; grilled fish with a cherry tomato and rugola salad; spaghetti with clams; and the best rum baba I've ever had. Geraldine said, 'You don't get food like this anywhere else.' A well-deserved compliment. The waiter intelligently wrote down our order and then read it back. London restaurant staff, please note.

Portofino is a tiny place. I've been going for years. I'd neither heard of, nor seen, **Concordia**. But I booked in after it was recommended to me by the guest-relations manager and the restaurant manager at the Hotel Splendido, both great professionals whom I like immensely.

If you walk towards the hills, away from the lovely harbour of Portofino, you enter a no-man's-land desolated by the town's only charmless buildings. Concordia is in one of them. There's no view, just cream walls, hideously bright lighting, a tiled floor and yellow tablecloths. The food wasn't awful, but considerably less good than you can get nearby. 'The setting is so dreadful I can't wait to get out,' I dictated. There's usually a good reason why an unknown restaurant is unknown.

ö Magazin is at the far end of the harbour in Portofino. Our table was a foot away from the water. You don't get the bustle of the square. Just little, bobbing boats and a view of the pine-tree-covered hill with its lovely castle. Very peaceful. The owner's charming daughter suggested the house appetiser – five kinds of fish. Only a tuna

Cont'd

sausage thing in the middle was horrid. The rest was very good. Then we had spaghetti with calamari, absolute perfection. Then delicious, juicy grilled prawns. I shall definitely return.

Puny, in Portofino, is an incredible restaurant with a stunning view, run with immense charm by 'Mr Puny', whose real name is Luigi Miroli. It looks like a minor trattoria, facing the little boats in the harbour and two tree-covered hills, one with a castle on it, the other with a church. Puny, aged 69, works day and night, sweating, moving with great speed, serving, preparing, hosting. He is a marvel.

Everything is staggeringly good. You can eat food identically described at many different restaurants. Some, like Puny, do it absolutely brilliantly, others don't.

I often see Silvio Berlusconi, the Italian prime minister, who has a villa nearby, dining at Puny. When he was elected the last time around he came to Portofino where the press photographed him in the square with his arm round Mr Puny. No fool Signor Berlusconi. He wanted to be sure of a good table.

The **Ristorante Delfino** is right on the waterfront in the lovely old harbour of Portofino. You sit facing one of the great views of the world. The totally preserved, tiny harbour, the multi-coloured houses with washing hanging from them, bobbing boats, fishermen unloading their catch, a hill, a castle, a church. It is just like an old Sophia Loren movie. Carmelo Carluzzo is the 34-year-old chef-owner here, and his beautiful wife Palma fronts the show. He knocked up a wondrous trofietto al pesto, sort of spaghetti and potatoes, all green and very good. Then a mixed grill of langoustine, lobster, sea bass and swordfish with courgettes, aubergines, seconi and onions. The fish was so fresh that you realise with great force the difference in flavour and texture of fish just from the sea as opposed to the London 'days-later' variety. I finished off with lemon sorbet and espresso. All pretty good.

I always rave about the hotel **Splendido** in Portofino. Every time I go there, *Sunday Times* readers come up saying, 'We're here because of you.' They're all happy!

I was given a beautiful new, larger suite, decorated with exquisite taste. But there was inadequate wardrobe space. I mentioned this to the marvellous manager, Maurizio Saccani, who came over as I was enjoying a peaceful lunch overlooking the bay. Mr Saccani went into overdrive to justify his meagre wardrobes. According to him people hardly carried luggage today. He invoked the name of his superboss James Sherwood – I expected to hear the Pope had blessed inadequate wardrobes.

There was only 17in of full hanging space in one cupboard and 50in for jackets in the other. Compared with 82in of hanging space in my older, smaller suite. And a massive 120in at the Cipriani, Venice, which James Sherwood sometimes inhabits. Geraldine was unimpressed with my measuring wardrobes. 'I don't know why you're bothering,' she said, 'the rubbish you bring could go in the bin.'

The food at the Splendido is superb. But on the first evening the extremely good, young restaurant manager, Carlo Lazzeri, said, 'Could I recommend a dessert for you, Mr Winner?' I said, 'Of course, Carlo.' Then regretted it. What arrived was tomatoes covered in hard chocolate! When I complained Carlo explained, 'We're testing it on you, Mr Winner.' I said, 'If you're offering me something as bizarre as chocolate-covered tomatoes, tell me in advance so I can flee.'

But the Splendido is one of my all-time favourites. Don't listen to me nit-picking. Go there.

Lo Stella is next door to the Delfino on the waterfront in Portofino, with the same incredible view. Vanessa had pansotti with nut sauce (ravioli filled with veg) and then langoustines. I had a salad and then fish ravioli, the house speciality, which they only do for two people. So I paid – and ate – a bit more! Finally, a very creamy tiramisù. During all this, a man with a guitar sang 'I Found My Love in Portofino', the old Dean Martin hit 'Volare' and a lot more. The singing is better than the food.

Santa Margherita, near Portofino, is a town where the clock has stood still. Grandly designed 19th-century hotels look out over the sea, their windows surrounded with shutters and ornately painted decorations. There's a delightful bistro called **Skipper** overlooking the port, where you sit in white directors' chairs and get marvellous local shrimp, mussels, cuttlefish and whatever. I assume it comes from the old-fashioned marble-slab-ridden market nearby, where the fishermen unload their catch and it's displayed for locals to buy. I had memorable mussel soup with white wine, tomato sauce, olive oil and pepper, and an excellent tart.

The **Caruso** is a reasonable addition to the thoroughbred stable that is the Orient-Express hotel group. It sits high on the hills above Amalfi. In its brochure and on its website there's a lovely view of tree-clad hills dropping to the sea. What they don't show (wisely) is that if you face the infinity pool and turn your head to the left there are mountains covered in tacky apartment blocks. It looks like a council estate. What they don't tell you is that the road down to the sea at Amalfi, a mere 4½ miles, can easily take an hour. More in high season.

The Caruso is beautifully decorated with restored 18th-century wall paintings and new ones done with great flair and taste. The furnishings are discreet and elegant. The traditional pictures on the walls are carefully selected.

However, I found it itsy-bitsy. A lot of public rooms. A sprawl. The balcony of my suite faced new, white-domed buildings, which looked like a reject for the touring version of ET: *the Extra-Terrestrial*. Why, when old stonework abounds, did they add these bright modern horrors? They're not helped by a cul-de-sac car park where the sun gleams off gaudily coloured motorbikes.

The grounds are spectacular. A great credit to the gardener, Gaetano Amato. There are rose arbours, white flowers rampant, lawns and trees.

The food is fantastic. Among the delights I stuffed down (and put on 7lb in six days) were risotto with pears and mussels; the best scampi I've ever eaten; 'cream of tarallo' bread flavoured with anchovies and served with local scabbard fish; incredible pizzas and perfect pasta. The desserts were a delight. With all this great food Geraldine was rightly appalled to find in our suite a kettle and two jars of Nescafé. That's what you expect at a Travelodge, not a five-star hotel. Why couldn't they have some fresh, ground coffee and a cafetière?

Ravello is full of tour buses and vastly overcrowded in the season, which means you're isolated in this generally lovely hotel. The Caruso staff are all exceptionally good and welcoming. However, the Caruso lacks community, if you know what I mean. It's undoubtedly glamorous, beautifully executed, reasonably well situated. But for me it sparkled much less than Orient-Express's other Italian jewels.

Atmosphere is every bit as important as food. In Ravello, visit a little local place called **Trattoria Cumpa Cosimo**, run by Netta Bottone. She looks like a pantomime dame. Ebullient beyond belief. She sails round her white-washed room like a grandmother on speed. She smiles a lot.

We ordered antipasti, then for me fettuccine with mushrooms and parsley, for Geraldine mixed pasta. The antipasti was gargantuan. Artichoke, ricotta cheese, ham, very good pieces of pizza, fried courgettes, fried zucchini, melon. The food comes to you in seconds. Netta cruised by, saying, 'piano, piano, bimbo', and pinched my cheek. Geraldine said, 'That means you're eating too quickly.' Netta arrived again saying, 'ah ha ha. Manga, manga, manga.' She always seemed to speak in threes. She meant I should eat. I was eating. Try and stop me.

'You would not call this place chic,' I dictated into my recorder. 'It's better than chic; it's real.' No pretension at all. A family place.

We lunched outside under an awning at **Dal Bolognese**, near the Piazza del Popolo in Rome. This restaurant is exceptionally good. I had tagliolini with shrimps and tomato, some mixture of fried brains, fried cheese and fried everything, and a good bollito misto. But the real miracle was the service. I've never seen everything brought so quickly or plates cleared so quickly. The plates went literally as the knife and fork were put down. The next course arrived in seconds. I want our waiter, Francesco Arcuri, to follow me wherever I go. I want him in every restaurant. I shall, in future, arrive with my own waiter.

People strain to hear every word I say in restaurants. They hope to see some lunatic complainer making a fuss. But in real life I'm very quiet. I shake hands with the staff when I leave. I often enter the kitchen and thank the chefs. Then I vanish into the night. People say: 'We were expecting a scene.' But reality is seldom as exciting as fiction. Only occasionally do I go bananas. It happened recently in Rome, at **Giggetto er Pescatore** in the bland suburb of Parioli. It's the most horrid place. The staff are miserable, there's no welcome, no charm, nil atmosphere. The customers are gloomy, mostly dull businessmen. So I did one of my very rare walkouts.

When I filmed in Rome in the 1970s, we used to go to the **Girrarrosto Toscano**, a very nice restaurant just off the Via Veneto. I returned there recently. It's decorated with wood and tiles. We had excellent bean and pasta soup. Then I had a steak and Georgina had a grilled veal slice. It was very pleasant.

Rome has never had grand hotels like the Ritz in Paris or Claridge's in London. The nearest to them was the Excelsior, which I stayed in when making movies. But the Via Veneto has gone downmarket and the hotel is now the Westin Excelsior. The **Hotel Eden** is where the stars mostly stay. It's pleasant. I was in the royal suite, which must be for quite small royalty. The bedroom was good, but the sitting room and separate dining room were tiny. At breakfast, the Eden had bottles of good mineral water free on the buffet. That's commendable. Also fresh banana juice. I liked that. My fellow guests looked like hitchhikers, except for Ed Victor, the sophisticated American literary agent. He provided social uplift.

In the world of movies Ivo Palazzi is greatly admired. He is the Mr Fixit of Rome. Every movie star visiting Rome fought to have Ivo in their contract. Burt Lancaster even had me take Ivo to Durango, Mexico, to be a Mr Fixit there. I hadn't been to Rome for a while, so I called Ivo. He took us to **Pierluigi**, on the picturesque Piazza dei Ricci. We sat outside on the cobbled street. The owner, Roberto Lisi, appeared and announced: 'You don't need menus, I'm here.' He brought us some delicious thinly sliced octopus, then a salad of crab, rugola and thinly sliced cheese. Then we got fried fish, fried artichokes, fried zucchini hearts and fried zucchini stuffed with mozzarella cheese and anchovies. Then we got lobster on top of some linguini, then sea bass. It was all excellent.

Santopadre, on the Via Collina in Rome, is a small, family-run restaurant with horse-racing pictures on the walls. On the table was some ham, some half tomatoes, cheese and pepperoni. Hot meatballs arrived in seconds. Then some chicory and mozzarella di bufala.

Cont'd

Bruno Santopadre, the owner, appeared. His fingers danced expressively with every description of food we might order. I can't remember what I had in the pasta department, but my notes say: 'My pork was so soft it fell off the bone. It was really, absolutely delicious.' I finished with apple strudel. They don't accept credit cards, so be warned.

Climb the steep hill that rises behind Santa Margherita and you'll eventually reach **La Stalla**, which has dramatic views overlooking the bay. You sit on the terrace. We had risotto with mushrooms, and 'Daddy fruit cake', which was like a sausage roll with fruit in it. The sorbet was more like a fruit frappé, rather liquid and in a tall wine glass.

The main square of Siena is one of the great masterpieces of the world. Breathtaking. Unfortunately the restaurants in it are beyond belief. We ate at **La Manga**. One of the worst meals ever. Close to us an English couple were having their wedding reception. If the marriage survives that food it'll survive anything. Our Bellinis were made with unripe, bitter peaches. The pan-fried shrimps with grapefruit and parsley were soggy, tasted old and horrid. The main course chicken casserole with Siennese herbs and carrot soufflé was ridiculous. Dry chicken, clammy soufflé. There may well be acceptable food in Siena. I've been there eight times and never found it.

We stumbled on a delightful lakeside place, the **Nilus** bar in Varenna on Lake Como. You sit right by the water on the edge of a pretty and totally unspoilt village. There are boats bobbing about, mountains opposite. Flowers in urns everywhere. It's idyllic. I had a great pizza. Geraldine had crêpes with artichoke and asparagus. Then I had chocolate and walnut ice cream. You can eat posh stuff there, but why bother?

Al Frati in Murano, the glass-blowing Venetian island, is in an old building with a deck overlooking the canal and the crumbling Palazzo da Mula. The view is wonderful, and Gi-Gi, real name Luigi Camozzo, who owns it, a totally charming host. I had fried scampi and granzella, which is spider crab. I then tried spaghetti with clams, and Vanessa had a mixed fish grill – the sort of thing they do particularly well around Venice. It's a place to go for lunch, and I thoroughly recommend it.

Luca di Vita is host and co-owner of **Alle Testiere**, a tiny 22-seat restaurant tucked away somewhere. No, not Golders Green. In a Venetian back street. It's one of my all-time favourite places. It was recommended by Lady Ruth ('call me

Ruthie') Rogers, co-owner of the River Café, also not in Golders Green. Or Venice. It's in Hammersmith.

At Alle Testiere the chef, Bruno Gavagnin, provided me with deep-fried soft-shell crab, which had been marinated in white vinegar and olive oil for three hours. Geraldine had gnocchi with scallops and fresh peas. Then I had ravioli with burata and basil and fresh tomato sauce, followed by prawns in spicy sauce. It was all totally, 102%, multi-historic. I finished with chocolate and liquorice ice cream with caramelised apple pie.

I was further delighted because the noisy child at the next table was taken out into the alley by the mother while hubby ate. Then hubby took him out while the wife ate. British parents please note and do the same.

I liked **La Caravella** in Venice even though it resembles a roadhouse in East Grinstead. Dark with silly nautical stuff on the walls. We booked for 8pm and out of courtesy I called to say we'd be there at 8.15. 'Come at nine,' said the maitre d'. 'No, no,' I replied patiently. 'I was booked for eight but shall be 15 minutes late.' 'Rather have you at nine,' he said in the great customer-service style now affecting restaurants everywhere. I came at 8.15 determined to hate it, but only the bread was awful. The calamari risotto, the carpaccio with spider crab, the drink of Titziano – fresh orange, strawberry and sparkling wine – all were good. So much as I wanted to, I didn't complain. Now that's something.

My favourite Venetian hotel is the **Cipriani**. It gets its name from Arrigo Cipriani's father who co-founded it. Then it was sold to the Orient-Express group. Now things are changing. The distinguished and superb long-serving general manager, Natale Rusconi, has retired. Maurizio Saccani has taken over. There are stories of mass staff resignations since Maurizio appeared. So what? If true, it's not unusual when a new man comes in if some of the old guard are ruffled.

I congratulate Maurizio on dropping the ludicrous dress code where, in the boiling heat of a Venetian summer, dining room guests sitting outside and sweltering had to wear a jacket. I'm less amused by Maurizio's plans to close the pool restaurant and enlarge the peaceful little dining area by the lagoon. That's where I eat. I don't want more people around me during lunch. 'If it ain't broke don't fix it,' I say. But then what do I know?

At the Cipriani, Maurizio has improved the food in their main restaurant and turned the pool restaurant into an elegant lounge snack place. The small pool dining area by the lagoon remains historic for food and setting. The view of St Mark's from the Cip's waterside restaurant is breathtaking. Maurizio even replaced the bloodstained carpet in my suite and revitalised the frayed curtains. He's doing a good job.

Da Ivo is a small place clinging to a canal in Venice. I bumped into my friend Lauren Bacall (Betty to me!) coming out. She liked it, but I found it claustrophobic and horrid. Tiny tables and an appalling group of tourists being slowly served. I got up and fled to the Cipriani pool. I returned later to Da Ivo for a full meal and it was pleasant, but not nearly as good as its admirers claim it to be. Too much salt on everything.

Lapping up the water music

Orchestras used to be everywhere when I was younger. A pianist and single violinist played in the teashop in Letchworth, just to the left of the mural of a stone balcony wall with flower gardens beyond. At the Criterion in Piccadilly, I remember at least eight men in evening dress, with a conductor, playing at lunchtime. Now the only regular place I visit with musicians is Claridge's.

Somewhere I visit less regularly, which has musicians galore, is Venice. In the Piazzetta, the bit you walk through to get to St Mark's, there's the **Gran Caffè** Chioggia, which advertises hot dogs and boasts a rather jazzy trombonist with a pianist and double-bass player, all too modern for my liking. But pass through into St Mark's itself, always a place of magic, and you are met with triple-stereophonic orchestras from three caffès – the Florian, the Quadri and the Lavena – which vie to attract passers-by on to the display of chairs and tables that face them.

My favourite has always been the **Florian**, which boasts, for most of the day and night at least, six musicians playing their hearts out with a selection of light classical and show tunes. Vanessa thought her vegetarian club sandwich was very good, my regular one was delicate and not bad, the wine was disgusting. But the service is exemplary, and to sit with a coffee or a citron pressé, listen to the music and look at the greatest architecture in the world is still a wonder. At night they floodlight the cathedral, the campanile (bell tower to you) and the two sides of the square, hung with lanterns, and called the Procuratie Vecchie and the Procuratie Nuove, dating back to the 15th century.

If it rains, the orchestra turns to face inside the cloistered archway and the restaurant beyond. You can sit in the glass-painted Caffè Florian and imagine you are in the 18th century when it was built, and even for a total realist like me it is the most romantic place ever. Guardi, Canova, Byron and Proust sat in the Florian while the **Quadri** opposite boasts the patronage of Alexandre Dumas and Wagner. There the band is dressed in rather bilious green and puts on more of a music-hall act. The clarinettist holds a note for ever and other musicians stare and mime surprise. The violinist twirls his violin before striking it dramatically with the bow to start the session. They get the crowd clapping with them in jolly, seaside fashion. Inside, paintings by Ponga of 18th-century Venetian life are modelled on those done in the Florian.

The **Lavena** seems to have a musician or so less than the others and the caffè itself is fronted with ice-cream cones and Venetian chandeliers. They speak of Franz Liszt and Rostropovich as their coffee-drinkers. At night, individually lit little stalls appear selling paintings and handbags and various twaddle, but quite like you see in Canaletto or Guardi paintings of centuries gone by.

It has been raining and a cold wind now runs through the square. The white tables are tipped up, most of the chairs are empty. It is 11 o'clock and the band turns, optimistically, from playing to inside to outside. A couple waltz through the puddles to Lehar's 'The Merry Widow'. I have stayed in Venice at Christmas when nobody else did (sadly it's now fashionable); then, mists swirled along the canals and the lights spilled from church doors into the alleyways as the choir sang. It really is the best place.

Harry's Bar in Venice is the best restaurant in the world. Not slightly, not marginally, not by a hair's breadth or whatever, but firmly, absolutely. It overlooks the start of the Grand Canal, but the windows are so small it doesn't matter. It was founded in 1931 by Giuseppe Cipriani, is now owned by his son Arrigio and has been a hang-out for Hemingway, Cole Porter, Joan Crawford and me – not in that order of importance, I might add.

It doesn't look much. A bar downstairs with some tables and a posher bit upstairs, both levels quite small. The Italians eat downstairs; tourists mingle with locals six-deep around the bar. The tables are so close together you need to be a contortionist to get in. Through it all, the white-clad waiters weave with dexterity. The room is genuinely chic, even though it has a linoleum floor and décor so plain I couldn't describe it. But it's a spirited place, noisy and cheerful. And it typifies the sort of food I like. Brilliant, natural ingredients, not over-fussed in the cooking or presentation, just direct.

Harry's Bar is famous for their Bellinis, a serious frothy combination of Italian champagne and tinned white peach juice. Giovanni Cipriani invented the Bellini in 1948, and the barman, Claudio Ponzio, has been making them meticulously for over 25 years. The taste is unbelievable. One day at the bar I knocked back three of them, some croque monsieurs, shrimp sandwiches and chicken patties. All were beyond belief superb – not like they sound, but in another stratosphere. On other visits for lunch or dinner, each meal was quite simply perfect. And desserts? Unbelievable! A chocolate cake that is definitely far and away the best I have ever tasted, and I consider myself the number-one world expert on chocolate cake! Even their bread is special.

Harry's Bar has lost its Michelin star. Why, I cannot imagine. To compensate, the Ministry of Culture has rightly declared Harry's Bar a national landmark.

My favourite restaurant in Venice is still Harry's Bar. Both for food and for service, which is precise and quick. The San Daniele ham was unbelievably thin, never tasted better. Ravioli with spinach, scampi and baby artichokes, all historic. Fantastic crêpes. Arrigo Cipriani, doyen of restaurateurs, said, 'We have 13 cooks here but no chef. Nobody knows who makes Armani clothes, but they know they're Armani.'

Arrigo Cipriani's first cloning of Harry's Bar is in Venice on the island of Giudecca. It's a bistro version called **Harry's Dolce**. Giudecca is also home to the Cipriani hotel. In summer you sit by the water in green canvas chairs, facing St Mark's Place and the Doge's Palace across the lagoon. We started with a Bellini. It wasn't nearly as good as those at Harry's Bar where it was invented. I had Harry's Dolce seafood appetiser. My main course was calf's liver and onions. It was good. The chocolate cake that followed it was quadruple historic.

Locanda Cipriani on Torcello is owned by Arrigo Cipriani's nephew (they don't get on) Bonfiacio Brass. His father, film director Tinto, married Arrigo's sister. Torcello used to be the largest and most important settlement in the Venetian lagoon. Now it's inhabited by an innkeeper (Bonifacio) and a few farmers. It's unbelievably peaceful. The 1000-year-old cathedral of Santa Maria Assunta and the attached church of Santa Fosca face the stone throne of Attila. Legend says anyone occupying it will be married in a year. I first sat on it in 1955. Still waiting. We ate in the gardens of the Locanda, cathedral in view. Veal escalope plus a stunning lemon meringue tart. Everything, and there was lots more, beyond belief good. Be sure to go there. It has six rooms if you want to stay.

A famous Italian clothes designer, one with his name on shops all over the world, advised a friend of mine, 'The best place in Venice, where all the Venetians go, is the hotel **Monaco & Grand Canal**.

The Monaco is on the Grand Canal, just across a tiny alley from Harry's Bar. It has a terrace with a spendid view of the church of Santa Maria della Salute, a 17th-century Venetian landmark. There's a large oil painting of it in my dining room. If you want to see the real thing, go there. If you want good food and ambience, don't. As for being the Venetians' favourite place, all the diners at the Monaco looked as if they'd come off a tourist bus. Except me and Geraldine, looking elegant as ever. Venetians were not to be seen. They were somewhere else. I don't blame them.

The *New York Times* once named the **Osteria Da Fiore** in Venice among the five best restaurants in the world, so I decided to try it. It is in a claustrophobic room with regency-stripe wallpaper, a low ceiling and no windows. The menu was all fish except for Parma ham. The freebie starter was baby shrimps, white polenta and zucchini. Polenta is the most over-rated stuff in the world. My main course was baked scallops with olive oil and thyme. I found it quite ordinary – I've had better scallops in my local Chinese. How this restaurant ever got into anyone's top five in the world I can't imagine.

San Pietro in Volta is an out-of-the-way Venetian island. At first you see only decrepit churches with a few boatyards thrown in, and you have a feeling of being lost. But it grows on you in a big way. The **Restaurant Nani** faces the old cathedral and the cobbled seaside square. It's a family business, legendary for its fish. As we entered, four of the family were preparing fresh lobsters and other fish at a table. Upstairs on the balcony, Joseph, son of Nani, looked after us superbly. Nice crusty bread, and then the most marvellous mix of lobster, crab meat, different types of shrimps, sea eels, everything. This was the best cold seafood starter I've ever had. I went on to noodles with fish, then a sort of mixed fish grill. We watched a man come from a shop and put some scraps on a plate on the dockside by a boat, then three cats walked over to eat them. It was so calm, the lagoon lapping on our left. At weekends, it's packed with locals who come from all over, but it's never touristy – except for me. And, if you're clever, for you as well.

In an alley off the Grand Canal and near the Rialto Bridge, the **Trattoria alla Madonna** is quite famous, although I only recently got there. The general manager is Lucio Rado and his father opened the restaurant in 1954. Dad, aged 76, is still working there. Seafood rice is their speciality and it's made with scampi and clams. It's like scampi and clam risotto really. Then we got black squid, and fried sardines that are put with onions for two days in vinegar. And then there was another plate of mixed fish, octopus, shrimps, grey fish, milk of the squid, little prawns and snails. Everything was boiled and superb. After all that I had an enormous soup called pasta e fagioli (pasta and beans), which was delicious. 'Very Bulgarian taste. I love it,' said Georgina of the soup. Then somewhere or other I had shrimps, monkfish and fried sole on a plate, and ended with a tiramisu. It's a bit cafeteria-like, very busy and bustly, very Italian. If you go to Venice, put this on your list.

In my 'other life' scenario I consider living on Burano, one of the many islands around Venice, or at least consider having a little brightly coloured house with a small garden leading down to the lagoon. Burano is very beautiful, but more peaceful than Venice. It has endless shops selling lace. There is also a fantastic restaurant called **Da Romana** owned by Orazio Barbaro, who is large, and his wife Linda, who is small. Both cook. They speak no English. Da Romana was started towards the end of the 1880s. Orazio is the grandson of the founders.

The menu exhibits signed drawings given by Henri Matisse, Joan Miro and others. Also letters of thanks from Ernest Hemingway, Charles Chaplin, Federico Fellini and Giorgio Armani. They list other folk who've eaten there, including Katharine Hepburn, David Bowie and John McEnroe. For some extraordinary reason they don't mention me.

Although it may sound grand, with such an incredible host of past diners, Da Romana is simple. It faces the town square with the church tower sloping over and with weeds growing out of the brickwork. Nearly all the shellfish and other stuff on offer came from the lagoon that morning. Recently it's gone downhill. It seems to do mostly weddings. I no longer go there.

The world gets uglier every day. More ghastly houses, more monstrous office buildings, more fields, woods and ponds covered with concrete. Wherever I go I see two views. The current one, which is usually obscene, and the one I used to see, which was beautiful. The airport in Nice used to be a hut. Behind it were vineyards and farmhouses with crinkly tiles. Now there are endless high rise apartments, hotels and convention centres. My own street was full of beautiful Victorian houses, all built by famous artists using new and innovative materials and designs. After World War II everyone wanted to go forward. Old buildings were pulled down, hideous rubbish put up. Most of the grand mansions in my street are gone. Replaced by tat. Portofino appears much as it always did. Until you look closely. Then, where they used to make fishing nets or sell freshly caught fish, there's Dolce and Gabana, Lara Piano, Brioni – the detritus of the super-rich. Oversized yachts dwarf the harbour.

However, if you go south on a boat (one hour journey), a train or a long hike, you get to Cinque Terra, five coastal villages. The best of them is Vernazza. This is really unchanged. No boutiques, no jewellery displayed behind unbreakable glass. Just laundry hanging from lines below the windows, crumbling multi-coloured exteriors of untouched 19th century buildings, an exquisite little harbour, high hills with vineyards, a lovely old church.

The food at **Gianni Franzi**, which looks like an ordinary trattoria, is beyond belief. Lady Ruth Rogers, chef and co-owner of the River Café comes regularly to work and learn in Gianni's kitchens. She had her son's 21st birthday there. The location is on the harbour, in a lovely little square facing the sea. The bread was crisp and fresh. Gianni was away. A handsome young man, Alessandro Cavazutti, served us. 'Are you Gianni's son?' I asked. 'No, I'm a long son,' Alessandro replied. 'Tiny village, we're all related somehow or another.' Our starter was fried fish balls, stuffed fried anchovies, breaded and fried anchovies, cheese croquettes, squid – I could go on. All incredible.

A little band was playing in the square. One woman played the flute, another the tambourine, a man the accordion. They were so good that when they came round with the hat I gave them 20 Euros. Alessandro said they were Croatian. Shortly after I'd coughed up 20 Euros, a policewoman with long blonde hair and high heels started a ruck. The band argued, the policewoman persisted. She sent them away. Lucky for the band she came after the collection and not before it. I should have given the policewoman the 20 Euros. Then the band could have played for a year.

My taped notes reveal: 'The meal continued with ravioli stuffed with bacola, stuffed with cod and is made in the black ink of the squid so it's black ravioli.' Figure that out. I can't. Then pasta potato and beans with pesto. 'This is real pesto, they made it this morning,' said Geraldine. At least one of us knows about food. Dessert was chocolate mousse, bavarese with citron and a panacotta. All marvellous. This place is more than a gem, it's the crown jewels plus. The cooks are Italian Angelo Sforza and Croatian Zeljko Vujicevic. I was told Zeljko organised the kitchen. As for the other one, Alessandro fluttered his hands around his head as if to say, 'The Italian is rather Italian.' Whatever. They produce food that's beyond historic. Not many do that.

Natale Rusconi, the Cipriani's eminent boss, arranged for Mauro Albrigi to show Georgina and me the best of Verona. Mauro escorted Margaret and Denis Thatcher for three days in Verona. We saw a great deal of it in six hours.

My lunch advice came from Arrigo Cipriani of Harry's Bar in Venice. Ignoring the two-Michelin-starred Il Desco, Arrigo suggested **Ciccarelli** in nearby Madonna di Dossobuono. It was basic, with well-spaced tables, wooden chairs, brown walls, vague panelling and overhead lights that must have come from a World War II prison-camp film – just bare bulbs with a tin shade. The clientele seemed to be local businessmen, mostly in shirtsleeves.

For the past three years, a pleasant man, Renato Castione, has been proprietor and chef. Renato was severely shocked when I ordered a Coca-Cola. He brought a Valpolicella Classico 1997 instead. 'The best year of the century,' explained Mauro. They produced, very speedily, a large bowl of tagliolini with a nice bit of melting butter on top. With it were bowls of superb, hot, sliced liver, and bolognese and tomato sauces. We could pick and mix. Georgina said: 'It tastes sensational.'

I'd ordered another house speciality, bollito misto. The waiter brought an enormous plate of boiled vegetables to the table. After that came the bollito misto, in Ciccarelli a mixture of boiled and roast meat served with 'the famous Beara sauce' and a grated root called cren. The meats were carved in front of me on the trolley, the problem being, as the trolley was open, none of it was terribly hot. Then they added a large number of sauces. I promptly spilt some on the table. It was all robust. Not much more.

LUXEMBOURG

When I went to Luxembourg to play a role for Steven Berkoff in the film of his riveting stage play, *Decadence*, I enjoyed dinner at a restaurant called **Saint-Michel**. It's in an extremely lovely setting, a 16th-century castle, and the food was more than excellent. We stuffed ourselves on lobster salad with mango and avocado, a fine foie gras d'oie maison, an exceptional ravioli of langoustines, pigeon stuffed with foie gras, a turbot with fine sliced potatoes and sauce persillée, a very good wine and tip-top desserts. If you feel an urge to rush off to Luxembourg, you should definitely visit the Saint-Michel.

MADEIRA

Net gains

We drove through the utterly uninteresting streets of Funchal, turned left after a car park, passing some tacky-looking open-air cafes, all fairly empty, and then between them to what is laughingly called the old section of town. This sports indeterminate, small-scale hacienda-type architecture. But there stirred a feeling of optimism as we walked toward **Arsénio's**. The first sight is of an open-air grill, a large display of fresh fish and a moustached man in a chef's hat with rimless glasses on the end of his nose. This is Arsénio, a restaurateur who cooks and works on the premises. We squeezed past the grill into a large, dim interior space with beams above the windows, arches, real cobwebs on the pillars and red tablecloths. It looked old, a very nice room. At the back, a man played a Yamaha keyboard.

The menu offered an enormous variety of fish. Arsénio brought some over to show us. I chose prawns with garlic, Vanessa melon with ham, but she only wanted the melon. To follow: mixed swordfish, tuna fish and 'squid fish on the skewer'.

The man left the Yamaha and turned down the lights. Two men arrived, one with a guitar and one with a mandolin. Then a lady in black joined them and started singing. She got a good round of applause. The music was local, called fado. Then a man with a moustache appeared and walked round the tables as he sang. It was very pleasant.

My prawns and garlic sauce arrived. Totally delicious. Memorable. Never mind that there wasn't some souped-up chef poncing about in the kitchen with Michelin stars in his eyes, this was a terrific first course.

Then a woman with grey hair and a black shawl sang and two men joined in from the back of the room. There was stereophonic live singing from all round the place as the various entertainers joined in. A delightful atmosphere.

My fish on the skewer was as good as you could ask for, genuinely fresh. A woman brought a plate of beans, potatoes and carrots, and some butter sauce. Outside, Arsénio was engulfed in a mass of smoke.

My dessert was flambéed bananas with vanilla ice cream. Superb. Local bananas, very good quality, excellent texture. Wonderful syrup with it all. This was a memorably first-class meal.

Oh Madeira!

I decided to visit the revered **Reid's Hotel** in Madeira for a long weekend. It's difficult to get there, so I took a private jet at £18,000 return. Within five minutes of leaving the airport in Madeira I had that sinking feeling. The key to buying property, and the same applies to hotels, is you need three things. Location, location and location. Reid's Hotel is set in a row of horrid modern hotels that loom over it. You look out of the windows of the suite, and that's what you see. Sit by the pool, that's what you see.

The public rooms had the faded desolation of a Bournemouth hotel on its uppers. It meant nothing to me they were to be redecorated. The suite was small with that awful hotel view. I asked to see something else. The general manager escorted us to a larger suite that didn't face the ghastly hotel cluster. I was considering it when Vanessa called me to the bathroom. The bath had a dirty watermark, the surround had been filled in with Polyfilla, a black line of dirt ran along the top and bottom of it. We decided to stay put.

We went down for the famous Reid's tea. I had received a severe letter from the general manager instructing me not to wear jeans, T-shirts or track shoes in any part of the hotel. I counted five T-shirts in seconds. The sandwiches were adequate, the scones good, the cakes utterly dreadful.

For dinner in the main restaurant, Mr Küng had informed me, in writing, the dress code was suit and tie; on the phone he said dark suit and most people wore evening dress. I started counting. There's a man in a light brown sports jacket, there another in a pink jacket and grey trousers, there... I gave up. They should learn that if they have a dress code, keep to it. Don't write telling people you have to dress a certain way when clearly you do not.

The wine waiter poured hot water into the decanter before decanting the wine. I found that odd. Not as odd as the wine list, which gave no date for any of the named wines. My tartare of tuna was bland and tasteless, Vanessa's smoked salmon tired. My soup was wishy-washy, Vanessa's okay. Of her John Dory fish she said: 'I don't think this is very fresh.' It clearly wasn't. I had ham, which I was told was a locally reared item. The chocolate cake dessert was even worse than the one at tea. The brown bread for Vanessa's smoked salmon stayed on the table until halfway through the dessert course when I asked for it to be removed.

At breakfast the next day, we ordered Earl Grey tea and got some undrinkable slush. They changed it for Earl Grey. Vanessa ordered mixed stewed fruits. Prunes arrived. The orange juice was the worst I have ever tasted.

It was all a nightmare. The brochure refers to: 'Attentive but discreet service, an unspoilt coastline, the last word in luxury and civilised elegance.' The last word it is. But not a word I care to mention in polite society.

MOROCCO

Al Fassia is owned by Saida, the daughter of Mohammed Chab, who is the deputy manager of the greatest hotel in Marrakesh, La Mamounia. The restaurant is modern Moroccan with oil paintings of Fez. It's very comfortable. The great thing about it is you can order what you like without having a set menu, which is almost mandatory throughout Marrakesh. It's also run by women, which is totally unique. The waitresses are women as is the owner. We had traditional Moroccan soup, which is tomato soup with lentils, chickpeas, celery, coriander and chopped lamb. I followed with roast lamb shoulder with onions and almonds on the top. And some plain rice. It's a very nice room, not pretentious. I would describe it as a no-nonsense restaurant. They brought a plate of dates and gave me some lemon to put in the soup. The lamb was enough to feed six people. Georgina said: 'It's so good I can't stop eating it.' We finished with Moroccan pancakes with melted honey and butter. The pancakes were superb. They've got little craters in them so they're not all that chewy. They were really some of the most exceptional pancakes I've ever eaten. What more could you want for dinner?

Aman is a splendidly run, super-posh hotel group. I visited its place in Phuket, Thailand. It has opened the **Amanjena** a few miles out of Marrakesh, adjacent to a golf course. It's a modern repro of old Morocco, but luxurious and much visited by Aman groupies and others. I find it cold and inhospitable. Although it does have a Thai restaurant as fine as any in Thailand.

Let the show begin

Being a poor boy from Willesden, I'm always greatly impressed by aristocracy. So when a marchioness at the Mamounia pool recommended some Marrakesh restaurants, I gratefully doffed my peaked Yankees' cap. The marchioness even sent a handwritten card to my suite confirming her choices, the card topped by embossed black letters giving her full title and a Belgravia address. I was all a-quiver. Top of the list was **Chez Ali**, which was 'great fun'.

When the aristocracy say something is great fun they could be referring to a public hanging, a day out in Harrods or pulling a Christmas cracker.

Chez Ali is a spectacular, enormous Moroccan restaurant and show palace. There are rows of Arab horsemen either side of a fake castle entrance. Once inside, hundreds of Arabs in different Moroccan tribal costumes blow some instruments and bang others. It's highly labour-intensive. There are camels, tents everywhere with people eating in them, a large, outdoor sawdust ring, more fake castles. It is the human row of extras that impresses. As you pass they come to life, dancing and playing music until you move to the next tribe and the old group relaxes waiting for new guests.

You recline luxuriously on rich cushions, dining off specialities described as harira, pastilla, tagine, mechoui, couscous, pastries, mint tea. An endless supply of tribespeople enter the tent bashing, blowing and dancing. Some of the Moroccan guests get up and jiggle around with them. It took some while before we were served a beef broth with beans and rice. Then an enormous plate of lamb with beef on skewers. The lamb was very good. After dinner, in the arena, the show started with a great display of stunt horsemen, guns going off and general pageant-type things. A bit later a man on a flying carpet appeared above one end of the arena, and all the stuntmen, camel-riders, horsemen and varied assorted tribes came forward and waved. The show was over.

As we headed back to Marrakesh, our guide Mustapha said: 'Once in a lifetime, everyone comes to Chez Ali. All the Moroccans.' 'Very nice for them too,' I said. And I meant it.

The **Comptoir Darna** is the only restaurant I found in Marrakesh largely populated with young people. Most of the restaurants are inhabited by extremely tedious-looking tourists. I'm sure they look at me and say the same thing.

The Comptoir Darna definitely has atmosphere. There are candles on the stairs, candles everywhere. It's all deep reds with cut-out metal lanterns housing more candles, which cast patterns of light on the ceiling. Four musicians in fezes sat on the stairs playing music.

I received a steak covered in lettuce. 'It's coriander,' explained Geraldine. To me any green vegetable is either lettuce or cabbage. There's no in-between. I had puréed potatoes on the side. The steak was very soft in texture and had no taste at all.

'How's that?' I asked Geraldine, referring to her fish. She pulled a face. 'Not bad,' she replied. Her fish was swimming in olive oil. She left almost all of it. 'I think this place is more for atmosphere than food,' I said. I can't think of much more to say about Comptoir Darna. But in a strange way I recommend it.

A good restaurant in Marrakesh is **Dar Marjana**, where the owner-host, Chaouqui Dhaier, walks around in a green robe with a hood, and has a marvellously chiselled face. It offered the best service I've encountered anywhere, a miraculous pigeon pie and a group of Swedes somewhat overjoyed after drinking the local wine.

The restaurant **Diaffa** in Marrakesh, owned by Brahim Rmili, was recommended by my guide, Mustapha Hussaine. Mustapha is the superb greeter for the Casino at La Mamounia, owned by my friend Willy de Bruyn, the only amusing Belgian in the world. We sat at a large round table, soon joined by the chief of police of Marrakesh, who spoke in confidential tones to Mr Rmili. It was like a scene out of *Casablanca*: the movie, not the town. I expected the police chief's eyes to flicker and I'd find Peter Lorre and Sydney Greenstreet eating sheep's eyes in the corner. Diaffa does a set six-course meal, which is superb. Moroccan salad, savoury pastries, lamb tagine with prunes and almonds. Marrakesh tangia meat stewed in a rich sauce . . . In the meantime, two musicians play and do a tap dance. Oh, I've got another main course now, meat and chicken done in herbs. Then the musicians changed and one of them, in red, dances round the room as if stoned. Finally, in comes the belly dancer and a good time is had by all.

The amber nectar

I'm extremely fond of Morocco and **La Mamounia**, although things happen there that turn me into Basil Fawlty. I asked for my regular driver and guide. I was assured they would be waiting. But when I arrived in the lobby, Mr Temsamani, the chief concierge, had directed them somewhere else. These are minor tribulations, however, compared to the overall delight of Marrakesh. You should consider going right now. Mr Temsamani, immaculate as ever, is waiting. Guests are sunbathing by the enormous pool with palm trees growing from an island in the middle. You lie facing grapefruit and orange groves set in lovely grounds.

Robert Bergé, the general manager (now replaced), rang me recently, amazingly distraught about a bad review in the Gullivanter Guide (whatever that is) for La Mamounia's Moroccan restaurant. 'They obviously have no palate,' I said. 'The room may be overlit, but the staff are sensational and the food is some of the best I've ever eaten.'

The most important person to know at any hotel with sun-loungers is the beach or pool attendant. A good location for getting suntanned, or in my case reddened like a lobster, is more essential than the right table in a restaurant. Luckily, Mustapha Rashid is a pool boss with real charm and energy. I see him from my balcony in the morning, setting out the loungers and placing an upright chair next to mine. I like to have a choice of seating. I make vast sweeping movements and Mustapha further separates my space from the people around me. I'm positioned beautifully, next to the flowerbeds and facing the orange grove.

Remember: when shopping in the Marrakesh souk, don't be too British. Knocking 10% off is not bargaining. It's possible to achieve 80% less than the asking price. The deeper you go into the labyrinth of magical alleyways, the cheaper the same thing will be. A supposedly old necklace made by Berber tribesmen caught my eye for Georgina. In frontal area of the souk, it started at £100. I got it for £30. Deeper in, the same necklace started at £40 and could have been had for £10. It's savings like this that keep me in private jets.

P.S. The Mamounia has had a massive overhaul. Took three years. I will return.

The best restaurant in Marrakesh is **Le Tobsil**, owned by a French lady named Christine Rio. This is one of the greatest places in the world. It's in an old Arabian mansion, where two local musicians in Berber robes play attractively 'stoned' music. The food is totally historic. I had a pastilla of vegetables, a sort of fried-vegetable pie. It was a major taste experience. Then we had a Moroccan salad – many bowls of everything from sheep's brains to mashed aubergine. The setting is deeply romantic, with balconies around an inner courtyard, beautiful hanging lights and lovely candelabra. The tables are large and placed well apart, with rose petals on the white tablecloths. Christine paces the room marshalling the traditionally dressed Arab staff. She's one of my all-time favourites.

When I discovered Marrakesh 10 years ago it was magical. Now signs of desecration are looming. More hotels, more building. One old-time favourite, **Yacout**, used to be terrific, but they now seat guests in an odd extension. The lovely Arab garden with pool, lanterns, palm trees and exotic bushes has been tarted up to make another restaurant.

La Roseraie, Ouirgane, is a hotel on the foothills of the Atlas Mountains, or higher up if you believe some people! It's extremely beautiful. If you like walking around mountains or swimming it could be very good for you. The food is no more than all right, but the look of the place makes up for a great deal. It's very popular with British people!

If you get fed up with the souk in Marrakesh, you can drive into the Ourika valley. This is spectacularly untouched. Mud houses cling to the mountainside. Have lunch at **Ramuntcho**, owned by Jamali Abbouo. The tall picture windows face the red earth of the Atlas mountains. I had toast with goat's cheese, a sliced-open roasted chicken, flattened like veal, and a meringue glacé à la Chantilly. On the way back I bought three Berber rugs from a hut, all wool, beautifully patterned, for £22 each. What? You're frightened to go there? That's your problem.

Gold standard

There are celebrated hotels in the world about which the cognoscenti speak in hushed tones. None is more regarded than **Le Gazelle d'Or** in Taroudannt, a small, unspoilt Moroccan town. Here, it is said, President Jacques Chirac spends every Christmas. Michael Portillo has been recumbent by the pool. A Saatchi, I know not which, definitely attended. It's where I met my childhood heroine, Valerie Hobson. We discussed her role in *The King and I*. Her husband, John Profumo, was charm itself.

I reach La Gazelle d'Or from Marrakesh, courtesy of Vincent Ducro, a tall, thin, angular pilot who looks like Harrison Ford. He flies a single-engined, old propeller plane with struts supporting the wings. The views over the Atlas Mountains are spectacular. After sheep have been chased from the runway, we land at a little-used airstrip. Adam Stevenson, manager of La Gazelle d'Or, meets us in a chauffeured Mercedes. We go to the Berber market in Taroudannt where a scarred man sells dead bats, dried lizards and other delights including amber, which I buy in bulk.

La Gazelle d'Or is owned by Mrs Rita Bennis, who spends much time at her flat in Notting Hill. The hotel was built in 1956 by a French baron; Mrs Bennis got it in 1981. It now consists of cottages set in large, beautiful and restful gardens. Wonderful flowers and shrubs vie with eucalyptus and jacaranda trees. Meals are served in the main house and by an idyllic pool. It is a magical world, very peaceful, near mountains, deserts and palm groves. The king of this domain is Adam Stevenson, a slim Englishman who was barman and pianist at the Colony Club in Soho. This was also known as Muriel's Club because of the celebrated owner, Muriel Belcher. A 1971 magazine shows him there with Francis Bacon, Lucian Freud, Annie Ross and Tom Driberg. The 1970s live on in Adam's persona and demeanour.

Life by the pool is serene. Under olive trees and bougainvillea, guests bask on sun-loungers while attentive staff in white flowing robes and white fezzes deal with everything, including a superb buffet lunch. Breakfast on the terrace outside the main building with a musical accompaniment of rare bird noises is spectacular. It falls silent until a cat walks by, clomping madly. Or thus it seemed, so utterly peaceful were the surroundings.

Before dinner you sit for drinks in a domed room with Moroccan pillars and an open fireplace, looking on to a terrace with candles and lanterns on the ground and the tables. There is the sound of crickets. It's very romantic.

In the dining room it was extremely posh. Everyone was very quiet. I had le magret de canard aux apricots and a purée de pommes de terre douces. Feeble. But a beautiful setting and excellent service. Vanessa continued with vegetable couscous with a side order of onions and raisins, which 'cheered the thing up no end'. This was not a meal to die for. The millefeuille dessert was okay.

Adam was playing the piano. Brilliantly. Superbly arranged. From the heart.

Melodies ranged from 'The Lambeth Walk' to Rachmaninov's Piano Concerto No 2. We adjourned to an outer room, where Adam sat at the grand piano. An old man with a white beard and a turban squatted in front of a bowl of mint. He broke up the mint sticks, put them in a teapot, and added sugar and hot water from a charcoal stove. Robed servants handed it round.

We went back to the suite and lit the log fire in the bedroom. There are few places left in the world like La Gazelle d'Or. Dinner may not have been three-star Michelin, or even one. Who cares.

P.S. Adam Stevenson is no longer the manager, but he still plays the piano every night. It is still very good.

PORTUGAL

The **Alcantara Cafe** in Lisbon is in a massive old warehouse. One of the best rooms I've ever eaten in. A lot of iron pillars and ironwork, vast mirrors, a great atmosphere. The food was average. Or worse.

I met the outstanding actor John Malkovich in the lobby of the Lapa Palace hotel, Lisbon. It was just before lunch. By coincidence, I was off to **Bica do Sapato**, a restaurant part-owned by John. He likes Portugal. I can leave it or leave it. Bica is on an estuary so it looks out over water. It's quite buzzy. The food is good but service was slow beyond belief.

Hotels are great, good or bad. There's an abyss of difference between great and good. **The Lapa Palace**, Lisbon, scrapes into 'good'. I'll deal with its better points first.

It's a lovely old 1870s villa that became a hotel in 1992. The decor and furnishings are antique, stylish and classy. The service is okay; the pool and gardens, lovely; the food, variable. I'm struggling to think of anything else. So I'll dish out the not-so-good.

Our suite was excellent in many ways. Lovely paintings, large rooms, an enormous terrace. The bathroom was ridiculous. Orient-Express hotels normally have terrific chrome fitted bulbs around the mirrors so you can see yourself well. We had two silly little lights set in a high ceiling. Useless. The toilet was open and in the bathroom. There was no bidet.

At our first dinner I asked Sandro Fabris, the general manager, what was typically Portuguese. 'Roast suckling pig,' he suggested. It came with small cooked onions and some stone-cold mashed potatoes. Not a flicker of heat in them. Who, in their right mind, serves cold mashed potatoes? Never mind the speeches about how the dining room chandeliers came from Venice, Mr Fabris. Show the chef how to turn the oven on.

Breakfast orders were frequently delivered wrong. Although Mr De Oliveira appeared on our terrace each morning with oranges and a squeezer, and made fresh orange juice in front of me. That was exceptional service.

In the main restaurant I dictated, 'This is a very flaky place.'

Sintra is one of those preserved villages that sit around everywhere. It wasn't a patch on the French or Italian ones. But nice. Old houses. Lots of tiles. The Portuguese like tiles. We crossed a tiny street to the **Hockey Cafe**, which was quite posh. They immediately gave me a terrace table for four. Although Geraldine and I ordered different variants of cod we both got the same. The cod was overcooked. Not a great meal but a pleasant setting, opposite what was once the old jail, the national palace and a blue-tiled 19th-century house.

SARDINIA

I'd been hearing forever about the **Pitrizza** on the Costa Smeralda in Sardinia. So I went. Ho-hum, I say. Great it isn't. The Pitrizza is not a thing of beauty. It was built in 1963 and re-done in 1990. The suites are in dumpy, stone buildings with greenery on the roof. They reminded me of World War II air-raid shelters.

Inside the furniture was pleasant but primitive. There was a television in the sitting room but not in the bedroom. Geraldine rightly said most of the public rooms, combined with the furnishing, looked like a Swiss chalet. I added 'gone wrong'.

The dining room ceiling is low and dark. When I first went there I asked for a table overlooking the bay and was told I couldn't have it. They showed me to an inferior table still on the edge but with a poor view. The chef is Agostino Vince. His food is definitely good – asparagus risotto, fried squid and scampi (too much squid, not enough scampi), grilled red snapper, lobster salad, that sort of thing.

At breakfast I chose a nice-sized table. The waiter said 'doo-ay' – Italian for 'two' – and indicated a smaller one. The restaurant was almost empty, so what's all that about? The butter was in tiny, foil-wrapped slivers; ridiculous for a hotel with suites at £5,500 a night. The breakfast display was poor.

There's a nice terrace facing a moderately good view where the Bellinis are superb and the staff exemplary. Geraldine gave the view seven out of ten. There's a wide bay with an island facing you, degraded by some ghastly houses being built on it and a yellow crane. On the right there's a low headland with some modern houses and scrubland. The hard sand beach is full of sharp, nasty little stones. They hurt your feet. This is not my idea of heaven.

The beach loungers are well spaced apart and you can walk straight into the sea. Except when I was there the water was so cold hardly anyone went in and it was too rough for a boat trip. So we visited the nearest town, Porto Cervo, which is boutique hell. All the architecture is modern. The whole coast is tacky. It's built for visitors and people wanting holiday apartments.

I got a glimpse of the real Sardinia thanks to the superb concierge, Domenico Columbano. The Sardinian interior is beautiful: white rocks and dark green vegetation. 'Before there was no money. People were poor but they were happy. Now there's much money and people are not happy,' explained Domenico. I said, 'I don't know why you even bother with a hotel, it's so lovely out here in the country.' 'I need the money,' said Domenico.

SOUTH AFRICA

It's very rare I go anywhere ahead of anyone else. So it's a miracle that I have recently been to the new 'in' place, Constantia and its surrounding areas, including Cape Town, in South Africa. There are leafy roads, pompous houses with flashy grounds, burglar-alarm displays and guard-dog shows. I was so impressed that when the actor Christopher Lee took me to **The Cellars**, a lovely country house hotel with 'breathtaking views across Constantia to False Bay', I couldn't remember anything I ate for dinner! This is not good for someone meant to be giving an opinion of the food! I vaguely recall it was pleasant, but unexceptional. Table Mountain looked impressive.

The Grill Room of the **Mount Nelson Hotel** in Cape Town is very 1950s, with banquettes of black and red-striped cloth, with jockey-and-horse prints on the wall and the plates. Some customers were in formal dress, others in open-necked shirts. The jovial, bearded chef-in-chief had prepared bobotie for me and Vanessa. I'd asked him what was a typical South African dish and here it came. Javanese-style minced lamb, bay leaves, cumin and other spices, washed with egg on the top and baked in the oven. A butternut and pumpkin bobotie for Vanessa. It was totally sensational. A tiny bit like cottage pie, but better. And I love cottage pie. Garth Stroebel, the head chef, gets my award for one of the best dishes ever. The restaurant manager, Arthur Claasen, was exemplary.

The Mount Nelson is a pink, white-balconied hotel of the old school. It is owned by the Orient-Express Group and that's about as good a recommendation as you can get. It looks out on to Table Mountain and villas. Soon the villas will be high-rises and Cape Town will be destroyed. But now it's beautiful. That's life, I guess.

Constantia Uitsig is a spectacular wine farm on the slopes of Constantiaberg, the first wine-producing area of South Africa. The bearded, bespectacled and cheerful chef, Frank Swainston, is from England. We had good local lobsters, and I greatly enjoyed the penne with olive oil, garlic and parsley. Frank did a classically good, creamy bread-and-butter pudding to finish.

Just outside Franschhoek we turned left at the Huguenot Memorial to find the restaurant, **La Petite Ferme**, with amazing gardens of roses and other flowers, lawns sloping down to a wooden-railed fence and then valleys with pine trees and, in the background, the mountains. The hot peppered mackerel was memorable. The 'Hunter's Choice' was springbok. Not as good as impala, but okay. The brandy tartlet was spongy and exquisite. The views are breathtaking, but all I could think was: 'Give it three years and this will be housing estates.' I've seen it happen to the south of France; in fact, I've seen it happen to the world.

Impala with everything

At **Mala Mala**, the most famous safari camp in South Africa, they understand things. The first-class visitors have nice little huts with bedrooms and suites overlooking the jungle, and a dignified dining room with a balcony near a flower-surrounded swimming pool. Opposite the main entrance is a separate area for the others. (I personally visited the plebeian side, walked among the diners and exchanged many jovial pleasantries. No snob, I.) But back to the 'select', and a fairly ropey lot they were. Aged Americans talking about Medicare and a South African cleric to whom the disappearance of apartheid was obviously a disappointment. Luckily, I was not asked to mix. You are given your very own white hunter. Mine, Jeremy Brooker, was a delightful fellow, so he, Vanessa and I ate on our own in the thatched room. There is an exterior compound with a camp fire where you usually eat, but the weather wasn't good enough.

At our first lunch, Jeremy showed us the terrace and said: 'Do you want to sit out in the wind?' 'We're English, we're used to that,' I replied, seeing tables were moved to the exact spot I wanted. Thus we settled on the wide, wooden veranda for the first of many excellent meals where I had least expected to find them. Lunch was impala, a lovely deer that leaps all around. It was delicate, not heavy like most venison. For dinner we had venison steak (impala to you). The next day we had venison curry (impala too!) and, later, deboned leg of venison with marula jelly, which was – surprise – more impala! Since it is unlikely to turn up on the menu at The Ivy, this didn't worry me.

The rest of the food was good, time-warp stuff, which is just what I like. Before cooking got too clever. There was red pepper soup, a brandy-snap basket with peach ice cream and, for Vanessa, who's almost vegetarian, delicious stuffed button-up courgettes with tomatoes, onions and mixed herbs. On the wall was a stuffed sable antelope; I searched the menu but he wasn't on it. Cheese and wine soup, very jolly; nutty baked bananas, ice cream and chocolate fudge sauce – to die for. Marvellous hazelnut and chocolate meringues, superb chicken pie and then cold sliced impala with salad and, on the final night, impala served with an oyster and mushroom sauce! Thus impala'd, I was served by Teddy Moodley, the superb bar steward, and Belinda van den Berg, who was called the Sable (our bit of the 'hotel') hostess. The only hostess I've met who wasn't cringe-making.

A private plane later and I was at **Ngala safari camp**, about an hour away. This was more nouveau, but still immensely pleasant. Our suite at Mala Mala had been, for one of my intolerably ludicrous demands, fairly basic. The one at Ngala was sensational. An enormous stilted house with wide balconies, a very large living room, a sizeable bedroom, everything but a telephone! So if you wanted something, you couldn't ask for it! The bottle of champagne that greeted us with profuse messages of welcome was removed while we had dinner. So when we felt like drinking, it wasn't there! And I behaved so well! The open-air dining room overlooked a river with reeds, trees and bushes. We'd missed sitting next to Oprah Winfrey and Michael Palin, but the almond tart, hard to cut, was totally historic, even though the turkey stir-fry didn't have enough gravy. The cauliflower soup was nice, but not hot enough. The guinea fowl, moderate. The fried camembert, excellent.

Mala Mala wins the food stakes. Ngala wins the shop prize – a store full of good safari gear and animal-embroidered shirts that even I could get into. The clothes were so comfy I went back and had a second portion of lemon tart.

Ah, the thrills of the jungle life under canvas! The hard sleeping bag on parched earth. The mosquitoes. The red water discoloured by sand. Thank goodness I never got any of that. It was enough that the hair dryer broke down for five minutes.

Soweto's finest

If you're ever in Soweto, I've got a terrific place for you. 'Why should we go to Soweto?' I hear you say. Well, I did. If you don't, it's your loss. Soweto is not as seen on TV. When I went my memory was people burning each other with rubber tyres. African tribes slogging it out with guns and machetes, white Afrikaner police looking decidedly nervous crouching by their armoured vehicles. I met a peaceful community, cheerful, decent, with housing ranging from posh to squatter camp. A spirit of genuine goodwill everywhere.

'Don't wear your gold pince-nez and chain,' cautioned Vanessa. 'If they want it, let 'em have it,' I said. 'They deserve it more than me.' Thus we got into a nice Mercedes driven by Edward Mtembu. Just in case, we took a charming security chap, Lovemore Mabena, with dark glasses, a black-striped shirt, a black bow tie and smart black trousers with black braces. I'm glad he came because he was delightful. As security, we didn't need him. The South Western Townships of Johannesburg house 5m black people. 'They say three and a half,' volunteers Ed. 'But they did the census from a plane and it's growing all the time.' It has 23 registered millionaires and a few more whose activities are such they're not keen on registration. We saw some of their houses, then Zulu hostels, fine schools with children in outfits far neater than their English equivalents and then into what was supposedly the danger zone. I never thought it would be, and it wasn't.

At Winnie Mandela's house, tough-looking guards sported a sign on their truck: Guns Not Peace. They were ever so jolly, shook hands and loved being photographed. I had my fortune told by a faith healer in a tin hut, saw where Nelson Mandela used to live and was arrested, and a lady carrying a cake said it was nice to see people like Vanessa and me in their area.

Wandie's Place, I was told, is Soweto's only restaurant. A sign on stilts also advertising Castle Lager tells you you're there. You go in through a wooden door to a tiny stone courtyard and on into a peaceful eating area with red and yellow tablecloths, two rooms interconnecting and a sign, 'No person under 21 allowed'. There's a good buzz and a Victorian print of a little girl writing and a cat pawing what she has written. Wandie Ndala comes over and recommends pap (maize) and stewed martin (lamb) with a salad. 'We can sit 60 people comfortably, sometimes 100 uncomfortably,' says Wandie and laughs. When he hears I directed *Death Wish*, the whole room falls into appreciative silence. I'm led to Wandie's wall of fame, where signatures include Pierre Cardin, Edsel Ford (grandson of Henry) and the Cuban ambassador, among other diminishing dignitaries. I am asked to sign in the middle.

Then we all sat and tucked in. Me, Ed, Lovemore and Vanessa. Wandie did the cooking, then joined us. The lamb fell apart as you touched it, tender and terrific. There was a pleasant, spicy sauce, some sliced bananas and the maize. The atmosphere was rather like a suburban rotary club.

They were very impressed I'd been flown to South Africa to judge Miss World. 'Give me one of your cards,' I said to Wandie. 'I'll wave it about when I'm introduced: 1.8 billion people will see this flash of red!' Wandie went to his office. 'He's gone to make a large card,' said Lovemore, but he came back with a normal one, and I waved it like mad when they announced us judges on TV. Well, it was a jolly meal and it was the least I could do. I don't suppose I'll go back, although Ed and I have corresponded a bit. There are days in your life you remember vividly. They mean something in a superb sort of way. They stand out. This was one of them.

Sun stroke

I have made two big mistakes in the past decade. One was taking financial advice from Adam Faith. The other was going to Sun City. Sun City is a complex in the South African veld, surrounded by nothing, about two hours' drive from Johannesburg. It consists of at least two hotels and a so-called entertainment centre, all of increasing ugliness. The supposedly class hotel in this bizarre setting is the **Palace**. It's a lost city, early MGM gone wrong, with a touch of *Indiana Jones's Temple of Doom*. Great towers belch forth from an infrastructure with domes and quasi-minarets. At the top of the main tower four antelopes appear as if leaping from the windows. Doubtless they went mad waiting for room service.

It is, if nothing else – and believe me there isn't much else – on a grand scale. Not staggeringly grand like Las Vegas, but big enough. Vast high-ceilinged lobbies and restaurants look out on to fake rocks and waterfalls, with some quite nice trees and plants and African birds mixed with fake alligators. It is all fake, and clumsily so. When we got to the suite there was no hot water. So a man came and said he was going to 'check the satellite heater station'. The water was erratic in its hot-potential thereafter. They kindly gave me a typewriter, but nobody knew how to work it – the lady who did was away and had left the instruction book locked in her drawer. After two nice ladies spent an hour and a half diffidently attacking it like it was a nuclear power plant, eventually someone came who got it right. A hotel messenger came to the door with a letter and said: 'I've been all over, they told me you were there,' indicating a distant wing. A letter I sent by hotel hand to Bruce Forsythe (thank God he was there, he's very funny) never got to him because the hotel got his room number wrong. It was endless.

I have never eaten such terrible food for seven consecutive days – and I lived through rationing and World War II, when we had powdered eggs! It is not a place for me, but some seemed to like it. The Crystal Court, the main centre of the hotel, has a fountain with six elephants in green holding it, a glass-balustraded double staircase and groups of tourists from other areas wandering through in short trousers and with rucksacks, videoing you as you eat.

There's a fake lagoon by the secondary pool, Egyptian-lunatic except that the surface around it is so hot you cannot walk without great pain. The lagoon produces a large wave every three minutes, and wending their way up a steep hill are dozens of ant-like tourists with large blue rubber tyres. I never saw them reappear. There was obviously a high cliff the other side over which they threw themselves in despair. Senior management were all over me, but when I left, signing my bill as always without looking, I sat in my private plane (show-off!) and found I'd been massively overcharged. First of all, they'd put all meals, laundry and other things on, when I was their guest to judge Miss World. Second, the difference between a junior suite and a luxury room (I'd said I'd pay for the suite increase) was down as being £2,303; when my office rang their English rep we learned it should have been £215.18!

After I threatened to sue Sun City, Sun International, Miss World, the Pope, Mickey Mouse and any passing tramp who would accept service of a writ, they apologised, knocked off the £215 room increase and finally reimbursed me £2,308 out of the bill of £3,340. A 62% overcharge! I should offer this to the *Guinness Book of Records*. It's what you call adding insult to injury.

SPAIN (including MAJORCA)

At the **Hacienda** hotel in Ibiza I was shown a room that could kindly be described as horrible, ill-decorated and impractical. There was no bath, just two tiny cubicles each with a shower – one produced steam – and a wash basin. There was a single toilet.

The decor was Indian. A hard wooden bench faced the television. There was a wood frame covered with ropes, on top of which lay sequined cushions. The small cupboards were so close to the bed that their doors scraped it. Outside was a whirlpool bath. Many of the wooden tiles you walked on to get in or out were not fixed and overlapped the steps. So they hinged forward, dropping you on to the hard balcony. Very dangerous.

By the swimming pool were four pillars with dried palm fronds circling out from the top for shade. One pillar had half its fronds missing, another had none at all.

To put it mildly, the Hacienda is a poorly run hotel. It cost £795 per night, just for the room.

Good things about the Hacienda include a spectacular hilltop view. The lunch service was excellent, the restaurant manager charming and efficient. The food was good.

Overall the Hacienda is bizarre. Nowhere near the standard of hotels I usually visit. You have been warned.

My friend the Hon Camilla Jessel, who is terribly posh and lives in Madrid said: 'You must eat at **Arzak** in San Sebastian. It's got three Michelin stars.' The meal was so nasty I'd rather not recall it. It was like having endless canapés. Nothing had any substance. A mussel came on a stick. And a fig with bacon, also on a stick. Every miniscule portion was irrelevant to life as I know it.

Cont'd

A ravioli of foie gras, melon and light cheese tasted like mild soap. There was txistrorra, a poached egg with a Basque sausage. That was okay. We had sautéed prawn and toast and an egg shaped like a flower with dates. Then monkfish with pistachios over a garlic cube! I ask you, what's all that about?

From the main courses, I had hot foie gras – two very small pieces! All this nonsense was accompanied by the roar of motorcycles and lorries from the main road outside.

The only nice thing about the place was the chef-owner, Juan Mari Arzak. He looked like a dentist, but was genuinely hospitable and cheerful. I just wish he'd simplify his cooking.

There's nobody more interesting, accomplished or nice than Andrew Lloyd-Webber and his wife Madeleine. His Lordship's talents are renowned. Just as formidable are the abilities of the lovely Madeleine. She's a marvellous influence on the mercurial Andrew. A wit, a great hostess. Nevertheless, I politely declined to stay in their villa in Deia, Majorca. I'm not cut out to stay with people in houses, boats, tents, caravans or any other accommodation. I opted for the hotel **La Residencia**. Each day we joined Andrew, Madeleine and their delightful family and guests for a meal.

Deia is a magically unspoilt medieval village on a hill. The area is not in any way overdeveloped. Except for a strange addition to La Residencia to which locals strongly object. The hotel is good. The management wobbly. An unset jelly is rock solid by comparison. One evening I was to visit Andrew for dinner. John Rogers, general manager of La Residencia, arranged a hotel car and driver. They had all day to check the route. The journey was under two miles. For the first time in 106 years, I was put with a driver (a hotel bellboy) who had no idea how to get to the destination. When I think of the trouble other hotel managers take to see any trip I embark on is properly serviced, this was just ridiculous.

We drove into the hills. Bellboy got lost. Eventually he found the right road and stopped at Andrew Lloyd-Webber's guest house. 'We want the real house, higher up,' I said. Bellboy, who spoke no English, looked baffled. 'Sod this,' I thought and got out. I knew there were stone steps leading from the guest house up to the main house. I started to climb. Soon Andrew's son Billy came charging down. Madeleine had seen the car on the wrong road, realised it was a cock up and acted. 'Can't I carry on walking?' I asked Billy. 'I'm out of breath and I'm only coming down the hill,' said Billy. I returned to the main gate where Andrew had a buggy. Bellboy followed him up to the real house. 'Would you come back at 10.15 and wait?' I said. That's not a difficult instruction, is it? I've given it thousands of times. Everyone's followed it. Not bellboy. It was beyond him.

Andrew played us the CD of the main aria from his *Phantom 2* musical, 'Love Never Dies'. It was beautiful. A few moments later, at 10.30pm, bellboy loomed on the terrace. He hadn't been asked to the party. Not even to after-dinner drinks. Madeleine went over. 'It's your driver. I told him you'll be going in five minutes,' she said. Bellboy either appeared because he came at 10.15pm as asked and felt he was too important to wait, or he came late at 10.30pm and thought he'd tell us he was there. Either way, incompetent.

Then there was the water drama. La Residencia, in their posh El Olivo restaurant, and everywhere else, offered the only still water worse than Hildon. The Spanish Solan de Cabras. 'Is this all you have?' I asked the waiters. All said, 'We have nothing else.' A few days later, while eating ghastly food on the snack terrace, I asked the food and beverage manager, Toni Bujosa, 'Do you really only have Solan water?' 'No, we have a water menu,' he replied. I said to John Rogers, 'If you have a water menu, why don't you show it to guests? Is it in a safe, marked "Secret – only to be opened on the outbreak of World War III?"' His answer was bizarre. 'It's quite new,' he said. On the water menu all the bottles cost around £14. The first was Fine from Japan. Dreadful beyond belief. The next Antipodes, 'from the Rotama Hills, which has a historically low human population density.' I'm not surprised. They probably drank the water and fled. Next was Elsenham, British, not terrible, not good. In the meantime Toni, on my recommendation, got in Evian. So I never got to try Lanquen, 'created by nature in the heart of Patagonia'.

On bottom of all that, the garden of our superb suite had four sun loungers. One was clearly broken on arrival. A wheel dropped off the second the next day. Once we got no bath mats. It's the first time I've ever had to lay towels on the bathroom floor. In the bedroom a TV came out of a unit at the base of the bed. Whether guests wanted it up or not, at night it was raised with Orient-Express ads showing. We pressed the switch by the bed to lower the TV. Nothing happened. At 11pm (boring, boring) we called down. Two maintenance men arrived. One bashed the TV on one side. His mate bashed the other side. Then the switch worked. The piped music in their El Olivo restaurant (Andrew hates piped music even more than me) was so funereal and gloomy you'd come into dinner cheerful and go straight up afterwards and take a cyanide pill.

It's a nice place in spite of everything. Most sloppy management ever. He's an extremely pleasant man, John Rogers. Softly spoken, very laid back. I don't care if my hotel manager is in the Nazi Youth, the Klu Klux Klan and the Stasi. I worship efficiency. I want a tightly run ship. If La Residencia was a ship, it would have sunk.

However, within a one-mile radius of La Residencia hotel which I also visited for Andrew Lloyd Webber's 60th-birthday bash, there were at least five great restaurants. The food is stupendous. I've never liked Spain. But Mallorca (or Majorca, as we English twits say) around Deia is fantastic, beautiful beyond belief, not overdeveloped. Mountains tower above it. I flew out Sir Michael and Lady Caine a day ahead of the official LW celebrations.

We dined first at **Es Raco d'es Teix**, in one of Deia's narrow streets, full of stone houses and thus far completely unspoilt. The chef Josef Sauerschell, used to be at La Residencia. He now owns this place and has a Michelin star. 'Let's up him to two,' said Michael, halfway through a stunning meal. I started with medallion of foie gras with pears and beans in a sauce of cinnamon, then pot-au-feu of fish, including lobster, scallops, red mullet and hake. There were four desserts; two of them took 20 minutes to prepare.

Dinner at **Sebastian** was another great meal, with profiterole of foie gras mousse with tartar of smoked duck breast, then spring roll of Mediterranean fish with mango salad, followed by veal fillet with a chive potato purée and truffle sauce. Sounds a bit pompous, but these places are very casual and absolutely lovely.

Lunch next day was at **Jaime**. Some of the best warm fresh bread I've ever eaten, with a white garlic pâté and a red tomato one. Then some white liquid stuff. 'Vichyssoise,' Michael kindly advised. Then a totally historic suckling pig. Soft, delicious pig, great crackling.

Another great place was **Xelini**, where we all sat at long outdoor tables. It was mid-March and sun all the way. It looked like a mafia wedding in old Sicily. I suppose I was the Godfather. Endless tapas.

Geraldine and I stayed on after the LW party left and had dinner at a restaurant called **Deia**. I had fried camembert with crust of almonds and blueberry marmalade. Geraldine, a tapas of that plus black sausage, cannelloni with crab and a pâté. My main course was rabbit with onion and wild mushrooms. Rabbit great; sauce tasty beyond belief. I finished with pear cake, whipped cream and ice cream.

I really should advise you to enjoy Deia, the foodie heaven. But it's unspoilt, even having had me loitering. So, please, stay away.

We went to Palma and had lunch in Puerto Portals nearby, at **Flanigan**, on the port. A simple place but excellent. I had fried anchovies, then shrimps in yellow rice, a lot of which ended up on my shirt. Everything we ate was fine, including the dessert of flat apple tart.

SWITZERLAND

We lunched in the main square of Bergamo, one of those beautifully preserved medieval towns. Or at least the old part is well preserved. The rest is horrid. At the **Trattoria Sant'Ambroeus** I had very pleasant ravioli with bacon and sage, followed by roast rabbit with polenta, except I changed the polenta for potatoes. We overlooked the enormous tower of the Santa Maria Maggiore basilica, which the waiter said was 13th century. I finished with a lemon sorbet. All good if not historic. The setting was definitely historic.

In Bergün I settled on the tiny **Hotel Restaurant Albula** for lunch. Although the village was almost deserted, this was quite busy. I ordered a Bergüner rösti mit Bergüner hauswurst. 'My rösti is like hash brown potatoes,' I dictated. 'On the top is an enormous, seriously tasty sausage. Most Germanic. Beautifully done hash brown, very light, not overcooked. Perfect.' I asked for apfel strudel, but they hadn't made any that day. So I chose 'zabione', which was excellent and, most unusually, had an ice cream in it.

Every time I go to Switzerland I think: 'Would it be nicer here, in this orderly, clean, well-run place, just sitting by a lake?' If I did go to live in Switzerland – please stop waving 'goodbye' and cheering, I haven't decided yet! – I could do worse than start in Cully. This is a small village on Lake Geneva with a row of beautiful Edwardian houses overlooking the tranquillity of the lake. There's a little hotel with a Michelin-starred restaurant, **Le Raisin**, owned by a chubby Swiss chef, Adolfo Blokbergen. Nothing has changed since before the war. The dining room, with its log fire, is homely. I've always found Swiss food exceptionally good. It's not too fussy. We had a marvellous meal in an atmosphere of peace and quiet.

I can recommend to you restaurant **Hecht** in Faulensee on Lake Thun, near Interlaken. Lovely view of the lake and mountains. The menu was only in German. Outside it said, 'English spoken'. Whoever spoke English was off that day, but we muddled along.

The village of Feurtesoey consists of a few chalets, one called the **Gasthaus Rossli**. Each night, like all the little Swiss places around Gstaad, customers of astonishing wealth try to look like locals. Which they are in a way, as Gstaad is second home to the rich and famous masquerading as ordinary folk. On the first floor of the Rossli is a very old-fashioned bowling alley with genuine locals drinking beer and playing bowls. Downstairs in the restaurant we were joined by the famous advertising boss of bosses, Frank Lowe. He represents Coca-Cola among other clients, but I decided not to bring up the matter of my letter to his super-boss about the different colour and taste of Fanta in Morocco compared to the UK.

I was sorry to see the old-fashioned inn-like dining room offering wrapped butter. It reminded me of a moment in the Palazzo Vendramin, an extremely posh outhouse of the Hotel Cipriani in Venice. At breakfast, Miss Lid the Second was reading the *Herald-Tribune*. 'There are so many terrible things going on in the world,' she sighed. 'Yes,' I responded, 'one of them in this room: wrapped butter.'

Then my enormous double portion of truite bleu arrived. Miss Lid the Third was having shrimps with saffron rice. Frank Lowe had truite japonaise. 'It's absolutely delicious,' he said. 'Bits of leek and a lot of ginger.' 'Onions?' I asked, noticing a vegetable I could actually recognise. 'Yup,' said Frank, 'onions, ginger and then green mustard.' Dieter was having cheese fondue and then putting fondued beef into chicken broth. For dessert we all liked the apple pie and ice cream.

I rented a boat to go round Lake Lucerne. It was a lovely trip. Past little villages, lakeside villas, old hotels. Snow on the mountains. We landed (if that's the word) at a village called Greppen. A field with a pathway beside it that led to old houses. One of them was the hotel **Sankt Wendelin**, built 400 years ago but much reconstructed in 1910. Lovely dining room with an old stove, views of the lake, wooden ceiling and, in the middle of nowhere, a lot of Swiss people having lunch.

I asked for bisque de crustacés soup. It was hot, tasty and totally superb. Apart from the fact it took a very long time to get my three main courses of fish – mind you, I wasn't exactly inundated with important things to do – they were all absolutely delicious. If I ever go back I'll ask them to plonk all three on the same plate.

For dessert I chose prunes in red wine with caramel ice cream. Geraldine had crème brûlée, which was very good but more like custard. I suppose crème brûlée is custard really, but this was particularly custardy. The desserts were excellent.

The glitterati of Gstaad have adopted **The Chesery**, an old-style chalet with a roaring log fire. Loup de mer was served in a vast shell of white, apparently the salt and whites of eggs in which it was baked. So large was the fish, they served us the top half first and then offered the second, which there was no room for. There followed a brie stuffed with mascarpone and truffles.

The picturesque hotel **Olden** was built in 1899. It's owned by Bernie Ecclestone, who also owns Formula One Motor Racing. I asked the general manager, Ermes Elsener, if Bernie ever showed up to help in the kitchen. 'He comes twice a year,' said Mr Elsener.

In the excellent downstairs front restaurant (as opposed to its other restaurants), the menu informs, 'Unless otherwise specified all meat is of Swiss origin'. I had mountain dried beef (Swiss mountain, of course) and shaved aged cheese (Swiss cheese, of course). Then a gourmet salad with beef steak tartare perfumed with cognac. I'm not sure if it was Swiss cognac. Finally I scoffed iced cappuccino Italian-style. Everything was superb.

Tough at the top

It costs £10,600 to join the **Eagle Club**. It looks like a war-time bunker, sitting on top of Mount Wasserngrad, near Gstaad. Thereafter, the carefully selected members give an annual donation of their own choice, which the club announces on its notice board. I observed that most people gave £211, although Mr Sackler and Mr Wolff stretched to £245.

The purpose of the Eagle Club is to provide rest and succour to the glitterati, so they don't have to mix with tourists at a similar-looking restaurant a few yards below. People often ask, when I go to ski resorts, 'Do you ski?' To which I reply: 'No, I eat.' I always enjoy going up and down in the ski lifts. You get a nice view of the snow, pine trees, mountains and villages. Occasionally over-virile skiers enter and pass a few bons mots. It's a thoroughly pleasant experience.

On the two occasions I have been taken to the Eagle Club – once by Roger Moore and recently by a German nobleman, Knautschi von Meister – it has been incredibly crowded. The trestle tables on the terrace look as if a contest is on, with a prize for the most-crammed-together bench seat. I was offered the best view, close to the rail, looking thousands of feet down the sheer icy drop below. Members' kids on a lower-level terrace threw plastic bottle tops into the ravine, which shows that vandals are the same whatever their class.

After waiting for ever at a door while overdressed skiers kissed each other and blocked it, we got to the terrace, where Januaria, Knautschi's friend, looked around. 'Very disappointing,' she said. 'I don't see one single royalty today. Victor Emmanuel of Savoy, he's often here; Maria Gabriella of Savoy, Gonzalo de Bourbon, he's the first cousin of Juan Carlos, king of Spain. Farah Diba was here two days ago; she was the wife of the Shah of Iran . . . .' She peered intensely and gave up.

'And King Constantine with his mobile phone,' added Dieter Abt, a successful fiction writer, once owner of the British caterers who did royal garden parties until things collapsed rather dramatically. Dear Dieter was accused of fraud on various counts. I always liked him: he once invited me to the Wimbledon finals. I knew he was too stupid to commit fraud and, indeed, on the few counts the judge didn't throw out, the jury found him not guilty with alacrity. He is now a key member of the Gstaad set.

Not only was it a bad day for royalty, it was a terrible day for food. Bipo, one of the few waiters, had an impossible task. Someone ordered spaghetti. 'Once you get the order in, it comes very quickly,' said Dieter. Over an hour later he looked pretty silly.

I fought my way to the buffet, which was like a Granada service station. What little there was left looked tinned and unpleasant. I did get some nice mackerel and filled my plate anyway, because I sensed food would not rush towards me.

After an hour and a quarter, the pasta, now cold, and some rösti arrived. 'The pasta wasn't good, was it?' observed Januaria. Even the rösti, a national food of Switzerland, was described by someone at my table as 'too greasy and not crunchy'. Still, it was a pleasant setting, and there's something endearing about seeing the super-rich putting up with conditions that would appal a coach party from Warrington.

I nipped back to the buffet and got the last of the meringues, all eight of them.

They were excellent. After that, everyone complained there weren't any left. By the time the coffee arrived, I'd decided, all in all, the Eagle Club was a terrific place. Bizarre, yes, a time warp, yes, but I liked it.

Apparently, there's a problem. The Wasserngrad ski lift runs at a loss. 'Three years ago it ran out of money, so the local people and the government put in money to save it,' said Dieter. 'It may not last much longer.' That would be terrible. The Eagle Club would be deserted, high in the mountains. Like the *Titanic* on ice. Where would Victor Emmanuel of Savoy go then? How would Gonzalo de Bourbon fill his days? Would King Constantine have to bring a picnic? Farah Diba, poor thing, would be inconsolable. So would I. It's too terrible to think about.

P.S. The Eagle Club is saved and is still there!

Millions were spent on the **Grand Hotel Bellevue** in Gstaad. Inside it resembled the 1930s gone wrong. It had none of the dignity or charm of the Palace hotel. And it's right in the middle of town so the views are minimal to non-existent.

The more I go to Switzerland, the more I like it. I drove around a great deal. At no time did we see even one tiny piece of litter. Everything was orderly. The views were spectacular.

The **Gstaad Palace** hotel is marvellous, because, like the country, it's in another era. The lounge is like an Agatha Christie set. An orchestra of two violinists, a double bassist, a clarinettist and a xylophone player offer Viennese waltzes at dinner and then wander through the lounge, where there's an enormous log fire and spectacular views of the snow-clad mountains. If you go in summer they're flower-filled. On Wednesdays Julie Andrews skips through them singing 'The Hills Are Alive'. I know that was Austria, but the mountains look the same.

The food under Peter Wyss, the chef, is not over-fussed, plate-decorated into extinction, or achieving anything other than simple quality. The restaurant manager, Gildo Bocchini, is as good as they come. I had great pea soup with truffles, fresh langoustine with rice, fusilli with tomato and basil, marvellous wild peach sorbet, superb petits fours and much more. The suites are tasteful. They don't yell, 'Isn't our interior designer chic beyond belief.' The view over the village to the mountains is historic. Although I found it odd that the excellently framed prints were of English hunting scenes. Surely the Swiss have their own period prints. Instead they offer TV in the bathroom.

It's also the only hotel I know where the sitting room is so cold you need a St Bernard dog with a flask of brandy. A gasp for help produced a hideous, white electric radiator. It was disappointing to get plastic spoons for sugar and cinnamon. Plastic shouldn't figure in a hotel of this quality. And why hand out tacky paper napkins in the lounge with the food service? Nor do I welcome sugar wrapped in paper. I was not put on earth to unwrap sugar.

The Gstaad Palace was built in 1913. Since 1947 it's been owned and run by the Scherz family. Andrea Scherz Jr is the general manager. He's come on well. He used to be invisible and rather nervous. Now he's a first-rate host.

I'm not a spa person, but I toured it and it looks great. Particularly the swimming pool and an exterior hot tub with steam pouring off it as guests sit amid snow and ice.

Mile-high club

'**P**eople are deserting the Palace and going now to the Park Hotel, Gstaad,' my occasionally omnipotent Swiss friend Dieter Abt told me. 'I'll book you a table.' There are moments when you arrive for an evening out and know it will be a disaster. But something propels you onward. A voice says, 'Run, get out!' but a second voice, which you know is stupidity incarnate, says: 'Don't be silly, you've made a booking. Stay, it'll be all right.'

That conversation ran in my head as I walked through the appalling lobby of the highly rated **Park Hotel**. It's a modern version of an overblown Swiss chalet gone madly wrong, full of unsuccessful attempts to retain Swiss charm in an ersatz, airport-anywhere interior.

In the restaurant we were given a table facing the door, near a central log fire largely blocked by two serving trolleys. Why not pile a few crates of Coca-Cola there as well, I thought. I went to look at their other restaurant featuring a cruise-liner buffet, which was horrible. Foolishly, I soldiered on.

The waiter objected to me saying I wanted to write on the menu. When I told him, rather tartly, that hotels from the Paris Ritz to the Splendido in Portofino and all places in between and around were delighted when I wrote on their menus, he changed and said: 'We're very happy for you to write on the menu.' 'No you're not,' I said. 'You made that very clear.'

There was a little terrine of cheese as a freebie starter. Vanessa pulled a face and left hers. I thought it bland. The maitre d' came over. 'Did you make your choice, gentlemen?' he asked. I pointed out that one of the two people facing him was a lady. The Swiss are usually good at dignified, old-style service: this proved there are exceptions. The foie gras and the pigeon were both tasteless and odd, the atmosphere sterile. Vanessa's turbot had no texture; it had obviously been in the deep freeze far too long. 'Did you enjoy your meal?' asked the maitre d'. 'No, the fish was definitely old,' I said. 'It's fresh,' he said. 'No, it's not fresh, it's frozen and it has been frozen for a very long time,' I replied. It's rare that I am less than gracious, but this place brought out the worst in me. They said they had a wonderful selection of cheeses and produced a trolley with eight – all uninteresting. About the dessert, I wrote: 'No special taste anywhere.'

The other diners were seriously anonymous. Some absurd pretend windows of chalet design gave it a basement air, even though we were on the first floor. If I had not been knocking back a bottle of Lafite-Rothschild 1985, I might have considered suicide.

When I got the bill, I noticed they didn't charge for Vanessa's fish. 'Is the service on?' I asked. The maitre d' said: 'The service is on, but the tip is up to you.' I've got a tip for them. Close the place down.

The **Sonnenhof** restaurant is the Ivy of Saanen, near Gstaad. Roger Moore first took me there years ago with French singer and nightclub owner Régine. It was full of the rich and richer who inhabit Gstaad. It's a chalet-type place, as is everything in and around Gstaad. Which is far better than the blob buildings we put up. There's a lovely view from its exterior tables on to pine- and snow-covered mountains and valleys. I had shrimps, which they peeled for me. Then I had veal Zurich. This was not veal with Swiss francs. It was with a creamy mushroom sauce. I added rösti. They were the best rösti potatoes in the world. Then I ordered their excellent chocolate mousse. It was a delightful meal. If you're in the area – and they let you in – go.

The **Grand Hotel Nationale** is only one of two hotels that seem to be right on Lake Lucerne. I had a very large suite overlooking the lake. An excellent view, good chandelier, nice curtains, well decorated. The hotel lobby is ghastly beyond belief. Whoever decorated the public rooms should be removed from society. The food is reasonable. Since the views are so lovely I'd give it a mild recommendation.

I wouldn't call Lucerne the culinary centre of the world. Nor, I guess, would anyone else. In my seven-day stay I only found one good place to eat. That was a three-star hotel, the **Hotel Schiff**, overlooking the famous old wooden bridge (recently burned down and re-built), a lovely church called Lady's Church and the River Reuss, which runs into Lake Lucerne.

The Schiff is in the old town, a quaint mix of buildings around Weinmarkt, a beautiful cobbled square where the houses have 18th-century paintings on their exterior stucco. The dining room is panelled and candle-lit. Tables are well apart. Very olde-worlde Swiss. Nice.

The owners are Sylvia Wiesner-Joller, who runs the front of house, and hubby Peter, who cooks. Sylvia recommended home-made pork hamburgers served with cream potatoes and gravy. She assured me Vaclav Havel, the former president of Czechoslovakia, came many times and ate them. 'May as well follow the president of Czechoslovakia as anyone,' I thought.

For starters Sylvia recommended the fish crackling. It was a load of fried fish from the lake. Very, very good. For dessert I had sweet wine ice cream from Piedmont (the wine, not the ice cream) and zabaglione.

I returned to Schiff twice and enjoyed horseradish soup with salmon and barley, veal with pasta, and apple fritters with ice cream. Everything was superb. If you find yourself in Lucerne – well, you never know – go there. You could even stay. They've got 17 rooms.

I first went abroad in 1946. To the **Palace** hotel in Lucerne, Switzerland. A grand edifice that opened in 1906. I walked along the corridor and into my room. On the balcony I literally gasped at the beautiful view of Lake Lucerne with the snow-clad mountains beyond.

Returning this year I gasped again. At the absolute awfulness of my suite. The view was much the same. But the sitting area of the suite was without doubt the ugliest room I've ever been in. The bedroom was only marginally better. Hilton hotel 1952 at its worst.

The hotel's grand lobby-lounge was full of ugly furniture that might have been bought in a cheap out-of-town warehouse. The hotel restaurant, Jasper, looked like an inferior impersonal, dated airport lounge. The food matched the furniture. Preserve childhood memories, I say. Never go back.

I visited the **Villa Principe Leopoldo** some years ago and was very impressed. I was less impressed visiting it recently. It has staggering views over Lake Lugano, but they've built a lot of modern buildings since my first visit in 1957. My suite was pleasant although the bathroom was too small. My friend John Cleese was not impressed with the gym. The food I thought was poor and very pompous. John summed the place up by saying, 'This hotel thinks it's wonderful but it isn't.'

Rougemont, near Gstaad, is the last French-speaking village before you get to the Germanic bit of Switzerland. It's olde worlde and surrounded by high mountains. **Le Comptoir d'Enhaut** is a panelled restaurant in a mid-19th-century chalet. Apparently the chef there fell in love with a Chinese girl for four months. Affected him deeply, so the food is oriental. Odd for a chalet decorated with cowbells, violins and accordions, with goat's skins on wooden benches.

I had soupe de poulet tom kha gai, which I was assured was the national soup of Thailand. I immediately poured some of it on to my shirt, which is quite normal. It was good, very spicy. Then Chinese noodles with duck and veggies. To finish I had a semifreddo châtaignes, whatever that is. Le Comptoir d'Enhaut is special. Go there.

The **Suvretta House**, situated just outside the Swiss town of St Moritz, is a grand, old-style hotel, poorly managed and pretentious. We liked our large room with views of snow-clad mountains and a frozen lake. But the bathroom looked as if it came from MFI on a bad day. The plastic-coated shelving was bizarre. In the restaurant, ludicrously called the Grand-Etage, guests were asked not only to wear a tie for dinner, but also a dark suit. You felt you were at an undertakers' convention. This might have been bearable were it not that I've never consumed four consecutive dinners of such bland, miserable food.

The hotel literature informed me: 'In January 1919 Vaslav Nijinsky gave his last major performance in the ballroom of Suvretta house.' In March 2003, so did I.

It was well past my lunchtime and I was weak from hunger. An oasis turned up in the form of a small roadside place called **Ristorante Sfazu** in the area of San Carlo. It's owned by the family Luigi Rossi-Gruber. Mrs RG suggested her home-made tagliatelle. It was absolutely historic. Done with fried onions, fried garlic, cheese and cabbage. Much fortified I drove back to St Moritz.

Thun is northeast of Gstaad and has a pleasant castle, a very attractive river bordered by lovely old buildings and a good parking place, reserved for guests of a riverside hotel, which I always use anyway. The **Cafe Reber am Plätzli** overlooks the river. It's delightfully old-fashioned. Geraldine chose Menu Two – soup and fish. I chose Menu One with sausage. I had cabbage and some sort of sauce. Everything was excellent.

Geraldine pointed out I wasn't eating cabbage, I was eating leeks. Why should I know the difference? I write about food!

The **Hotel Baur au Lac** in Zurich is a splendid, old-fashioned-type grand hotel in the very best sense of the word. It is definitely a place to stay if you can get in. The rooms are beautifully decorated, as are the corridors and communal rooms. There are large gardens running down to the lake. The very pleasant dining room, like a summer house, is in the gardens. I thought on the whole that the food was excellent. The butter was not wrapped, which is good. They also had an excellent chocolate mousse. What more could anyone ask for?

THAILAND/BURMA

At Ayutthaya, a Thai capital of old (they kept being attacked by the Burmese and burnt down, so new capitals abounded), there are incredibly preserved temples and royal palaces and, even better, hardly any visitors. The **Krungsri**

River Hotel reminded me of a canteen in old Czechoslovakia. There was no sign of a river, but a glorious, totally uninterrupted view of the motorway. The dining room was large and busy. All orientals. Our guide, Sirirat Norseeda, ate Thai noodles, braised cabbage, hard-boiled egg, flying fish, chicken curry with sauce and rice, and veg. I followed her lead. All perfectly tasty. For dessert there was pineapple and watermelon on display, but – goody, goody – four different Thai jellies too. A green one, a black one, a red one and a strange wispy one in coconut cream, all topped with spoonfuls of sugary syrup. The jelly was in little strips, not rabbit-moulded as in my youth, but scrumptious none the less.

Thai to die for

When referring to the **Oriental Hotel Bangkok**, people say to me: 'The service is so good you never get to press the elevator button!' Even though this is true, it is not a great hotel achievement. Pressing elevator buttons is one of the few things I can do myself. My first sight of the hotel was in an old book: small, colonial architecture, gardens leading down to the Chao Phraya river. Then I saw modern photographs showing two ghastly tower blocks like those East End council flats we see blown up because they are such a blot on public life. When I arrived, my first thought was, this is a seriously big hotel. The marble lobby is from the grand-airport school of design. It looks out on to a swimming pool, flowering bushes and horrible enormous buildings across the river.

I had been advised to take one of the authors' suites in the old building, named after visitors such as Somerset Maugham, Joseph Conrad and others. Melvin J J Robson, the English manager (Kurt Wachtveitl, the famed general manager, had the sense to be on holiday), led me to the Presidential Suite atop the large tower. 'You asked for a view,' he explained. 'The authors' suites don't have one.' I later discovered the 'old' hotel is attached, Siamese twinlike, to the smaller block. The original lobby is used for tea with cane chairs, two musicians in evening dress on flute and guitar – and shops off it staffed by the rudest assistants I have ever found, which is surprising as most Thais are immensely lovely and charming.

The Presidential Suite had a huge living room, two large bedrooms, a dining room for 12, a kitchen, an enormous hall, two bathrooms, various lavatories and washrooms, and a cupboard full of electrical things where our floor butler pressed endless knobs in an unsuccessful attempt to stop the air conditioning from being deepfreeze level. There were terraces all around, with impressive views over an ugly, overbuilt, high-rise city.

My first meal was in Lord Jim's restaurant, one of seven places to eat provided by the hotel. Piped music everywhere – the Thais are very fond of that. They even blast it from loudspeakers attached to trees as you walk around their old palaces. There was a nice view of the river terrace, food certainly good, a high-class buffet, service remarkable. You could not sit down without staff holding your chair for you. The moment you neared the end of a Coca-Cola they asked if you wanted another. Good curry, excellent sushi bar, lovely apple flan. I wish there was something like it in London.

My favourite turned out to be their Thai restaurant, the Sala Rim Naam, to which you are ferried on the other side of the river. At night, the terrace, flower-bedecked and looking over to the hotel, is a terrific place to eat. There are trees with fairy lights and, inside an adjacent room, a costumed Thai dance troupe. We peeked in to admire, not wishing to join 200 people sitting on the floor. The prawn soup with coconut milk, chicken with lemon grass and steamed sea bass were all very good. On the terrace over the water is an Italian restaurant and a sort of grand carvery.

The hotel is too large to be my all-time favourite, but it works superbly well. It's just that when I see tour groups in the lobby, I feel queasy. The Oriental has been voted the Best in the World many times by serious magazines. 'Best' is a non-word. I prefer boutique hotels, small and exclusive. But as large ones go, you'd be hard-pressed to beat the Oriental.

My stay was made particularly pleasant through the immense charm and expertise of Melvin J J Robson, who even guided us into town, at my request, to see things I would not even hint at in the *Sunday Times*. He also provided me with a list of visitors who had inhabited the Presidential Suite: Richard Nixon, Pierre Cardin, Sean Connery, Michael Jackson, the Duke of Edinburgh, the Prince and Princess of Wales and George Bush, to name but a few. Just as well I stayed there. They could do with someone important.

The **Sinvana** resort in Phitsanulok, the 13th-century capital city, is a beautifully gardened Thai-style complex outside Bangkok. Nobody else there. Stir-fried Thai water mimosa, a sort of fried water spinach, very nice. Fried fish with garlic and pepper, stir-fried Thai watercress, both jolly. The waitresses watched cartoons on the telly.

The new boat people

There's no doubt about it, I am the guest from hell. I don't want to be invited, I don't want to have to worry about being endlessly pleasant, about keeping to times and events planned by my host. I want to order what I want when I want it, not to have to eat what is served at times not of my choosing.

I care not what it costs to avoid all this. A good hotel nearby is fine. A bedroom in someone else's house is ugh. So I looked hard at the beautifully embossed card that read 'James and Shirley Sherwood request the pleasure of the company of Michael Winner aboard the **Road to Mandalay** from Pagan to Mandalay Burma'.

The 'Road' is not an old Bob Hope–Bing Crosby movie but an elegant vessel that once glided up the Rhine. Now poshed up no end, it is a terrific Orient-Express adventure that goes up and down the Irrawaddy river. While I was considering my position, a letter arrived signed by James B Sherwood, super-chief of one of my all-time favourite hotel groups, with a tick on a little box at the bottom denoting 'this is a personal letter'. With it, a list of 88 other guests, a highly exclusive group of international importants, ambassadors, titled folk – you name them, they had them. Vanessa looked worried as she checked the names. 'Well, basically, darling,' she said, 'you're going to have to be very well behaved.' This is not something I am good at.

They must have been nervous, because when I arrived in Rangoon (now Yangon) all the others were booked for one night into a ghastly Russian-built thing called the Inya Lake hotel, whereas I, alone, was put in the Strand hotel, a lovely old colonial spot run by the excellent Aman group. The next day we flew to Pagan (now Bagan) – one of the most beautiful sights ever. A biblical landscape dotted with endless Buddhist temples and pagodas. Oxen drew carts along dusty streets, life unchanged by supposed progress.

The Orient-Express buses took us to the wide Irrawaddy river where was moored the elegant boat. I sought out the only brilliant PR lady I know, Nadia Stancioff. 'I do not wish, ever again, to go on your buses!' I said cheerfully. Nadia's smile wavered just a touch. 'I'd like, please, my own car, my own driver and my own guide. Where the others go in the morning, I will go in the afternoon. I wish to relish these sights undisturbed. On one day I hear we are to go by smaller boat, I would like my own boat.' 'They'll come off their buses, see you and gnash their teeth,' said Nadia. 'I don't give a damn,' I replied.

Let me be absolutely clear, the Road to Mandalay is one of the great excursions of the world. Even if you go on the bus (and you'll be overjoyed to hear I got my car!), see it before it vanishes. Burma is hardly touristed at all, the people are beautiful, the atmosphere serene, the architecture old and breathtaking. But there are nasty signs. A big hotel starting here, posters encouraging visitors there. To cruise up the Irrawaddy seeing bamboo rafts floating by, canoes, bamboo tents, wooden huts, life being lived as it has for centuries, is mind-blowing. The food on the boat was excellent, mostly European and prepared by a Welsh chef! It was all tasty, from fish soufflés to English tea. The cabins are small but nice. The few staterooms bigger and nicer. Mine had satellite television and telephone. The service was all-over superb. James Sherwood, in peaked cap, looking like the manager of a successful baseball team, drank endless cups of black coffee and hosted guests like mad. His wife, Shirley, dark, petite and full of energy, is everyone's favourite aunt. She bustled about making sure we'd all seen everything.

Only problem was the sun-loungers grouped around the deck pool. There were 14 of them for 90 guests. 'Do I get an alarm call for 3am and put my paperback and towel on those two?!' I said to Carl Henderson, charming boat boss. 'Or can you suggest...' 'I'll do my best, Mr Winner,' he said. 'That strikes terror into me,' I responded ungraciously. 'I've only just met you, I don't know what your best is. I'll have the alarm call. Outdo the Germans!' 'It won't be necessary,' said Carl, and he pulled it off.

I have previously written of James Sherwood as my hotel hero. I've had more wonderful times at his places, from the Splendido, Portofino, to the Cipriani, Venice, to the Mount Nelson, Cape Town, than anywhere else. He is now my boat hero, too. Nothing else left for him to achieve really, is there?

USA

Loving Las Vegas

The Brits recently opened a hotel-casino in Las Vegas – and boy are the natives laughing. They point at the hugely over-budget **Aladdin Casino** and pour scorn on our efforts. They criticise the design, saying much the same that has been said of other casinos opening in Vegas. But it is London Clubs, a major British gaming organisation, that's now facing the flak.

I last went to Vegas in 1967 to see my hero, Dean Martin, at the Sands. It's different today, with 5000-room hotel-casinos fronted by unbelievable creations. The Paris boasts a half-size Eiffel Tower and Parisian streets. The Venetian offers near full-size replicas of the Doge's Palace, the campanile and the Rialto bridge, complete with gondoliers to glide you along. Aladdin, which I greatly enjoyed, has meticulously built Arabian streets with a sky so real you think you're outside. There's even a believable thunderstorm with rain, which, sensibly, doesn't get you wet.

P.S. The Aladdin has now re-opened as a Planet Hollywood hotel and casino.

The Bellagio in Las Vegas has a massive lake surrounded by crinkle-tiled Italian villas and a stunning water display from its fountains. It also has an excellent restaurant called **Le Cirque**. The original Le Cirque is a highly fashionable restaurant in New York, founded and owned by Sirio Maccioni. In Las Vegas, you reach their Le Cirque after walking past endless slot machines. It is a small haven of elegance amid the casino din. I started with stone crab, a traditional American shellfish from Florida. It was superb. Then I had braised rabbit in riesling wine with spaetzle, which is pasta from Alsace. With it were little sweet peas from California and fresh morels. I can see the rabbit now. It was in a bowl. A cross between thick soup and a stew. The taste was historic. Unfortunately, since I was on English time, and it was four in the morning for me when I ate it, I cannot remember what I had for dessert. I do recall the very courteous Italian restaurant manager, Vincenzo Granata, and the chef de cuisine, Brian Konopka.

My meal at the **Stage Deli** in the MGM Grand in Las Vegas was extremely disappointing. I like the original in New York, where I've enjoyed their chicken soup with lokshen and kneidlach. The MGM version was a gloomy corner of the casino. The chicken soup was terrible, made worse by the spoon being plastic. My doughnuts were unspeakable. The hot-dog sausage was okay, but the bun was dreadful.

TRAVEL

PROMOTER: "WE'VE GOT THESE LECTURE DATES, THERE'S A MOTORWAY" WINNIE: "I DON'T DO MOTORWAYS". PROMOTER: "WE'VE GOT A JAGUAR" WINNIE: "I ONLY DO ROLLS OR BENTLEYS".
PROMOTER: "THERE'S THE TRAIN. WINNIE: "I DON'T DO TRAINS." PROMOTER: "HOW WILL YOU GET THERE?"
WINNIE: "HELICOPTER".
I GIVE UP!
A TRUE STORY, HONESTLY!!

PLANES AND TRAINS

Taking liberties

There is nothing more sanctimonious than a reformed smoker. Except a reformed thief. I am both. I stopped smoking 14 Monte Cristo Number One cigars a day in 1994 when my cardiologists said: 'If you keep going there's no point in us putting in new arteries.' This saved me £25,000 a year and meant I could run up stairs without getting out of breath on step three. I stopped stealing when I was 17 and went to Cambridge. This was not the expectation of the joys of academia, it just happened that way. Now, although I frequently take towels, soap, cutlery etc from hotels, restaurants and airplanes, I always ask permission first!

It was food – believe it or not – that set me on the road to larceny. At my Quaker school, during the war, sweets were rationed. The government issued coupons to be exchanged for a limited amount of sweets and chocolates. Needless to say, the official quota fell far short of the demands of young Winner. Thus I needed extra coupons and extra cash. To get this I would go round the boys' discarded clothing during the games period and nick money from their pockets. It was always a great disappointment to me when I found another boy had beaten me to it. With the money thus disgracefully gathered, I would buy my fellow students' sweets coupons and then more sweets. When even that wasn't enough, we would buy fish and meat paste from the corner post office and scoop it out of the little glass jars with our fingers!

My thieving worried me greatly in later life. A few years ago, remembering I had nicked 10 shillings (50p now) from a boy called Clotworthy, I found his number and phoned him up. I expressed my great sorrow and told him I would send him a cheque for 50p plus compound interest since 1950; and this I did. I also invited him and his wife, at my expense, to come to London for three days and attend one of my film premières; and this they did. But he was appalled to receive my cheque! He didn't remember the event at all and sent it back saying he hoped the money had in some small way helped in my success. I returned the cheque begging him to keep it, and at last he obliged. This was reported in a national newspaper, where I offered to give money to any boy who was at St

Christopher School, Letchworth, with me. It says something (good or bad) about the boys of St Chris's that none came forward.

Nearly all of us take something or other from hotel rooms. Soap, used or unused, towels, bottles of this or that, even cutlery. I have a terrific collection of airline and hotel cutlery. There's nearly a complete set from the Pierre Hotel, New York. As I'm leaving I always say: 'Got two forks and a spoon in my bags, OK?' Nobody has ever said 'No'. And at a thousand quid a night for a decent suite, what's 20p worth of second-hand cutlery? Especially to a charming, regular guest! There was a lovely old man named Mr Durcos on reception at the Pierre when it was managed by Forte – and incidentally far better managed than it is now by the Four Seasons Group – who saw me on a New York talk show going on about my set of Concorde cutlery, and that I needed six knives to complete my Pierre Hotel set. When he next gave me my room key, six knives were handed over with it!

Concorde used to have its own special cutlery, then it changed to the British Airways regular with a C on it. Now it's not distinctive at all. I've got a lot of that through all its periods. I use it for the staff. Only last week coming back from Nice I admired the new Air France cutlery, which has plastic handles with a nice blue and white stripe. I cautiously put aside a fork and spoon. 'I'd like to take these,' I said to the steward. 'Let me get you some clean ones, sir,' he replied. Mine were clean, but anyway he went to an unused tray and gave me a whole set!

Sadly, few hotels use their names on ashtrays now. But I have some rare, old Beverly Hills Hotel and Beverly Wilshire ones. Or rather, did have. On checking recently, I found a lot of my 'donated' cutlery, ashtrays and the like have been genuinely nicked from my house! Unbelievable! Nobody ever asked my permission as they were leaving.

P.S. Now nobody's allowed to smoke anywhere. Since I don't, sod 'em.

I don't admire **BA**. The seats where you supposedly stretch out as if in bed were immensely uncomfortable. I can sleep anywhere – in the office, in cinemas, in theatres, in the middle of a conversation, during a meal – but not in these seats. Which was unfortunate, because I was on a night flight. I checked the other passengers, all sleeping in their BA pyjamas. They looked ridiculous.

British trains have never been my favourite place to dine. Recently I ventured on a train to Bognor for a newspaper article. Bognor stinks. There were no restaurants on the train!

At Nice I forewarned **BMI** I was on heat and they whisked me onto the plane smoothly. Once there, however, oh dear. Those nasty, narrow little seats, same in Diamond Class as Economy. And the tray of dinner, beyond belief. A hot bowl with a tinny cover

Cont'd
when unpeeled left me confused. 'What is this?' I asked the hostess. 'Fish,' she said, 'salmon, I believe.' It didn't look like salmon to me, and it smelt not nice. There were some odd potatoes and stringy spinach, a rubbery bread roll and a chocolate egg with sickly-goo stuff in the middle. All in all these were the worst tastes ever to insult my persona. The cutlery was so awful I didn't even bother to ask if I could take some.

I had to lunch with some Canadian film people in Paris, so I decided to take the **Eurostar** train. Door-to-door from my house, it would probably be an hour longer than flying, but it might be an adventure. And I could eat breakfast on the way.

The food was totally beyond human belief. It made British Airways look like Nico Ladenis. The croissant was cold and rubbery; there were harmless corn-flakes in a plastic container; the cutlery was a new low and I nicked a fork to remind myself of this later. Then I tried a rubbery chocolate brioche thing, followed by what the menu called a 'traditional hot breakfast (scrambled eggs with smoked salmon, hash browns, button mushrooms and tomato)'. When I say unbelievable, I mean unbelievable! I cannot remember anything worse ever being placed before me in my entire life. Tasteless, horrid, strange texture, a mad knife murderer disguised as food. On the plus side, the three girls serving were exemplary. They were elegant, charming, professional and lovely.

The food on **Thai Airways** was pretty normal airline fodder. Vegetable spring roll, not crisp, gooey. Prawn cracker, very bad indeed. Chicken consommé where the bits of chicken, even immersed in liquid, managed to be dry. Fish curry appeared in some leaves, swimming in sauce. But I forgive them everything for there, in a large tin, was Sevruga caviare. Such a sight has not been seen on British Airways in living memory. You could have seconds, thirds, even fourths. I know, because I did. After that, the dodgy ice cream gateau didn't matter. And when I told the stewardess I collected cutlery, she said: 'Can I get you a bag to put it in?' 'No thanks,' I responded, 'I've got two forks and a spoon in my briefcase.'

Richard Branson is my hero. British Airways senior personnel are toilet fodder at best. For years I travelled to Barbados on BA. Because I like its ground crew and cabin staff, I wrote articles complimenting the company.

But each year when I asked my travel agent in January to book my return flights, leaving 11 months later, it was told the plane was full. How, you may ask, could a plane be fully booked 11 months ahead? I believe because nice Geoff Moss, chairman of Elegant Resorts, and various other Caribbean tour specialists grab seats ahead of the public. We're left with zilch.

I put this to Theresa Sabin, PA to BA's current chief executive, Willie Walsh.

'I don't think that's what happens, Mr Winner,' she said in a voice snooty enough to remove entrails from a rabbit.

The bosses of British Airways have often behaved like tacky gangsters. They succeeded in putting Sir Freddie Laker out of business when he dared to start a new airline. The same idiots tried every dirty trick possible to sink Branson's **Virgin** airline.

They were rightly and successfully sued by Branson, who won substantial damages, which were upheld on appeal. Whereupon Lord King, then BA's chairman, uttered the immortal words, 'I'd have taken Richard Branson more seriously had he been clean shaven and worn a suit.' My case against British Airways rests.

This year I turned to Virgin. Not only considerably better, but £2,737 less per person for a top-class Barbados return. Thus I saved £5,474.

I'd only flown Virgin once, to St Lucia. When I arrived at Gatwick there was a personally signed letter from Richard Branson welcoming me, thanking me for flying with his company and giving me his phone number on Necker Island, where he was, 'in case you need anything'. I thought of ringing up and saying, 'I'm in the lounge Richard, my coffee hasn't arrived.' But everything was vastly efficient so I didn't have to.

This time Virgin flew from Heathrow. Much better. No letter from his Richardship, but we were chauffered to the airport in a lovely Mercedes. In its superb lounge, Virgin offers massage, beauty treatments, a hairdressing salon, shoe polishers and a menu (all free) including slow-cooked duck leg, seared sea bass and shepherd's pie.

On the plane Virgin's upper class layout knocks British Airways' first class into the proverbial cocked hat. There are fewer seats, more space, and the best cabin crew I've ever come across. Our waitress (okay, stewardess), Ashleigh Fisher, was speedy, charming, polite, elegant, smiley. She'd grace any hotel or restaurant.

The menu recited the usual airline twaddle: 'The wealth and quality of British food today has prompted us to devote the next month to celebrating the great tastes of British cuisine.' Come off it, this is an aeroplane. The days when Trans World Airlines had lashings of beluga caviar followed by great vanilla ice cream with chocolate sauce and nuts are over. Although, as a main course, TWA once offered a duck covered in green mould. The Virgin food was fine. Geraldine thought it was well above British Airways standards.

Virgins for ever I say. Even though in my younger days I never used to.

HOTELS AND RESTAURANTS INDEX

(page numbers are in italics)

LONDON

Alain Ducasse at the Dorchester, Park Lane, W1K 1QA •020 7629 8866 *3*
Almeida, 30 Almeida Street, N1 1AD •020 7354 4777 *4*
Al-Dar III, 221 Kensington High Street, W8 6SG •0871 971 7004 *4*
Alounak, 44 Westbourne Grove, W2 5SH •020 7229 4158 *5*
Amaya, Halkin Arcade, Motcomb Street, SW1X 8JT •020 7823 1166 *3*
Angela Hartnett's Menu, Connaught Hotel, 16 Carlos Place, Mayfair, W1K 2AL
  •020 7592 1222 *82*
Aroma II, 118 Shaftesbury Avenue, W1D 5EP •020 7437 0377 *6*
Asia de Cuba, St Martin's Hotel, 45 St Martins Lane, WC2N 4HX •020 7300 5544 *7*
Assaggi, 39 Chepstow Place, W2 4TS •020 7792 5501 *8*
Aubergine, 11 Park Walk, SW10 0AJ •020 7352 3449 *8*
Avenue, The, 7–9 St James Street, SW1A 1EE •020 7321 2111 *9*
Awana, 85 Sloane Avenue, Chelsea, SW3 3DX •020 7584 8880 *10*

Balans, 187 Kensington High Street, W8 6SH •020 7376 0115 *11*
Bellamy's, 18 Bruton Place, W1J 6LY •020 7491 2722 *11*
Belvedere, Holland Park, off Abbotsbury Road, W8 6LU •020 7602 1238 *12*
Berkeley Square Café, 7 Davies Street, W1K 3DA •020 7499 7791 *13*
Biagio, 15–17 Villiers Street, WC2N 6ND •020 7839 3633 *13*
Bibendum, Michelin House, 81 Fulham Road, SW3 6RD •020 7581 5817 *13*
Bistrot 190, 190 Queensgate, SW7 5EU •020 7581 5666 *14*
Bloom's, 7 Montague Street, WC1B 5BP •020 7323 1717 *15*
Bombay Brasserie, The, Courtfield Road, SW7 4UH •020 7370 4040 *16*
Boxwood Café, The Berkeley, Wilton Place, 87 Knightsbridge, SW1X 7RL
  •020 7235 1010 *17*
Brass Rail Salt Beef Bar, Selfridges, 400 Oxford Street, W1A 1AB •0800 123 400 *17*
Brasserie, La, 272 Brompton Road, SW3 2AW •020 7584 1668 *18*
Brasserie St Quentin, 243 Brompton Road, SW3 2EP *18*
Brilliant, The, 72–74 Western Road, Southall, UB2 5DZ •020 8574 1927/0276 *19*
Brinkley's, 47 Hollywood Road, SW10 9HX •020 7351 1683 *19*
British Home Stores, Oxford St, W1C 1DL •020 7855 4300 *19*
Brown's hotel, Albermarle Street, W1S 4BP •020 7493 6020 *20*
Brunello, Baglioni hotel, 60 Hyde Park Gate, SW7 5BB •020 7368 5900 *21*
Bumpkin, 209 Westbourne Park Road, W11 1EA •020 7243 9818 *21*
Byron, 222 Kensington High Street, W8 7RG •020 7361 1717 *22*

Cafe Anglais, Le, 8 Porchester Gardens, W2 4DB •020 7221 1415 *22*
Cafe Pasta, 229 Kensington High Street, W8 6SA •020 7937 6314 *23*
Cafe Tarte, 270 Kensington High Street, W8 6ND •020 7371 6003 *23*
Capital Hotel and Restaurant, 22 Basil Street, SW3 1AT •020 7589 5171 *24*
Caprice, Le, Arlington House, Arlington Street, SW1A 1RT •020 7629 2239 *25*
Caraffini, 61–63 Lower Soane Street, SW1W 8DH, •020 7259 0235 *25*
Carluccio's, Heathrow airport, terminal 5, UB3 5AP •020 8759 6850 *26*
Carpaccio, 4-6 Sydney Street, SW3 6PP •020 7352 3435 *27*
Cecconi's, 5A Burlington Gardens, W1X 1LE •020 7434 1509 *27*
China Tang, Dorchester Hotel, 53 Park Lane, W1K 1QA •020 7629 9988 *28*
Christopher's, 18 Wellington Street, WC2E 7DD •020 7240 4222 *28*
Cinnamon Club, The Old, Westminster Library, 30-32 Great Smith Street,
  SW1P 3BU •020 7222 2555 *29*
Cipriani, 25 Davies Street, W1K 3DF •020 7399 0500 *29*
Clarke's, 124 Kensington Church Street, W8 4BH •020 7221 9225 *30*
Club at the Ivy, 9 West Street, WC2H 9NE •020 7557 6095 *30*
Club Gascon, 57 West Smithfield, EC1A 9DS •020 7796 0600 *30*
Coast, 26b Albemarle Street, W1X 3FA •020 7495 5999 *31*
Coco Momo, 79 Marylebone High Street, W1U 5JZ •020 7486 5746 *31*

Petersham Nurseries Café, off Petersham Road, Richmond, TW10 7AG
•020 8605 3627 95
Petite Maison, La, 54 Brooks Mews, W1K 4EG •020 7495 4774 95
Philpott's Mezzaluna, 424 Finchley Road, NW2 2HY •020 7794 0455 96
Pied à Terre, 34 Charlotte Street, W17 2NH •020 7636 1178 97
Planet Hollywood, Coventry Street, W1D 7ER •020 7437 7639 97
Poissonnerie de l'Avenue, 82 Sloane Avenue, SW3 3DZ •020 7589 2457 98
Polish Centre Restaurant, 246 King Street, W6 0RF •020 8741 3225 98
Pont de la Tour, Le, 36d Shad Thames, Butlers Wharf, SE1 2YE •020 7403 8403 99
Il Portico, 277 Kensington High Street, W8 6NA •020 7602 6262 100
Poule au Pot, La, 231 Ebury Street, SW1W 8UT •020 7730 7763 100
Promenade, The, 53 Park Lane, W1A 2HJ •020 7629 8888 91

Quo Vadis, 26–29 Dean Street, W1A 6LL •020 7437 9585 101

Racine, 239 Brompton Road, SW3 2EP •020 7584 4477 101
Rasoi Vineet Bhatia, 10 Lincoln Street, SW3 2TS •020 7225 1881 102
Red Fort, 77 Dean Street, W1D 35H •020 7437 2525 103
Rhodes W1 Brasserie, The Cumberland Hotel, Great Cumberland Place, W1H 7DL
•020 7616 5930 104
Rib Room at the Hyatt Carlton Tower Hotel, 2 Cadogan Place, SW1X 9PY
•020 7824 7053 105
Richard Corrigan at Lindsay House, 21 Romilly Street, W1D 5AF •020 7439 0450 106
Richoux, 41a South Audley Street, W1K 2PS •020 7629 5228 107
Ritz, The, 150 Piccadilly, W1J 9BR •020 7493 8181 107
River Café, Thames Wharf Studios, Rainville Road, W6 9HA •020 7381 8824 108
Rivoli bar, The Ritz, 150 Piccadilly, W1J 9BR •020 7493 8181 91
Roast, The Floral Hall, Stoney Street, SE1 1TL •0845 034 7300 109
Roka, 37 Charlotte Street, W1T 1RR •020 7580 6464 109
Rules, 35 Maiden Lane, WC2E 7LB •020 7836 5314 110

St Alban, 4-12 Regent Street, SW1Y 4PE •020 7499 8558 111
St John Bread and Wine, 26 St John Street, EC1M 4AY •020 7251 4090 112
Salloos, 62–64 Kinnerton Street, SW1X 8ER •020 7235 4444 113
San Lorenzo, 22 Beauchamp Place, SW3 1NH •020 7584 1074 113
Scalini, 1 Walton Street, SW3 2JD •020 7823 9720 114
Scott's, 20 Mount Street, W1Y 6HE •020 7629 5248 114
Sheekey's, 28–32 St. Martin's Court, WC2N 4AL •020 7240 2565 115
Shogun, 44 Grosvenor Square, W1K 4AG •020 7493 1255 115
Simpson's-in-the-Strand, 100 Strand, WC2R 0EW •020 7836 9112 116
Sketch, 9 Conduit Street, W1S 2XG •020 7659 4500 117
Snows on the Green, 166 Shepherd's Bush Road, W6 7PB •020 7603 2142 117
Sotheby's Café, 34–35 New Bond Street, W1A 2AA •020 7293 5000 118
Spoon, The Sanderson Hotel, 50 Berners Street, W1T 3NG •020 7300 1444 119
Square, The, 6–10 Bruton Street, Mayfair, W1X 7AE •020 7495 7100 119
Sticky Fingers, 1a Phillimore Gardens, W8 7QB •020 7938 5338 119

Tamarind, 20 Queen Street, W1X 7PJ •020 7629 3561 120
Teatro, 93–107 Shaftesbury Avenue, W1V 8BT •020 7494 3040 120
Terrace Cafe, Royal National Theatre •020 7401 8361 120
Theo Randall, InterContinental hotel, 1 Hamilton Place, Park Lane, W1J 7QY
•020 7318 8747 121
Timo, 343 Kensington High Street, W8 6NW •020 7603 3888 121
Tom Aikens, 43 Elystan Street, SW3 3NT •020 7584 2003 122
Tom's Deli & Café, 226 Westbourne Grove, W11 2RH •020 7221 8818 123
Toto, Walton House, Walton Street, SW3 2JH •020 7589 0075 123
Tramp, 40 Jermyn Street, SW1Y 6DN •020 7734 0565 124
Trompette, La, 5 Devonshire Road, W4 2EU •020 8747 1836 124
Truc Vert, 42 North Audley Street, W1K 6ZR •020 7491 9988 125
2 Veneti, 10 Wigmore Street, W1U 2RD •020 7637 0789 125
202, 202 Westbourne Grove, W11 2RH •020 7727 2722 126

UK AND IRELAND

England

Dorset
Bournemouth: Oscar's, Royal Bath Hotel, Bath Road, BH1 2EW ●01202 555 555 *150*
Cranborne: The Sheaf of Arrows, 4 The Square, Cranborne BH21 5PR
  ●01725 517 456 *150*
Gillingham: Stock Hill House, Stock Hill, SP8 5NR ●01747 823626 *151*
Highcliffe: Bertie's Fish & Chips, 331 Lymington Road ●01425 274727 *149*
  Linda Attrell *150*
Mudeford: Ship in Distress, 66 Stanpit, Christchurch, BH23 3NA ●01202 485123 *151*

Durham
Almshouses Café, Palace Green, DH1 3RL ●0191 386 1054 *152*
Durham Marriott Hotel Royal County, Old Elvet, DH1 3JN ●0191 386 6821 *153*

Gloucestershire
Kingham: Daylesford Farm Shop, Nr Kingham, GL56 0YG ●01608 731 700 *153*
Lower Slaughter: Lower Slaughter Manor, GL54 2HP ●01451 820 456 *155*
Southrop: Swan, Lechlade, GL7 3NU ●01367 850 205 *155*
Stow-on-the-Wold: Kings Arms, Market Square, GL54 1AF ●01451 830 364 *153*
  Wyck Hill House, GL54 1HY ●01451 831936 *155*
Upper Slaughter: Lords of the Manor, Nr Bourton on the Water, GL54 2JD
  ●01451 820243 *154*

Hampshire
Brockenhurst: Thatched Cottage, 16 Brookley Road, SO42 7RR ●01590 623090 *157*
Lymington: Egans, Gosport Street, SO41 9B ●01590 676165 *153*
  The Mill at Gordleton, Silver Street, Hordle, SO41 6DJ ●01590 682219 *156*
New Milton: Chewton Glen, Christchurch Road, BH25 6QS ●01425 275341 *155*
Nomansland: Restaurant and Bistro Les Mirabelles, Forest Edge Road, SP5 2BN
  ●01794 390205 *157*
Winchester: Lainston House, Sparsholt, SO21 2LT ●01962 863588 *156*

Hertfordshire
Aldbury: Greyhound Inn, 19 Stocks Road, HP23 5RT ●01442 851228 *160*
Ayot St Lawrence: Brocket Arms, AL6 9BT ●01438 820 250 *159*
Barley: Fox and Hounds, High Street, SG8 8HU ●01763 848 459 *160*
Barnet: Loch Fyne, 12 Hadley Highstone, EN5 4PU ●020 8449 3674 *161*
Buntingford: Bull of Cottered, Cottered, SG9 9QP ●01763 281 243 *159*
Frithsden: Alford Arms, Nr Hemel Hempstead, HP1 3DD ●01442 864480 *157*
Gosmore: Bird in Hand, High Street, SG4 7QG ●01462 432 079 *159*
Letchworth: Simmons Bakers, 10 Eastcheap, SG6 3DE ●01462 684 511 *162*
Hitchin: Just 32, 32 Sun Street, SG5 1AH ●01462 455 666 *161*
St Albans: Sopwell House and Country Club, Cottonmill Lane, AL1 2HQ
  ●01727 864 477 *162*
Tring: Pendley Manor Hotel, Cow Lane, HP23 5QY ●01442 891891 *162*
Welwyn: Auberge du Lac, Brocket Hall, Brocket Park, AL8 7XG ●01707 368 888 *158*
  Wellington, 1 High Street, AL6 9LZ ●01438 714 036 *163*

Kent
Ramsgate: Kent International Hotel, Harbour Parade, CT11 8LZ ●01843 588 276 *164*

Manchester
Lal Qila, 123–7 Wilmslow Road, M14 5AN ●0161 224 9999 *164*
Lowry hotel, 50 Dearman's Place, Chapel Wharf, M3 5LH ●0161 827 4000 *164*
Meridien Victoria & Albert, Water Street, M3 4JQ ●0161 832 1188 *164*
Nutters, Edenfield Road, OL12 7TT ●01706 650 167 *165*
Yang Sing, 34 Princess Street, M1 4JY ●0161 236 2200 *165*

Middlesex
Teddington: Trattoria Sorrento, 132 High Street, Teddington, TW11 8JB
  ●020 8977 4757 *165*

East Grinstead: Gravetye Manor, Vowels Lane, RH19 4LJ •01342 810567 *180*

West Yorkshire
Leeds: Malmaison hotel, 1 Swinegate, LS1 4AG •0113 398 1000 *180*

Wiltshire
Castle Combe: Manor House Hotel, Chippenham, SN14 7HR •01249 782 206 *182*
Ford: White Hart Inn, Ford, New Chippenham, SN14 8RT •01249 782213 *184*
Lacock: King John's Hunting Lodge, Tea rooms and guest house •01249 730313 *181*
Lucknam Park: Colerne, SN14 8AZ •01225 742777 *182*
Melksham: Tollgate Inn, Ham Green, Bradford-on-Avon, BA14 6PX •01225 782 326 *183*
Warminster: Jacqueline's, 28 High Street, BA12 9AF •01985 217 373 *181*

Worcestershire
Broadway: Buckland Manor, Buckland, WR12 7LY •01386 582626 *185*
Kidderminster: Brockencote Hall, Chaddesley Corbett, DY10 4PY
   •01562 777 876 *184*

Scotland

Easter Ross: Oystercatcher, Main Street, IV20 1YB •01682 871 560 *188*
Fort William: Inverlochy Castle, Torlundy, PH33 6SN •01397 702 177 *186*
Glasgow: Malmaison, 278 West George Street, G2 4LL •0141 572 1000 *185*
Gretna Green, Dumfriesshire: Old Smithy Restaurant, DG16 5EA
   •01461 338 365 *186*
Lairg: Kylesku, Sutherland, IV27 4HW •01971 502 231 *188*
Lochinver: Lochinver's Larder, Main Street, IV27 4JY •01571 844 356 *188*
Spean Bridge, near Fort William: Old Station Restaurant, Station Road, PH34 4EP
   •01397 712 535 *190*
Sutherland: The Carnegie Club at Skibo Castle, Dornoch, IV25 3RQ
   •01862 894 600 *189*
Ullapool, Rosshire: Morefield Motel, North Road, IV26 2TQ •01854 612 161 *190*

Wales

Betwys-y-Coed: Women's Institute fête *190*
Crickhowell: Nantyffin Cider Mill Inn •01873 810 775 *191*
Hay on Wye: Oscars Bistro, Oscars High Town, HR3 5AE •01497 821 193 *192*
Llyswen, Powys: Griffin Inn, LD3 0YP •01874 754 241 *192*
   Llangoed Hall, LD3 0YP •01874 754 525 *193*
Seion, Caernarfon: Ty'n Rhos Country House and Restaurant, Llanddeiniolen,
   LL55 3AE •01248 670 489 *194*

Ireland

Dingle, Co Kerry: Dick Mack's, Green Street •00353 66915 1960 *195*
   Milltown House, by Slea Head Drive •00353 66915 1372 *195*
Dromoland Castle, Newmarket on Fergus, Co Clare •00353 613 8144 *199*
Dublin: Balzac, La Stampa Hotel & Spa, 35 Dawson Street, D2 •00353 1 677 8611 *195*
   Locks Restaurant, Number 1 Windsor Terrace, Portobello, Dublin 8
   •00353 1 454 3391 *196*
   Messrs Maguire, O'Connell Bridge, Burgh Quay, D2 •00353 1 670 5777 *196*
   Patrick Guildbaud, 21 Upper Merrion Street, D2 •00353 1676 4192 *196*
   Shelbourne hotel, St Stephen's Green •00353 1663 4500 *197*
   Thornton's, 128 St. Stephen's Green •00353 1478 7008 *197*
Kenmare, Co Kerry: Park hotel •00353 64412 00 *197*
Mallow, Co Cork: Longueville House •00353 2247 156 *198*

AUSTRIA
Filsmoos a Dachstein: Hotel Hubertus •0043 64 53 82 04 *203*
Salzburg: Hotel Sacher •0043 662 88 977 *203*
   Hotel Schloss Fuschl •0043 6229 22530 *204*

Carcassonne: Hôtel de la Cité ●0033 4 68 71 98 71 228
Deauville: Brasserie Miocque ●0033 2 31 98 66 22 229
    Hôtel Normandy ●0033 2 31 98 66 22 229
Eze: Le Château Éza ●0033 4 93 41 12 24 231
    La Chaumière ●00 33 493 017 768 231
Fayence: La Moulin de la Camandoule ●0033 4 94 76 00 84 231
Fleurie: Le Cep ●0033 4 74 04 10 77 232
Fontjoncouse: Auberge du Vieux Puits ●0033 4 68 44 07 37 232
Golfe-Juan: Bistrot du Port ●0033 4 93 63 71 16/63 76 82 232
    Tétou ●0033 4 93 63 71 16/63 76 82 233
Gréolières: Le Cheiron ●00 33 4 93 59 98 89 232
Haut-de-Cagnes: Le Cagnard ●0033 4 93 20 73 21 233
Honfleur: Ferme Saint Siméon ●0033 2 31 81 78 00 234
L'Isle-sur-la-Sorgue: Le Jardin des Quais ●0033 4 90 38 56 17 234
Joigny: La Côte Saint Jacques ●0033 3 86 62 09 70 235
Lyon: Château de Bagnols ●0033 4 74 71 40 00 235
Mougins: Moulin de Mougins ●0033 4 93 75 78 24 236
Nice: La Petite Maison ●0033 93 92 59 59 236
St-Etienne-de-Baïgorry: Arcé ●0033 5 59 37 40 14 237
St-Jean-Cap-Ferrat: Bistro du Port ●0033 493 760 446 237
    Grand Hôtel du Cap-Ferrat ●0033 4 93 76 50 50 237
    Hôtel Royal Riviera ●0033 4 93 76 31 00 238
    Le Provençal ●0033 4 93 76 03 97 238
    La Réserve de Beaulieu ●0033 4 93 01 00 01 238
    Le Sloop ●0033 4 93 76 03 39 240
    La Voile d'Or ●0033 4 93 01 13 13 240
St-Paul-de-Vence: La Cocarde de St-Paul ●0033 4 93 32 86 17 240
    La Colombe d'Or ●0033 4 93 32 80 02 240
    Mas de Pierre ●0033 4 93 59 00 10 241
St Tropez: Auberge de la Môle ●0033 4 94 49 57 01 241
    Byblos ●0033 4 94 56 68 00 241
    Résidence de la Pinède ●0033 4 94 33 91 00 242
    Tahiti beach restaurant ●0033 4 94 97 18 02 243
Tournus: Restaurant Greuze ●0033 3 85 51 13 52 243
La Turbie: Hostellerie Jérome ●0033 4 92 41 51 51 243
Vence: Chez Guy ●0033 4 93 58 25 82 244
Villeneuve-sur-Yonne: Auberge La Lucarne aux Chouettes ●0033 3 86 87 18 26 244

GERMANY
Aschau im Chiemgau: Residenz Heinz Winkler ●0049 8052 179 90 246
Dinkelsbühl: Hotel Restaurant Eisenkrug ●0049 9851 577 00 247
    Café Extrablatt ●0049 9851 247
Kraftshof near Nuremberg: Gasthaus Schwarzer Adler ●0049 911 34 56 91 247
Nuremberg: Belm Schlenkeria ●0049 911 22 54 74 248
    Gasthaus Rottner ●0049 911 612 20 32 248
    The Grand ●0049 911 232 20 248
Ramsau bei Berchtesgarden: Gasthof Rehwinkl ●0049 8657 347 249
Rothenburg: Hotel Meistertrunk ●0049 98 61 60 77 249

ITALY
Amalfi: Lido Azzurro ●0039 089 871 384 249
    Da Gemma ●0039 089 871 345 249
Apricale: Apricale da Delio ●0039 0184 208 008 249
Bellagio, Lake Como: Grand Hotel Villa Serbelloni ●0039 031 950 216 250
Capri: La Capannina ●0039 081 83 70 732 250
    Feraglioni ●0039 081 83 70 320 251
    Da Gemma ●0039 081 83 70 461 251
    Quisiana ●0039 081 83 70 788 251
Cernobbio, Lake Como: Trattoria del Vapore ●0039 031 51 03 08 252
    Villa d'Este ●0039 031 34 81 252
Chianti: Restaurant La Vigne (Radda) ●0039 0377 73 86 40 252
    Villa Sangiovese (Panzano) ●0039 055 85 24 61 253

LUXEMBOURG
Saint-Michel •00352 22 32 15 276

MADEIRA
Arsénio's •00 351 91 22 40 07 276
Reid's hotel •00 351 91 76 30 04 277

MAJORCA
Deia: Deia restaurant •0034 971 639 265 293
  Es Raco d'es Teix •0034 971 639 501 292
  Jaime •0034 971 725 943 293
  La Residencia •0034 971 639 011 291
  Sebastian •0034 971 639 417 293
  Xelini •0034 971 639 139 293
Palma: Flanigan •0034 971 679 191 293

MONACO
Monte Carlo: Avenue 31 •00 377 97 703 131 244
  Chez Gianni •00 377 93 30 46 33 245
  Hôtel de Paris •00 379 92 16 29 66 245
  La Piazza •00 377 93 50 47 00 245
Rampoldi •00 377 93 50 43 84 246

MOROCCO
Marrakesh: Al Fassia •00 212 44 43 40 60 278
  Amanjena •00 212 4 40 33 53 278
  Chez Ali •00 212 4 30 77 30 278
  Comptoir Darna •00 212 524 437 702 279
  Dar Marjana •00 212 4 44 11 10 279
  Diaffa •00 212 4 42 6898 280
  La Mamounia •00 212 4 44 89 81 280
  Le Tobsil •00 212 4 44 49 52 281
  Yacout •00 212 4 38 29 29 281
Ouirgane: La Roseraie •00 212 44 48 56 93 281
Ourika valley: Ramuntcho •00 212 44 48 45 21 281
Taroudannt: Gazelle d'Or •00 212 8 85 20 39/85 20 48 282

PORTUGAL
Lisbon: Alcantara Café •00 351 213 621 226 283
  Bica do Sapato •00 351 218 810 320 283
  Lapa Palace •00 351 213 182 791 283
Sintra: Hockey Café •00 351 219 235 710 284

SARDINIA
Porto Cervo: Pitrizza •00 390 789 930 111 284

SOUTH AFRICA
Cape Town: The Cellars •0027 21 194 2137 285
  Mount Nelson hotel •0027 21 23 1000 285
Constantiaberg: Constantia Uitsig •0027 21 794 6500 286
Franschhoek: La Petite Ferme •0029 21 876 3016 286
Mala Mala and Ngala safari camps •0029 110784 6832 286
Soweto: Wandie's Place •0027 11 982 2796 288
Sun City: Palace •0027 14 557 10 00 289

SPAIN
Ibiza: Hacienda •00 34 971 33 45 00 290
San Sebastian: Arzak •00 34 943 278 465 290

SWITZERLAND
Bergamo: Trattoria Sant'Ambroeus •00 39 035 237 494 293
Bergün: Hotel Restaurant Albula •00 41 81 407 11 26 294